# Praise for *Lost in Trans Nation*

"Dr. Miriam Grossman lays bare the criminal misbehavior of the medical professionals and counselors perpetrating the 'gender-affirming care travesty.' In doing so, she brings solace to those terrified that the children they love will fall prey to the demented excesses of the latest and worst of the contemporary psychological epidemics. In a time characterized by a shameful dearth of courage among medical professionals (and their counterparts in the field of psychology), Miriam Grossman has the courage to say what needs to be said."
— **Dr. Jordan B. Peterson, author, psychologist, online educator, and professor emeritus at the University of Toronto**

"Dr. Miriam Grossman is a rare truthteller. This book is a necessary guide for everyone, especially parents, battling gender ideology today."
— **Debra Soh, PhD, author of *The End of Gender*, featured in the *Daily Wire*'s "What Is a Woman?"**

"*Lost in Trans Nation* is the compass and map today's parents need to navigate the treacherous and inescapable gender-bending waters that engulf our youth from preschool forward. Written in her usual engaging and direct style, Dr. Miriam Grossman has crafted an indispensable tool to prevent and heal transgender indoctrination in children and young adults. Parents, grandparents, educators, health professionals, attorneys, and policymakers should all give this book a close read."
— **Michelle A. Cretella, MD, cochair of the Adolescent Sexuality Committee of the American College of Pediatricians, Advisory Board Advocates Protecting Children**

"Thank God for Dr. Miriam Grossman. Thanks to her, we may finally have the book that begins our exit from a madness in which America finds itself. That madness is the belief that men can become women and women can become men.

*Lost in Trans Nation: A Child Psychiatrist's Guide Out of the Madness* is mandatory reading for all parents who are enduring the indescribable trauma of having their beloved daughter insist she is a boy or whose beloved son insists he is a girl. It can literally be lifesaving and, at the least, sanity-saving and family-saving. For families who have a gender-distressed child, Dr. Grossman provides practical advice on how to respond to the child's demands, how to find a non-ideology-driven therapist, and how to talk to the schools, teachers, physicians, and hospitals all collaborating in ruining their child's life.

All good in history has been accomplished by outliers. Miriam Grossman is such an outlier."

**— Dennis Prager, nationally syndicated radio talk show host, cofounder of PragerU and author of ten bestselling books**

"The mind virus of gender ideology is coming for your children, and it has captured the medical, educational, and legal institutions meant to protect them. Dr. Grossman's *Lost in Trans Nation* serves as an essential resource for parents in a culture intent on confusion and chaos."

**— Matt Walsh**

"American parents face a new epidemic: the sudden declaration by children of a transgender identity, with demands for a new name, pronouns, and risky medical interventions. Dr. Grossman arms parents with the science and practical guidance they need to survive this nightmare, or better yet, prevent it altogether. America needs this book."

**— Stanley Goldfarb, chairman, Do No Harm and former associate dean for curriculum the University of Pennsylvania's Perelman School of Medicine**

"We are the largest support network in North America for parents of rapid-onset gender dysphoria (ROGD). As parents who have been through this nightmare with our own kids, we are canaries in the coalmine. Parents need to understand that their children are being bombarded with gender ideology relentlessly. It is promoted in their children's schools, among their friends, in the media, on the Internet, and even by the very medical professionals they turn to for help. Dr. Grossman's book will help parents understand the depth and breadth of the problem and provide them with skills to protect and guide their children safely through."

**— Jane, national organizer of Parents of ROGD Kids**

"Dr. Grossman warned parents about the gender movement a decade ago. Now that it's in full force, her book arms parents with the tools to fight the gender hydra that lurks around every bend. A must-read."

**— Erin Friday, Esq., co-lead of Our Duty-USA, a support network for parents who wish to protect their children from gender ideology.**

"Parents, are you aware of the gender indoctrination happening in your child's classroom? You better be—it's a pipeline to a gender clinic, keeping you in the dark. Don't be blindsided like so many parents in Dr. Grossman's practice. Her explosive book provides a roadmap and practical guidance to safeguard your child's physical and emotional health. Read this book, absorb every word, and inoculate your family against the scourge of transgender ideology.
— **Tina Descovich and Tiffany Justice, cofounders Moms for Liberty**

"Dr. Miriam Grossman has done the public a tremendous service with this harrowing recounting of the ethical corruption of the medical profession and the devastation wrought by radical gender ideology on the lives of countless young and vulnerable Americans. If you want to know how the United States got to this crisis point, read this book."
— **Josh Hammer, opinion editor,** *Newsweek*

"In twenty-five years of experience as a health care policy expert at the state, national, and international levels, I have rarely met a more determined, strong, and courageous person than Dr. Miriam Grossman. *In Lost in Trans Nation: A Child Psychiatrist's Guide Out of the Madness*, Dr. Grossman provides us with much needed information and ammunition to support what we already instinctively knew but were struggling to articulate. In the name of 'affirmation' and health care, a horrific tragedy is being perpetrated on humanity's most vulnerable, impressionable, and malleable—our children. Dr. Grossman's book is a crucial resource, a scientifically sound treatise, and a necessary call to action for all those who care about the future of our children, our culture, and our country."
— **Dianna Lightfoot, North Carolina Physicians for Freedom; White House Appointee USAID-Global Health 2017–2021**

"*Lost in Trans Nation* is a ground-breaking book, and required reading for anyone who cares about our school-age generation. Dr. Miriam Grossman details the war being waged over our children's identities, with everyday parents and community members on one side, and proponents of a radical new 'gender-affirming' ideology on the other that is spreading like a contagion and is tearing apart families, threatening the fabric of society. She explains how this is a wholly different phenomenon than the rare cases of gender identity disorder seen in the past.

In many cases the gender-affirming movement's proponents are well-meaning teachers, guidance counselors, doctors, and even parents buying into the 'need' for incredibly invasive medical interventions that are grounded in, as we learn, corrupted science and driven by powerful organizations and government policy. Parents are terrified that if they don't support their children's 'transition' to an ambiguous or opposite sex, their children's lives will be at risk.

In *Lost in Trans Nation*, Dr. Grossman charts a path for navigating the madness of our times, a path that will help keep children safe, families whole, and society functional. Through this captivating work, readers will also find the courage to stand up for reality and truth, and for future generations."

— **Jan Jekielek, senior editor at The Epoch Times and host of American Thought Leaders**

# Lost in Trans Nation

## A Child Psychiatrist's Guide Out of the Madness

MIRIAM GROSSMAN, MD

FORWORD BY DR. JORDAN B. PETERSON

Skyhorse Publishing

Skyhorse Publishing books may be purchased in bulk at special discounts for sales promotion, corporate gifts, fund-raising, or educational purposes. Special editions can also be created to specifications. For details, contact the Special Sales Department, Skyhorse Publishing, 307 West 36th Street, 11th Floor, New York, NY 10018 or info@skyhorsepublishing.com.

Skyhorse® and Skyhorse Publishing® are registered trademarks of Skyhorse Publishing, Inc.®, a Delaware corporation.

Visit our website at www.skyhorsepublishing.com.

10 9 8 7 6 5 4 3 2 1

Library of Congress Cataloging-in-Publication Data is available on file.

Hardcover ISBN: 978-1-5107-7774-3
eBook ISBN: 978-1-5107-7775-0

Cover design by Brian Peterson

Printed in the United States of America

The information presented in this book is for educational purposes only and not intended to serve as a substitute for diagnosis, treatment, or advice from a qualified, licensed medical professional or therapist. Neither the author nor the publisher bears any responsibility for the accuracy or content of the sites, books, or resources listed or for the therapeutic approach of mental health providers listed therein.

# CONTENTS

# Dedication

This book is dedicated to the parents of kids with Rapid-Onset Gender Dysphoria and to the groups who support them.

I spoke with you from your cars, basements, and bathrooms. You huddled and whispered behind closed doors, as if seeking my help was criminal behavior. You're not criminals, you are heroes. The criminals are the therapists, teachers, school counselors, and sex educators who indoctrinate your children with falsehoods, and the doctors who then disfigure and sterilize them. They are guilty of crimes. Their day will come.

## USA / Canada

@AudraMcDonald13
@fullowl and husband in NY
@onemoremother, yetanotherfather
@realitygirlzine
@SciMom22 from Niagara
@screaminlesbianmom &
  Chitownmom, IL
2014 OG Mom
A – Michigan
A grieving mother: Janet Marshall,
  Clermont, Florida.
A Mother Minnesota
A mother surviving and living on in
  spite of the loss.
A. Carnes - Missing him & still
  hoping, SC

Accidental Activist, Pennsylvania
ADM
AEJ from Upstate New York
AGA
Aggie in Bklyn
Amanda J.
Amber in Tampa
Amelie
Andrea D., Texas
Angeles Green
Angry in TX
Anita and Andrew, loving parents
Anita Green
Ann Best
Ann Smith USA 27-year-old male to
  female, devastated

Anne
*Anonymous (24 people)*
Anonymous from Canada
Anonymous from Charlotte, NC
Anonymous in CA
Anonymous in Massachusetts
Anonymous in Ohio.
Anonymous in Philadelphia
Anonymous in the US
Anonymous mother in St. Louis, MO
Anonymous- Oklahoma
Anonymous USA
Anonymous, Florida
Anonymous, Ithaca, NY
Anonymous, Midwest, United States,
Another crying mother, Los
  Angeles, CA
Apollo Beach, FL
April from Central Illinois.
Athena, Oregon

B. Graham
Barbara Petruccelli
Begbie
Beleaguered parents, Oregon
Beloved in IL
Ben Mason, Sheridan, Indiana
Beth Kristin Brown, Davis
  California
Betty Ventura, somewhere in rural
  red state America
Bizzie
Boris Spider
Breezy, Fort Worth, TX
Broken Father, East Coast,
  Canada.
Brokenhearted mom and dad in NH
Broken-hearted in Arizona
Butterfly

C in Canada
C Lynn Ay, NJ, US
California caring mom fighting this
  battle for way too long.
Canada Mom
Canadian Mom Fighting for my Kid
Carole M. in Kentucky
Carrie Smith, southeastern
  Pennsylvania
Cassie Blanc - South Carolina
Cathleen
Charlène K, San Francisco Bay Area
CHG
Chicago, IL
Chris in New Orleans
Christen Redding - Florida
Christine and Rob from NY
Cindy in Florida
Claire F.
ClayMom
Concerned Parent and Citizen in VT
Connie and Randy from PA
Cordelia
Courtney W.

D&M
D.B - dedicated mom in Canada
Daisy Grace
Daisy101
Dan Giles
Danielle O'Neill
Dee E. Sacramento
Dee from Toronto
Deedee long island
Devastated parent
Donna M.
Donna, Lethbridge, Alberta,
  Canada

Dr. Lorraine, pediatrician from NY
Dr. Neil Gupta
Duly Noted

E2Texas
EE
EL in Chicago
Eldon's Mom
Elizabeth from Washington state
Elizabeth W. Minnesota
Ellen C
Ellie in Florida
Emily A.
EP
Erin Friday, California
Erin Lee, mother from Colorado
 (@erinforparentalrights)
Erin Loving Mother from IL
ES and I am from California

F. L.
FAD in CA
Father of a beautiful girl in
 Cincinnati
Fierce Boy Mom
Flannon Shee
Francesca

Gay Johnson
GBR from WA
Grace Almighty
Grieving in Minnesota
Grieving Parents in NC

Hailee Harris, Austin TX
Hanna Vasilieva, Canada
Harry Instinct
Hazel and Ana in MA
HBgirl

Heartbroken but hopeful mom in
 the US
Heartbroken Mom, Charlotte, NC
Heartbroken physician mom from
 Florida
Heather - I live in Super Woke
 Durham, NC
HisMom CT
HMH
Hope Springs
Hope42day & Anonymous in
 Austin
Horrified left wing Berkeley liberal
Hurting Mom in the Carolinas

In the California weeds 319
Irene D.
Isabel Rodriguez Wosina
Isabelle Katya

J. Butler from Cary, NC
J. J Grimes, Johnson City,
 Tennessee
Jackalynn Lopez
James from USA
Jane S.
Jane Williams & Father of a beauti-
 ful girl in Cincinnati
Janet Marshall, Clearmont, Florida
January Littlejohn
JAO
JB
JB in Utah
Jean Driscoll
Jeannette Cooper – PEC
 Co-founder
Jeannie B, FL
Jen in Brooklyn
Jen Schmidt-Missouri

Jen Todino
Jennifer @nogenderpredtrs
  Washington State
Jennifer B. FL
Jennifer Dellasega, PEC co-founder
Jennifer Hayward
Jennifer in Illinois
Jennifer Van Outer, Washington DC
Jeremiah P Reilly
Jessica from California
Jessica S.
JG
JH from Kentucky
Jolene Brown, Chicago, IL
Jose Zamora
Josh & Katie in Seattle, the PNW
Josie Armstrong
Joy Flores, Michigan
JR
Judy C
Jules Smith
Julie F.
JV Thank you for this opportunity.
JvB

K in Northern VA
K squared and Loscar
K.M. and the late J.M.
Karen
Kari
Kate, Metro-Boston
Katherine
Kathleen Rogers
Kathy K
Katie Kerr, Southfield, Michigan
Katy and Mark in Atlanta.
KC
KC Bishop.
KD

Kevin Ingalls
KG - HTX
KLG — Mom of Desisting
  Daughter
KMC
Kristie - NC
Kristin Cole Kalamazoo, Michigan.

Laura in California
Laurie from Florida
Laurie S.
LC in TN
LeaundLilly
LinOak
Lisa A
Lisa T, Lumberton NJ
Lisa, Long Beach, CA
Lori K Canada
Lost in Lake Wylie, SC
Lost in SF.
LOVAL
Loving Mom in Asheville NC
Lydia M. from CA.

M Ballesteros
M. O'Brien, S. O'Brien
MA mom living in reality
Mad mom in Samo
Mama in the Bay Area
MamaBear in Vermont
Mamazilla in LBC
Marcy W.
Margaret in Seattle
Maria Gray
Martha J
Marth Shoultz - PEC
Mary
Mary McDevitte
Matilda F. from Tennessee

Maybelrose, MN

MBR

Melanie, fled from WA to avoid medical kidnapping

Melissa McArthur

Mem Larson

MGWard

Michele Blair

Michelle B., Canada

Mike and Patricia, Raleigh, NC

MK Allen, CA

MM, Charlotte, NC

MM, Georgia

mom fighting for her child in Colorado

Mom in N. Palm Beach, Florida

Mom of 16yo ROGD female with ADHD and PTSD in South Carolina

Mom of a desisted teen

Mom of a Minnesota Girl

Mom of P, USA

Mom to UC

Mom2seven in Indiana

Momdog, Southwestern US

Monique Rwanda

MoominMamma USA

Mother in Canada

Mother of 17 y natal female/ trans-identifying man, NC

Mr. and Mrs. Smith, Oregon

Ms. Mom

Mungeri Lal

Mw

MW, Portland Oregon

N, BC, Canada

Nana

NGL - Tallahassee, FL

Nicki D

NJ

No name USA

Noli Timere

NoMalarkeyMom

P.A.

Pacific Northwest

Page Sampson, Bellingham, WA

Patricia

Paul R

pc hc

Perdita

QuestionPDX

Rachel's mom

RetiredKTeacher, IL

RN from CA

Robert B - South Carolina

ROGD parent, Boston

Ronli Moses

Rose F

runningmind

Ruth Arliss from Virginia

S NC, USA.

S.B. California

S.R.F.

S.T

Samantha Parker

SarahD

SarahJami

SCA and BSA

Scared Mama- Chattanooga, TN

Sheila from Minnesota

SheIsHis

SK

Skeptical Mom in PA

Sophia's Mom, Portland, OR
Sorrow and despair in Maryland
South Carolina Dad
Stacy Williams
State is OK- NYS
Stella's mom
Step-mother in Texas
Susan Martin
Susan Z, Virginia
Susan, mother to Levi, who is my son.
Susanna Bellotti, Virginia
Susie White, Devoted Mother, MI
Suzanne L

T Jardine, Nova Scotia, Canada
T.T.
The Nelsons
Therapist and ROGD mom in
   Charlottesville, Virginia.
TN mom
TOmom
Torie Jaynes
TRW
Trying to save my son in PA.

Unresolved Grief in Vancouver

Vermont Rational Dad
Victoria Hall I'm thrilled to be
   named. I'm not hiding

William Mahoney
William Potts
WT

**Australia**
A mum in Queensland
Amy Samuels Australia
Anonymous in Perth

C.C Australia
Joselyn in Sydney
Jude in Australia
K O Australia
Kate Johnson Rowville, Victoria
Kiwimum
Lisa
LW
Nikki in Melbourne
Parent, NSW
RB from Australia
ROGD parents' group for Victorian
   parents
SL and RD
Tess, Western Australia.
@blackthugcat -Australia, Victoria.

**Austria**
Sabine O.

**Brazil**
TM - Rio de Janeiro

**Chile**
@unamadremas21 - Santiago de
   Chile

**Ecuador**
Oma y Tata Sin Perder la Esperanza
Tia Andi Waiting for Redemption

**France**
Suzanne from Ypomoni

**Germany**
A father from Germany
Alexa
Concerned German mother of a
   confused daughter

Desperate mother of a girl.
J. Germany
Loving Papa from Berlin
Mother, Germany
Parents from Bavaria
PartOfheSolution @ROGD_GER
Ulrike, mother of an 18 year old
  daughter
Germany, Rheinland-Pfalz
Vater Elch, Hamburg
Wilhelmina Tell
You'll always be my baby GIRL

**Ireland**
Deravara

**Italy**
Anonymous
Benedetta, mamma di Bea, 14 anni
Dolphin in storm
Noraa speranzosa
Vittorio - Trento
Worried parent of ROGD FTM
**New Zealand**
N P from Christchurch
PhD scientist Mum & Academic
  Dad

**Spain / España**
#NoContabanConLasMadres
@comseraquan
Agusto sin queer
ALC
AMANDA, (Agrupación de Madres
  de Adolescentes y Niñas con
  Disforia Acelerada, de España)
Amat madre desbordada de España
  (overwhelmed mother)
Amatxu

Ambu
AML LaMadre
AMR
Anayenci
Angela
Angeles T
Anónima
Anónima
Anónimo
Anónimo
BBG
Beta
Bluelinx1
Brenda E.
BSG
C.Torres
Carmen.
Claudio M. Martínez
Cloe
Como anónimo
Confianza y coraje! (Trust and
  Courage)
Crrj
D y P
EAP
Elena Navarro y mi hijo Julen
Estibaliz 1975
F.V.G.
Fixyou
G.A.
GGB
I.L.
Irene Arias
IUFG
L. G. I.
La madre
Ll. De España
Lydia N.
M Isabel C Saez

M. Félix
M.A. Mallorca
M.A.R.
M.I.J.
M.J.A.G.
M.J.L.
Madre anónima
Mamá anónima
Madre d
Madre España
Madre en España
Madre Española
Madre guerrera
Madre luchadora de España (fighting mother)
Madres leonas (Mother lionesses)
Mago
María
Marisol
MayRS
MCMP
Meme
Merrita
Mimi
MLLL
MMJ
Mp
MR
MRV (Isabel's mom)
Muchas gracias de España
MVRR Spain
MYSR
Necesito un completo anonimato
Nuria Hernández – Encantada de aparecer con mi nombre real
P. L. V.
P.S.A., MADRID, ESPAÑA
Padres anónimos
Paloma

PAT
RCR
Rosario Trasobares De Dios. (Using my real name. I am her mother and she needs to know that I always did everything possible to protect and defend her)
Sin mención
Sin nombre
Sole desde España
Sonia
Su mamá
SUPER MRC 72
T.B.
TGM
Twitter: @emege_2
Una madre más
Yolandascpcervera

**South Africa**
Struggling South African mom

**Sweden**
Liberal mom

**Switzerland**
Lori from Switzerland

**UK**
Beth - Kent
LovingMum
Mum of male desister
Paul and Janet M
Sarah Buchanan, Scotland
T.T.
Tristia,
UK50

❋    ❋    ❋

**Parent Support Groups**

**International**

Genspect

Gender Critical Resources Support
Board

Partners for Ethical Care

Oasis: A Place for Parents (Facebook
group)

Our Duty

Parents of ROGD Kids

**By Country or Region**

**United States** – Cardinal Support
Network

Advocates Protecting Children

**Belgium** – Cry for Recognition

**Brazil** – No Corpo Certo

**Finland** – Kirjo

**France** – Ypomoni

**Germany** – Transteens Sorge
berechtigt

**Italy** – GenerAzioneD

**New Zealand** – Aotearoa Support

**Norway** – Genid: Gender Identity
Challenge Norway

**Spain and Latin America** –
AMANDA Agrupación de Madres
de Adolescentes y Niñas con
Disforia Acelerada

**Sweden** – Genid: Gender Identity
Challenge Sweden

**Switzerland** – AMQG

**United Kingdom** – Bayswater
Support Group

# Foreword
## Dr. Jordan B. Peterson

We are all familiar—at this point in time, far more than we want to be—with the epidemics caused by viruses, bacteria, and parasites, but their equivalent can also emerge on the psychological front—and this has been the case for a very long time.[1] As the great Swiss analytical psychologist Carl Gustav Jung stated in 1957:

> Just as people can catch measles and scarlet fever from one another, so can they catch the ways of feeling, thinking, and behaving. The more people live together in heaps, the less each individual counts, and the more he or she will be inclined to take his or her cue from the collective rather than pursue an individual ideal.[2]

The rapid exchange of information, which perhaps above all else characterizes the age we now live in, has increased the speed at which social contagions can spread, as well as producing a more varied plethora of forms. It is the case with viruses that the faster a given pathogen can spread, the more deadly its form, at least under certain conditions,[3] and that the same could well be true on the psychological front. How deadly can such epidemics become? We are, no doubt, in the process of finding out. Hopefully, the answer won't be "universally fatal." But that possibility certainly beckons.

Three relevant kinds of transmissible psychological disease appear to exist—or, at least, such might be argued on historical grounds. The first kind is transmitted through the general population. Examples of those, which abound, include multiple personality disorder[4] (whose cycles of sporadic emergence and social dissemination have been traced back centuries[5];)

hysteria (big in Freud's day, although more complex than originally considered[6];) cutting or other forms of self-mutilation;[7] eating disorders,[8] including anorexia and bulimia; trichotillomania;[9] Tourette's symptomatology;[10] and, more recently, bodily dysmorphia of the form that manifests itself as cross-sex identity.

The pattern underlying the emergence of such social contagion is this: sufferers, typically young women, suffer disproportionately and more generally and primarily from elevated levels of trait or state neuroticism, including its clinical and subclinical variants, depression, anxiety, self-consciousness, and confusion.[11] This tendency toward a basic and undifferentiated psychopathology then seeks a socially acceptable form of expression.[12] That form varies with the times. In Freud's time[13]—which, at least among the upper classes from whom Freud drew his clients, was obsessed with the theater—depressed, anxious, neurotic young women had dramatic fits of weakness and fainting (which would often attract the attention of young men, striving to be knights on horseback, but which also sometimes resulted in hysterectomy, as a consequence of medical misdiagnosis). More recently, young women in similar straits found themselves exchanging photos of their emaciated bodies and tips on self-starvation on social media channels.[14]

The second kind of transmissible psychological disease might be considered political. National Socialism spread like a virus. So did communism. The former, like smallpox, has been virtually eliminated. The latter has mutated very effectively and continues to make its terrible effects known. Much has been written on both; we won't spend much time on this variant here, although the topic at hand has its ideological element, as the ideology that fosters the development of the stunningly immature, philosophically shallow, and incoherent, hedonistic, and narcissistic claims of absolute subjectively defined "identity" underlying the trans/gender-dysphoria/gender-affirmation movement is in part ideological and political.

The third kind of transmissible psychological disease spreads among medical professionals and their clinical colleagues (psychologists and counselors first and foremost among them). These diseases emerge when poorly trained clinicians entice themselves into leaping on the latest "medical" bandwagon. Unaware of the literature on psychological contagion, or otherwise incompetent, greedy, manipulative, narcissistic, or downright sadistic, they offer unproven treatment to those in dire straits, creating tremendous damage in their wake, lining their own pockets, trumpeting their incompetence as cutting-edge clinical wisdom, and demonizing those who dare to question their ethics. Up to 40,000 people were lobotomized in the US between the 1930s and the 1950s. Walter Freeman introduced the procedure in the US (importing it from Portugal). He and his colleagues developed a variant involving the insertion of a long, thin, sharp metal implement (imagine an ice pick) through the eye socket into the prefrontal cortex of the "patient" and slicing through the brain—with all the accuracy one might imagine would accompany such a procedure.

They outfitted vans to travel from town to town offering lobotomies, which could be done in a very short period of time, to all takers. These "surgeries" were often performed without anesthesia, and in the absence of proper consent. Post-surgery, the "patients" were not so much cured as rendered permanently docile, as the prefrontal cortex is the part of the brain that makes plans before they are implemented, so that damage to its structure is very likely to decimate higher-order will.

These variant forms of transmissible psychological disease can interact, or dance, with one another. Medical personnel played a key role during the Nazi regime in the euthanasia programs and the Holocaust. The Nazis relied on the public trust in and perceived expertise of nurses, doctors, and other medical professionals to justify and implement its policies of public and racial "hygiene" and then genocide. Physicians, in particular, were instrumental in the selection of individuals for euthanasia and genocide and developed the methods and techniques used to kill them. This typically involved identifying disabled or chronically ill individuals deemed "life unworthy of life." Often, justification for such identification was couched in the language of compassion.

One prominent example is the Nazi propaganda film titled *I Accuse* (*Ich klage an*), released in 1941, which depicted a fictional case of a woman suffering from multiple sclerosis. The film aimed to evoke sympathy and promote the idea of "mercy killing." In the film, a husband pleads for the euthanasia of his wife, who is depicted as suffering greatly and being a burden on him and society. The film's narrative portrays euthanasia as an act of compassion, presenting it as a way to end the woman's suffering and release her from her deteriorating condition. The systematic killing of disabled people started with child "euthanasia" in 1939, and quickly expanded to include adults, and then whole classes of peoples. This was common language and practice in the lead-up to the genocides. Is there anything worse than torture and murder masquerading as compassion? It is a long and hard search indeed to find a deeper and more contemptible pit of hell, or worse demons native to that abyss.

Doctors in the National Socialist era were responsible for completing the appropriate questionnaires and determining which patients would be sent to the killing centers (after completing the requisite questionnaires). They were also recruited (or signed up) to administer the lethal injections or organize the gassing of patients in gas chambers. Medical professionals played key roles in the genocide of Jews and other minorities during the Holocaust. They also helped plan and carry out medical experiments on prisoners in concentration camps, which involved testing new drugs, surgical procedures, and sterilization techniques. Such experiments were often performed without consent and resulted in the death or permanent injury of the subjects. Doctors and their professional compatriots also helped identify prisoners too weak or sick to work, so that they could be sent to the gas chambers.

Why did this happen? Why, indeed? And why have we failed to learn? To begin with, there is no reason to assume that physicians, et al., would be particularly less prone than any other class of persons to fall prey to the blandishments of demented ideologues, and there is some evidence to suggest that they may in fact be more rather than less likely to participate in the perpetration of political and other forms of horror. Medical personnel have access to vulnerable people, at the points in their life when that vulnerability is most magnified. This can create opportunities for those characterized by the darkest of personality traits. Surgeons and anesthesiologists, in particular, may exhibit higher levels of narcissism, Machiavellianism, psychopathy, and sadism than those typifying the general population.[15] These traits, collectively referred to as the "Dark Tetrad," are characterized by callous disregard for others, manipulative behavior, desire for power and control, and a positive delight in the subjugation and suffering of others.

This all creates a very toxic brew—psychological and political, with regard to victim and perpetrator—and one whose analysis sheds substantive light on the newest set of transmissible diseases plaguing our current culture. There has been a substantive increase in the number of young people presenting with so-called gender dysphoria in recent years. This has been caused, in all likelihood, by the same mechanisms operative when other psychogenic epidemics have spread through the population: that is, by the marshalling of social forces, for oft-political reasons, to shape the manifestation of an underlying non-specific proclivity to anxiety, depression, and hopelessness among a vulnerable subset of children and adolescents. This marshalling is done under the rubric of hypothetical "compassion" for young people suffering through the increased self-consciousness and negative emotion commonly associated with puberty (particularly among girls[16]—particularly if they reach puberty earlier).

What is the cause, in more detail—and the outcome, individually and socially? This is precisely what Dr. Miriam Grossman outlines in the present work, documenting as she does the rapidly increasing prevalence of "gender-affirming treatment" for vulnerable children and adolescents, the role political and ideological ideas play in shaping that treatment, and the oft-terrible consequences for confused children, destroyed physically and psychologically by those who should be caring for them, and for the parents of such children, betrayed in the most profound sense by precisely the professionals that they should most be able to rely on when dealing with the very real distress of their children.

She begins by documenting the appalling case of Dr. John Money, whose now-widely-discredited efforts laid the groundwork for justifying the current butchery of children. He developed the idea of "gender identity"—the idea that there was a separate subjective element to sex, purely psychological in nature—an idea that has infiltrated the psychiatric and other medical sub-professions, to the great detriment of those most practically affected by it (and that would be children and adolescents subject to "gender reassignment" protocols, ranging from the "therapeutic" to the hormonal and surgical).

The consequence: a veritable explosion in the number of child and adolescent referrals to psychiatric and other medical clinics for "gender dysphoria" (the subjectively defined mismatch between biological sex and "gender identity"). It is now the case that in many jurisdictions in the Western world the theory that sex and subjective "gender identity" are separate is now enforced by law, and therapists and medical professionals are therefore compelled to "affirm" the subjective identity claimed by their clients and patients in preference to their—in the terrible lingo of the times—"sex assigned at birth" [17]—the sex designation recorded on an infant's birth certificate, typically as either "male" or "female," based on an assessment of the infant's external anatomy.

Dr. Grossman details the fact that although endless assurances have been delivered that children will be subjected to the proper evaluation prior to any dramatic medical intervention, assessment for "gender dysphoria," prior to the initiation of hormone treatment (and, too often, subsequent surgery) such assessment often occurs in the most cursory and unprofessional of manners, producing the implicitly and explicitly desired catastrophic outcome. She also discusses the now-discredited[18] "Dutch Protocol" that hypothetically established the standards for so-called "gender-affirming" care, as well as the terrible Tavistock scandal that rocked the UK (the now-disgraced Tavistock Clinic was practicing at the forefront of "gender-affirming" care provision, following precisely that "Dutch Protocol") and others similar scandals in the US.

Grossman spends some time, as well, discussing the most egregious and evil lie told to the parents of so-called "trans children": "Would you rather have a live trans child or a dead child?" There is, to put it mildly, no evidence that the only alternative to early medical transition for a child with gender dysphoria is suicide. Providing desperate parents in a time of crisis with this appalling piece of utterly unjustified "medical" advice is professional misconduct of the most unforgivable sort. Equally egregious lies are now disseminated by schools and other institutions, including—as Dr. Grossman also details—the courts and the social work systems nominally devoted to the protection of children. It should be noted in this regard that it is not only the lives of children that are being irreparably damaged by their subjugation to the terrible processes of psychological and physical transformation accompanying the "affirmation" of their new "gender." All of their family members suffer dreadfully, watching a child they love being harmed in an irrevocable manner and being changed into something false and foreign—finding themselves, as parents and grandparents and other loved ones, in the position of those who are damned if they do and damned if they don't. Furthermore, the availability of trans-hormonal and surgical procedures have added another weapon to the arsenal of narcissistic parents perfectly willing to use their children either to emphasize the purity and extent of their terrible compassion or to wage war against their estranged spouse in an all-out custody or divorce battle. If you are one of the naive ones who don't think that such things can and do happen, then you are setting yourself and those dependent upon you for your security for a serious fall at the hands of some malevolent actor perfectly willing and able to exploit your blind faith in the goodness of man—and woman.

"I had beautiful breasts. Now they're in the incinerator. Thank you, modern medicine": so laments Miss Chloe Cole, pioneering detransitioner, currently dragging various members and corporate bodies of the medical establishment (including Kaiser Permanente) deservedly through the courts for the barbarities perpetrated upon her when she was a minor. Such enterprise is a growth industry, trumpeted for its economic possibilities by the marketing types who will line themselves up to make money regardless of the source. Global Market Insights, for example, has estimated a greater than 11 percent compound annual growth rate in the possibility of services to be offered and outlined the money, money, money to be made.[19]

Get in while the getting's good: the mad physician and counsellor gold rush continues apace, providing an ever-expanding source of money (opportunity abounds!) to those perfectly willing to exploit miserable, wretched, unhappy children and their desperate, clueless parents: $632 billion in the US in 2022; $1.9 billion in 2032 (projected). Thus, the absolute worst of capitalism meets the most dismal and destructive of ideologies in a truly unholy alliance.

What the hell is wrong with us? And why won't more nurses, physicians, and counselors speak up? There is a cowardice, mendacity, and self-serving "morality" making itself manifest in our society at the individual, political, and medical levels that makes previous psychogenic epidemics look like a walk in the park. Dr. Miriam Grossman has courageously stood up for the victims and victims-to-be of this appalling growth enterprise and written a book bound to be both welcome and of clear practical use to parents and others who have had bloody well enough of this miraculously hypocritical, self-serving, and truly near-murderous lying and butchery.

Hopefully, her book will put another nail in the coffin of the so-called "gender affirmation" movement. Hopefully, it will serve to expose its stunningly cynical co-opting of the civil rights movement, its greedy exploitation of confused children, its offering of the cheapest and most contemptible virtue to its adherents and promoters. Hopefully, it will awaken sleeping parents, teachers, nurses, physicians, counselors, legislators—and, most of all, police officers and members of the judiciary—to the reality of the horrors being perpetrated by the delusional, mendacious, corrupt, narcissistic, and, indeed, psychopathic (particularly on the counselling and medical front) on the most vulnerable members of our deeply confused and more-than-metaphorically possessed and increasingly willfully blind society.

# A Note on Language

At the start of this project, I had to decide whether to comply with my profession and use a newly mandated vocabulary. To me it's a language without clarity: even the word "gender" has no coherent definition, to say nothing of "non-binary" and "cisgender." I was also aware that the newly invented terms erase an ancient one—woman. If a man can be a woman, then "woman" means nothing.

I considered my options. I could follow the herd and do as I'm instructed. I could decide case by case, calling a man "she" under certain circumstances. Maybe if "she" lived as a woman for decades? Or made great efforts to appear female? Or perhaps, call any man a woman who declares himself one, just to be kind?

Without question, had I been presented decades ago with a "pronoun dilemma," I'd have called a man "she" without hesitation. I am respectful and compassionate by nature, as reflected in my career choice. She would have been extraordinarily rare, and extending the courtesy wouldn't impact others, so why not?

But times have changed. We face a crusade, a juggernaut, that seeks to demolish male and female, and its success hinges on the control of language. Under those circumstances, to call a man "she" is not a kindness, it's a concession—to a scheme to control our beliefs and advance an agenda, one pronoun at a time.

In this book, I emphasize that male and female, after being established at conception, are permanent. I urge parents to be honest and consistent with their children, and to at all times stay grounded in biological reality. I have always done that in my office, and I'm not going to stop now.

Could I write "she" while quietly holding on to my truth? I could, but that presents a few problems. One, it's living a lie, and that injures the soul.

Two, co-opting the word "woman" is offensive to me. I am not a belief or a costume.

Finally, with each pronoun capitulation—whether for Jazz, Marci Bowers, or Rachel Levine (all of whom you will meet)—another boy thinks, *If "she's" a woman, I can be too.* I will have fostered his delusion, perhaps moving him further along a dangerous path. All because of words and "kindness."

Humans require meaning and connection to thrive, but the trans belief system leads to disconnection: words stripped of substance; minds dissociated from bodies; youth estranged from their names, families, histories, and futures.

While cumbersome, in this book I avoid pronouns for transgender-identifying persons. I reject the new vocabulary because I've seen the suffering to which it leads. I've seen it up close, day after day, for years. I will have no part of it.

# Introduction

When I graduated from medical school, I took an oath. I stood up, raised my right hand, and vowed to prevent disease whenever I could. At the time, I expected to go to war against cancer and schizophrenia. But after forty years, I've realized my most challenging fight is not against dangerous diseases, but dangerous ideas.

The beliefs that man and woman are human inventions, that the sex of a healthy newborn is arbitrarily and often incorrectly "assigned," and that as a result the child requires "affirmation" through risky medical interventions—these ideas are divorced from reality and therefore hazardous, especially to children. They are, in fact, a mockery of twenty-first-century science and cause immeasurable harm to young people and their families. I know, because I'm a psychiatrist and they're my patients.

I don't have the words to describe the sorrow of parents I know whose young daughter was removed by a government agency, placed in foster care, and started on testosterone. Their crime? Insisting she's a girl. Or the anguish of a young man I see, who sought castration to become his "authentic self" and now, after the fact, regrets it. Or the rage of a twenty-something woman going through menopause due to "gender-affirming" removal of her reproductive organs.

Are these atrocities really happening in our country? They sure are, and you must protect your loved ones from joining the multitude of victims.

I discovered how children were being indoctrinated with gender ideology while writing my 2009 book[1] *You're Teaching My Child WHAT?* I wanted parents to know that the powerful sex ed industry has agendas that undermine the health and safety of children. Widely used curricula and teen-friendly websites promoted sexual freedom, not sexual health, placing students' well-being at risk.

In the final chapter, I cautioned parents about "Genderland," comparing it to the upside-down world of *Alice in Wonderland*:

> Parents, fasten your seatbelts. If what you've learned so far about sex education horrifies you, and you believe it can't get any worse, I caution you: it can and it does. . . . Welcome to Genderland, where the madness of sex education reaches a peak, and everything you know is turned on its head.[2]

"Madness" was the right word. I'd discovered the nation's flagship sex ed organization, the Sexuality Information and Educational Council of the US (SIECUS),[3] was informing students that people "have an internal sense that they are female, male, or a variation of these"; Planned Parenthood instructed them, "your gender identity may shift and evolve over time"; and Advocates for Youth[4] claimed "being transgender is as normal as being alive."[5] All those outrageous statements were made with astonishing certainty.

As a child psychiatrist, I was alarmed. A coherent sense of self requires knowing who you are. Struggling with identity is a handicap. Those are fundamental premises of psychology—why, I wondered, are bizarre and destabilizing ideas about identity being taught as facts to vulnerable students?

After refuting the sex educators' claims, I warned:

> Genderland is a dumbfounding departure from reality. . . . Every parent needs to visit Genderland, ahead of his child, and carefully observe the landscape. Many will feel, as Alice did, like they've fallen down a black hole and landed in a truly bewildering place. . . . [It's] a recipe for physical and emotional disaster for our kids.[6]

The disaster is here. We are in a freefall down a black hole, with no landing in sight. Girls who claim to be boys and boys girls are almost as common, it seems, as teenagers with acne. But it should come as no surprise: after years of bombardment with the notion that the "gender binary" is false and oppressive, and encouragement to explore whether they're male, female, both, or neither, lo and behold, the number of teens with recent-onset discomfort with their sex is up 4,000 percent.

In 2004, there were two clinics *in the entire world* for these exceedingly rare cases. Now there are at least one hundred clinics in the US alone, and preteen girls learn from American Girl's guide *Body Image*, "If you haven't gone through puberty yet, the doctor might offer medicine to delay your body's changes, giving you more time to think about your gender identity."[7]

And how does a girl do that? She might flatten her developing breasts with a tight elastic binder she can easily find—at Walmart,[8] Target, or at school.[9] She goes through the day in pain, feeling lightheaded and short of breath. She may "pack" her underwear to create a bulge emulating the look of a penis.[10] A boy might shave his arms, legs, and chest to erase signs of masculinity. To achieve a flat, feminine crotch he'll push his testicles into his inguinal canals, then tape his penis and scrotum together behind his legs.[11] This maneuver can cause severe pain, infection, and testicular torsion—an acute condition requiring emergency surgery.

I know, it's hard to believe, but that's what's going on. The gender utopians have colonized not only super-liberal Berkeley, but Knoxville and Plano. I know the devastation that results and consider it a duty to warn and educate parents, grandparents, aunts, and uncles—anyone with a child in their lives—about the mess we are in.

I want the following truths—recognized by everyone on the planet aside from gender studies professors and grad students until about two weeks ago—to be acknowledged in the first pages of this book: Sex is not assigned at birth; it's established at conception. Brains always match the bodies to which they are attached; we are not Legos or Mr. Potato Heads that might be improperly assembled. Sex is binary. Sex is permanent. Males cannot become females and females cannot become males.

Doctors, therapists, and others who lead young people to believe otherwise are guilty of malfeasance. They must be stopped and held responsible for the damage inflicted on children and families.

Having said that, I will also state outright that there are individuals for whom living a life consistent with their biology is a life of torture. We do not understand the condition from which they suffer, but it is real and unrelenting. I firmly believe their chronic disembodiment is a disorder of the mind and that they deserve our compassion and respect. Hormones and surgery? Maybe, but we cannot predict with accuracy in whom the benefit will outweigh the harm.

This book is not about those extraordinarily rare people, who have been written about for almost 100 years. This book is about the kids whose new identities are the result of a hysteria fueled by the Internet, social media, Hollywood, and the gender medical and government establishment that mushroomed out of the ideology I discovered in sex education fifteen years ago.

For me this is a black-and-white issue. Most things in life are nuanced, but this is not one of them. This is—and here's a word you don't expect from a doctor—evil. It's evil to indoctrinate children and young adults with falsehoods and to drive a wedge between them and their loving parents. It's evil to encourage them on a path that leads to harm. And it's evil to describe it all as a journey to authenticity, and to entice children with glitter and rainbows.

We are a nation lost in trans madness; the price we are paying is staggering.

This is a guide out of the madness. If you're a parent, you needed it yesterday, because the crusaders are at your door, they've already conquered Disney and Target, your kids' school, camp, and pediatrician.

I wrote this book to arm you for battle against the blitz of transgenderism, because no family is immune. Yes, "battle" and "blitz": I use military terms intentionally. The trans issue is not a debate with reasonable and moral people on both sides, it's a war. It's a destructive, cult-like crusade that targets your children 24/7; there's hardly a place that's free from indoctrination, slogans, flags, and emojis. You must gird yourselves with knowledge, confidence, and support and oppose the onslaught as much as possible.

Wake up, parents: you know it makes a difference if someone's male or female, but depending on how indoctrinated your child is, he or she may think it's completely inconsequential. I have patients who are indignant when I inquire if someone is a boy or girl: "You mean what they were assigned at birth?" they answer indignantly. "What difference does it make?"

I want you to understand who and what you are fighting, and to avoid being blindsided like so many families who were bewildered by their child's sudden announcement: *Mom, Dad—I'm not your daughter, I'm your son,* or by the gender therapists' emotional blackmail: *Do you want a live daughter or a dead son?*

Starting with new names and pronouns and ending too often in the operating room, the trans journey is an assembly line. One step leads to another, and it's difficult to get off, so your goal is to prevent your child from even climbing on. With each step they believe their goal will be reached, they'll finally feel good about themselves. When the "high" fades, they take the next step, and the next.

Scott Nugent is a forty-eight-year-old female-to-male transgender person who underwent seven surgeries in her* sex reassignment surgery, followed by life-threatening complications. Scott regrets her decisions and warns:

---

* Scott told me she doesn't care which pronouns I use in referring to her.

Each step is like a Christmas present. You open the present and it's exactly what you wanted, but then the elation wears off. Testosterone, top surgery, bottom surgery . . . then the Christmas party is over, you look around, there are no more presents left to open. And you realize: this didn't work.[12]

And there's no scientific foundation that the ever-lengthening list of "Christmas presents"—a new name and pronouns; hormones; breast, facial, and Adam's apple surgeries; and the construction of a faux vagina or phallus—provides a solution for the perceived "mismatch" between body and mind, what's called gender dysphoria.

The new names and pronouns seem harmless, but they can end with surgery, so that's why I chose to have surgical instruments on the cover of this book: to highlight what for many is the disastrous endpoint—disfigurement, sterility, and mental health issues. For many, it seems, their post-transition lives are not filled with glittery rainbows, but with pain, infection, and urine bags.

My wish is for your child to reject the falsehoods from the get-go. If he or she is already on a "gender journey," the goal is therapy that will facilitate him or her to love themselves as they are, without harming their bodies. I want to preserve your child's health, sexual pleasure, and fertility. No child is born in the wrong body, their bodies are just fine; it's their emotional life that needs attention and healing. In this book you'll find the ammunition to protect your children while raising them in Trans Nation: information, parenting strategies, and hope.

## What You'll Learn

I'm going to teach you what you must know about gender but aren't taught. I regret to inform you that with this matter, the sources you've always trusted—your child's school, pediatrician, and therapist—will likely provide ideologically driven misinformation. They will direct you and your child down a perilous path. I've spoken to hundreds of parents who regret following the advice given them by schools, pediatricians, and therapists.

Whether your child is five and perfectly content, or eighteen and demanding a double mastectomy, you will be savvier than he or she.

I'll explain that transgender ideology is a system of beliefs, like a religion. It has a unique language and Articles of Faith. While the language and beliefs are bizarre, they are taught as sacred facts. The core belief—that biology can and should be denied—is a repudiation of reality.

When your fourth grader brings home a diagram of the genderbread person,[13] you'll say with confidence, "This is interesting. Let's look and see if it's true." When she claims intersex is as common as red hair, you will gently correct her.[14] Ditto when she argues that half of transgender youth have tried to commit suicide. I'm teaching you to recognize the falsehoods your kids are absorbing, discuss them calmly, and rectify them with confidence.

You'll understand that not only is your child misinformed, but so are his teachers, guidance counselor, therapist, and doctor. Might as well throw in the American Academy of Pediatrics, the American Psychological Association, the Endocrine Society, our president, and officials at HHS. They are all a part of, or have been led to believe in, the "Castro consensus"[15] that has a tight grip on medical, educational, and governmental institutions, to say nothing of popular culture. A Castro consensus is when there appears to be agreement about an issue when in fact, due to extreme polarization and squashing of dissent, there's no true agreement. You will learn why the only consensus that exists about the care of kids with gender distress is a Castro consensus.

I will provide the historical underpinnings of gender theory. You'll learn about Dr. John Money, distinguished psychologist and researcher, who in the 1950s coined the term "gender identity" and proposed that biology doesn't matter—one of the dangerous ideas to which I referred. But John Money was an arrogant psychopath; he destroyed a family and distorted his "research" to prove gender theory and further his fame. An entire field was built on his false claims. It's because of John Money and his disciples that transgender ideology is hitting homes such as yours like nuclear bombs.

You'll learn how today's science proves Money's theory is categorically false: from conception, there is a wide-reaching, permanent impact of biology on every system of the body. Each of our seventy trillion cells with a nucleus is stamped "XX" or "XY," and hard science demonstrates the enduring influence of that biological reality on the brain and every other organ system.

Nevertheless, John Money's falsehoods are central to the success of the gender blitz. You'll learn how to prevent his ideas from invading your home and harming your family.

I will introduce you to the powerful World Professional Association for Transgender Health, whose standards of care are followed by just about everyone: clinicians, hospitals, courts, and governmental agencies (Admiral Dr. Rachel Levine, deputy secretary of Health & Human Services, is a huge fan). WPATH exercises dominion over global policy regarding all transgender issues. When you read my exposure of the lies emanating from that organization, of their consumerism, and normalization of deviance, your jaws will drop.

I will explain how the American Psychiatric Association (APA) reclassified gender disorders as a normal variation of human expression—another dangerous idea. Hint: there was no referendum of its members. It was about politics, stigma, and insurance coverage.[16]

You'll get to know the work of Stephen Levine. I doubt there's another clinician alive who understands transgender-identified patients better. How do I summarize Dr. Levine's expertise? His resume is twenty-four pages long.

Dr. Levine is clinical professor of psychiatry at Case Western Reserve University and Distinguished Life Fellow of the American Psychiatric Association. He founded the Case Western Reserve University Gender Identity Clinic in 1974 and has served as codirector since that time. Dr. Levine was given his Department of Psychiatry's Hall of Fame Award in 2021 and has been named to America's Top Doctors consecutively since 2001. He is the author of five books, forty-four chapters, and 146 papers about sexuality and gender.

Dr. Levine has treated transgender-identifying individuals for fifty years. He's an outspoken critic of gender-affirming care (GAC)—the immediate social and medical affirmation of what could be a young person's temporary identity. Levine calls professionals out for failing to inform patients and their parents that the current approach is sorely lacking in quality research and fraught with uncertainty.

Levine's battle takes place in the pages of academic journals and in the courtroom, where he is a formidable advocate for the health and well-being of young people. If there is a hero in this ghastly tale, it is he.

I will review basic biology you may have forgotten [Appendix One: "Biology 101"]. You'll learn the significance of puberty and why blocking it is a risky experiment.

I promise, when you're done reading, you will be an expert on all things trans—including the dangers of giving testosterone to girls and estrogen to boys and the perils of what's euphemistically called "top" and "bottom" surgery, operations that would make Mengele proud.

Can minors provide informed consent for those life-altering interventions? I'll explain why I, and others, think not.

*But all the medical organizations say gender affirmation is the only safe and ethical treatment! If you don't support your child, he's at high risk of suicide.*

Plan on hearing that from just about everyone. I'll demonstrate how the suicide myth is a distortion of the data; teens identifying as transgender have just about the same risk of suicide as LGB kids and kids with mental health issues. You'll learn how mainstream medical organizations are just mouthpieces propping up the woke narrative. The disfiguring and steriliz- ing treatments for which medical groups like the American Psychological Association (APA) and the Endocrine Society (ES) advocate are poorly researched and controversial, and without careful follow-up to determine long-term outcomes. Despite this, no debate is allowed. Doctors who ques- tion are shut down. That includes the American Academy of Pediatrics, whose guidance and policy positions your pediatrician most likely follows. No worries. I provide talking points. She won't get the truth from the AAP, that's for sure, but you'll be able to enlighten her if you wish [Appendix Two: "Key Scientific Papers"].

You will immediately recognize when the same empty arguments are being regurgitated and biological truths denied.

Washington wants you to think there's a medical consensus on these issues and that the science is settled. Again, it's a Castro consensus. You will learn there is a severe lack of knowledge, and a debate rages. Professional standards and treatments are all over the map, and they're being disputed in court cases and medical conferences. I will explain what the experts (on both sides) are arguing in those venues—you have a right to know. Parents must be extremely cautious.

Take the "affirmation" model. It's based on one small study from Holland conducted in the 2000s. Subjects had to have developed gender identity disorder as children, and those with mental health issues were excluded. Yet the Dutch study is now used to justify medical treatment of a very different population: those who developed discomfort with their sex as teens, and most of whom have an emotional or neuro-atypical condition such as ADHD, autism, anxiety, and depression. I will describe instances when even psychotic and suicidal kids have been placed on the trans assem- bly line.

So, while Joe Biden and Rachel (originally Richard) Levine (not to be confused with Stephen Levine, and henceforth to be called "the Admiral") tell parents that hormones and surgery are "crucial and life-saving care" for their kids, one of the authors of the Dutch study recently asked, "Why is the rest of the world blindly adopting our research? We need more data."

Yes, we need more data, that's for sure. In in the meantime, doctors should "do no harm." You'll learn that countries like Britain, Sweden,

Finland, and Norway are doing exactly that: after rigorous reviews of existing studies, they decided to severely restrict, even ban, medical interventions for minors. But in the US and Canada it's full steam ahead.

## Trust Your Gut

"Experts" with lots of diplomas instruct you to begin using your child's new name and pronouns at once. Your gut screams, *no!* But maybe you doubt yourself.

I'm saying in this instance—and I am an expert with lots of diplomas on my wall—believe your gut. Trust your parental instincts. The entire world is telling you to put your gender-questioning child in the driver's seat, but you will learn they're wrong.

Arrogant teachers and therapists believe they know better than you what's best for your child. They believe all kids should question their identity, that feelings trump reality, sex is on a spectrum, and all the rest of it—this is healthy, they think, so they teach the ABCs of gender ideology to your children when they've yet to learn their real ABCs. My advice: run the other way and don't look back. You know your child best, never forget that.

It's vital you are confident in your convictions. You must be free of the ideology; you must know it's false and dangerous. There's no one-size-fits-all approach, but the more certain you are, the more you can stay true to yourself, the better. This is challenging to say the least, when it seems like the whole world is steering you in another direction and claiming you are harming your child. But it can be done. Might the outcome be negative? Of course, there are no guarantees. You are fighting a monster while trying to keep your child close—a Herculean task.

You're in unfamiliar, bizarre territory and need a roadmap. The good news is you're not alone. Many parents have navigated the same shark-filled waters and have excellent advice for you [Appendix Seven: "Responses to International Parent Survey"]. You will hear about parents who felt no choice but to use their "nuclear option": homeschooling or moving to another state or country. Parents like you have taken extreme measures to save their child from irreversible medicalization and are pleased with the results.

Sooner or later, whether it's about your child's classmate or cousin, the topic of being "trans," and new names and pronouns, will come up at your house. You'll be prepared and know how to respond.

What if it's your own child who is struggling? What do you say, and refrain from saying, when your child announces she's "pansexual," "gender queer," or "nonbinary"? How do you enter and get control over her social media and Internet access [Appendix Six: "Guide to Internet Accountability Tools"]? What do you do when she gets a buzz cut and starts shopping in the boys' department? That's addressed in Chapter Thirteen.

Schools cannot be trusted; they are a major site of indoctrination. Teachers and counselors can undermine your parenting and drive a wedge between you and your child. Stories abound of parents discovering their child has been using the opposite sex bathroom, or that teachers have been calling her by a boy's name and using male pronouns without their knowledge. Schools are being sued for active deception of parents and facilitation of a student's double life—Daniel at home, Daniella at school.

You'll learn that schools can be a minefield, one of your most difficult challenges. Each family has a different situation, but other parents have come before you and you don't need to reinvent the wheel. There are also courageous and brilliant lawyers fighting for your rights as parents with whom I have worked. I will provide you with guidance and a list of resources [Appendix Three: "Dealing with Schools"].

The transgender blitz is causing American families to endure horrific ordeals. You will learn about Hank, a dad who wouldn't accept his fourteen-year-old emotionally disturbed daughter's male identity. Protective Services deemed his home unsafe, placed her with a male couple, and facilitated testosterone therapy. Hank hasn't seen his daughter in three years.

You will learn how to protect your family if a state agency interferes with your parenting [Appendix Four: "Dealing with Child Protective Services"].

I will describe the grief and trauma of parents, and their abandonment by the mental health profession. You will learn about finding help and support for yourselves.

## Returning to Reality

You may ask, is this a futile situation? Are we up the creek? Absolutely not. Trust me, there is reason to hope. You'll read about the positive outcomes I've seen. It's altogether possible to bring your son and daughter back to reality and acceptance of their sex. It's possible to survive, albeit with scars.

I receive frantic emails from parents of gender-confused kids every day. They're all the same: *We are losing our child and we are desperate. The doctors and therapists say we are the problem. We have nowhere to turn.*

Here's how it goes. Let's say twelve-year-old Ariana is seeing a therapist; maybe she has ADHD or her parents are divorcing. One day, out of the blue, Ariana announces to her therapist that she's "Ash," a boy. She's unhappy about her breast growth and nervous about getting her period. Two of Ava's online friends take medicine to stop their development, and Ariana wants the same. The therapist believes her client is expressing a variant of normal development. She affirms her new identity on the spot, referring to her as Ash and he/him in conversations and in her records, and suggests referral to an endocrinologist. If Ariana's parents refuse to go along with the treatment plan, the therapist believes their lack of support places her patient at risk of suicide. She tells the parents so, perhaps in Ava's presence.

Parents turn to me because I have a different approach.

I'm old-fashioned. After practicing psychiatry for forty years, and making it into my seventh decade of life, I have more knowledge and wisdom than my young patients. First of all, I'm curious about everything: their family, school, and friends, as well as their worries and dreams. Everything is connected to everything, and nothing is unimportant. Their new identity serves a purpose, and together we unravel what it is. We slowly explore the source of their distress, and I guide them toward self-acceptance. That's what therapists were once trained to do before gender ideology laid siege to the mental health profession. Now I am instructed to respect children's self-diagnoses and to follow *their* plans, to implement *their* solutions for their unhappiness.

I will not stand back and allow my patients—whose brains are immature and prone to make emotional decisions instead of rational ones, who cannot fathom the consequences of medically "transitioning" to the opposite sex (as if that's possible), who have not experienced the pleasure their sexed bodies can provide and cannot imagine the joy and meaning that parenthood brings—to call the shots and make the most important decision of their lives.

But helping patients to accept themselves might be professional suicide. In June 2022 President Biden signed an executive order[17] instructing his administration to end non-affirming therapy. America's leading medical organizations called on the government to "investigate and prosecute" doctors like myself. For prioritizing my patients' life-long well-being, and for keeping the oath I took to do no harm and to prevent disease, I might face investigation or even loss of my license. Yes, I worry about that. Still, I won't stop.

❋ ❋ ❋

You will be reading about several of my patients: all names and identifying details have been changed to protect confidentiality. Some portrayals represent a composite of several individuals.

I have tried to understand how this predicament came to be and will share what I discovered. But I am neither a scholar nor an investigative journalist—far from it. I am a doctor who sees patients all day, who's scratching her head, seeking to comprehend how her profession lost its way. This book has limitations.

It is not by any stretch a comprehensive review of the history and literature pertaining to gender identity, gender dysphoria, or transgenderism. It also does not include detailed discussion about the comorbid conditions associated with gender distress or the role of pornography.

I'll briefly mention that the link between transgender identities and autism spectrum disorder is undeniable. If your child has autistic traits such as social impairment, difficulty adjusting to change, obsessive interests, all-or-nothing thinking, and sensory issues, he or she may be vulnerable to transgender ideology. People with autism often feel different, misunderstood, and isolated. Their thought patterns and non-conformity likely predispose them to recruitment. This subject alone could fill an entire book. Because of the sheer volume of material and limited time as well as space, I could not cover it and many other topics. I hope others will attack that project.

I regretfully was not able to include the work of some of the giants in this field and the many researchers, writers, and journalists whose contributions have been critical. I hope you understand the tight spot in which I found myself.

Of necessity, I had to choose just a few of the many detransitioners with whom I spoke and read about. I wish I could have included more of your testimonies—you deserve your own genre of books. I look forward to the deluge that's coming.

With the help of AC, a warrior mom, a parent survey was conducted. I was overwhelmed by the response: 500 parents from seventeen countries. Parents: *thank you.* Your heartfelt words will help other parents navigate the dystopian gender landscape. It was tough to select the few that are included in Appendix Seven.

I've struggled with understanding the gender belief system. Who and what is behind it? Is it a social movement? A political movement? A system of faith, a crusade? Something else? From where does the funding come? What's the role of the transhumanism movement—that seeks to "free" the body and mind of their biological limitations and augment human capabilities with technology? Jennifer Bilek[†] and others have done a great job explor-

---

† https://www.the11thhourblog.com/about.

ing these issues. I'm not going to pretend to know things I don't. I'm sticking with what I see in my office, giving parents a voice, and providing the information they need to protect their families and avoid being ambushed.

I've done my best but am sure there are errors and omissions, for which I take complete responsibility.

A mother consulted with me about her twelve-year-old daughter. She told me when she goes to websites to learn more about her daughter's struggles, she feels physically ill. "I can't go on," she told me, "I have to stop. Reading about what they do to kids, sterilizing them, I feel sick."

"That's a fitting response," I told her. "You should feel sick. I do, too."

Decent people have a visceral reaction when they learn children are being harmed. You will be troubled by what you read in the pages ahead; you will probably need to take a break. Well, join the club. Take care of yourself, then come back and do what you must to protect your child, all children, from a perilous social movement that erases "male" and "female" and aims to revolutionize what it means to be human.

# Articles of Faith

Behold GENDER IDENTITY; it liberated you from oppression, from the harsh constraints of biology.

GENDER IDENTITY is sacred; thou shall not question it; thou shall not turn away from it to hard science, for GENDER IDENTITY is jealous and cannot tolerate the scientific method.

Remember GENDER IDENTITY, to keep it holy. Behold, it is both fixed and fluid; healthy and needing drugs and surgeries; do not admit the contradictions.

Thou shall consider "male" and "female" arbitrary assignments; thou shall deny their establishment at conception.

Thou shall affirm all gender identities with all your heart and all your soul, so that you will be an ally and keep your livelihood.

Do not misgender.

Do not deadname.

Thou shall not explore anxiety, ADHD, trauma, or autism; thou shall always invoke the minority stress model.

Thou shall honor the self-diagnosis and judgment of minors and young adults. Thou shall not recognize their emotional and cognitive immaturity.

Gatekeeping is an abomination. Thou shall therefore scorn psychotherapy, and place your trust in breast binding, penis-and-testicle-tucking, pills, patches, syringes, scalpels, implants, and prosthetics.

# CHAPTER ONE

# John Money's Dangerous Idea

*I was betrayed by the medical profession . . . they put my life on the line so that they could hold on to their theories.*
—David Reimer[1]

During the nine years it took to become a doctor, a psychiatrist, and a child psychiatrist, I spent thousands of hours in lectures and saw innumerable patients of all ages. I went to countless Grand Rounds, Journal Clubs, and conferences in which unusual cases were presented. Board certification was a grueling review of mountains of material followed by oral and written exams. During that entire time, my exposure to individuals distressed by their sex was limited to a description of them in the *Diagnostic and Statistical Manual of Mental Disorders,* the DSM. Gender identity disorder (GID), as it was then called, was so incredibly rare*—and I studied medicine at Bellevue Hospital in New York City, the world's magnet for rare medical and psychiatric conditions—that I didn't expect to ever come across a case in my career.

Thirty-five years later, that's all I do. My entire practice is composed of kids unhappy with their sexed bodies and their parents, and I'm forced to turn down many other families' requests.

My young patients, who have anxiety, autism, depression, and other challenges, are certain the solution to their woes is a deeper voice and flat chest, or boobs and soft skin.

---

* In 2013, the DSM-5 estimated the incidence of gender dysphoria in adults to be at 2–14 per 100,000, or between 0.002 percent and 0.014 percent.

They yearn to "transition" to the opposite sex, along with their friends, many of whom either take hormones to alter their bodies or count the days until they can start. In chat rooms, they vent about their breasts, hips, and body hair. They binge on YouTube videos, mesmerized by their peers' transformations into synthetic opposite-sex personae. One such influencer, a woman living as a man, says the most common question she gets is *How do I know if I'm trans?* Her response: *If you think you may be trans, you probably are.* She's a superstar with over 385,000 subscribers.

Ten years ago, psychiatry, following cultural trends, declared that what was once an extraordinarily rare psychiatric disorder was a normal variant of child development,[2] and guess what. Since then, the numbers have skyrocketed.

London is home to the world's largest gender clinic for minors. Serving the entire United Kingdom, it opened in 1989 and over its first decade saw an average of fourteen patients a year.[3] By 2021–2022, that number exploded to 3,585 patients a year[4] with a waiting list exceeding 5,300.[5]

But it's not only the astonishing rise in cases. Gender ideology has become a powerful social-political movement. It has taken over our once-trusted medical, educational, and governmental institutions. It has co-opted our language and, in some places, compels our speech[6]. We are blitzed 24/7 with its lexicon and symbols: gender neutral names, pronouns, and bathrooms; "nonbinary," "gender-fluid," "gender-queer"; the ubiquitous flags and rainbows on buildings, clothing, cereal boxes, and ATM machines. Tampon machines next to urinals. Drag queen shows for toddlers, and honors at the White House.

How did this happen? It all rests on one man's theory about what makes us male and female. The entire edifice was built on his idea: it's the foundation of today's madness. And the foundation, as you will learn, is rotten.

❋   ❋   ❋

John Money[†] grew up on a farm in New Zealand. He studied psychology at Harvard, where his 1952 doctorate thesis was about hermaphrodism,[‡] a rare medical condition found in one in 5,000 births. Money was fascinated by these cases, in which a newborn's genitalia is ambiguous—not clearly male

---

† A few individuals preceded Money, such as Magnus Hirschfeld and Harry Benjamin. I believe John Money's influence has had the greatest long-term impact.

‡ Now called intersex or disorders of sexual development (DSD), but I will use historically the accurate term.

or female—and pioneered the work in "sex assignment," the complex decision of whether to raise a hermaphrodite as a boy or a girl.

In those days, perhaps less now, parents of a baby with ambiguous genitalia faced a real dilemma: boy or girl? Back then, the blankets in hospital nurseries were either blue or pink, not the striped variety we now have. Which blanket would wrap the new baby—blue or pink? What about a name, and what should parents tell the older siblings, family, and friends?

In such instances, or in other cases in which it becomes clear later that there's a disorder, it's accurate to say sex is or was "assigned." Instead of the *recognition* of male or female that occurs in 99.98 percent of infants, the circumstances required a decision.

Money established the country's first clinic for treatment of hermaphrodites, including their surgeries, at Johns Hopkins University. His clinic later became the first in the United States to provide sex-change surgery for adults.

Money had a theory. Not only about hermaphrodites—how many were there, after all?—but about humanity. He believed chromosomes and anatomy were irrelevant to the development of masculine and feminine identities, behaviors, and interests. Instead, he suggested children develop male or female qualities in the first years of life, based on how they are treated and on the expectations of others: *boys don't wear dresses or express their feelings. Girls aren't competitive or good at building things.* To describe the identity imposed from without, or "socially constructed," he coined the term "gender identity."[7] The year was 1957.

"[M]en impregnate," Money wrote, "women menstruate, ovulate, gestate, and lactate." All other distinctions are due to socialization.[8]

Before Money, the notion of divorcing identity from biology did not exist.§ If you had XX chromosomes, you were female. If you had XY chromosomes, you were male. There was no thought given to whether you *felt* female or male, because . . . that's what you *were*. What was there to talk about?

John Money changed that. He proposed the existence of a psychological sex, separate and more consequential than the body's sex. He named the psychological sex "gender." Infants are blank slates when they're born, he claimed, without a predisposition to think, feel, or behave in a masculine or feminine manner. Sex, he said, was determined by nature, but gender was

---

§ Yes, there were rare cases of transsexuals, almost always men, who sought SRS [sex reassignment surgery]. They were understood in various ways to have a disorder. There was no sweeping theory like Money's, denying the role of biology.

determined by nurture. Sex and gender—two different things, get it? Now there's a lot to talk about.

With his theory, Money made a huge leap. A hermaphrodite may have been exposed to abnormal levels of hormones in utero. Their genitals developed atypically; there was uncertainty how the child would eventually identify and how to facilitate their adjustment and well-being. Because of the uncertainty, they did indeed require "assignment" at birth as male or female.

From those rare infants—as I said, less than .02 percent of births—Money speculated about *all* babies, 99.98 percent of whom develop normally in utero, with normal hormone levels and normal genitals. You see why his theory was a big leap. But as you'll learn, Dr. Money was a daring fellow who pushed limits; he thrived on being in the limelight with shocking views.

John Money had an idea. Since, according to his theory, newborns are gender neutral, a child could be raised successfully as the opposite sex. If masculinity and femininity are man-made, social constructs imposed on children without basis for them in biology, why couldn't a boy be raised as a girl, or a girl as a boy?

Of course, reassignment of a child's sex would necessitate reproductive organs be removed and refashioned. The child would become a sterile adult dependent on hormones his entire life, but Money's clinic could take care of all that. Money's only caveat was that the process start by the age of two and a half or three at the latest, because, he explained, by the age of three gender is fixed.

Stated differently, Money declared we are all psychological hermaphrodites at birth, with the potential of being male or female. Our identities are externally imposed, unrelated to X or Y chromosomes, genitalia, or reproductive roles. He introduced his revolutionary theory in 1955, and he dedicated his life to changing how people think about a central aspect of humanity. As we will see, he succeeded beyond what could have been imagined.

When a person is zealous about a particular cause, when they're convinced of a truth the world must recognize, and their life mission is defined by it, it's worth asking, why this cause? I never met John Money, but his writing suggests an answer.

John had a traumatic childhood. He was a thin, delicate boy who was bullied at school. His father, who was prone to explosive acts of violence, terrorized his mother and abused John. In later life, Money described his father as a brutal man who shot the birds in his fruit garden and whipped four-year-old John over a broken window. It was that incident, Money wrote, that helped establish his lifelong rejection of "the brutality of manhood."[9]

John was eight when his father died, after which he was raised by his mother and unmarried aunts in a strictly religious home. It's fair to wonder if the absence of a positive male role model during John's early life, and repression of his sexuality by his religious mother and aunts, contributed to what would today be called his "gender dysphoria"—*rejection of his male genitals*:

> I suffered from the guilt of being male, he wrote. "I wore the mark of man's vile sexuality. . . . I wondered if the world might really be a better place for women if not only farm animals, but human males also were gelded⁵ at birth.¹⁰

That's troubling, isn't it, coming from a doctor to whom parents turned for advice about having their sons castrated?

Again, I never met John Money, but it's fair to suggest his vision of gender divorced from sex served a purpose in the subconscious management of his childhood trauma. In his child's psyche, not only his father but all men were cruel. He didn't understand cruelty isn't part of manhood; it's a character trait—women can be cruel, too.

I venture that as a child, John wished to be more like his mother than his father. But there he was—defined by his anatomy, a member of a group little John considered monsters. He didn't realize he could accept his genitals and be a man, just not the type of man his father was.

His theory provided a solution to his inner conflict: anatomy doesn't count. Dismiss biology and be free of the terrible burden of being male. Even though he had the same "vile" genitals as his father, it didn't mean he was an out-of-control Neanderthal who went after vulnerable women, children, and birds.

Money wished to flee nature, to escape how he was made. I propose that was the source of his *biophobia*—an irrational fear and hatred of biology. His invention of a psychological sex untethered to chromosomes and genitals is consistent with his deep-seated biophobia. It defined his life's work and the subsequent development of gender ideology. In its absence, today's transgender epidemic wouldn't exist.

To further understand Money, it's important to know he was a member of a group of sex researchers and academics, several of whom were disciples of Alfred Kinsey. Kinsey, one of history's most deviant and public personalities, campaigned against traditional sexual morality. The consortium that included

---

⁵ castrated

Money argued that "all forms of consensual sexuality are good, or at least neutral; problems arise not from sex but from guilt, fear, and repression."[11]

Like the gender activists of today, Money grasped the power of language to influence how we think. He disliked the psychiatric term "perversion" and suggested "paraphilia" in its place, arguing the latter was "less prejudicial and judgmental when describing people with unusual sexual behavior problems."

"Unusual sexual behavior?" What could that mean? Which activities did Money believe we shouldn't judge?

Forgive me, you might wish you could unread what's ahead. I regret the necessity of quoting the vulgar material that follows and describing offensive subjects, but I know of no other way to support my claims.

One of the innovations SIECUS (Sexual Information and Education Council of the United States) brought to sex ed was called sexual attitude reassessment (SAR).[12] To help patients with intimacy problems, they argued, doctors and therapists must be knowledgeable of, and comfortable hearing about, anything and everything. The assumptions upon which SAR is built include: "We have a right and obligation to know objectively the range of human sexual behavior. . . . Each person has a right to his/her own beliefs and convictions."[13]

But professionals are uncomfortable discussing sexual issues. Said the sex ed crusaders: the professional must examine and change their attitudes. How?

In the 1940s, Kinsey suggested that sexually explicit material (i.e., pornography) be used for educational purposes. He in fact turned the attic of his home at Indiana University into a studio where he filmed his colleagues and their wives.

In the 1970s, John Money devised lectures for medical students including slides of unusual sexual behaviors. There's that word again—"unusual." Here's what it means:

> Money introduced the films to the Johns Hopkins Medical School Curriculum
> in 1971. The show featured explicit photographs of people engaged in bestiality,
> urine-drinking, feces-eating, and various amputation fetishes. . . . Money had
> also screened a stag film of five women and three men having group sex. . . .[14]

Money was a depraved human being and advertised it to the world. Now we understand his campaign against the "perversions" category in psychiatry's bible, the DSM. In fact, the term was dropped in the DSM-3, and "paraphilias" was adopted.[15]

Money's immorality extended to children. He claimed that from an early age, children must be exposed to explicit images, in order to understand the difference between male and female sex organs. He publicly endorsed pedophilia and incest, calling the former "a love affair between an age-discrepant couple."[16] About incest he wrote, "a childhood sexual experience, such as being the partner of a relative . . . need not necessarily affect the child adversely."[17]

You get the picture. Like Kinsey, Money was a degenerate, disturbed man. Like Kinsey, he crusaded to rid society of repressive Judeo-Christian taboos. Stir up controversy. Break down restrictions and taboos. Create a new world where anything goes. And be in the limelight, confident and self-satisfied, during the process.

Money aggressively promoted his gender theory, but it remained speculation. How could he demonstrate that nurture, not nature, determined gender identity? How could he prove beyond doubt that chromosomes and genitals don't matter? He couldn't, until a family with a unique dilemma showed up in his office.

The following incredible story was documented in an article in *Rolling Stone*, then the book *As Nature Made Him: The Boy Who Was Raised as a Girl* by John Colapinto. It's a real page-turner, required reading; I can only give you the bare bones here.

In 1965, a young couple from Winnipeg, Canada, by the name of Janet and Ron Reimer gave birth to identical twin boys, whom they named Bruce and Brian. At birth the boys were fine, but after a few months a doctor recommended circumcisions due to an issue with the twins' foreskins. During Bruce's procedure at eight months of age, an electrocautery needle was used instead of a scalpel, and his entire penis was burned beyond repair.

The Reimers were desperate for months, until one day they heard a famous professor on TV confidently explaining that gender was more important than anatomy, and therefore a boy could be successfully raised as a girl. Finally, there might be an answer for poor Bruce. They traveled to Johns Hopkins to see John Money when the twins were twenty-two months old.

The Reimers may have thought Dr. Money was the answer to their prayers, but the opposite was true: Bruce and Brian were the answer to his: they were the perfect test case for his theory. Brian was Bruce's quintessential matched control, a genetic clone raised in the same home. If Bruce could be successfully raised as a girl, Money could prove his theory to the world.

Money was known for his intellect, speaking skills, and confidence. He was one of the most highly respected sex researchers in the world at one of the world's premier medical centers. He was the authority on ambiguous genitalia, and he knew how to promote himself. He also did not tolerate disagreement.[18] He was known for his tantrums and violent reactions; apparently Money was like his father after all.

When the Reimers first met Dr. Money at the Psychohormonal Research Unit he directed, Ron was twenty and had finished seventh grade; Janet was twenty-one and had completed ninth grade. Janet said decades later, "I looked up to him like a god, I accepted whatever he said."[19] The doctor told them if they followed his instructions, Bruce would identify as a girl and grow up to be a happy, well-adjusted woman.

The outcome of their consultation was hardly surprising: Bruce was castrated, and surgeons constructed female-appearing external genitalia. He was renamed Brenda and clothed in pink dresses. When Brenda was older, Money explained, she would need an operation to construct a vagina, and hormones to go through female puberty. Dr. Money emphasized that for the success of the sex change, Ron and Janet eradicate any doubts they may have about the treatment, as that could weaken Brenda's identification as a girl.[20] He also warned they were not under any circumstances to tell Brenda she'd been born a boy.

Money's approach can be summed up in this way: "I have an idea. Let's raise this boy as a girl and see what happens." Bruce was the first child in the world born with normal genitals to have sex reassignment surgery.

Every year, the Reimers would travel to Baltimore to see Dr. Money. In between visits, Janet kept him informed with letters and phone calls. When Brenda and Brian were six, in 1972, Money revealed his "twins case" to the public at an annual meeting of the American Association for the Advancement of Science in Washington, DC. He told the capacity crowd of over one thousand[21] that a normal male infant had been raised as a girl, and the experiment was a resounding success. They could learn more about it, he told them, in his book published that day, *Man and Woman, Boy and Girl*.

Describing the book, Colapinto writes,[22]

> [T]he account portrayed the experiment as an unqualified success. In comparison with her twin brother, Brenda provided what Money variously described as an "extraordinary" and a "remarkable" contrast. Brian's interest in "cars and gas pumps and tools" was compared with Brenda's avid interest in "dolls,

a doll house and a doll carriage"; . . . Brenda's interest in kitchen work was placed alongside Brian's disdain for it. . . . All in all, the twins embodied an almost miraculous division of taste, temperament, and behavior along gender lines and seemed the "ultimate test" that boys and girls are made, not born.

Money's announcement was groundbreaking, and he made certain it got exposure in both professional and lay publications. The twins' story became a landmark case and brought John Money fame and funding for the rest of his life.

There were a few dissenters. One was Milton Diamond, a professor of anatomy and reproductive biology at the University of Hawaii. Diamond's position was that male and female identities are hardwired in the brain during the initial months of pregnancy. In the sixties he published challenges to Money's theory of psychosexual neutrality and voiced concerns over sex reassignment surgery in babies. When Money reported the twin experiment a success, Diamond insisted his conclusion was premature, as the twins were only six.

Diamond remained one of the few longtime vocal critics of Money, but Money fought hard against opponents and intimidated editors from giving a voice to Diamond. There's evidence Money was a tyrant at Hopkins, too.

Even when an alternative, less invasive, treatment was developed for infant boys with underdeveloped genitals, Money refused to present it to parents as a possibility. In his opinion, sex reassignment surgery was the sole option.

Quentin Van Meter, a pediatric endocrinologist who was trained at Johns Hopkins in the early eighties, recounts an infant who was born with a micro-penis. He had normal XY chromosomes, so the endocrinologists suspected the issue was his pituitary gland, in which case he might develop normal genitalia in response to hormones. He was placed on a six-week scientific protocol requiring an initial week of hormone therapy in the hospital followed by five weeks of hormone injections at home, then a return to Hopkins to evaluate the response.

Dr. Van Meter (from YouTube transcript):

[T]he baby goes home and comes back six weeks later, I went out to call the baby and the family back to the clinic office, and there was the mom . . . but sitting on her lap was a child dressed in a pink, frilly outfit with a white bonnet on its head . . . I said, "I thought you were bringing your baby boy this time," and she said, "Oh, Dr. Money met with us before we left the hospital."

Now we did not invite Dr. Money in to see this patient because we did not need his consultation. But he found out the child was there, grabbed the mother, sat her down and said to the mother, "These endocrine doctors don't know what they're doing. This protocol will not work. It has never worked. You need to go home. Tell your family that you have a baby girl. Change the name, dress the child as a female. You can come back and we'll prove to those silly endocrinology doctors that they don't know what they're doing." [23]

But upon examining the baby, Dr. Van Meter recalls, his penis was normal. His mom had heeded Dr. Money's instructions and dressed him in girl's clothing, but the boy had also received the hormone injections per the endo-crinologists—and his penis had responded as they'd hoped:

. . . everything that we had planned and hoped for and used our scientific experience and logic and previously established protocols worked perfectly. This was a boy who was going to be perfectly fine and raised as a boy and the baby went home and was raised as a boy.

And so it went. Money remained in the limelight for decades, and his theory was taught as dogma in the fields of pediatrics, child development, psychology, sociology, and many other disciplines. For decades and all over the world, parents of sons with abnormal genitalia were advised to castrate and raise them as girls.[24] How could they make such a fateful decision? They trusted the doctors who said with certainty, "there's a medical consensus."

The consequences of Money's gender-neutral, biology-denying narrative on science, academia, and—as you'll see—the kids in my office cannot be overestimated.

In 1974 Money published *Sexual Signatures*, written for the general public, and again reported the twin's experiment a total success. While Money acknowledged Brenda's tomboyish traits, he nevertheless called Bruce's transformation into Brenda a "metamorphosis." A review in the *New York Times* described Brenda as "sailing contentedly through childhood as a genuine girl." It also portrayed her parents as blissfully content.

In 1978, the twin case was still the single most compelling evidence proving nurture was more important than biology in determining gender identity. That year, Edward Goldwyn, a documentary filmmaker with the

BBC, was investigating gender identity. Goldwyn visited Johns Hopkins and heard the twin case may not have been exactly how Money portrayed it.[25]

Colapinto quotes Goldwyn, "I was getting vibes from people in Baltimore being quite embarrassed by Money and the prominence of this case in the literature. . . . I could tell that these people were getting increasingly worried."[26]

Goldwyn located the Child Guidance Clinic treating Brenda in Winnipeg. Keith Sigmundson, the psychiatrist who supervised Brenda's case, agreed to be interviewed by Goldwyn only under conditions that guaranteed the Reimers' and their clinicians' anonymity, and that the program wouldn't be sold in Canada or the US. When Goldwyn asked about the prognosis for Brenda's sex reassignment, Sigmundson paused.

Describing his hesitation years later to Colapinto, he said: "After all, it was still Hopkins. Money was the guru."

Following his silence, Sigmundson replied:

> I don't think all the evidence is in. . . . At the present time, however, she does display certain features which would make me be very suspicious that she will ever make an adjustment as a woman.[27]

Fast-forward nineteen years to 1997. Brenda, age thirty-two, went public, but she was then "David," a janitor in a slaughterhouse, married to a woman and father to three adopted children. The whole thing was a hoax—the experiment had been a complete failure. Far from accepting his gender reassignment, David had fought against it tooth and nail from the beginning. He had refused to play with dolls, ripped his dresses off, and preferred wrestling to cooking. He even urinated standing up when possible. Brenda had been teased relentlessly for the boyish way she moved, spoke, and gestured. Kids called her "cavewoman." In second grade she wanted to be a garbage man, and in eighth a car mechanic. As puberty started, Money began pressuring "Brenda," who was already on estrogen, to grow breasts, to have surgery to construct a vagina. Brenda was fiercely resistant—to her that was a nightmare.[28]

After years of this ordeal—not only for Brenda but for the whole family—Brenda's psychiatrist urged her parents to reveal the truth. Despite Money's warning to never do so, they gave in. It was 1980, and the twins were fourteen when Brenda was told she'd been born a boy. Speaking about that moment years later, David said, "I was relieved. Suddenly it all made sense why I felt the way I did. I wasn't some sort of weirdo. I wasn't crazy."

Brenda returned to living as a boy at once. He chose the name David because he felt that his whole life, he'd been courageously fighting Goliath.

His mother reported the development to Dr. Money.[29] But Money always insisted, at least publicly, that the case was lost to follow-up and continued to advocate for sex reassignment surgeries for infant boys.

When David learned of his fame in the medical literature and of Money's false reports of success, he was shocked. David was especially concerned that, because of Money's claims about him, the medical protocol for other boys was to get same treatment—sex reassignment.

David explained, "By me not saying anything the medical community was under the impression that my case was a success story. I was shocked when I heard that people thought that my case was a success story."[30]

At that point David and his parents agreed to be interviewed by Diamond, who had been contacted years earlier by the BBC.

In 1997, Diamond and Sigmundson published a bombshell paper:[31] the landmark case of the boy who'd become a normal, happy girl, was in fact bogus. *The present findings*, Diamond and Sigmundson wrote, *show the individual did not accept this sex of rearing.* So controversial were the findings that it took the authors two years to find a journal willing to publish them.

How did Money respond? He didn't. The esteemed professor simply stopped mentioning and writing about the case.[32]

Interviews with David and Brian about their yearly childhood visits to Dr. Money revealed—you won't be surprised—they'd been sexually abused by him until they refused to return to Baltimore. Unimaginable damage had been inflicted on the Reimer family. Brian overdosed at age thirty-six, and David committed suicide when he was thirty-eight. Their parents blamed John Money for the loss of their sons.

One might think that when the disaster came to light, doctors and academics would reexamine—if not completely reject—gender theory. After all, Bruce a.k.a. Brenda a.k.a. David was supposed to be Money's proof of concept, and it had failed miserably.

Instead, it's been David's story that's been rejected. Instead of acknowledging the critical role of biology, students at all educational levels are taught they can dismiss it, and authorities remain loyal to Money's biophobic theory—identity trumps nature.

There are many lessons to be learned from the Reimer family's tragedy.

First, it illustrates the arrogance of a scientist in a powerful position, and how he exploited and ultimately destroyed a family with the aim of furthering his ideology and gaining fame and fortune. Second, *we see the readiness of the medical profession and of academics to adopt ideas because they support the social movements of the day.*

The lesson most relevant to this discussion is that Money's biophobic theory was wrong: David was not born gender neutral, with an equal potential of identifying as male or female. That's what Money wanted the world to believe, but it wasn't true.

Despite years of sincere effort by his parents, relatives, and school staff to enforce his identity as a girl, David preferred stereotypical boy play and behavior. He walked like a boy, he talked like a boy, his interests were boyish. It is remarkable that he wanted to learn from Ron how to shave, and he preferred to urinate standing up.

Apparently, the presence of a Y chromosome, instead of two X's, had a huge, lasting impact. It was the also definitive factor in his identification: he never felt like a girl.

If anything, the experiment demonstrated that more than any other factor, David's *biology* dictated his identity. Even under the extraordinary conditions in which his anatomy resembled a girl's and he was socialized as one from before the age of two, his psychological sex, his "gender identity," was consistent with his chromosomes.

Bottom line, with the help of two doctors and a journalist who cared about the truth and understood the catastrophe that resulted and would continue to result from covering it up, John Money was exposed as a fraud. But Money never came clean. He went to the grave knowing he destroyed a family and duped the world, without any accountability.

You could say Money was just another blemish of many in my profession, I accept that; there are bad apples. But you know what I can't understand? The adulation he received through the years, upon his death and to this day.

At a 1987 NIH meeting, John Money was honored as a scientist funded for twenty-five consecutive years: "infant sexual reassignment surgery was one of his most important clinical contributions to medical science."

Following Money's death in 2007, Anke Ehrhardt, a psychologist who was his colleague and coauthor, wrote " . . . [he made] extraordinary contributions . . . scholars are indebted to him for his brilliance, his scientific contributions, and his passionate commitment to research and clinical care."[33]

No surprise, the Kinsey Institute called Money "an extraordinary pioneer . . . a visionary researcher." They established The John Money Collection of his personal and professional papers: "We are most honored to have been the fortunate recipient of his support and his exceptional collection."[34]

"Most honored?" No. John Money was an emotionally disturbed, deviant child abuser who, seeking the recognition and fame he craved, exploited a simple working-class family who'd suffered a terrible tragedy. He was a public supporter of pedophilia and incest. Yet to this day, he's celebrated by at least some academics, physicians, and mental health professionals. Next time you're getting advice from someone with lots of diplomas, it's something to keep in mind.

# CHAPTER TWO

# Psychiatry's Dangerous Idea*

At the 1997 meeting of the American Academy of Child and Adolescent Psychiatry (AACAP), the Belgian film *Ma Vie en Rose* was screened and discussed. It told the story of Ludovic, a seven-year-old boy who yearned for femininity: pink toile dresses, earrings, lipstick. Ludovic insisted that he was a girl and would one day be a man's bride. He and his family suffered humiliation and disdain; his father lost his job. It was a superb film, and it evoked compassion for the boy and his family.[1]

Following the film, I expected a discussion about the boy's delusion that he's a girl and will become a woman. According to psychiatry's *Diagnostic and Statistical Manual of Mental Disorders* (DSM), he suffered with gender identity disorder (GID).

Instead, my colleagues focused on Ludovic's victimization in a society with rigid definitions of male and female. If his culture did not insist on a black-and-white understanding of sex, my colleagues argued, he would have had an easier time. The implication was that society must change.

I sat in the audience and thought, wait a minute. Sure, there are feminine boys whose personalities and interests are not stereotypically male, and that's fine. But this was different: *Ludovic insisted he is a girl.* An actual girl. When his belief was challenged, he had a meltdown and escaped to a fantasy world of glitter and princesses.

I raised my hand to say it was the boy who was disordered, not society. I looked around and listened. It dawned on me that my comment would

---

* Psychologists are included.

not be well received. I didn't have the guts to be the sole challenger, and I lowered my hand. Something had changed in psychiatry. I needed to figure out what—and how.

## Gender Identity, Then and Now

Sooner or later the term "gender identity" will be used in your home, and I want you to thoroughly understand its meaning. You see, during the decades since John Money, the idea morphed into something altogether different.

Money proposed that an identity of either "male" or "female" is imposed on a child by society and that by age three it's permanent.

Your child has been taught differently. Let's say you have a daughter. Her femaleness, she's been told, is an internal sense. She might also be male, both male and female, or neither—she's been told there are dozens of possibilities. She believes her identity can change over her lifetime. Regarding the "gender binary"—male and female, fixed in childhood—to her, that's false and transphobic. There are so many people like her, she'll tell you, there always have been, whose gender identities do not match their genitals. It's a normal variant, like red hair. But they're a marginalized and oppressed group, and that's why so many trans people commit suicide.

OK, hold on a minute.

How did John Money's idea, exposed in 1997 as bogus, without scientific foundation, evolve into what seems like an entirely new concept?

The original belief went like this: girls are passive and emotional, and like make-up and dresses, because of society's expectations. Now the ideologues insist: a guy who *says* he's a girl *is* a girl, and an oppressed minority.

To review, then and now:

**Then:** Male and female. **Now:** Limitless possibilities.

**Then:** Imposed by culture. **Now:** An inner experience.

**Then:** Fixed at age three. **Now:** Fluid throughout life.

**Then:** An academic theory. **Now:** A turbocharged crusade.

In my own quest to understand the bizarre evolution of gender identity, I discovered the process would require studying post-structuralism, first-wave feminism, queer theory, gender schema theory, second-wave feminism, Marxist feminism, anti-essentialism, radical feminism, third-wave feminism, and radical gender theory.

That's not going to happen. I'm not going to pretend I even know what any of those are.

What I do know is the concepts and terminology have been ever-changing and increasingly radical. Even as I write these words, more and more inane ideas are introduced and foisted on me. For example, the world's foremost authority on transgender health (WPATH, more about them later) tells me that eunuchs—castrated boys—are a sexual orientation like gay and lesbian.

I have also seen over and over the real-life consequences of a phony psychological theory that became the foundation for a global social justice movement. And I know, boy do I know, about the current and future victims of that movement: the young people who are disfigured and sterilized, their lives and their family's shattered.

I'm going to stick to what I do know, and here's what I've figured out: During the decades after Money's theory was institutionally embraced, and Brenda/David was living in torment, male and female came to be seen in an entirely new way.

The two-sex option, or "binary," it was argued, is a lie; sex is a spectrum. People rejecting the "binary" are oppressed. Gender and sex are instruments of power, and the system must come down. As journalist Christopher Rufo explains,

> Radical gender theorists argue that white, European men invented the "gender binary," or division between man and woman, in order to oppress racial and sexual minorities. They believe that this system of "heteronormativity" must be exposed, critiqued, and deconstructed in order to usher in a world beyond the norms of heterosexual, middle-class society. In order to facilitate the destruction of this system, radical gender activists promote synthetic sexual identities. . . . The goal is to replace notions of biological sex, the male-female binary, and the nuclear family with "queer alternatives" and "a world beyond binaries."[2]

With that paragraph, I'm reminded why I studied biology and chemistry in college, not political science. What is this gobbledygook? How did it become mainstream?

People think the gender ideology blitz is new and developed at breathtaking speed. No. While the number of young people identifying as "gender variant" has exploded recently, the groundwork was in place before they were born. Examining that groundwork helps understand today's madness.

## It Didn't Start Yesterday

Regarding "trans," so many parents, journalists, and others wonder: What is happening all of a sudden? Where did it come from? How did these way-out ideas reach my kid?

Listen up: no one should be surprised. Kids have been indoctrinated with gender ideology since at least the nineties. Anyone who believes the craze suddenly appeared has not been paying attention.

Today's version of Money's gender identity—limitless options, fluid throughout life, a normal variant, oppressed by society—was hatched decades ago in the minds of activists. They opposed the structure, order, and morality of traditional society. Their strategy was and is to attack and destroy, without providing a constructive, truth-based alternative. If you can't make sense of all this, I can't either. That itself is the goal: confusion and chaos.

Yet I kept seeing one phrase stand out in their writings and lectures over the decades: *our understanding of gender is evolving.* Evolve it did—into something unrecognizable. And as it evolved, always in the absence of substantive scientific foundation or medical consensus, the ideological crusade marched through our institutions—medicine, mental health, sex ed, education, government—all this, years before the current outbreak of youth who believe they can defy biology.

To explore how these incoherent theories managed to take over institutions, I began pulling volumes off my shelves, and papers from my files. I have a library compiled from decades of work in child and adolescent psychiatry—and, book by book, paper by paper, it demonstrates the defeat of science and common sense in my profession.

Here's what it looked like.

Until the 2000s, the professional organizations remained old-school: two sexes, identity fixed by age three, persistent distress over one's sex calls for psychological evaluation.

For example, on my shelf are psychiatry textbooks published in 1979[3] and 1989.[4] They both state male and female identities (the only possibilities back then) are fixed at age three. Children uncomfortable with their sex are called "troubled" and are seen as having "extreme pathologies."[5] Various treatments are discussed, including family therapy.

Yet during the final decades of the twentieth century, new concepts appeared in gender and feminist studies, ideas like "gender variance" or "the gender binary is oppressive." These ideas began flourishing on campuses and in sex education.

Compare these two books, both published in 1998, the year after David Reimer went public.

The first is the American Academy of Child and Adolescent Psychiatry's *Your Child: What Every Parent Needs to Know About Childhood Development from Birth to Preadolescence.*[6] In this 400-page volume that addresses parent questions from A to Z, gender concerns are off the radar. Nothing. No sex "assigned" at birth, no "gender identity," no ink given to children unhappy with being male or female, non-binary identities, fluidity, or oppression.

The second is *My Gender Workbook: How to Become a Real Man, a Real Woman, The Real You, or Something Else Entirely.* This book isn't for professionals, it's an activist tract recruiting kids. The cover resembles a grade-school workbook and features a doll that's half Ken and half Barbie:

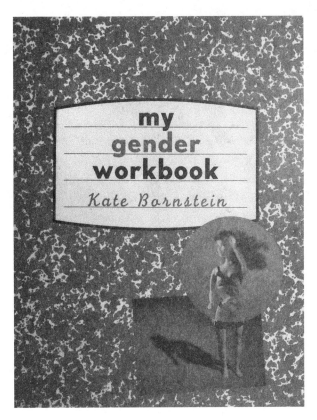

The author is Kate Bornstein, who explains he was born Albert but as an adult "became a woman" for a few years, then "stopped being a woman and settled into being neither." His lover, Catherine, decided to "become a man," David. Kate and David stayed together as a "heterosexual couple."

Kate writes that "she" now identifies as "something else entirely" and hopes to "dismantle the 'gender system' on the planet as we know it." His message to young people: the gender system has a "death grip" on them and identifying as a boy or girl is "neither natural nor essential."[7]

Yes, that was 1998, the full-blown modern version of gender theory: non-binary, fluid, oppressive. Sure, you recognize it: it's precisely what your child learns at school, from his guidance counselor and very likely his pediatrician. A quarter of a century ago, Kate/Albert was proclaiming the Articles of Faith, which are now regurgitated by all the institutions we once trusted. *It didn't start yesterday.*

While activist literature was marketed to children, pediatricians and psychiatrists hadn't budged. The *Textbook of Pediatrics*[8] from 2000 and the 2002 *Textbook of Child and Adolescent Psychiatry*[9] reiterate that male and female (note: only two options) identities are "firmly established and resistant to change" after thirty months.

Regardless, the culture raced ahead of the medical and mental health establishments. Kids were instructed it's normal to feel they're the opposite sex. Activist literature presented radical gender beliefs with finality—*these are the facts, the binary is false and oppressive.* For at least a decade, there was a chasm, it was the Wild West. The views of doctors specializing in children and adolescents didn't matter. Activists—particularly among sex educators—forged ahead with astounding confidence.

"Being transgender is as normal as being alive," students were instructed in 2002 by Advocates for Youth,[10] who were and still are a flagship sex ed organization, along with SIECUS (Sexuality Information and Education Council of the United States) and Planned Parenthood.

To a seventeen-year-old boy who wrote, "I want to be a girl, what do I do?" Planned Parenthood responded in 2010, "[I]t is not uncommon for a person to identify strongly with the other gender . . . talk to someone who you can trust, and understands gender identity issues."[11]

On a site recommended to youth by SIECUS: "[T]hrough your adult life you'll likely find that your personal gender identity . . . changes and grows, and becomes more clear (and more murky!) with time and life experience . . . gender isn't anything close to binary, but like most things, is a wide, diverse spectrum, a varied, veritable genderpalooza."[12]

It's no surprise that sex educators like SIECUS were at the forefront of gender indoctrination. From the start they were about social reform, urging students to question adult beliefs, reject tradition, and make their own decisions about sexuality: *Explore and experiment,* students are told, *it's your right.* In the sixties sex ed taught students: "it's healthy to question to whom you're attracted and explore the possibilities." A few decades later, they added, "it's normal to question if you are male, female, neither or both."

For decades, American children have been told, *your mind and body may be mismatched, like a pair of socks—it's perfectly normal.*

By the way, in 2019 SIECUS dropped it's spelled-out title and added the tagline: *"sex ed for social change."* [13] They don't hide their ambition; they never did.

Before we go on, I want to acknowledge the vast difference between people with gender dysphoria and individuals with personalities and interests more typical of the opposite sex. Gender ideologues lump them all together under an enormous "gender variant" umbrella, sufficiently wide to cover tree-climbing, math-loving girls, ballet-loving boys, and the very small number of severely dysphoric individuals who wish to permanently alter their bodies and live as the opposite sex.

The humongous umbrella serves their purpose to hoodwink you into believing this is all about inclusivity and acceptance, and that a man who desires castration is in the same category as a girl who loves STEM and sports.

The strategy extends to language. Those who control the language control the outcome. The Orwellian manipulation of language influences how we think. An example you just read and probably missed: activists use "gender" and "sex" interchangeably.

Look again at the quote above from Planned Parenthood. They didn't say it's common to identify with the other *sex*, but *gender.* This switcheroo happened in the past 10–20 years on driver's licenses, doctors' forms, school records, everywhere. Expectant parents shouldn't have *gender* reveal parties; surely, they don't know their unborn child's "inner sense of male or female, both or neither." What they know is their baby's *sex.*

The conflation of sex with gender was a critical development, but like so many things it escaped the radar of most.

It was a deliberate weaponizing of language, but to what end? Gender, we are told, is subjective, fluid, on a spectrum, multidimensional. If sex and gender are interchangeable, then sex is all those things too—subjective, multidimensional, nuanced, blah blah blah. In the end, "male" and "female" mean nothing.

*They want sex to be synonymous with gender, so they can destroy it.*

As explained in Appendix One, sex is *not* vague, not fluid, not multidimensional—and it's critical you and your children know that. Mammals are either male or female based on the presence or absence of the SRY ("sex determining region") gene on the Y chromosome, which establishes the production of sperm or eggs.[14] Yes, it's that simple. Genderists argue sex is endlessly complex and nuanced. No, it's not. They insist it's on a spectrum. No, it's not. That it's "assigned at birth" No, outside of .02 percent of births, it's not.[†]

In 2004, I attended a UCLA conference on transgenderism, and student speakers were angry. A woman living as a man described her challenges getting a pelvic exam and picking up medicine for endometriosis. Staff at the clinic and pharmacy are confused—and that, she told the audience, is unacceptable. "I am a male with a vagina, and I should be able to talk about it."

Therapists should not be gatekeepers, I was informed at the meeting: if student requests hormones, write the letter. (This is now known as gender-affirming care [GAC], the unquestioning acceptance of a patient's self-diagnosis and provision of requested medical interventions. You'll hear more about it later.)

The culture and language are evolving, students reported. Society restricts us with the gender binary, and we must break free. Gender is fluid, there are more than two options, and exploring those options is normal. One student explained, "My gender is a sliding scale. It's the rejection of male and female that I find attractive."

Like at the AACAP meeting seven years earlier where I had raised my hand to say Ludovic, not society, was disordered, I sat in the audience at UCLA bewildered, the only one it seemed. *No gatekeeping, just write the prescription? What am I, a rubber stamp?*

Someone on the staff of the University took the podium. *"How little we know,"* he observed. *"Students are leading us."*

"Students leading us?"—that's not science and that's not medicine; that's a political movement. And the political movement has been at the helm all these years, steamrolling the medical and scientific establishments with their radical, biophobic belief system. Witnessing the process was like watching a stone edifice crack and crumble to pieces in slow motion.

In 2005, a physician who was a man living as a woman spoke at the annual meeting of the American College Health Association.[15] Dr. Jamie Buth from Tulane University School of Medicine told the audience, "transsexualism[‡] is a variation of being alive, not a disorder." How should doctors and nurses care for the transgender students on their campuses? Dr. Buth instructed the

---

† One can only properly say sex is "assigned at birth" in the exceedingly rare circumstances of a child with a disorder of sexual development, born with ambiguous genitalia.
‡ Earlier psychiatric term for transgenderism

audience: validate them. Again, don't be a gatekeeper. Provide the treatment they request to feel congruent with their bodies.

This time, the guidance wasn't coming from a student activist. Gender-affirming care was presented as the only option for health professionals *in 2005 by a physician.* There was no debate. There was no new science. There was just, *this is how it's done.*

In 2006, the American Psychological Association's (APA) *Answers to Your Questions About Transgender Individuals and Gender Identity* informed readers that some people have "blending or alternating genders," and that GID "is highly controversial."[16]

*My Gender Workbook* was recommended by a presenter at the 2006 annual meeting of the American Association of Child and Adolescent Psychiatry. Remember, that's the book for students by Al, who became Kate, who became not male or female, but "something else entirely."

A 2008 flyer published by University of Massachusetts asked *What Does Transphobia Look Like?* One answer: *assuming everyone is male or female.*

So you see, I hope, that gender madness was going on right under your noses for a long, long time. Years before the teens and young adults who now stand in line for blockers, testosterone, estrogen, and operations were born.

## Compassion, Stigma, Insurance Codes

The medical establishment was caving to a mighty social movement. A revision of the DSM[17] was a watershed moment in that decline.

A full understanding of the significance of that moment and how it came about will, I hope, shed light on where we are today.

The DSM is a handbook published by the APA that describes psychiatric conditions. Psychiatrists use it to diagnose and treat their patients. To put a complicated system simply, a formal diagnosis in the DSM also allows for specific conditions to have billing codes—necessary for billing insurance companies.

Gender identity disorder was added to the DSM in 1980. Note the word *disorder.*

There were two components of gender identity disorder; both were needed to make the diagnosis. The first was a strong and persistent desire to be, or the insistence that one is, the opposite sex, as manifested by cross-dressing, cross-sex roles in play, and preferring stereotypical activities and playmates of the other sex.

The second component was persistent discomfort about one's sex. There also had to be evidence of "clinically significant distress or impairment in social, occupational, or other important areas of functioning."

Age of onset was between two and four. For prevalence, the DSM referred to data from Europe suggesting that roughly 1 per 30,000 adult males and 1 per 100,000 adult females seek sex-reassignment surgery. The DSM noted: Only a very small number of children with gender identity disorder will continue to have symptoms that meet criteria for gender identity disorder in later adolescence or adulthood.

By 2008, the DSM-4—the fourth version of the manual—still included "gender identity disorder," classifying Ludovic, Kate Bornstein, Jazz Jennings, and Rachel Levine "the Admiral" as patients with an emotional problem.

Clearly, that wouldn't work. Not when so many authorities had been claiming for years that opposite sex identities are "as normal as being alive."

There had been calls to remove GID from the DSM since the nineties. In 2006 a debate raged within APA with some contending the diagnosis must be eliminated, and others arguing for its retention "because the health care system in the United States requires a diagnosis to justify medical or psychological treatment."[18]

Again, there was no new science or studies. The debate was driven by politics. To be sure, doctors also felt compassion toward transgender-identifying individuals and believed social change would improve their patients' lives.

Good news for them: by 2008, it was time to plan the the next edition of the DSM. Many wondered: What will happen to GID? Toss it? Keep it? Revise it?

A task force was announced. The overarching issue was whether GID should be retained. "Disorder" was stigmatizing, but access to medical and psychological care was essential. And for access (read: insurance coverage) a diagnosis, along with a code, is needed.

Psychiatrist Jack Drescher, perhaps the most highly regarded voice for LGBT issues in psychiatry, described the dilemma well: "[I]t is difficult to find reconciling language that removes the stigma of having a mental disorder diagnosis while maintaining access to medical care."[19]

The word "disorder" was particularly distasteful, explained Dr. Kenneth Zucker, one of the most prominent experts in the field:[20] "Many transgendered activists and some clinicians . . . argu[ed] that GID was not a mental disorder. . . . [T]ranssexualism was nothing more than a normal variant of gender identity, that its classification as a mental disorder contributed to stigma, and that there was nothing inherently 'wrong' with a gender identity that was incongruent with one's biological sex."

## A Violation of Human Rights

In 2010, the World Professional Association for Transgender Health (WPATH), said it's not just wrong to believe gender confusion is a disorder, it violates human rights: "Gender variance is not in and of itself a psychiatric disorder and, therefore, the label of gender identity disorder as a mental illness/mental disorder is not appropriate. Such labeling may undermine human rights in that it undermines legitimacy of identity and creates and sustains social stigma."[21]

WPATH went further in 2012. Attempting to "change gender identity and expression to become more congruent" with biological sex is ineffective and "unethical."[22]

To assist with their decision, the DSM task force conducted an international survey[23] on issues related to the GID diagnosis. To whom was it sent? Perhaps to the tens of thousands of board-certified psychiatrists like me?

Hardly. It sent the survey to organizations "concerned with the welfare of transgender people." Of the forty-three groups completing the survey, only five were categorized as associations of medical professionals. Five.

The results: 55.8 percent of respondents believed GID should be excluded from the new DSM. The major reason for its retention was health care reimbursement: "The survey revealed a broad consensus that if the diagnosis remains in the DSM, there needs to be an overhaul of the name, criteria, and language to minimize stigmatization of transgender individuals."[24]

How to solve the thorny issue?

It would be solved with a new perspective: the focus must be on a patient's distress, not their identity. If your son experiences his body as wrong, it's not pathology. It's not cause for concern. It's his associated distress—his dysphoria—that's of clinical significance. If a "mismatch" is present free of distress, your son has no diagnosis. Insurance coverage remains, stigma is gone. Good-bye gender identity disorder, hello gender dysphoria.

It was a brilliant idea. Unlike GID, GD would no longer fall into a "disorder" category. It was given a category of its own. It was a brilliant idea, yes—but also a dangerous one.

## Mudslinging Psychiatrists

Some insights into the creation of DSM-5—the entire process, not just the GID issue—are in order. When it was being drafted, Dr. Allen Frances and Dr. Robert Spitzer—two leaders in the field of psychiatry who directed the drafting of earlier versions of the DSM[25]—issued a letter of condemnation: the leadership group writing the update was "sealing itself off from advice and criticism."

"DSM 5 leadership has lost contact with the field by restricting the necessary free communication of its working groups," the pair of doctors wrote, calling the drafting of the diagnosis manual a "secretive and closed DSM process" that is "insulting to the other mental health professions." The resulting DSM, they warned, "would haunt the field and the APA for decades."[26]

Following publication in 2013, Dr. Frances told physicians to use the manual "cautiously, if at all."[27]

I'm not telling you about DSM-5 and clashes between psychiatrists because it's colorful history. The point is that with the normalization of gender distress, my profession caved to ideology or, if you prefer, caved to compassion. And that capitulation set the stage for the disasters I see daily.

The "downgrading" of GID to GD by psychiatric authorities leads parents like you to believe there were rigorous studies and discussion of the matter, culminating in a majority agreeing that your son's biology has no bearing on his identity. After all, that's what the DSM says.

Wrong. There was no agreement about it in 2013, and there is none now. As Stephen Levine put it to me, "Diagnosis in psychiatry is supposed to be based on studies, not politics or well-intentioned concepts of how to make the world a better place."

To this day mental health professionals are at one another's throats over the proper approach to patients with gender dysphoria. There is no consensus.

✳   ✳   ✳

After the DSM made distress, and not incongruence of mind and body, the focus of psychiatric concern, one of the most powerful lobbying organizations in Washington changed its course. The Human Rights Campaign (HRC) spent years working to redefine marriage, and they won in 2015. What to do next?

In 2014, HRC's annual report barely mentioned the word "transgender."[28] The latest annual report mentions "trans" or "transgender" nearly 100 times in thirty-three pages.[29] HRC had abruptly pivoted, and now its trained workforce waves the trans flag.

HRC isn't just a powerhouse with a roughly $45 million annual budget.[30] It raises those millions from the influential mainstream brands: Amazon, Apple, Google, Morgan Stanley, Target . . .[31] The Articles of Faith have big-name devotees.

The federal government is in the game. The Department of Health and Human Services tells us "gender identity is an inborn self-perception. It can be male, female, both or neither; it can change throughout life."[32]

The International Classification of Diseases (ICD) lists diagnoses and includes codes for health records and billing. The latest version was promulgated in 2022, and gender dysphoria was removed. In its place was "gender *incongruence*." Just like with the DSM, this change wasn't based on evidence, but on activists with an agenda.

Using "incongruence" de-pathologizes gender confusion even further. Gender incongruence is considered a "sexual health condition," in the same category as pregnancy. The message:

Rejecting your biology is a healthy and ordinary process, like giving birth. This change will, in turn, be reflected in the next DSM because it publishes the corresponding ICD codes for each mental health diagnosis.

The World Health Organization (WHO) went further, removing "gender identity disorder" from its global manual of diagnoses altogether. Activists celebrated a big win. This "will have a liberating effect on transgender people worldwide," Graeme Reid, the LGBT rights director at Human Rights Watch, said.[33] *Worldwide effect.*

Parents, you must understand these aren't just words on paper. We all want to trust authorities to inform us what's cause for concern and what's not, when we must intervene medically and when we can wait. Having confidence in professional medical organizations, parents sign on the dotted line for puberty blockers and young adults seek castration. *They're being misled and misinformed.*

What began as a monster psychologist's idea, then became a fringe movement in radical feminism and gender studies, has taken over the medical establishment and beyond—almost without resistance. Their victory is now almost complete.

## Biology Doesn't Care About Your Inner Sense

Over the past two to three decades as our institutions fell to gender tyranny, scientists explored a new field of medicine: the biology of sex. Their discoveries refute the Articles of Faith, they contradict the ideas with which your children are being indoctrinated. They demonstrate the inborn, unchanging, binary nature of male and female.

To elaborate: "Inborn"—sex is established at conception; "unchanging"—sex is permanent; and "binary"—sex is male or female, there is no spectrum.

While ideologues insist that men menstruate and give birth, draining the word "woman" of meaning, cell biologists, embryologists, and other hard-core scientists bring into sharp focus the permanent anchoring of male or female in every cell.

In the research lab there's only one reality, and it's found under the microscope, not in hearts and minds. Here I provide you with a tiny taste, just a few crumbs really, from the incredible smorgasbord of what for me is the most exciting science ever, and critical ammunition for your discussions with your child about the meaning of male and female.

To begin, you and your kids must understand the difference between hard and soft science.

Hard science explores the natural world, for example biology, chemistry, physics. Soft science explores intangibles—behaviors, thoughts, and emotions. Psychology, sociology, anthropology are examples of soft sciences.

Hard science is based on the scientific method, in which experiments have controlled variables, objective measurements, critical analysis, and verification. In the hard sciences, the scientific method is straightforward. In the soft sciences, it's difficult.

Many kids swept up by gender ideology are whizzes in STEM subjects. One would hope they'd be receptive to the distinction between hard and soft science. The degree to which he or she is indoctrinated will determine the ability to tolerate a discussion that challenges their beliefs.

But remember, you are planting seeds. They may listen in silence or dismiss you—take it in stride. Even if they refuse engagement now, it doesn't mean they won't recall what you've said in the future. It could make a difference.

Regardless, rest assured you have mountains of evidence on your side.

When gender theory was proposed seventy years ago, there was no way to closely examine chromosomes. It was believed the Y chromosome had only a few genes regulating male sex characteristics such as anatomy, body hair, and lower pitched voice. Aside from that, the Y chromosome was considered "a genetic wasteland."

With limited knowledge, the "nurture is more important than nature" theory was not unreasonable. Scientists might have taken Money seriously when he proposed "women menstruate, gestate, and lactate," and all other differences between men and women are due to socialization.

That was the traditional "bikini" medical model—based on the premise that differences between male and female are limited to their reproductive systems. Now we know that's utterly wrong. Distinctions are found in each organ system, are determined in the earliest stages of development, and have lifelong impact.

It was the biotech revolution in the nineties that opened the door to those discoveries. With new technology, we learned the Y chromosome is filled with DNA that is unique to males. It's far from a genetic wasteland.

A male embryo develops testes that secrete testosterone, the male hormone, beginning at eight weeks after conception. The testosterone travels to every part of the body: the entire growing organism begins to be masculinized at eight weeks after conception. This includes the brain. David Reimer, the castrated twin abused by John Money, was born with a masculinized brain, and that could not be changed by naming him Brenda, giving him Barbies, and dressing him in pink (what we would call today "social transitioning").

The testosterone surge places the fetus on a masculine trajectory. Both the presence of a Y chromosome in each cell, and the effects of testosterone traveling through the fetal bloodstream, have effects on every system of the body. For example, the male brain has more space devoted to centers for action, aggression, and sex drive. These are facts, not theory. (As mentioned earlier, there are varying degrees of masculinity and femininity, and there are very feminine boys and masculine girls. This does not deny the biology presented here.)

Listen to Larry Cahill, an internationally recognized professor of Neurobiology at the University of California, Irvine: "The mammalian brain is clearly a highly sex-influenced organ. Both its function and dysfunction must therefore be sex influenced to an important degree."[34]

Or Dr. Louann Brizendine, a neuropsychiatrist, founder of the Women's Mood and Hormone Clinic at University of California, San Francisco, and author of *The Male Brain: A Breakthrough Understanding of How Men and Boys Think*[35] and *The Female Brain*: Males and females "have a distinct biology . . . there is no unisex brain."[36]

The impact of sex specific chromosomes and hormones is not limited to the brain. "All Cells Have Sex" is the title of a paper by three researchers at Chicago's Medical School Department of Physiology and Biophysics: "Not only does an individual have a sex, but each and every cell within that individual's body also has a sex. As we embark on an era of so-called 'personalized medicine,' consideration of the impact of pharmacological therapies on 'male' and 'female' cells needs to be made."[37]

In 1990, the National Institutes of Health created an Office for Research in Women's Health in recognition that *men and women are unique* and the medical and research communities can no longer assume otherwise.[38] Here's an example of the language on their website: "Sex makes us male or female. Every cell in your body has a sex—making up tissues and organs, like your skin, brain, heart, and stomach. Each cell is either male or female . . ."[39]

You know what's astonishing? Sex differences have been discovered even *before* a fetal male's testes begin secreting testosterone. They are seen remarkably early—prior to the embryo's implantation in the uterus.[40]

That fact, and many other observations, indicate that the presence of XX or XY chromosomes impacts all cells and organs, independent of hormones like estrogen and testosterone. Gender ideologues want us to believe your daughter can be given testosterone and voilà—she's your son. Not quite.

Name the medical condition, and I will describe a difference in the response of each sex. Women are better at fighting bacteria, fungi, and parasites.[41] Menstrual cycles impact symptoms of irritable bowel syndrome, migraines, and other conditions. Men are more likely to survive severe burns.[42] Over 80 percent of autoimmune diseases are in women.[43] Until menopause, women have a lower risk of hypertension and cardiovascular disease. Women are more likely to develop certain heart rhythm abnormalities. There are critical sex differences in the therapeutic power of drugs and their side effects.

Do you see why there's a medical specialty called "Gender-specific medicine"? It's "a new science studying the differences in the normal function of men and women."[44]

Researchers now recommend that if possible, women needing kidney transplants receive the organ from a female donor. They are more likely to reject male kidneys because the Y chromosomes are seen as foreign.[45]

Sex differences are observable at birth. At one day, boys look longer at a mobile, while girls show stronger interest in faces.[46] At one year, girls are drawn, again, to videos of faces and boys to videos of racing cars.[47] At year one and two, girls make more eye contact with their mothers than boys.[48]

Male and female are social constructs? Gender differences were created by European men? Not quite.

Neurobiology confirms what experts observe in cultures across the planet. From *Sex Differences in the Brain: From Genes to Behavior*:[49] "across cultures, girls more than boys are interested in and engage with dolls and doll accessories, arts and crafts, kitchen toys, fashion, and make-up, whereas boys more than girls are interest in and engage with transportation toys, electronics, blocks (especially complex building sets), and sports."[50] These preferences emerge at nine months, are stable by eighteen months, and remain pervasive and consistent.[51]

The explosion of data demonstrating sex differences prompted the development of a new specialty, as mentioned: gender-specific medicine, with leading researchers and clinicians producing the seminal text *Principles of Gender-Specific§ Medicine: Gender in the Genomic Era.* Vivian W. Pinn, the founding director of the NIH's Office of Research on Women's Health, wrote matter-of-factly in the book's forward, "The expansion of knowledge about sexual dimorphism and sex-based biology . . . characterizes the future of improved health care."[52]

That's what the science says, but the gender ideologues are dug in. Dr. Marci Bowers, the president of WPATH, dares to say: "Assigning gender identity on the basis of genitalia makes about as much sense as assigning it on the basis of height. Biologically, we're much closer to each other because everyone starts out with a primordial female anatomy, so everything a male has, a female has, and vice versa. It's just a matter of how the cards are shuffled."[53]

Dr. Bowers, your biophobia is showing. John Money would be proud.

Dr. Bowers is right that, at conception, humans are anatomically similar. But it's not just that "cards are shuffled." It's more like early in fetal development, babies hit a fork in the road—male or female. Those paths lead to vastly different places, and you can't choose a new one once you've started.

If John Money lived today and not decades ago, I highly doubt—given our awareness of the enormity of sex differences at every level of functioning, in every system of the body, and from before birth—that anyone would believe his theory that we are born "gender neutral." Back then, with limited knowledge, one could believe the Y chromosome was nearly empty and almost everything was up to nurture. In this era, it impossible to defend such a position.

Dr. Christiane Nüsslein-Volhard, 1995 winner of the Nobel Prize in medicine, said it best. Referring to the idea that an individual is whatever gender he or she claims to be, she declared, "That's nonsense! . . . There are people who want to change their gender, but they can't do it"[54] because it's

---

§ Note: the terms "sex" and "gender" are, surprisingly, used synonymously in the title, introducing confusion to a field centered on the dimorphic nature of sex. The title should read *Sex-Specific Medicine*. I am also perplexed to find some chapter authors refer to "sex assigned at birth," when a preponderance of the textbook is based on the indisputable fact that sex is determined at conception.

built into every single chromosome in the human body and affects each individual's development from the moment of conception.

In 1997, I put my hand down. No longer. Decades of hard science utterly invalidate John Money's theory, yet young people are being sacrificed at his feet. These aren't just bad ideas. These bad ideas have a body count, and the body count is rising.

# CHAPTER THREE

# Rosa

Two events preceded Rosa's "non-binary"* identity, her mother told me: a boy she loved dumped her, and COVID lockdowns.

Rosa was a gifted fifteen-year-old from San Diego who'd until recently been a compliant and easy child. She had always been anxious, especially in social situations. Her mother saw her as naive and easily manipulated.

With high school's daunting social scene ahead of her, Rosa's anxiety peaked the summer before ninth grade. But the first week of school, she met Sean in AP English and fell for him at once. They went out all year, and she truly thought he was The One. Rosa wore a sexy gown to prom and thoroughly enjoyed the glitz and glamour. That summer, she and Sean spent their free time surfing. But on Thanksgiving, he suddenly broke up with her, and she cried for a month.

With COVID lockdowns Rosa was separated from her friends. She discovered a new group online and during every free moment was talking, texting, and FaceTiming.

That's when her transformation began.

Rosa used to hang out in the kitchen in a camisole and shorts, cooking, eating, and gabbing with the family. According to her mom, she'd always loved make-up, hair, manicures, and, more recently, Victoria's Secret. She once bought a barely-there bikini that her parents made her return. There was never a hint of discomfort with being a girl.

---

* In *The Gender Book*, recommended by the AAP, nonbinary is defined as "those whose identities fall outside of the widely accepted gender binaries" (*The Gender Book*, 24), but I prefer the more scientific definition provided me by one of my patients, fifteen years old: "It basically means you're still figuring this sh*t out."

But over the months as Rosa isolated in her room, joining the family only for dinner (her parents insisted), she turned into a different person.

She wore an oversize hoodie and baggy sweatpants. She was irritable and withdrawn. She was stuck to her phone and iPad. Rosa's sister, with whom she shared a room, reported she was sucking her thumb.

"Rosa stopped doing that when she was eight!" her mom exclaimed.

Rosa began to talk about gender being fluid. "Girls and guys are just two options," she told her parents, "I don't fit into that strict binary." We didn't know what to make of that, her mom told me. Then she started saying she wasn't a girl. When her father said that's ridiculous, she had a meltdown, accused him of being biased, and didn't speak to him for three days.

This was not the girl they'd raised for fifteen years. It was someone else, someone they didn't recognize.

"Just so you know," her mom told me, "my husband is the sweetest, most tolerant person you'll ever meet. He campaigned for gay marriage. His brother is gay, and we are very close to him and his husband."

They took Rosa to see a therapist, but they felt slighted. The therapist met with Rosa alone first, spending more time with her than with them—she didn't seem interested in Rosa's history and put little value on the fifteen years of history they had with their daughter. The therapy didn't help.

"We didn't know at the time," Rosa's mom told me, "but a few of her new online friends were non-binary and transboys. Back then, I didn't even know what those words meant. I'm a lot smarter now." One day Rosa came home with a buzz cut, and her mom nearly fainted. "I'm pangender and non-binary, and my name is Glen," she emailed her parents. "I need hormones. Please make an appointment at a gender clinic."

"I had no idea what all that meant," her mother told me, "but I saw my daughter's not herself. It felt like we were losing her and we all needed help. I found a clinic in a major medical center two hours away. We truly believed they'd have answers for us. We walked in with hope."

But the first thing the clinic staff asked was, "What pronouns do you use?"

This wasn't what her parents expected. "We couldn't believe it," her mother told me. "They weren't interested in all she'd gone through—the years of anxiety, then the break-up and the lockdowns. I knew in my gut those things had really affected her. I knew she was still hurting from what happened with Sean. She was so confused and angry."

Something didn't sit right with her. "I'm a real-estate broker, not a therapist, but anyone could see Rosa needed therapy. In under six months she'd become unrecognizable. But the gender therapist kept telling us 'Glen' was non-binary and we must support 'them.' I'm telling you, they would have put her on hormones that same day."

Rosa's mom and dad knew that something must have happened to their daughter, and the solution couldn't be as simple as using new pronouns and a boy's name. At that moment, they faced a wrenching choice: Listen to the professionals, or trust their guts?

"It was the scariest day of my life," her mother said. "We got up and left."

## Different Types of Gender Dysphoria (GD)

A few years ago, the world's largest gender clinic, London's Tavistock Gender Identity Disorder Service (GIDS), was overwhelmed. They saw only eighteen patients in the five years between 2000 and 2005. In 2009–2010, they saw

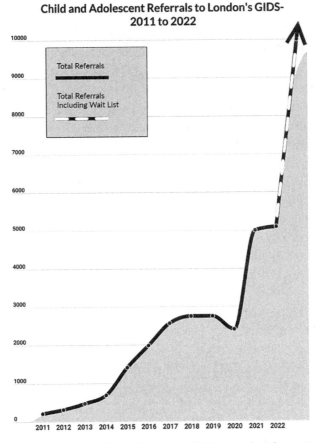

*Data sourced from NHS Tavistock and Portman,[1] GIDS- Gender Identity Development Service,[2] SEGM,[3] Michael Biggs, "Suicide by Clinic-Referred Transgender Adolescents in the United Kingdom."[4]*

seventy-seven.[5] By 2021–2022, that number exploded to 3,585 patients[6]—an increase of 4,555 percent in just over ten years. But the true number is even higher, because the waiting list in 2021 exceeded 5,300.[7]

The graph above gives a snapshot of the growing stampede of patients to GIDS.

Note the graph in 2011. If it were extended farther to the left (earlier in time), you'd need a microscope to read it, that's how few patients they had.

Similar remarkable surges have been documented in Canada, Denmark, Sweden, Norway, and Finland.[8]

Cases in the US have exploded as well, but accurate documentation is challenging. Our healthcare system is decentralized, and we lack standardized national data collection tools enabling analysis of these trends at a state or local level. Yet we do know in 2021, 2 to 9 percent[9] of the roughly 15 million[10] US high school students identified as transgender, and 8 percent[11] of the nearly fourteen and a half million[12] college students identified as "gender-diverse"—not male or female as those terms have always been understood. That same year, about 42,000 children and teens across the United States received a diagnosis of gender dysphoria (GD), nearly triple the number in 2017, according to data Komodo compiled for Reuters.[13]

These numbers are likely undercounted because they only include treatment covered by insurance of pediatric patients with a GD diagnosis. Other patients may not have a formal diagnosis, are cash pay who turn to private clinics, or are uncounted in insurance data when medical professionals deliberately miscode diagnoses.[14]

To put it differently, according to DSM-5 prevalence rates, of the approximately 1.73 million living in the Pittsburgh metropolitan area[15] in 2010, there would have been well under 200 people with gender dysphoria. Ten years later, you could find over 300 among just the 3,168 students in thirteen high schools in that city.[16] A 2021 study reported almost 10 percent of Pittsburgh high school students self-described as "gender diverse"—about three in a class of thirty.[†]

More and more adolescents and young adults in first-world countries do not consider themselves male or female. Many are convinced they inhabit the wrong bodies and are disembodied from their physical realities. Aside from brief declines during COVID, cases of GD swelled like a tidal wave.

Rosa was drowning in it. She started believing she's a boy in 2020. If a graph like the above for GIDS existed measuring US cases, Rosa would be

† I acknowledge the difference between GD and "gender diverse," but the numbers are still striking.

one of the thousands in the surge to the right—near what I can only hope is the high-water mark.

To speak of this matter with accuracy, we must make distinctions. The eighteen patients at Tavistock in London from 2000 to 2005 are not the same as the hordes of adolescents in gender clinics today. If your child complains of gender distress now or in the future, you must know to which group he or she belongs.

Gender dysphoria is a symptom, and symptoms can be caused by a variety of conditions. A fever, for example, can be caused by the flu, infection, heat exhaustion, cancer, and other ailments. Some fevers don't need much attention; they resolve by themselves. Others require investigation and treatment. Fevers cannot be lumped together as one entity.

Gender dysphoria is complex and not well understood, but we know there are multiple, distinct types and pathways to it. There are variables such as age at onset, and there are influences like adoption, abuse, and autism. Each group is different, and research and data pertaining to one group don't apply to another. Some want to make gender dysphoria an entity with one-size-fits-all treatment. This is a blunder.

University of Toronto psychologist Ray Blanchard, a prominent researcher in the field for forty years, warns:[17]

> . . . failure to make scientifically valid and functional distinctions among different types of gender dysphoric persons can only prevent progress toward finding the best approach to helping each.

For the purposes of this discussion, I will distinguish between three types of GD.

The first is exemplified by Admiral Levine.

I've never met the Admiral, but in an interview with the *New York Times*,[18] Levine described becoming more introspective and exploring gender identity after marrying and having two children. This is typical of what's called adult-onset gender dysphoria.

Two other types of gender dysphoria are early-onset in young children, and late- or adolescent-onset in teens and young adults.

Born in 2000, Jazz (originally Jared) Jennings is the posterchild for childhood-onset GD. I never met Jazz, a public personality with a well-publicized biography—important enough to be interviewed on Barbara Walters's *20/20* in 2007.

Jazz insisted he was a girl at age two and, despite his parents' efforts, could not be convinced otherwise. To the extent that he loved mermaids, unicorns, and princesses, Jazz consistently rejected all things masculine, not the least his anatomy.

His convictions, feminine preferences, and behaviors persisted, no matter what they tried. Jazz was diagnosed with gender identity disorder at age five. The year Jazz was diagnosed, only about 80 children were seen at the sole clinic in the western hemisphere specializing in kids with GD, Toronto's Gender Identity Service at the Centre for Addiction and Mental Health.[19] Children like Jazz were so rare, only three such clinics existed worldwide at the time.

Jazz's rejection of his maleness began prior to socializing with similar children—he was only two, and children with GID were few and far between. What caused a toddler like Jazz to insist in 2005 that he's the opposite sex? We didn't know then, and we don't know now.

Because kids with GID were so rare, we have scant information on them, and the studies we do have are poor quality. But we know this: A vast majority were boys; their dysphoria began before the age of seven, and it resolved, in most cases, before adulthood; a majority ended up gay or lesbian. The resolution of gender dysphoria is called desistance.

As the DSM-4 put it in 1994, "only a very small number of children with gender identity disorder [as it was called then] will continue to have symptoms . . . in later adolescence or adulthood."[20] Eleven studies over four decades have shown a majority of patients become comfortable with their biological sex by puberty or young adulthood.[21] James M. Cantor, PhD, explains that large scale follow-up studies indicate transgender kids such as Jazz "generally turn out to be regular gay or lesbian folks." Despite large discrepancies in definitions and methodologies, the majority of research shows desistance rates above 70 percent and reaching 90 percent during puberty.[22]

Take note, parents, here's the zinger: *We have no way of knowing if a child's or adolescent's gender dysphoria will persist into adulthood.* I'll have more about that later.

Returning to the current epidemic, it's not due to a sudden increase of children and adults lining up at the doors of gender clinics. The lines aren't made up of individuals like Jazz and Rachel. They are nearly all teenagers like Rosa.

Rosa is a minor with GD, as Jazz was, but the similarities end there. Rosa's an adolescent, not a toddler, insisting she's a boy precipitously following social stressors and internet immersion. The new identity was followed by a plunge in her mental health. She withdrew from her family and previous friends.

Also unlike Jazz, Rosa grew up in a trans-celebrating environment. When she was three, a pregnant "man" gained fame after appearing on Oprah. When Rosa was seven, California passed SB 48, a bill mandating that transgenderism be taught beginning in kindergarten.‡ Books in her school library such as *10,000 Dresses* ("a modern fairy tale about becoming the person you feel you are inside")[23] introduced the idea of being born in the wrong body in a matter-of-fact way and celebrated the "coming out" of children her age.

In 2014, when Rosa was nine, Jazz was named a "most influential teen" by *TIME* magazine.[24] Bruce Jenner became Caitlyn when Rosa was ten, and the same year millions began to watch Jazz's reality show chronicling the road to genital surgery and beyond.

How could Rosa have escaped being impacted by the radical social change? In fact, several of her girlfriends believe they are boys, actual boys who will become men. Their false beliefs are affirmed by everyone they know. They use the boys' bathrooms at school and dorm with boys on overnight trips. At least one of them, Rosa's parents later learned, was on testosterone and planning a double mastectomy.

And don't forget, all those years Rosa was also absorbing the belief that anyone who questions the transgender narrative is a bad person—biased and hateful.

If your preteen or teen announces a new identity, he or she is almost surely in Rosa's group, not Jazz's. If your child had early-onset gender dysphoria, you would have known years ago.

Like all parents I see, Rosa's parents were anguished but also dumbfounded: "We know there are transgender people, and we support and respect them. But what in the world happened to our daughter and how did it happen so fast? And why, for God's sake, why did the gender clinic rush to validate and medicate her?"

I told them what I'm going to tell you: your child is not another Jazz or Rachel. Like a fever, the symptoms may be the same, but the causes are different. Your family is a casualty of a social epidemic, some would say a cult. This is a whole new ballgame.

---

‡ More on the impact of SB 48—and my testimony against it—will be covered in Chapter Eight.

## A Curious Doctor

In 2018, Brown University physician, researcher, and academic Lisa Littman noticed an unusual trend in her small Rhode Island town. As Dr. Littman explained, "Teens from the same friend group were announcing transgender identities on social media, one after the other, on a scale that greatly exceeded expected numbers."[25]

The onset of GID in teen girls was practically unheard of: before 2012, there was next to no research about them. Given how uncommon adolescent gender dysphoria[§] once was, multiple transgender teens in the same friend group was bizarre. Even one instance would be a statistical anomaly. More than one? Inconceivable. Dr. Littman decided to investigate.

Online, she found parents describing the same phenomenon: Teens and young adult children, a majority girls without previous gender dysphoria, came out in quick succession. Sometimes *entire friend groups* identified as transgender at the same time.

These weren't Jazzes or Rachels, but something entirely new. Littman's town had a growing crowd of Rosas—and it was far from the only one.

Yet no one asked why a previously rare condition of primarily young boys was skyrocketing in teenage girls. Even worse, gender therapists were focused on names and pronouns, instead of the real question: *What is going on here?*

Dr. Littman sought answers to the real question. She conducted an online survey of 256 parents about their teen or young adult's gender dysphoria that had appeared "out of the blue."

"In online forums, parents have been reporting that their children are experiencing [gender dysphoria] . . . appearing for the first time during puberty or even after its completion," Dr. Littman wrote in her report, labelling these kids as "adolescent and young adult" children, or AYAs.[26]

Parents described "clusters of gender dysphoria outbreaks occurring in pre-existing friend groups" coupled with "immersion in social media, such as 'binge-watching' YouTube transition videos and excessive use of Tumblr." This type of gender dysphoria was novel, Littman wrote, "inconsistent with existing research literature."[27]

To describe this new phenomenon, Dr. Littman coined the term "Rapid Onset Gender Dysphoria," or ROGD: the development, over a short period, of gender dysphoria in an adolescent or young adult with no

---

§ "Gender Dysphoria" and "Gender Identity Disorder" refer to the same condition. How the name changed—and why—was covered in Chapter Two.

significant earlier history. Her data, gleaned from the parent survey, were both intriguing and troubling.[28]

To begin, 83 percent of the kids were girls, and four in five had no evidence of gender dysphoria in childhood. This was a dramatic shift in demographics compared to the male-dominated, early-childhood dysphoria of Jazz Jennings.

Prior to their gender distress, a large majority suffered psychologically. Nearly two-thirds had at least one mental health disorder or neurodevelopmental disability; over two-thirds suffered from social anxiety, and well over half had "poor or extremely poor ability to handle negative emotions productively." For many, their lives were shaped by trauma: Half of the parents reported a "traumatic or stressful event" preceded the dysphoria, such as divorce, death of a parent, rape, a bad break-up, bullying, or psychiatric hospitalization. Dr. Littman posited that these kids may have rapidly adopted a transgender identity as a "maladaptive coping mechanism to avoid feeling strong or negative emotions."[29]

The profile fit Rosa to a "T." And like Rosa, many had suboptimal mental health evaluations by the clinicians they saw, despite a history of psychiatric problems.

In 2012, the American Psychiatric Association (APA) Task Force on the Treatment of Gender Identity Disorder advised that teens be "screened carefully" for trauma as well as for other psychiatric disorders that may produce gender confusion.[30] But the screenings parents described to Dr. Littman were anything but careful.

Dr. Littman told an interviewer: "The therapists really weren't interested in hearing . . . that the kid had a mental health history . . . or that the kid had experienced rape recently and that this [gender dysphoria] only came right after. . . . The clinicians basically said . . . get on board with transition and otherwise you're transphobic."[31]

Elsewhere Dr. Littman explained that providers "were only interested in fast-tracking gender-affirmation and transition and were resistant to even evaluating the child's pre-existing and current mental health issues."[32]

Over 70 percent of parents reported clinicians did not explore their child's mental health and nearly the same percentage failed to request previous medical records. One parent said, "When we tried to give our son's trans doctor a medical history . . . she refused to accept it. She said the half hour diagnosis in her office with him was sufficient, as she considers herself an expert in the field."[33]

A new demographic of girls with mental health issues, a majority believing that medical transition will solve all their woes,[34] and clinicians who failed to properly assess them—those findings alone were alarming. Even more explosive were Dr. Littman's data on "cluster outbreaks" of gender dysphoria, and her hypothesis explaining them: social contagion.

Social contagion is the swift spread of activities, behaviors, or even emotions through a network. When your daughter will only wear Reeboks and your son demands a high-fade haircut, those are benign forms of social contagion.

But eating disorders and self-injury can spread the same way. As Dr. Littman put it, "an individual and peer [can] mutually influence each other in a way that promotes emotions and behaviors that can potentially undermine their own development or harm others."[35]

Teens, especially girls, are vulnerable. They copy their friends, for better or worse.

Dr. Littman provided strong evidence that social contagion driven by peer group and online influence is a key determinant in the development of adolescent gender dysphoria. Over 86 percent of parents in her survey reported their child, like Rosa, became dysphoric after binging on social media, having one or multiple friends come out as trans in quick succession, or both.[36]

Based on earlier studies, only 0.7 percent of young adults identify as transgender. But in a third of the friend groups Littman researched, 50 percent or more of the members became transgender in a brief time. In other words, compared to the general population of young adults, these friend groups had *seventy times* more trans-identifying members than would be expected.[37]

Littman was careful to point out that it's unlikely that friends and the Internet can make people transgender, but it is plausible that certain beliefs "can be initiated, magnified, spread, and maintained." She specified the following beliefs:

1. that nearly any symptom, including those that accompany normal puberty, is GD and proof of being transgender;
2. that medical transition is the sole solution and must be pursued urgently;
3. that anyone who does not accept the self-diagnosis or the plan to transition is "transphobic, abusive, and should be cut out of one's life."[38]

Regarding the first belief, Littman found the following advice on Tumblr, one of two sites, the other being YouTube, that a majority of parents reported influenced their child:

"Signs of indirect gender dysphoria," read one post on Tumblr. "1. Continual difficulty with simply getting through the day. 2. A sense of misalignment, disconnect, or estrangement from your own emotions. 3. A feeling of just going through the motions in everyday life, as if you're always reading from a script. 4. A seeming pointlessness to your life, and no sense of any real meaning or ultimate purpose 5. Knowing you're somehow different from everyone else, and wishing you could be normal like them. . ."[39]

Difficulty getting through the day? We used to call that depression, being down, or just having a bad day.

Estrangement from your emotions? We're supposed to believe it's odd that teenagers—or heck, even adults—don't understand their emotions?

Feeling like you're going through life reading from a script? No meaning or purpose? Different from everyone? Oh, come on. Not to minimize the unpleasantness, but these could all be normal teenage angst.

Ty Turner is a woman living as a man with hundreds of thousands of followers.[40] Turner's YouTube video "Female to Male Transition—1 Year on Testosterone" has 4.1 million views.[41] Turner instructs your child: "If you're wondering if you might be trans, you probably are."

## Just Lie to the Doctor

Believing that transition is the only solution and that time is of the essence, teens seek ways to get past parents and clinicians who don't share their sense of urgency. The blogs Dr. Littman discovered proposed a simple strategy: lie.

"Find out what they want to hear if they're gonna give you T [testosterone] and then tell them just that. It's about getting treatment, not about being true to those around you," one person wrote.

"Get a story ready in your head . . . like how you were feeling, but was [*sic*] too afraid to tell anyone. . . ."

Another poster recommended: ". . . look up the DSM for the diagnostic criteria for transgender and make sure your story fits it."

One parent who responded to Littman's survey wrote: "Being trans is a gold star in the eyes of other teens," referring to the positive attention and increased status after coming out. But there was a dark side to that too, which goes back to the third belief that Littman suggests can be spread by peers and the Internet: the assumption that "anyone that is critical about being trans-gender (even just asking questions) is either ignorant or filled with hate."

Dr. Littman observed once AYA kids come out as trans, they "became increasingly sullen, withdrawn and hostile toward their families."[42] Nearly two-thirds of parents surveyed had been called "transphobic" or "bigoted" by their children for the smallest perceived transgressions like using sex-specific pronouns, calling a child by his or her birth name, or even for calling for more time to think about gender issues.[43]

"If they aren't mocking 'cis' people,[¶] they are playing pronoun police and mocking people who can't get the pronouns correct," one parent reported.[44]

And don't think for a moment that the parents were staunch members of the GOP. In fact, 86 percent favored extending marriage to include gay and lesbian couples, and nearly nine in ten believe that transgender individuals "deserve the same rights and protections as other individuals in their country." But their own children call them bigoted and transphobic.

❁   ❁   ❁

Helena Kerschner took testosterone in her teens. She writes about how the online world adopts ideas of intersectionality—where combinations of factors like race, gender, and sexual orientation make one privileged or marginalized. The privileged cause the world's problems. The marginalized are the victims. [45]

"Since Tumblr users are mostly biological females," Kerschner explains, "the 'cishet[**] white girl' holds the position of most privileged and therefore most inherently bad group. In this climate, you are made to feel guilty and responsible for all the horrors and atrocities of the world."

Helena mocked the online narrative: "LGBT people and POC[††] can't even walk out of their houses without being murdered by cishet white people just like you!"

According to Kerschner, heterosexual white girls often despise what makes them "privileged." They can't change their sexual orientation or race. But they *can* change their gender. Transgenderism offers a way for adolescents to be absolved of privilege and join the ranks of the oppressed.

---

¶ "Cisgender" describes someone whose identity corresponds to their sex: no dysphoria, no need for "alignment"—it's all good.

** This term means someone is cisgender (someone who identifies with his or her biological sex) and heterosexual.

†† People of color.

"The beauty of gender ideology is it provides a way to game this system, so that you can get some of those targets off your back. . . . It's as easy as putting 'she/they' in your bio. Instantly you are transformed from an oppressing, entitled, evil, bigoted, selfish, disgusting cishet white scum into a valid trans person who deserves celebration."

Is it any wonder that Rosa and her white, heterosexual, middle-class teenage friends transitioned within a short period?

Rosa's parents were caught off guard. They didn't know she was spending hours on YouTube, Reddit, and Tumblr. Like the families in Dr. Littman's survey, Rosa's relationship with her parents derailed. Any time Rosa's parents questioned her new identity, Rosa prepared for war. And like most of those families, Rosa's parents are pro-LGBT. Yet their open-mindedness and progressive politics didn't spare them from her wrath.

Rosa's parents asked: Will she grow out of this? Can we ride this rough patch out and go back to normal?

I had to say we don't know because long-term studies on ROGD kids don't exist. Dr. Kaltiala, Finland's gender expert: "The phenomenon [of adolescent-onset gender dysphoria] is new, and there is therefore no research data on the permanence of experience."[46]

## Proceed with Extreme Caution!

Dr. Littman acknowledged the limits of her research. Relying on parental reports alone, she explained, was "incomplete," and some parents she surveyed were found on websites for those worried about their child's gender dysphoria. That might have introduced bias.

Likewise, Dr. Littman made clear the existence of ROGD does not imply "that no AYAs would ultimately benefit from transition." She was describing a phenomenon, not offering a treatment plan. More than anything Dr. Littman urged caution, calling for more research while warning that distressed teenagers should be carefully evaluated because their self-assessment may not be 100 percent accurate.

While recognizing the limits of her research, Dr. Littman nonetheless concluded that clinicians treating gender dysphoric kids suffer from hazardous blind spots.[47] First and foremost, they must recognize adolescent-onset gender dysphoria is not the same as early-onset—*and doctors should stop treating them as if they were.* Again, Rosa's path to GD was altogether different than Jazz's. Like patients with fevers, we can't lump them together just because they have the same symptom.

Dr. Littman warned it's unknown if "gender dysphoria occurring in young adults [is] transient, temporary or likely to be long term." So clinicians need to slam on the breaks—"extreme caution should be applied before considering the use of treatments that have permanent effects such as cross-sex hormones and surgery." [48]

She further called them out: "The majority of clinicians described in this study did not explore trauma or mental health disorders as possible causes of gender dysphoria or request medical records in patients." Some clinicians refused to communicate with parents about their own child, despite the fact that parental insights are a "pre-requisite for . . . fully informed diagnosis." Dr. Littman called these problems "alarming"—they put AYAs "at considerable risk." [49] I couldn't agree more—what parents described indicated a dereliction of duty.

Dr. Littman confronted the gender establishment narrative and suggested that social and medical affirmation may cause "an iatrogenic persistence of gender dysphoria in individuals who would have had their gender dysphoria resolve on its own." [50]

"Iatrogenic": A word I want you to remember. It's when a medical intervention—including something a health professional says or implies—causes harm.

To put it differently, Littman suggested affirmation may not help ROGD kids embrace their authentic identity; it may entrench a false one.

Those were the stakes facing Rosa's parents. They may have been unaware at the time, but if the gender clinic put their daughter on hormones, Rosa could have locked in her gender dysphoria for good.

Proponents of affirmation relentlessly promote transition of kids like Rosa because they believe, per the Articles of Faith, that her gender identity is innate, that everyone with gender dysphoria is transgender, and that there's only one path to relief.

Littman's research blew a hole in their creed. ROGD sees GD as a symptom, a coping mechanism, with various paths to and away from it. It is *not* always innate and unchangeable. The self-diagnoses of minors are *not* always accurate. Every instance of GD does *not* require transition.

The notion of ROGD violated the medical establishment's creed. That made Lisa Littman a heretic—a heretic deserving punishment.

# CHAPTER FOUR

# The Castro Consensus

Lisa Littman observed an unusual trend, so she asked questions, gathered data, crunched numbers, and generated a hypothesis. Acknowledging the limitations of her data, she published her findings and highlighted the urgent need for more research.

Dr. Littman did precisely what good, ethical researchers should do. How was her paper received?

The assaults began swiftly.

## "Junk Science"

Like many studies, Dr. Littman's was first published as a short abstract. Without waiting for the entire paper, activists claimed her methodology was faulty. "Some folks saw [the abstract] and were very ready to write about how this couldn't possibly be true, couldn't possibly happen . . . without having read the paper, because the paper didn't exist yet," Dr. Littman recalled.[1]

After the full paper was released, the gender medical establishment worked to discredit and quash her findings.

The *Journal of Pediatrics* conducted their own study, declaring it "did not support the rapid onset gender dysphoria hypothesis."[2] A statement issued by the Coalition for the Advancement & Application of Psychological Science (CAAPS) went further, calling for "eliminating the use of ROGD and similar concepts for clinical and diagnostic application."

Their statement was signed by over sixty professional associations, including the America Psychological Association, the Society for Behavioral Medicine, and the American Psychiatric Association.[3]

The Human Rights Campaign (HRC) declared Dr. Littman's study "junk science."[4]

How about the professional group to which I as a child psychiatrist once belonged? Even four years after Dr. Littman's paper, the American Academy of Child and Adolescent Psychiatry (AACAP) denies ROGD. At their 2022 meeting, a two-hour lecture—"Trans Youth: Evolving Gender Identities and Detransition"—omitted any mention of it.[5]

Reacting to Dr. Littman's paper, the World Professional Association of Transgender Health (WPATH) pointed out in 2018 that ROGD is not listed in any official classifications of diseases like the *Diagnostic and Statistical Manual of Mental Disorders* (DSM) or International Classification of Diseases (ICD). How could it be? The process takes years, and Dr. Littman had just introduced the concept.

Nevertheless, they declared "the term 'Rapid Onset Gender Dysphoria (ROGD)' is not a medical entity recognized by any major professional association. . . . Therefore, it constitutes nothing more than an acronym."[6] The Australian division of WPATH issued a similar statement.[7]

While the gender establishment fumed against Littman and ROGD, many clinicians embraced it. In a 2018 paper delineating ethical issues in the informed consent process, Stephen Levine wrote about "adolescents with ROGD."[8] He explained to me his readiness to adopt the term: "I use ROGD because the vast majority of boys and girls seen for gender issues describe, as do their parents, onset at puberty or several years after. ROGD just described the phenomenon."[9]

## "This is how it's going to be."

One of the primary goals of this book is to pull the curtain back and provide parents with a glimpse of the ferment and quashing of debate regarding how best to help youths with gender dysphoria. Affirming care appears to be a settled science, but it is neither science nor settled.

In 2021, Erica Anderson—the first transgender president of WPATH's American associate, USPATH—wrote a *Washington Post* op-ed criticizing the medical community's blind embrace of affirming care for minors.[10] In response, WPATH and USPATH issued a joint statement that they "opposed the use of the lay press" to discuss these issues.[11] Internally, USPATH proposed a six-month moratorium on its members talking to the press.

In response to the gag order, Anderson quit her position on the board, denouncing their "tactics of muzzling leaders in the USPATH/WPATH."[12]

The Endocrine Society (ES) also crushed debate. The Society's 2017 guidelines, calling for puberty blockers at an early age followed by cross-sex hormones, leaves patients infertile. Whoa, that's a big deal. There must have been lots of discussion about that. Right?

Dr. William Malone is an endocrinologist who treats adolescents and a founder of the Society for Evidence-Based Gender Medicine (SEGM), an international group of over 100 clinicians and researchers. He described the ES meeting at which the 2017 guidelines were introduced.

They "rolled out a set of guidelines for gender dysphoric adolescents and children that had really no evidence base, and essentially said that okay, your job as endocrinologists now is to medically affirm children—well [i.e., healthy] adolescents—with puberty blockers and cross-sex hormones. . . . There was no discussion at all. It was difficult even to submit questions after they presented the guidelines. It was done under an atmosphere of 'This is how it's going to be, and if you ask questions, you're a bigot.'"[13]

In 2020, Dr. Quentin Van Meter, a pediatric endocrinologist and member of the ES, proposed the Society host a debate on the treatment of transgender youth at their annual meeting. He offered to set up everything—all he asked was the ES allow open dialogue.

Informed that he missed the deadline, Dr. Van Meter tried again in 2021 but received no response. In 2022, again, no response.[14] You get the picture.

If dialogue was permitted, doctors critical of the ES guidelines could voice their objections. They could point to studies with troubling results. Young adults could be brought in to share their stories and express their regret. Other doctors could learn about other countries' systematic reviews and their conclusions that the risks of hormones outweigh the benefits. Perhaps the media would have reported on the controversy. Maybe there would have been no need for this book.

The American Academy of Pediatrics (AAP) has also been taken over by gender zealots. In 2018, the AAP endorsed gender-affirming care (GAC) for all gender dysphoria, no matter the age of the child. This included immediate social transition* before puberty.[15] AAP policy is considered the gold standard for child treatment. If your child has gender distress, your pediatrician will mostly likely follow the AAP's playbook.

How was their policy crafted? Contrary to what you're led to believe by mainstream media and trans-activists, rank-and-file AAP members had

---

\* Social transition, or "affirmation," refers to telling people about a new identity, adopting a new name and pronouns, changing one's presentation (hair, clothing, etc.), using opposite sex restrooms and other facilities, and sometimes changing one's legal name. Social transition does not necessarily include all of these, nor does it happen all at once.

nothing to do with it. AAP members don't even get to vote on new policy statements prior to release. In fact, all AAP policy statements are produced, passed, and publicly released by a maximum of thirty pediatricians who sit on the board of directors and a few self-selecting committees pertinent to the issue being considered.

The 2018 gender affirmation-only policy, for example, was written by a Brown University pediatrician and child psychiatrist, Jason Rafferty, who had affirmed and transitioned children for years; it was then edited, approved, and released by other long-time LGBQT activist pediatricians including at least one other gender-affirming colleague, and the AAP board of directors.

The remaining 66,000 AAP members—those who spend long days taking care of children—had no voice in the matter. In fact, most AAP pediatricians first read the new policy on "affirming care" at the same time you did—when it was released to the media.[16]

One might argue it is necessary to have policies written by small groups of "expert pediatricians" to guarantee that they are scientifically sound. There's just one problem: the AAP's policy statement contradicts the very studies it cites.

The AAP did not count on being fact-checked by Dr. James Cantor, a psychologist and GD expert who practiced in Kenneth Zucker's Toronto clinic.

Dr. Cantor knew almost all clinics used a "watchful waiting approach" because the vast majority of childhood GD cases desisted by late adolescence; clinics would not consider medical interventions prior to age twelve, and often not before age sixteen. This prompted him to hunt down and read AAP's purported evidence.

Cantor made three important observations. First, he found AAP relied heavily on a claim that "conversion therapy" was being foisted on children unhappy with their sex and needed to be rejected. Cantor pointed out this was a fallacy since "conversion therapy" only applied to sexual orientation; indeed, that is precisely what the studies AAP cited pertained to—attempts to change sexual orientation in adults; not one citation pertained to GD. Second, he noted that the AAP "simply disappeared" the eleven follow-up studies of GD children in the psychiatric literature that revealed high rates of natural desistance. Finally, he noted that the references AAP cited as supporting gender-affirmation only actually "outright contradicted that policy, repeatedly endorsing *watchful waiting*."[17]

Cantor summarized the AAP statement this way: "AAP is, of course, free to establish whatever policy it likes on whatever basis it likes. But any assertion that their policy is based on evidence is demonstrably false."[18]

Quite an accusation. Has the AAP responded to Dr. Cantor? Of course not. Is your pediatrician aware of this fiasco? I highly doubt it. She's been trained to trust the AAP.

In the meantime, AAP bullies stifled debate. It even rejected SEGM's application to set up an information table—just a table with pamphlets manned by SEGM members, something dozens of organizations, drug companies, and other businesses do without obstacles—at its 2021 annual meeting.[19]

Joseph Zanga is a past president of both the AAP and the American College of Pediatricians.[20] The latter is an organization formed by AAP members in 2002 who were fed up with the organization's capture by ultra-liberal agendas, such as over-the-counter contraception and abortion rights for teens without parental consent. Their dissent was silenced, so they went off and formed their own professional group.

Dr. Zanga explained to me that the AAP holds a conference every year, the Annual Leadership Forum, ALF. The AAP Board of Directors as well as the president and vice president of all the chapters of AAP attend. The ALF discusses resolutions submitted to them.

In 2021, pediatrician and AAP member Julia Mason submitted a resolution suggesting the Academy halt their promotion of medical transitions for minors until research demonstrated long-term benefit.[21]

What could be more reasonable? The resolution called for a hiatus until doctors, patients, and families have sufficient evidence of safety and effectiveness. Rank-and-file pediatricians agreed: "Because of the pandemic, they had [the resolution] online and it got a lot of engagement," Dr. Mason said. "It was in the top five in terms of pediatrician engagement, and it was four-to-one positive versus negative votes."[22]

Dr. Mason's resolution was submitted to a Reference Committee at the ALF for discussion and vote on whether to submit to the ALF itself. It received 80 percent "yes" votes. That was about the highest support for any resolution in that Committee. But when the Committee itself sat to discuss what resolutions would be presented, they had "no recommendation" for that resolution, and the resolution disappeared.

In 2022, Dr. Mason submitted another resolution calling for caution. AAP leadership invented a rule that resolutions "unsponsored" by a chapter or committee cannot be reviewed.[23] "There were four other pediatricians who coauthored [the 2022 resolution] with me, but it got buried. Nobody could give it a 'yes' or 'no' vote, and very few could even read it," Dr. Mason said.[24] It was bureaucratic trickery. The previously nonexistent sponsorship rule seemed designed to block the resolution questioning affirming care.[25]

Being a persistent fellow, Dr. Zanga personally asked AAP leadership to change course. He told me, "The Academy of late has been unwilling to even discuss the transgender issue. It's something that I as a past president, a member of the Past Presidents Advisory Committee, have asked the Committee to consider and discuss. It unfortunately never gets added to our meeting agenda. I stand here and say, I'm disappointed. . . . The science says that children and adolescents are not capable of making these kinds of decisions."

Note the AAP's description of their committees as "a trusted source of expert opinion on scientific principles and pediatric health care delivery."[26]

Dr. Zanga submitted an article to the Georgia AAP newsletter, urging discussion of unproven affirmation therapies and return to the principle of "do no harm." The chapter rejected his submission.[27] I remind you, Dr. Zanga is *a previous president of the AAP*.

OK, let's examine this for a moment. The AAP takes time in its leadership forum to address racism in medical education, cultural headwear discrimination among children, and "promoting recycling."[28] While these issues may warrant attention, so does the permanent disfigurement and sterilization of kids without strong evidence of lasting benefit.

Dr. Mason summed up the medical establishment's endemic problem: "When we hear that 22 professional organizations support affirmation, this is not the voice of the average pediatrician. It's the position of a few activists that have captured key committees at these medical societies and are using the bureaucracy to ensure the voice of regular pediatricians isn't heard." [29]

## Learning from Fidel

The APA, the Endocrine Society, WPATH, AAP. . . while leading the public to believe their policies are reached following robust research and exchange of ideas, these groups act as a monolithic mouthpiece regurgitating the Articles of Faith.

It's a fraud. Doctors and researchers are at war over gender treatment. There's no medical consensus on treatment of transgender-identifying people; only a Castro consensus.[30]

How did Fidel Castro rule Cuba for over four decades? Easy—he banned opposition. There were no authentic elections, so Castro always "won" in a landslide. Then he proclaimed to his country and the world that, once again, he had the full support of the Cuban people.

The medical community has adopted Fidel's methods. Policymaking is dictated by a small number of ideological bullies who silence dissenting voices like those of Drs. Malone, Van Meter, Cantor, Zanga, Mason,

Anderson, Levine, and others. Only one approach is permitted, gender-affirming care (GAC). Then the establishment institutions proclaim the science is settled, everyone agrees.

How does this affect parents? It affects you big-time. You trust your pediatrician and turn to her for guidance and information. But your pediatrician is busy and cannot possibly keep up to date on every topic in her field. So she turns to the AAP for guidance; *she* trusts *them* and assumes their positions have been rigorously reviewed, otherwise they wouldn't have been adopted. That's how your pediatrician adopts the AAP positions as her own. But now you know the pro-affirmation lobby is running things at the AAP; as Dr. Van Meter put it to me, "the AAP is a lost cause." When you reach the end of this book, you'll likely know much more about transgender-identifying kids than your pediatrician.

❋ ❋ ❋

Pro-affirmation activists discovered Dr. Littman worked with the Rhode Island Department of Health on projects supporting the health of pregnant mothers and premature babies—completely unrelated to transgenderism. Nonetheless, they wrote a letter demanding she be fired.[31]

The paperwork had already been submitted to renew her contract for another year, but Dr. Littman wasn't rehired. [32] Followers of the Articles of Faith sent a clear message: contradict us, and you'll be out of work. Dr.Littman was also rebuffed by Brown University, where she was an assistant professor. After the attack on her research, Brown removed her paper from its sites and apologized. "Brown community members [were] expressing concerns that the conclusions of the study could be used to discredit efforts to support transgender youth and invalidate the perspectives of members of the transgender community,"[33] the Dean of Brown's School of Public Health said.

Brown's mission is to "serve the community, the nation, and the world by discovering, communicating, and preserving knowledge and understanding in a spirit of free inquiry."[34]

Brown University, what happened to your "spirit of free inquiry" when it came to Dr. Littman's paper?

*PlosOne*, the journal that originally reviewed, approved, and published Dr. Littman's research, also cracked under pressure, initiating an uncommon postpublication re-review.[35]

Dr. Littman stood strong. She eventually republished her paper with minor changes and the same conclusion: social contagion may be a factor in the development of adolescent-onset gender dysphoria.[36]

It didn't matter to activists that Dr. Littman's results stayed the same. They continued to smear her research. The Human Rights Campaign claimed her paper needed additional review because it was riddled with issues.[37] Southern Poverty Law Center asserted that Brown University took it down because the data were bunk.[38]

## Interesting Spin

Affirming care proponents propose the striking rise of GD is due to society's increasing acceptance. There were *always* this many trans people. They just never had the words to express themselves or faith that society would accept them.

As psychology professor Phillip Hammack put it to the *New York Times,* the spike in trans-identifying teenagers "signifies a new confidence among a new generation to be authentic in their gender identity." The *Times* wasn't sure "whether that jump [in the number of those identifying as trans] reflects inaccuracies in the previous estimate, a true increase in the number of transgender adolescents, or both."

"That's the bewildering question of why this is all happening," Dr. Jody Herman added in.[39]

Dr. Herman, are you unaware of Lisa Littman's paper and her robust evidence for social contagion as a contributing factor to adolescent GD? Or are you simply dismissing her critical contribution?

If the rise in gender dysphoria is due to social acceptance, where are the hordes of eager, newly identified trans, nonbinary, gender-fluid adults in their thirties, forties, fifties, sixties, and seventies? Why do we see only teens and young adults coming out with their friends after binging on social media?

Let's say for argument's sake that the soaring rates among youth are due to increasing social acceptance. How then do we explain the alarming rates of mental health issues in youth of "diverse" gender identities?

Now here's an interesting spin—their emotional problems are due to society's transphobia. Yup—that's what we're supposed to believe. The rates of transgender-identifying teens have skyrocketed because society is *more accepting,* but those same people who are more accepted suffer from anxiety, depression, and increased suicidality because . . . there's so much transphobia.

This is intellectually dishonest. It's one or the other, you can't have it both ways.

Blaming Rosa's anxiety on society's transphobia is based on the minority stress model: the idea that sexual minorities are victims of hate and discrimination and, as a result, suffer mental health burdens like anxiety, bipolar disorder, and suicidal thoughts and attempts.

If the minority stress model was valid, we expect the mental health of transgender people to improve with increasing societal acceptance.

But we don't see that. In 2020, the authors of a thirty-five-year chart review of 8,263 Dutch patients at Holland's primary gender clinic noted an increasing cultural acceptance of transgender persons over the past nearly half century, but little impact on suicide rates.[40]

The minority stress model is also, conveniently, the go-to explanation for the phenomenon of detransition. A speaker at the AACAP 2022 annual meeting[41] explained that when, after social transition and medical treatments, people decide to turn back and live in congruence with their sex, it does not necessarily mean they regret transitioning. "For a small minority, gender trajectories are non-linear and dynamic." These individuals have "evolving paths." It is simply "a shift in expression," and "internal and external factors" must be considered, including family and society stigma. Conservative homes and the military were mentioned.

This is astonishing to me. I am told by AACAP to immediately affirm a four-year-old without considering the context or complexity of the child's life, without asking what factors may have led to his wish to be, or his insistence that he is, the opposite sex. But when a twenty-five-year-old woman claims, "I made the mistake of my life, I am infertile and have a beard, am filled with regret, my therapist and doctors failed me," these mental health professionals call for a complex analysis of internal and external factors including what they call internalization of transphobia—she's rejected her male identity because she hates herself.

No, my esteemed colleagues, she rejected her male identity *because she is a woman.*

It seems to me if their primary concern was these young people in distress, wouldn't the AACAP, instead of invoking "internalized transphobia," invite detransitioners to speak at their meetings, and to describe their experiences at the hands of psychiatrists, psychologists, social workers, and counselors, so we might learn from them and help others seeking our aid?

The attacks on Dr. Littman had a silver lining. Her paper has been viewed or downloaded nearly half a million times,[42] unheard-of success.

That success came at a price. She lost one of her jobs. The institutions that published her work turned their backs on her. She had her research dragged through the mud. To her credit, Dr. Littman isn't bitter: "I just feel, as a scientist, as a responsible person, that, despite the noise, I have to get where the truth is."[43]

## Silencing Other Voices

Dr. Littman wasn't the only one targeted by gender activists for violating the Castro consensus.

In 2020, Abigail Shrier wrote the bombshell book *Irreversible Damage* based on Dr. Littman's research and families of ROGD kids. For endorsing and publicizing ROGD, Shrier was boycotted. When she appeared on the popular podcast *The Joe Rogan Experience*, employees mounted a campaign to cancel the show.[44]

Amazon blocked advertising for *Irreversible Damage* the month it was released.[45] The next year, Amazon employees circulated a petition to ban sales of the book on the platform.[46] They had reason to hope for success: Target pulled Shrier's blockbuster book from its shelves months before, only to return it after a public outcry against censorship.[47]

The controversy surrounding *Irreversible Damage* was heated, but not new. The pro-affirmation inquisition existed years before Dr. Littman's research. One of their most prized victims: Kenneth Zucker.

As discussed, Dr. Zucker is a long-acknowledged authority on children with gender dysphoria. He founded Toronto's Child Youth and Family Gender Identity Clinic (GIC), arguably the first such clinic in the world, and is one of the most cited names in the literature.[48]

Dr. Zucker was once as much an insider of the gender establishment as possible. But he failed to follow every detail of the Articles of Faith.

Dr. Zucker's approach was a cautious one: to help his gender-dysphoric patients, sometimes as young as three, to reach a sense of comfort with their own bodies without affirming an opposite-sex identity. This is called "watchful waiting."

Remember, between 61 and 98 percent of young children with gender dysphoria eventually embrace their biological sex. Given those numbers, and the medical and psychological risks of social and medical interventions, Zucker's cautious approach makes sense.

For his views, Dr. Zucker was accused of practicing conversion therapy. The term originally applied to therapy for individuals who were struggling with their same sex attraction and wished to develop a heterosexual orientation. Twenty states and the District of Columbia ban conversion therapy.[49]

Although sexual orientation is entirely different from gender identity, the same term has been applied to any therapy that is not 100 percent affirming of the patient's stated gender identity, based on the Article of Faith that gender identity is inborn and unchangeable. (I know, it's "unchangeable" but also "fluid"—if you still expect consistent and sensible thinking on this topic, you're going to continue being disappointed.)

Canada officially banned conversion therapy for gender-distressed people in 2021[50]—their prime minister, Justin Trudeau, called the practice "despicable and degrading."[51] Yet in 2015, long before the law officially made Dr. Zucker an outlaw, he was removed from his position, and the clinic was shuttered.[52]

The hospital that hosted Dr. Zucker's gender clinic did an external review. They ambushed him on vacation, calling him back to the office, where they accused him of practicing conversion therapy and of shaming and traumatizing patients.

Dr. Zucker denied the accusations, but he was fired the same day.

An investigation exonerated Dr. Zucker and found activists wanted his removal solely because he helped children come to terms with their sex. He was awarded substantial damages and a public apology.

From his fifty years in the field of transgender care, this is how Stephen Levine sees the battle:

> Nowhere in medicine has free speech been as limited as it has been in the trans arena. Skeptics are being institutionally suppressed. Critical letters to the editor . . . are refused publications, symposia submitted for presentation at national meetings are rejected, scheduled lectures are cancelled, and pressure has been exerted to get respected academics fired.[53]

## The Madness of Knee-jerk Affirmation

I was contacted by lawyers in Salt Lake City about a thirteen-year-old boy whose divorced parents were in litigation over his social transition. Zach had recently declared himself a girl, and his mother was 100 percent on board—new name, pronouns, dresses. His father wasn't going along with it.

I reviewed the records from Zach's recent psychiatric hospitalization. Staff listed gender dysphoria as one of his diagnoses and consistently used his girl's name and female pronouns, but the reasoning for those clinical decisions was absent. The hospital records indicated Zach heard voices and saw "ghosts." I searched for more information about the voices and the ghosts but found none.

Was it possible no one had asked? Psychotic symptoms such as auditory or visual hallucinations always warrant further questions. An obvious one: What did the voices say? Was Zach hearing voices telling him he's a girl?

These were questions that demanded attention from his clinicians prior to affirming a new identity. Maybe Zach's gender dysphoria was related to his disordered thinking and hallucinations. Perhaps instead of lip gloss he needed Risperdal (anti-psychotic medication).

I found similar madness in the care of seventeen-year-old Nicole in Boston. Nicole's life had been chaotic; her father left when she was two, her mother had five other kids with two other men, she was sexually abused by a neighbor, and her family had been homeless for months on several occasions. She had an IQ of 68 and was on three psychiatric medications to treat hallucinations, ADHD, and depression. When she discovered her mother was pregnant, Nicole came out as a boy.

At the time I was consulted, Nicole was in foster care due to charges of physical abuse by her mother.

Nicole wanted testosterone. I was asked by the court to provide my professional opinion regarding "gender-affirming" care, including testosterone, for her.

Having read this far, I trust you can figure out what I said. No testosterone for Nicole.

❋    ❋    ❋

Zach lives in Utah and Nicole in Massachusetts—both states that ban "conversion therapy" for minors.[54] As we saw with Dr. Zucker, that means any approach that fails to immediately affirm a child's new identity is prohibited.

Like Dr. Zucker, I put myself at 1 risk when I argued that Zach and Nicole should not be affirmed but instead have their long-term mental health issues treated.

At least with those two consultations, my role was to provide my professional opinion. But that wasn't the case with David, a patient in Colorado with whom I worked directly.

One day David told his parents that he is transgender and asked to be called Zoe, "she," and "her." He wanted blockers because the hair sprouting over the corners of his lips and his cracking voice reminded him he's a boy. If only he could take estrogen, he told me, having breasts and wider hips would make him feel confident and secure.

The medical establishment, the DSM-5, and the state of Colorado say the only permissible response I'm allowed is to act as if he was a girl. David must be in the driver's seat—forget about "Do no harm." If he picks a different gender identity, name, and pronouns next week, I must use those. I am to instruct parents to tell everyone—family members, school staff, his piano teacher and dentist—to do the same. His mom, dad, and I are all supposed to celebrate what doctors at Johns Hopkins call David's "evolving sense of self." [55]

Celebrating an evolving sense of self sounds fine and dandy. But I happen to know that when David first appeared at a family event in a dress, his mother—a strong feminist and lifelong liberal who supported gay marriage and survived 9/11 and breast cancer—had to flee to a restroom, where she had the first panic attack in her life. I also know puberty blockers might be followed by estrogen and perhaps even orchiectomy—castration.[†] He could end up disfigured and infertile and still not be satisfied with his body.

When David is ready, I must share those dangers with him. I took an oath to prevent harm, no matter what the gender medical establishment or the state of Colorado might say.

For refusing to validate the opposite-sex identities of Rosa and David, I risk an investigation like Dr. Zucker's, but I'll live with that. I'm going to do what's best for my patients.

## Discord on Discord

On my advice, Rosa's parents dug into her social media, specifically Discord.

They discovered that for the past five months, their daughter was part of a group of four girls, two of whom identified as boys. They played Roblox and Minecraft but also spoke of harming themselves with knives or cigarette lighters. Rosa was in an intense emotional and sexualized relationship with one of the transgender girls, "Fletcher," who lived in the Midwest. They spoke and FaceTimed day and night.

Among the messages from Fletcher to their daughter: "I'm nibbling your neck. I'm making you moan." It was Fletcher who'd suggested to Rosa that she may be a boy and instructed her on how to come out in a text to her parents.

Rosa told me Fletcher was trans and gay, and one of her favorite people on the planet. They understood each other, she explained; she could tell "him" everything—Fletcher knew how to help her and was her therapist. "I need him in my life, I need to be able to speak with him at any time."

---

[†] The troubling effects of puberty-blocking drugs and cross-sex hormones is detailed in Chapter Five.

Her parents further discovered that a month earlier, their daughter had received a video of one of the older girls in the group masturbating. The following day, Rosa had searched the Internet for ways to harm herself.

I saw her at once for a full assessment. She described severe anxiety, depression, and thoughts of ending her life in a few months if she didn't feel better—she was going to wait two months. She had no intention of harming herself now and was willing to switch to a stronger medication and to sign a no-harm contract.

But it was also necessary to sever the harmful relationships. Her parents blocked the Internet and changed the WiFi.

Dad made a contact list on her phone that couldn't be edited. Rosa protested and sobbed. She tried to reach Fletcher on her mother's phone and by using the Discord app on the VR Oculus. Her primary concern was that without her, "he" would commit suicide.

There was a lot of work to do.

She learned and began to practice some coping skills. We dived into her long history of social anxiety, her relationship with Sean, and lockdowns. We spoke about her loneliness, turning to Discord, and meeting Fletcher and the other girls, and their profound influence on her thinking and feelings. She began to realize her attachment to Fletcher had been unhealthy: "It was like I was under a spell." The medication took the edge off her anxiety and irritability. She didn't care so much about names and pronouns. She grew her hair out.

After few months off the Internet, Rosa was feeling better and reconnecting with her family. She wasn't yet out of the woods and back to wearing a bikini—that took about a year. But it happened.

In the end, Rosa wasn't "trans." Her gender dysphoria was precisely as Lisa Littman theorized: it was a coping mechanism in response to multiple complex factors including long-standing anxiety, social isolation, and social contagion. If her parents hadn't walked out of the gender clinic, Rosa might have soon been on blockers and testosterone, with her emotional issues unaddressed. Rosa and her parents may have joined the many unsuspecting families who become casualties of gender clinics—a frightening situation the public is only beginning to understand.

# CHAPTER FIVE

# The Whistleblower

Thank God for Jamie Reed.

Many of us were aware of gender clinic malfeasance for years. Finally, in February of 2023, a courageous whistleblower provided an eyewitness account from the belly of the beast.

From 2018 to 2022, Reed worked as a case manager at the Washington University Pediatric Transgender Center at St. Louis Children's Hospital, where she was responsible for patient intake and oversight.[1] Reed saw around 1,000 patients flood through their doors during her tenure.[2]

"I took the job because I support trans rights and firmly believed I would be able to provide good care for children at 'the Center' who are appropriate candidates to be receiving medical transition," Reed wrote. "The center's working assumption was that the earlier you treat kids with gender dysphoria, the more anguish you can prevent later on. This premise was shared by the center's doctors and therapists. Given their expertise, I assumed that abundant evidence backed this consensus."[3]

She assumed wrong. The "abundant evidence" didn't exist. There were no formal protocols for treatment at the clinic, and the physician codirectors were the sole authorities.[4] The "care" she witnessed profoundly troubled her.

Reed self-describes as a "queer woman, and politically to the left of Bernie Sanders . . . now married to a transman." Yet in January 2023 this progressive, tattooed, pro-trans woman hired a pro-family Christian lawyer and provided sworn testimony to the suit-wearing, conservative, Republican attorney general of red-state Missouri.[5] His office swiftly launched an investigation.

What could have propelled Reed to join forces with her political enemies? What pushed her to risk being labeled a "traitor to the trans community" by her compatriots on the left?[6]

Reed saw a parade of malpractice and deception inflicted on vulnerable children and their parents that she called nothing less than "morally and medically appalling."[7]

The following is taken from her sworn affidavit and public statements after she left the St. Louis clinic and exposed the sordid reality of the gender medical establishment.[*]

Reed:

> One of my jobs was to do intake for new patients and their families. When I started there were probably 10 such calls a month. When I left there were 50, and about 70 percent of the new patients were girls,[8] many with no previous history of gender distress.[9] Sometimes clusters of girls arrived from the same high school.[10]
>
> Social media is at least partly responsible for this large increase in children seeking gender transition treatment from the Center. Many children themselves would say that they learned of their gender identities from TikTok.[11]
>
> In just a two-year period from 2020 to 2022, the Center initiated medical transition for more than 600 children. About 74 percent of these children were assigned female at birth.[12]

Sound familiar? Reed is describing Rapid Onset Gender Dysphoria (ROGD): mostly girls, influenced by social media, coming out in peer groups. But the doctors running the clinic clung to the Articles of Faith:

> When I said the clusters of girls streaming into our service looked as if their gender issues might be a manifestation of social contagion, the doctors said gender identity reflected something innate.[13]

As Littman described in her 2018 paper, although patients at the St. Louis clinic suffered from serious psychiatric issues, clinicians rushed to affirm and medicalize.

Reed:

---

[*] While Reed's words have been arranged thematically from different sources for clarity and additional context, block quotes within this chapter are all direct quotations.

> Most children who come into the Center . . . have serious comorbidities including, autism, ADHD, depression, anxiety, PTSD, trauma histories, OCD, and serious eating disorders. Rather than treat these conditions, the doctors prescribe puberty blockers or cross-sex hormones.[14]
>
> There were diagnoses like schizophrenia . . . bipolar disorder, and more. Often they were already on a fistful of pharmaceuticals. . . . Yet no matter how much suffering or pain a child had endured, or how little treatment and love they had received, our doctors viewed gender transition—even with all the expense and hardship it entailed—as the solution.[15]
>
> In hundreds of . . . cases, Center doctors automatically issued puberty blockers or cross-sex hormones without considering the child's individual circumstances or mental health.[16]

Reading Reed's affidavit, I wondered how the center represented their practice to parents in need. (To be honest, after so many years in this field, I knew their claims and could have recited them in my sleep.) Just for the record, from their website:[17]

> Gender-affirming care is the gold standard of pediatric gender care. Research shows that when transgender kids receive support that upholds their gender identity, they have better mental health. Not receiving that support puts their physical and mental health at risk.
>
> Most experts, including our team, believe that puberty blockers are safe.

They cite the Endocrine Society's and the World Professional Association for Transgender Health's support of puberty blockers and inform parents the US Food and Drug Administration has approved puberty blockers for children who start puberty at a young age. From the center's website:

> Every person is different, so we work closely with each patient to determine whether hormone therapy is the right choice.

Sounds good, right?

Reed:

> One teenager came to us . . . when he was 17 years old and living in a lock-down facility because he had been sexually abusing dogs. . . . Somewhere along the way, he expressed a desire to become female, so he ended up being seen at our center. From there, he went to a psychologist at the hospital who

was known to approve virtually everyone seeking transition. Then our doctor recommended feminizing hormones.[18]

. . . Children come into the clinic saying they want hormones because they do not want to be gay. Children come in changing their identities on a day-to-day basis. Children come in under clear pressure by a parent to identify in a way inconsistent with the child's actual identity. In all these cases, the doctors decide to issue puberty blockers or cross-sex hormones.[19]

In one case, a child came into the Center identifying as "blind," even though the child could in fact see (after vision tests were performed). The child also identified as transgender. The Center dismissed the child's assertion about blindness as a somatization disorder but uncritically accepted the child's statement about gender and prescribed that child with drugs for medical transition. . . . No concurrent mental health care was provided.[20]

The clinic has the audacity to claim, "we will take a personalized approach that addresses your specific needs,"[21] but according to Reed, it was anything but personalized: A trans identified girl with significant autism? Hormones. A "nonbinary" boy with a history of sexual assault? Hormones. Teens who don't want to be gay? Hormones. A boy practicing bestiality, who claims to be a girl? Hormones.

This is reckless. Doctors at the clinic should have been aware of the heated international controversy surrounding their one-size-fits-all model of care. Littman urged medical and mental health professionals to hit the brakes, warning that medical interventions like blockers and cross-sex hormones could solidify gender dysphoria that might otherwise have resolved. But St. Louis clinicians acted like the therapists she described: they dismissed their young patients' emotional disorders, as well as their parents' concerns.

It's as if Dr. Littman had witnessed a car pileup on the expressway, families crashing in at eighty miles per hour. She ventured out to the road, waving a red flag: "Caution, danger ahead, slow down!"

Littman wasn't out there by herself. Stephen Levine has expressed concern about the welfare of "transitioned" individuals since the early eighties. In 2009, he noted how the rhetoric of many in the field was "remarkably certain about the long-term value of gender transition," adding that such certainty requires "carefully established sophisticated follow-up. . . . These are lacking."[22]

Researchers in 2011[23] and 2016[24] concluded that postoperative patients continue to suffer emotionally and need psychiatric care. In his 2018 paper Dr. Levine wrote,

> When clinicians are cheerleaders for transition, their behavior indicates to the patient that this is the best solution. . . . They may lead patients and parents to believe that there is scientific certainty about the wisdom of transition. This is not what the ethical principle of honesty means.[25]

In 2019, world-renowned child and adolescent psychiatrist Christopher Gillberg charged that unproven treatment of gender-distressed children is "possibly one of the greatest scandals in medical history." Professor Gillberg's neuropsychiatry group at Sweden's Gothenburg University called for an immediate moratorium on puberty blockers because of their unknown long-term effects.[26]

Did clinicians at the St Louis center even hear of Littman's landmark paper, Dr. Levine's persistent warnings, and many other voices alerting the medical profession? Maybe they would have thought a minute and reconsidered their approach. Perhaps they might have informed patients, and their parents, of the controversies? Maybe some kids could have been saved from the wreckage.

Sadly, according to Reed, there was no thinking and no reconsidering.

## Geriatric Skeletons

Reed:

> I have seen puberty blockers worsen the mental health outcomes of children. Children who have not contemplated suicide before being put on puberty blockers have attempted suicide after. Puberty blockers force children to go through premature menopause. Puberty blockers decrease bone density.[27]
>
> In July 2022, the FDA issued a "black box warning" for puberty blockers, the strictest kind of warning the FDA can give a medication. It issued the warning following evidence in patients of brain swelling and loss of vision. Despite this warning, doctors at the Center continued their automatic practice of giving kids these drugs.[28]

There are very few good data on the use of blockers in healthy children. Most of what is known about them comes from their use in adults with disorders such as endometriosis or prostate cancer.

Puberty blockers are also used for the relatively rare disorder of central precocious puberty. Side effects include mood changes, headaches, nervousness, anxiety, agitation, confusion, delusions, insomnia, depression,[29] mood swings, suicidal ideation,[30] early menopause,[31] lung disease,[32] sexual dysfunction,[33] inability to experience orgasms,[34] and genital atrophy.[35]

Puberty blockers can cause osteoporosis, the loss of bone density.[36] In Sweden, the puberty blocker-induced osteoporosis of a trans-identified young girl sparked a national controversy in 2021.

Eleven-year-old "Leo" was referred to Karolinska University Hospital, one of the world's top medical centers. The doctors told her parents, "The earlier you stop puberty, the better." Eager to help their distressed daughter, but inadequately informed of the risks, they agreed to the medication.[37]

As her mom, Natalie, described it, at first "Leo" was happier. Then her mental health worsened. She attempted suicide several times. Her back, shoulders, and hips ached every day, but nothing was done.[38] While the recommended length of treatment is two years, she stayed on blockers for over four years, eventually being sent for a bone-density test and scans due to ongoing pain. The results: fifteen-year-old "Leo" had osteoporosis, spinal fractures, and vertebral damage.

According to the drug manufacturer, those tests should have been done regularly. Normally, bones are strengthened during puberty, but Leo's puberty had been blocked, and her bones were weak, like an old woman's.

A Swedish National TV documentary[39] (available with English sub-titles) on "Leo's" story sparked a national outcry. Investigators discovered eleven other children injured by hormone treatment at the Karolinska University Hospital. The hospital conducted its own investigation and at its end acknowledged that Leo and others faced "serious injury." It issued an apology, admitting families were not properly told of the side effects and that the scientific basis for use of blockers in children like "Leo" is weak and that it is not possible to know whether the treatment is useful or safe.

One doctor opined that based on "Leo's" psychiatric problems, she should have never received puberty blockers.[40]

Natalie: "looking back, I feel such anger. . . . We trusted the doctors when they said 'This will help your child'. . . . First they told us nothing about side effects, now they're gaslighting us about how badly he's been injured by those drugs . . . we are guinea pigs."[41]

Sweden was the first country to legalize sex reassignment. Yet as a result of the fiasco just described, Sweden's National Board of Health and Welfare reviewed the evidence and cracked down, effectively banning medical transition of minors in May 2021. Board Department Head Thomas Linden said, "The uncertain state of knowledge calls for caution."

In March 2022, France joined the UK, Finland, and Sweden in urging "great medical caution" with the use of PBAs:

> [G]iven the vulnerability, particularly psychological, of this population and the many undesirable effects and even serious complications that can be caused by some of the therapies available. . . . If France allows the use of puberty blockers . . . the greatest caution is needed in their use, taking into account the side-effects such as the impact on growth, bone weakening, risk of sterility, emotional and intellectual consequences and, for girls, menopause-like symptoms.[42]

The documentary, the hospital apology, and the decision by Swedish medical authorities to ban gender-affirming care—all were international news in 2021–2022. Were the directors of the St Louis clinic aware? It's their field, after all.

Aware or not, the center directed more families onto the expressway toward the pileup.

Another disaster, this one in New York. Two years after an eleven-year-old was put on blockers, her bone density plummeted. "I worry we've done permanent damage," her mother said.[43]

Likewise, when a teenager in Texas went on blockers for a year, scans revealed the patient's bone density dropped *below the first percentile*[44] (see records below). Touted by the gender medical establishment as nothing much, just a "pause button," it appears that puberty blockers at least in some instances give teenagers geriatric skeletons:

INTERPRETATION:

L-Spine (L1 to L4) 0.575 g/cm2 Bone Mineral Density (BMD), -5.7 T-Score, -4.9 Z-Score.

Based on the patient's age and weight, the patient's bone density is below the 1st percentile.

IMPRESSION:

Bone mineral density below 1st percentile indicating osteoporosis.

RECOMMENDATIONS:

Since the diagnosis and treatment of osteoporosis in children is usually associated with other disease processes, the referring physicians should determine individual treatments based on the need of each patient.

*Records show teen with low bone density after a year on blockers.*[45]

## "Very Low Quality"

The Endocrine Society recommended in 2009, 2014, and 2017 that doctors prescribe puberty blockers and cross-sex hormones to adolescents, and their stance has become a pillar of the gender medical establishment. But take a close look at their guidelines. You'll discover the evidence supporting their recommendations is ranked either "very low-quality" or "low-quality."[46]

Hormone treatment before puberty—"Low-quality."

Puberty blockers in adolescence—"Low-quality."

Hormone treatment for under sixteen-year-olds—"Very low-quality."

Of the twenty-two recommendations with evidence ratings, nineteen are rated "low" or "very low-quality" and only three are rated "moderate quality." Not a single recommendation was supported by "high-quality" evidence.[47]

We're supposed to believe gender-affirming care is evidence-based medicine? The evidence is terrible!

As the Gender Exploratory Therapy Association (GETA) put it, "The 'low quality' rating indicates that it is unclear whether the benefits of interventions outweigh the risks."[48]

And take a look at the Endocrine Society Guidelines' disclaimer:

"The guidelines should not be considered inclusive of all proper approaches or methods, or exclusive of others. The guidelines cannot guarantee any specific outcome, nor do they establish a standard of care. The guidelines are not intended to dictate the treatment of a particular patient."[49]

Do parents seeking care for their gender-distressed kids who visit the website of the St Louis Children's Hospital Transgender clinic learn of the debate and uncertainty in which "affirming" care is mired? To the contrary. They are informed the clinic's approach is "research-based," and that:[50]

> Most experts . . . believe that puberty blockers are safe:
>
> The Endocrine Society and the World Professional Association for Transgender Health support the use of puberty blockers for kids who want to delay or prevent unwanted physical changes.
>
> The U.S. Food and Drug Administration has approved puberty blockers for children who start puberty at a young age.[†]

How do they get away with it?

---

† This is a medical condition unrelated to gender dysphoria.

Dr. Zucker has seen 2,000 kids in his Toronto clinic. He decries "a vexing problem: there are no randomized controlled trials of different treatment approaches, so the front-line clinician has to rely on lower-order levels of evidence in deciding" how to treat gender dysphoric patients.[51]

The United Kingdom's National Institute of Health and Care Excellence assessed the quality of evidence for puberty blockers as "very low certainty"[52] and Professor Carl Heneghan, director of the Centre of Evidence Based Medicine at Oxford University, was even more blunt: He called the quality of evidence "terrible."[53]

How in the world, given all that, can parents be reassured that "puberty blockers are generally considered safe"?

For the gender establishment puberty blockers are dogma, and doctors better toe the line. For example, the American Psychiatric Association (APA) require psychiatrists take continuing medical education courses. One included this scenario:[54]

"A thirteen-year-old transgender girl is significantly distressed by the experience of masculinizing puberty, including having suicidal ideation. Which of the following statements related to these symptoms is best supported by the available evidence?"

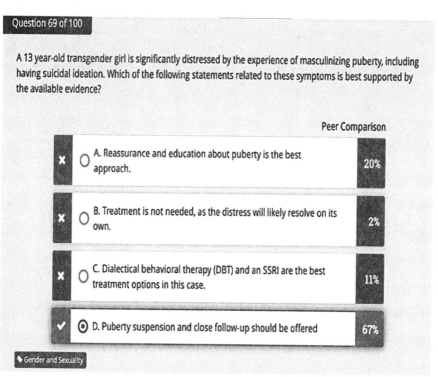

Question 69 of 100

A 13 year-old transgender girl is significantly distressed by the experience of masculinizing puberty, including having suicidal ideation. Which of the following statements related to these symptoms is best supported by the available evidence?

Peer Comparison

| | | |
|---|---|---|
| ✗ ○ A. Reassurance and education about puberty is the best approach. | 20% |
| ✗ ○ B. Treatment is not needed, as the distress will likely resolve on its own. | 2% |
| ✗ ○ C. Dialectical behavioral therapy (DBT) and an SSRI are the best treatment options in this case. | 11% |
| ✓ ◉ D. Puberty suspension and close follow-up should be offered | 67% |

Gender and Sexuality

Four choices of answers are provided, but they are all wrong. The correct answer is to conduct a thorough assessment of the patient and his family, including a suicide assessment, identify and treat comorbidities and family issues, and start exploratory psychotherapy.

The available evidence for prescribing blockers in this instance is, as you already know, terrible. But the APA is entirely captured by gender ideologues. The "right" answer is: "puberty suspension and close follow-up should be offered."

## Puberty Is Not a Disorder

Puberty is not only about developing breasts or growing facial hair. It impacts nearly all organs and systems of the body. It's a complex biological process that we are far from understanding.

Too many of my medical colleagues have forgotten that the body has its own wisdom. That's one of the things that's gotten us into this mess.

In 2015 I joined doctors Den Trumbull and Michelle Cretella—pediatricians and leaders of the American College of Pediatricians (ACP eds)—to write a letter to the journal *Pediatrics*. The letter was titled "Puberty Is Not a Disorder":

> We submit that children who dread the development of secondary sex characteristics are emotionally troubled. . . . In fact, puberty brings relief for the vast majority of children receiving therapy for GID [gender identity disorder] because hormone surges propel the development of their brains as well as their bodies and they come to identify with their biological sex.[55]

Puberty isn't an illness. We cannot presume that interfering with a complex biological process such as puberty, turning it on and off synthetically, can be accomplished without paying a price.

Nowhere could that price be higher than with the brain.

I wrote about this fourteen years ago in *You're Teaching My Child WHAT?*:

> During the second decade of life and into the third, a period of 'explosive growth and restructuring' takes place. There is a "dramatic metamorphosis of the brain," writes a leading developmental psychologist. "The magnitude of these brain alterations is difficult to fathom."[56]

It's like *Extreme Makeover: Teen Brain Edition*. Before puberty, your son has the brain of a child. It will take about fifteen years, well into his third decade of life, to develop the brain of an adult. The hormones of puberty, estrogen and testosterone, drive puberty's explosive growth and restructuring of the brain. Puberty blockers interrupt a natural process and could have cognitive and emotional consequences.

Consider the ability to rationally weigh actions, predict results, and balance pros and cons. The prefrontal cortex is the area of the brain that governs these executive functions. Consider it the CEO of the brain. You don't need a PhD in neurobiology to know the executive functioning of teens isn't the greatest. They easily forget their actions have consequences, and just how damaging those consequences might be.

The prefrontal cortex is the last area of the brain to fully mature.[57] If it is the thinking and planning part of the brain, the amygdala is the feeling part. It too is transformed by puberty.

Over the years, the prefrontal cortex and amygdala develop and integrate. Puberty puts these systems into balance, helping young adults regulate their emotions, control impulsivity, and make better decisions.

How does "pausing" puberty with blockers affect the development of your child's pre-frontal cortex, amygdala, or, for that matter, any other part of her brain? We have no idea.

What about the young adults who were old enough to legally consent to hormones and surgery but by their midtwenties have desisted, and regret those decisions?[58] The timing suggests brain maturation may have played a role.

As three physicians wrote in a letter to *Archives of Disease in Childhood* titled "Use of puberty blockers for gender dysphoria: a momentous step in the dark": "blockers are now being used in the context of profound scientific ignorance."[59]

*Profound scientific ignorance.* Well said. Don't parents have a right to know?

The sole animal study we have suggests puberty blockers may threaten brain maturation and cognitive maturity.[60]

Not only that, but puberty blockers also potentially trap kids in a permanent gender-identity crisis. Remember, a majority—in some studies a large majority—of kids grow out of their gender confusion *in puberty*. Is it due to the hormonal surges, estrogen in girls and testosterone in boys? Maybe. The point is *we don't know*.

As Dr. Littman observed, medical affirmation may cause "persistence of gender dysphoria in individuals who would have had their gender dysphoria resolve on its own."[61] Did the medical establishment's dismissal of Lisa Littman in 2018 prevent the doctors supervising Jamie Reed from reading her research?

Aren't the AAP, ES, WPATH, and other medical organizations obligated to keep gender clinicians informed and up to date? Did staff at the St. Louis clinic hear about Leo's geriatric skeleton? Again, they were either innocently unaware or purposely kept in the dark.

## "I Was Just a Kid"

Affirming care places children in the driver's seat. Aside from perhaps enlisting in the military, and in some states getting an abortion, I cannot think of another instance of permitting teenagers to make independent life-altering decisions.

Chloe Cole, a prominent detransitioner, described with emotion the discussion with her endocrinologist about puberty blockers:

> It was like, "are you aware that you may experience vaginal atrophy?" Or "are you aware that this may affect your ability to have children as an adult?" And I just went along with it. It was like, "Oh yeah, I know that, I don't plan on having kids."
>
> And I also had never had sex at that point, so I didn't know what effect any of that would have on my body. But I was being treated as if I were an adult with the mental faculties to be able to consent to all this and understand what I was consenting to."
>
> [Cole paused for a moment, the pain and anger welling up in her voice.] But I wasn't. . . . I was just a kid.[62]

Dr. Daniel Metzger, an endocrinologist associated with the World Professional Association for Transgender Health (WPATH), acknowledged there's "reproductive regret" in young adults left infertile from medical transition: "I don't think any of that surprises us. . . .It's always been a good theory that you talk about fertility preservation with a fourteen-year-old, but I know I'm talking to a blank wall," he told other medical professionals. Observing that "the parents have it on their minds," Dr. Metzger admitted, ". . .when we're doing informed consent, I know that's still a big lacuna [empty space]. . . . Most of the kids are nowhere in any kind of brain space to really, really, really talk about [fertility] in a serious way."[63]

Chloe Cole and Metzger are Exhibit A supporting Dr. Stephen Levine's argument in his article "What Are We Doing to These Children?" He writes, "the consent process for youth gender transition is so problematic . . . that it can no longer be considered 'informed.'"[64]

How does Dr. Metzger justify sterilizing minors when he is aware they have no idea what they're forfeiting? His answer: "We still want kids to be happier in the moment, right?"[65]

This is astonishing. *We want kids to be happier in the moment?*

Ecstasy makes people happier in the moment. So does unprotected sex and driving 100 miles per hour. Honestly, Dr. Metzger, do you have children? Do you allow them to make decisions with lifelong consequences because it makes them happier in the moment?

What's come over my colleagues? This is not practicing medicine.

Experts around the world agree. The High Court of the United Kingdom: "There is no age-appropriate way to explain to many of these children what losing their fertility or full sexual function may mean to them in later years."[66]

The Swedish Pediatric Society: "Giving children the right to independently make vital decisions whereby at that age they cannot be expected to understand the consequences of their decisions is not scientifically founded and contrary to medical practice."[67]

Anthony Latham, chair of the Scottish Council on Human Bioethics: "The young brain is biologically and socially immature, tends towards short-term risk taking, does not possess the ability to comprehend long term consequences and is highly influenced by peers. . ." He concluded, "Children cannot consent, and therefore should not be asked to consent to being treated with puberty blockers for gender dysphoria."[68]

Yet like Leo's parents, many are misled by "experts" in white coats claiming puberty blockers are safe and reversible. After all, hospitals,[69] establishment medical organization,[70] and even the federal government[71] all say that blockers safely "pause" puberty. It's not true.

From Reed:

> The doctors at the Center tell the public and tell parents of patients that puberty blockers are fully reversible. They really are not. They do lasting damage to the body.[72]

You can't pause puberty without a price. It's a biological process, not a song on Spotify. How high is the price? Ask me in ten or twenty years.

Reed:

> The Center tells the public and parents of patients that the point of puberty blockers is to give children time to figure out their gender identity. But the Center does not use puberty blockers for this purpose. Instead, the Center uses puberty blockers just until children are old enough to be put on cross-sex hormones. Doctors at the Center always prescribe cross-sex hormones for children who have been taking puberty blockers.[73]

The St. Louis clinic is no outlier. Ninety-eight percent of kids on blockers go straight to the next stage: testosterone for girls and estrogen for boys.[74]

## The Danger of Synthetic Puberty

Gender-affirming care (GAC) rests on the assumption that a synthetically induced, so-called "opposite sex puberty" has the same effects as one that's natural. And where's the evidence for that?

You're aware that puberty changes every body system, but let's center on the brain. Where are the yearly brain imaging studies and psychological and cognitive evaluations of youth whose hormone levels are abnormally elevated due to gender-"affirming" care?

A girl's testosterone should not be over 45 ng/dL; a boy's estrogen should be under 40 pg/mL. But girls on "T" might have levels up to 700 ng/dL, and boys on "E" up to 200 pg. While the boys' estrogen levels are sky-high, their T is decreased to below 55, using an additional medication.

Their brains are exposed to these abnormal levels during the most critical time of brain growth and restructuring since the womb, where—as you learned in Chapter Three—the fetal brain was placed on either a male or female trajectory.

So—where are the studies? There are none.

In 2019, the Endocrine Society concluded the only evidence-based indication for testosterone for women is for the treatment of hypoactive sexual desire disorder—a low sex drive—and that "There are insufficient data to support the use of testosterone for the treatment of any other symptom or clinical condition, or for disease prevention." Also, "The safety of long-term testosterone therapy has not been established."[75]

But in gender-"affirming" care, patient autonomy comes first. No gatekeeping by doctors allowed—it's one of the Articles of Faith. If your daughter wants testosterone and your son estrogen, there are few or no obstacles.

At eighteen, Helena Kirschner saw herself as a "transman." She was prescribed testosterone after a twenty-minute meeting at Planned Parenthood. On her Substack, which includes images of her intake, consent, and dosage, she describes the remarkably casual decision-making process around her starting dose:

> When the nurse practitioner suggested a lower dose to start, I objected, saying I believed I had "higher estrogen than most AFABs" (people "assigned female at birth"), citing the size of my thighs and breasts as evidence. This was acceptable to the nurse practitioner, and she asked me what dose I would like to start at. Nervously, I said something along the lines of, "well what's the highest we can go?"
>
> Most female transitioners I've known have told me they started at 25mg, or even less. Some of my FtM [female-to-male] friends who are still on testosterone and look remarkably like natal males, are only on 50mg. I was prescribed 100mg of testosterone, to be self-injected into my thigh muscle weekly, starting that very day.[76]

Reed testified:

> During the time I was at the clinic, the WPATH Standard of Care Version 7 stated that children be at least sixteen years old to start using cross-sex hormones. The Center deviated even from this most lenient standard and routinely prescribed cross-sex hormones to children as young as 13.[77]
>
> I witnessed children experience shocking injuries from the medication the Center prescribed.[78]
>
> I doubt that any parent who's ever consented to give their kid testosterone (a lifelong treatment) knows that they're also possibly signing their kid up for blood pressure medication, cholesterol medication, and perhaps sleep apnea and diabetes.[79]
>
> Most patients who have taken cross-sex hormones have experienced near-constant abdominal pain.[80]
>
> I know of at least one patient at the Center who was advised by the renal department to stop taking Bicalutamide [a drug to produce the effects of estrogen] because the child was experiencing liver damage. . . . The parent said they were not the type to sue, but "this could be a huge PR problem for you."[81]
>
> When a female takes testosterone, the profound and permanent effects of the hormone can be seen in a matter of months. Voices drop, beards sprout,

body fat is redistributed. Sexual interest explodes, aggression increases, and mood can be unpredictable.[82]

Girls were disturbed by the effects of testosterone on their clitoris, which enlarges and grows into what looks like a microphallus, or a tiny penis.[83]

Children who take testosterone as a cross-sex hormone experience severe atrophy of vaginal tissue. One patient on cross-sex hormones called the Center after having sexual intercourse. The patient experienced vaginal lacerations so severe that in less than an hour she had soaked through an extra heavy pad, her jeans, and a towel she had wrapped around her waist. She had to be sedated and surgically treated in St. Louis Children's Hospital emergency room. She wasn't the only vaginal laceration case we heard about.[84]

Most of the data we have on long term effects of opposite sex hormones come from treating adults since long-term follow-up of treated children has not been reported. In males, cross-sex hormones can lead to decreased muscle mass and strength, decreased sexual desire, decreased sperm production, voice changes, decreased testicular volume,[85] erectile dysfunction, infertility,[86] deep vein blood clots,‡ stroke,[87] coronary artery disease, and cerebrovascular disease.[88]

Compared to untreated men, men on cross-sex hormones are forty-six times more likely to get breast cancer,[89] twice as likely to have a stroke, sixteen times as likely to have deep vein clots. As compared to women, they are two times more likely to have a heart attack.[90]

The list is just as awful for women on testosterone. They face hair loss, elimination of menstruation, deepening of the voice,[91] severe acne,[92] high blood pressure, high cholesterol,[93] and increased risk of type 2 diabetes,[94] erythrocytosis[95] (which includes symptoms of blurred vision, headaches, confusion, high blood pressure, nosebleeds, itching, weakness, and tiredness),[96] cerebrovascular disease, hypertension, pelvic pain, and uterine cancer.[97] Pap smears to detect early cervical cancer are more than three times more likely to be unsatisfactory. That means less likely to detect cervical cancer.

One systematic review of seventy-six studies showed that while females on testosterone developed breast cancer less often than other females, in the former group it occurred twenty years earlier than expected, even though most had mastectomies before the diagnosis.[98]

---

‡ Known as venous thromboembolism.

There have been reports of intracranial hypertension in women on testosterone. This is an uncommon cause of severe headache that can cause visual loss from damage to the optic nerve.

As compared to women not on testosterone, those treated with testosterone are almost four times more likely to have a heart attack.[99] As compared to men, they are four times more likely to have a stroke.[100] Clots in the veins, which can cause life-threatening pulmonary embolism, are five times more likely to happen in women treated with testosterone.

## A Generation of Sterile, Frustrated Gen Zers

GAC calls for blockers at the first sign of puberty. As mentioned, when followed by cross-sex hormones, the result is infertility. To mature and be viable for reproduction, sperm and eggs ("gametes") require the testosterone and estrogen surges of natural puberty. Blockers followed by cross-sex hormones prevent eggs and sperm from reaching full maturation, making reproduction impossible.[101]

Keep in mind as well that with early hormonal interventions your son's genitals will never appear normal—he will forever have a micro-penis. And according to gender-affirming surgeon Marci Bowers, he will not be able to orgasm.[102] This is guaranteed.

Can all this be reversed? Stop the blockers and synthetic hormones and allow the natural ones to kick in? We don't have the answer because close to 100 percent of kids put on blockers continue to cross-sex hormones.[103]

Sure, your teen may know all about reproduction and sexuality, but he or she can't fathom the implications of infertility.

As Reed put it:

> After working at the center, I came to believe that teenagers are simply not capable of fully grasping what it means to make the decision to become infertile while still a minor.

Even the UC San Francisco Gender Affirming Health Program warns, "the issue of infertility is often far more problematic for parents and family members than for youth, especially at the beginning stages of discussing moving forward with gender-affirming hormones."[104]

How problematic? Parents, if you allow your child to go on puberty blockers, you are closing the lid on your biological grandchildren's coffins before they have a chance to be conceived.

The Children's Hospital Los Angeles warned parents in a consent form, "If your child starts puberty blockers in the earliest stages of puberty, and then goes on to gender-affirming hormones, they will not develop sperm or eggs. This means that they will not be able to have biological children."[105]

The Children's Hospital provided a list of issues boys may face: "sperm will not mature, leading to infertility. The ability to make sperm normally may or may not come back even after stopping taking feminizing medication. . . . Erection may not be firm enough for penetrative sex . . . testicles may shrink 25 to 50 percent.[106]

Sure, as Dr. Metzger observed, blockers and hormones make kids happy in the moment. But that moment will pass. We doctors must focus on the big picture: your child's long-term health and well-being.

In an interview, the Admiral shared: "If I transitioned when I was young, then I wouldn't have my children. I can't imagine a life without my children."[107]

It sounds like the Admiral was talking about biological children, can't imagine life without them, and is grateful for transitioning later in life.

But Admiral, don't you see? Your fervent endorsement of GAC is creating a generation of sterile young adults.[108] Children for me, but not for thee?

## "Wow, We Hurt This Kid."

As for the kids from the St. Louis clinic, how are they faring? How many have brittle bones and sexual dysfunction? How many regret what was done to them?

We don't know, and we may never know.

From Reed, who by the way has a master's in clinical research management:

> The Center . . . refuses to track complications and adverse events among its patients. . . . And the Center actively avoids trying to learn about these adverse events.[109]
>
> On my own initiative, I have tracked some patients on a case-by-case basis, but the Center discouraged me from doing so. I wanted to track the number of our patients who detransition. I wanted to track the number of our patients who have attempted suicide or committed suicide. The Center would not make either of these tracking systems a priority.[110]

We should be tracking desistance and detransition. We thought the doctors would want to collect and understand this data in order to figure out what they had missed. We were wrong. One doctor wondered aloud why he would spend time on someone who was no longer his patient.[111]

Why spend time on a former patient? Because doctor, you're treating your current patients with the same risky approach.

Reed continued:

Because I was concerned that the doctors were giving cross-sex hormones and puberty blockers to children who should not be on them, I created a "red flag" list of children where other staff and I had concerns.[112]

It was an Excel spreadsheet that tracked the kind of patients that kept my colleague and me up at night.[113]

The doctors told me I had to stop raising these concerns. I was not allowed to maintain the red flag list after that.[114]

It is my belief that the Center does not track these outcomes because they do not want to have to report them to new patients and because they do not want to discontinue cross-sex hormone prescriptions. The Center never discontinues cross-sex hormones, no matter the outcome.[115]

Reed told of a particularly awful case:

I have heard from patients given testosterone that their clitorises have grown so large that they now constantly chafe against the child's pants, causing them pain when they walk.[116]

I counseled one patient whose enlarged clitoris now extended below her vulva, and it chafed and rubbed painfully in her jeans. I advised her to get the kind of compression undergarments worn by biological men who dress to pass as female. At the end of the call I thought to myself, "Wow, we hurt this kid."[117]

While recounting the horror show she witnessed for years at the clinic, Reed made a profound observation:

There are rare conditions in which babies are born with atypical genitalia— cases that call for sophisticated care and compassion. But clinics like the one where I worked are creating a whole cohort of kids with atypical genitals.[118]

John Money studied rare cases of children with abnormal genitalia. The goal at that time, for better or worse, was to normalize their appearance to look clearly male or female. Reed points out that today, against reason, we witness the reverse. Doctors take youth with *normal* genitalia and, with "treatment," cause them to appear abnormal.

Back on the gender affirmation expressway, while the pileup of cars mounted, more clinicians, researchers, and journalists came out waving red and yellow flags. But at clinics like Reed's, the flags remained green. Staff continued to wave one car after the next, full speed ahead.

CHAPTER SIX

# A Dangerous Dutch Idea

Jamie Reed's testimony begs the question: From where did the model of affirming, one-size-fits-all treatment of adolescent GD come? It is based on a small study from Holland that led to what's known as the Dutch Protocol.

## The Dutch Protocol

In the Netherlands, sex reassignment was available for adults since 1972. The number of patients was limited, and almost all were middle-aged men. For their work and research in this highly specialized field, a few Dutch clinicians achieved worldwide prominence.

Following their patients over time, they discovered they had significant mental health issues including suicidality—perhaps, researchers thought, because the men had gone through male puberty and had masculine bone structure, muscle mass, hair growth, and voices. It was therefore difficult to pass as women.

The Dutch researchers had an idea: identify kids whose GD will probably persist to adulthood, prevent their masculinization from puberty, then use estrogen and surgery to achieve a feminine appearance. The doctors were well-intentioned: perhaps puberty suppression of these extremely rare individuals would produce an improved quality of life.

The means to chemically prevent puberty already existed. Children with a medical condition called precocious puberty begin sexual, bone, and muscular development early: girls before the age of eight, and boys before nine. Because their premature development causes social and emotional difficulties, they are sometimes given a medication called a GnRH agonist, which acts on the brain to prevent the release of estrogen and testosterone from the ovaries and testicles. At the appropriate time the medication is stopped, and with time puberty resumes.

As discussed in Chapter Three, there's no way to determine with certainty which children will persist with gender distress. Nevertheless, the Dutch hypothesized that those with severe dysphoria from very early childhood, whose conditions worsened into midadolescence, would most likely remain gender dysphoric the rest of their lives.

Researchers started administering puberty blockers to 111 such youth at an average age of fifteen,* cross-sex hormones roughly at age seventeen, and breast and genital surgeries around age nineteen.[1] The patients also received ongoing psychological support.

An article about their experimental interventions was published in 2006, supported financially by Ferring Pharmaceuticals,[2] the manufacturer of triptorelin, a puberty-blocking agent.[3]

In 2014, the researchers published groundbreaking claims: puberty suppression and surgeries were associated with marked reduction or resolution of GD, improved mental health, and overall functioning.[4] Their guidelines became known as the Dutch Protocol, and the one study is the basis for all gender-affirming care, including of course the care on which Jamie Reed blew a whistle.

## Salivating Doctors

Michael Biggs, a professor of sociology at Oxford, recently undertook a comprehensive investigation of the Dutch study.[5] Published in 2022, he describes its history, claims, and rapid international adoption.

Biggs writes that in the mid-to-late nineties, two of the Dutch researchers were elected to the board of directors of the Harry Benjamin International Gender Dysphoria Association, later called WPATH. In 2001, more than a decade *before* the Dutch experiment's results were published, puberty suppression entered WPATH's standards of care.

One would think the recommendation for a non-FDA-approved medication acting on the brains of children with no medical illness would have been founded not on gold-, but platinum-quality evidence. But I learned from Dr. Biggs that was not the case at all. The *only published evidence* in 2001 for the benefits of puberty suppression was a case study of one patient, "FG."[6]

---

* The protocol allowed for treatments at the ages of twelve, sixteen, and eighteen, but on average they began later.

The Dutch Protocol arrived in the US in 2007, when Harvard affili-ated pediatric endocrinologist Dr. Norman Spack cofounded the Gender Management Service at Boston Children's Hospital, which was the first dedicated clinic for gender dysphoric children in the US. Its program was based on the Dutch model; the hospital sent a psychologist to Amsterdam for training.[7] From the outset, the Boston clinic offered puberty block-ade with no minimum age,[8] specifying only that the child reach Tanner Stage II—marked by the first growth of pubic hair and for girls by budding breasts, and for boys by growing testicles.

As reported in 2015 by the *New York Times*,[9] Dr. Spack recalled being at a meeting in Europe fifteen years earlier, when he learned that the Dutch were using puberty blockers in early adolescents.

"I was salivating," he recalled. "I said we had to do this."

Why were all these doctors in a hot rush? I propose they shared Dr. Money's approach: "I have an idea. Let's do this to patients and see what happens."

Spack joined three Dutch researchers on the Endocrine Society's com-mittee tasked with writing their first clinical guidelines[10] for "transsexual persons," the earlier term for transgender persons. In 2009, the ES recom-mended puberty suppression for children in early puberty.

So as early as 2009, doctors, clinics, hospitals, and drug companies could point to prestigious organizations like WPATH, ES, and Boston Children's and say, "puberty suppression is an internationally accepted treatment for children with GD." The assumption was based on the Dutch study that was seriously flawed.

"Replicability" means obtaining the same result when an experiment is repeated. It is foundational to medical research. The Dutch study has never been replicated. Clinicians in London tried; from 2011 to 2014, forty-four teens were given blockers. Results were presented at a 2016 WPATH con-ference: the patients didn't do well. But the bad news wasn't publicized, as Biggs explains: "These conference papers were not published as articles, fol-lowing the typical fate of medical experiments that fail to produce positive results."[11]

The results were published, Biggs explains, only in 2021 as the result of a protracted campaign "involving media publicity, complaints to the eth-ics committee that approved the research, and a judicial review." For the London cohort, puberty suppression "brought no measurable benefit nor harm to psychological function in these young people," and gender dyspho-ria likewise did not improve. [12]

The failure to reproduce the Dutch results was only one of many red flags.

Along with Biggs's paper, E. Abbruzzese, Stephen Levine, and Julia Mason provide insight into the flaws and widespread adoption of the Dutch Protocol in a 2023 paper titled "The Myth of "Reliable Research" in Pediatric Gender Medicine: A critical evaluation of the Dutch Studies—and research that has followed."[13] They discuss "runaway diffusion": "the phenomenon whereby the medical community mistakes a small innovative experiment as a proven practice, and a potentially nonbeneficial or harmful practice 'escapes the lab,' rapidly spreading into general clinical settings":[14]

> "Runaway diffusion" is exactly what has happened in pediatric gender medicine. "Affirmative treatment" [i.e., the Dutch Protocol] . . . rapidly entered general clinical practice worldwide, without the necessary rigorous clinical research to confirm the hypothesized robust and lasting psychological benefits of the practice. Nor was it ever demonstrated that the benefits were substantial enough to outweigh the burden of lifelong dependence on medical interventions, infertility and sterility, and various physical health risks. . . . The speed of the "runaway diffusion" accelerated exponentially when pediatric gender dysphoria . . . went from a relatively rare phenomenon before 2015, to one that impacts as many as 1 in 10–20 young people in the Western world.[15]

*A small innovative experiment is mistaken by the medical community as a proven practice, and it escapes the lab.* Sounds like John Money and the twins again.

## Scrutinizing the Dutch Protocol

The authors describe numerous flaws in the Dutch study and submit its results are not applicable to today's teens and young adults. Aside from the failure to replicate results mentioned above, they point to poor research design, bias, confounding variables, and lack of control group:

- A careful selection process skewed the sample population "toward the most clinically straightforward and stable cases."
- 111 subjects were chosen, but the number was whittled down to seventy, then fifty-five. In doing so, the researchers excluded

patients who stopped the treatment, refused to participate in follow-up, developed serious medical problems, or had "complicated personal situations," per Dr. Levine. As a result, key outcomes were available for as few as thirty-two patients.

- One of the subjects excluded was killed by necrotizing fasciitis after vaginoplasty. Like Jazz, the eighteen-year-old's penis was too small due to puberty suppression, so an intestinal graft was needed to construct a "vagina."[16] Biggs points out: "A fatality rate exceeding 1 percent would surely halt any other experimental treatment on healthy teenagers."[17]

- *Patients with mental health issues (such as Rosa) were disqualified.* The current demographic has high rates of psychiatric disorders and neurodivergence.

- All subjects had severe GD, "lifelong extreme and complete cross gender identity"[18] (like Jazz), which worsened with puberty. Current demographic is characterized by sudden adolescent onset (like Rosa).

- All subjects received psychotherapy that could have led to improvement, not the medical treatments. In today's GAC therapy is optional and considered potentially harmful.

- The Dutch assumed blockers are fully reversible, we know this is incorrect.

- The Dutch did not consider effect of blockers on physical health, libido, sexual development; attention to fertility was meager.

- The average age of starting blockers was fifteen, currently children as young as eight are eligible.

- The scale used to measure GD pre and post treatment was highly problematic. The claim of improved GD—the linchpin of the protocol—could have been an artifact of measurement error.

- The follow-up was premature, medical complications and regret can take years.

Regarding the study's strict mental health criteria, Reed pointed out the irony.

> Medical transition practice for children and adolescents is based on . . . the "Dutch study," [which] excluded participants who presented underlying mental health issues.[19]

> But nearly all children who came to the Center here presented with very serious mental health problems. Despite claiming to be a place where children could receive multidisciplinary care, the Center would not treat these mental health issues. Instead, children were automatically given puberty blockers or cross-sex hormones even though the Dutch study excluded persons experiencing mental health issues.[20]

Today, the Dutch Protocol is the foundation for GAC calling for medicalization of youth like Rosa and the patients Reed described. But with their psychiatric issues and recent onset of GD, none of them would have met the Dutch study's criteria. They would all have been excluded.

In 2021, Thomas Steensma, one of the primary authors of the Dutch studies, seemed astonished that doctors assume their conclusions are applicable to today's youth with GD. "We don't know whether studies we have done in the past can still be applied to this time. Many more children are registering [for transgender care], and also a different type," he said. "The rest of the world is blindly adopting our research."[21]

Annelou de Vries, another principal researcher, also expressed concern, warning psychotherapy may be better than life-altering hormones in these situations: "Longer-term follow-up studies . . . are needed to inform clinicians so that an individualized approach can be offered that differentiates who will benefit from medical gender affirmation and for whom (additional) mental health support might be more appropriate."[22]

What about the claims of improved mental health? When examined closely, we discover they were minimal, and only in certain categories.

According to the Gender Exploratory Therapy Association (GETA), "Of 30 psychological measures, there was no statistically significant improvement in nearly half of the measures, and the balance only evidenced small changes of questionable clinical relevance. Importantly, there was no improvement in anxiety, depression, and anger scores."[23]

In the words of Levine and his coauthors, it is "impossible to determine whether gender reassignment, therapy, or the psychological maturation that occurs with the passage of time led to these few modest 'improvements.'"[24]

Now here's a fascinating tidbit: remember, due to strict eligibility criteria, the subjects with serious mental health or family problems were turned away. What happened to them, the rejects?

Well, what do you know! Most found ways to deal with their GD, and it diminished significantly. [25] Only 22 percent had gender surgery as adults.

Among those rejected from the study and medically untreated as adults, almost 80 percent were okay about having been rejected.

Levine and his coauthors pointed out these findings

> raise the possibility that the majority of those rejected from hormonal interventions not only were unharmed by waiting but benefited from "nontreatment" with gender reassignment in adolescence. Unlike the medically and surgically treated subjects, the "rejects" completed uninterrupted physical and psychological development, avoided sterility, maintained their sexual function, eliminated their risk of iatrogenic harm from surgery, and avoided the need for decades of dependence on cross-sex hormones.[26]

Thousands of minors have been funneled through affirming clinics in the aftermath of the Dutch Protocol, yet the Dutch didn't announce their long-term follow up until 2022.

The study had a response rate of only 50 percent, so a good number of negative outcomes likely went unrecorded.

The follow-up study showed that in their early thirties, over half who responded were single—not unmarried, but without a partner at all, an extremely high rate of singleness indicative of much larger issues. Nearly 60 percent were ashamed of their genital appearance. Significant numbers—44 percent of females and 35 percent of males—regretted losing their fertility.[27]

Of the males who underwent transition, three quarters had problems with libido, over 70 percent experienced pain during sex, and two-thirds had difficulty achieving orgasm.[28]

These unfortunate individuals aren't shining examples of success. Their lives are cautionary tales of the high price of denying biology.

One statistic is especially compelling. Twenty percent of respondents reported a change in identity over time. Remember, they all had severe GD from early childhood through mid-puberty. Nonetheless their opposite sex identities were not fixed.

To repeat: one in five people who were gender dysphoric in early childhood and went through medical "affirmation" described a change in their self-perception over time. Does that mean they desisted? Or identified as "non-binary" instead of a woman or man? It's not clear.

We must ask, what will happen to today's cases who develop GD in adolescence and in response to stress and social contagion? In how high a percentage will identity remain unstable? We don't know.

## Reckless and Sloppy

Demonstrating the lack of consensus among professionals who treat GD, psychologist Erica Anderson disclosed in an interview[29] with Abigail Shrier that "many transgender healthcare providers [are] treating kids recklessly." Asked if children in early puberty should be placed on blockers, a treatment considered standard of care by professional groups such as the World Professional Association for Transgender Health, vaginoplasty surgeon Marci Bowers, their incoming president, said: "I'm not a fan."

In the same interview, Anderson said: "due to some of the, I'll call it just 'sloppy,' sloppy healthcare work . . . we're going to have more young adults who will regret having gone through this process."

Anderson elaborated on what was "sloppy":

> Rushing people through the medicalization . . . and failure—abject failure—
> to evaluate the mental health of someone historically in current time, and to
> prepare them for making such a life-changing decision.

When you hear confident claims from the gender medical establishment claiming the science is settled, remember: the widespread use of puberty blockers and hormones is based on a study riddled with deficiencies and bias, some of the original authors openly question why ROGD kids are being treated under their model, and two prominent advocates of GAC, who themselves identify as transgender, call it reckless and sloppy.

From her experience at the St. Louis gender clinic, Reed described how children are put on a medical assembly line. It begins with the elimination of comprehensive psychological evaluations.

Reed:

> A criterion to receive puberty blockers or cross-sex hormones is that the
> child have a letter of referral from a therapist. This requirement is supposed
> to ensure that two independent professional clinicians agree that medi-
> cal transition is appropriate before a child is given medication that causes
> irreversible change. But nothing about this process at the Center involved
> independent judgment.[30]
>
> The Center steered children toward therapists that the Center knew
> would refer these children back to the Center with a letter supporting medi-
> cal transition. The Center had a list of therapists we would send children to,
> and a therapist could be on that list only if the Center "knew they would say
> yes" to medical transition.[31]

We also instructed the therapists what to say in their letters to us. I was instructed to draft and send language to the therapists for them to use in letters they then sent to us, and most therapists on the list had a template letter drafted by the Center that they could fill out to return to the Center. [32]

The next stop was a single visit to the endocrinologist for a testosterone prescription. That's all it took.[33]

A one-hour consultation with Endocrinology or Adolescent Medicine . . . is little more than a box-checking exercise. One hour is not sufficient time to fully assess these children.[34]

The Center tells the public and parents that it makes individualized decisions. That is not true. Doctors at the Center believe that every child who meets four basic criteria—age or puberty stage, therapist letter, parental consent, and a one-hour visit with a doctor—is a good candidate for irreversible medical intervention. When a child meets these four simple criteria, the doctors always decide to move forward with puberty blockers or cross-sex hormones. There were no objective medical test or criteria or individualized assessments.[35]

"Gender-affirming care is the gold standard of pediatric gender care," the center's website claims. "Gender-affirming care isn't meant to influence people in any particular direction. We don't 'treat' anyone's identity or tell anyone what they should or shouldn't do."[36]
Reed testifies to a different scenario:

I personally witnessed Center healthcare providers lie to the public and to parents of patients about the treatment, or lack of treatment, and the effects of treatment provided to children at the Center.[37]

The Center tells the public and parents that it provides multidisciplinary care. The Center says that you can come to the clinic and get transition hormones, if that is needed, but you can also get psychological and psychiatric care. [38]

That is not true. . . . [T]he Center placed such strict limits on Psychiatry and Psychology that I was almost never allowed to schedule patients for those practices. . . . Even when psychology was available, it was only to write a letter of support for the medical transition treatments and never for ongoing therapy.[39]

The public has been led to believe that a "team" has considered their child's care and that the "team" had ruled it best for the cross-sex hormones to be initiated, but the public was not told the truth.[40]

This Center did have members who would advocate for different options for the patients with concerning gender histories, concerning comorbidities, and attempt to raise the serious concerns regarding patient care. Patients and their parents, however, were never informed that the team did not have consensus on the treatment. The staff members on the team that were not universally in support of immediate cross sex hormones were not supported and were told to stop questioning the prevailing narrative.[41]

## That wasn't the only way the clinic misled the public. Reed continued:

Doctors know that cross-sex hormones (immediately after puberty blockers) make children permanently sterile. The doctors did not share this information with parents or children.[42]

Another disturbing aspect of the center was its lack of regard for the rights of parents—and the extent to which doctors saw themselves as more informed decision-makers over the fate of these children.[43]

The center downplayed the negative consequences, and emphasized the need for transition. As the center's website said, "Left untreated, gender dysphoria has any number of consequences, from self-harm to suicide. But when you take away the gender dysphoria by allowing a child to be who he or she is, we're noticing that goes away. The studies we have show these kids often wind up functioning psychosocially as well as or better than their peers."

There are no reliable studies showing this. Indeed, the experiences of many of the center's patients prove how false these assertions are.[44]

[Yet] a common tactic was for doctors to tell the parent of a child assigned female at birth, "You can either have a living son or a dead daughter." The clinicians would tell parents of a child assigned male at birth, "You can either have a living daughter or dead son." The clinicians would say this to parents in front of their children. That introduced the idea of suicide to the children. The suicide assertion was also based on false statistics. The clinicians would also malign any parent that was not on board with medicalizing their children. They would speak disparaging of those parents.[45]

## Reed detailed further the way clinicians manipulated and bypassed parents:

Doctors at the Center routinely pressured parents into "consenting" by pushing those parents, threatening them, and bullying them.[46]

Parents would come into the Center wanting to discuss research and ask questions. The clinicians would dismiss the research that the parents had found and speak down to the parents. [47]

When parents suggested that they wanted only therapy treatment, not cross-sex hormones or puberty blockers, doctors treated those parents as if the parents were abusive, uneducated, and willing to harm their own children. [48]

These assertions about abuse and suicide were used as tools to stop parents from asking questions and to pressure parents into consenting. [49]

The Center has a team culture of supporting the affirming parent and maligning the non-affirming parent. [50]

Parents routinely said they felt they were being pressured to consent. Often parents would give "consent" but say they were only doing so because "you guys are going to do this anyway." [51]

The Center routinely issued puberty blockers or cross-sex hormones without parental consent. [52]

Other centers who prescribe cross-sex hormones and puberty blockers require parents to issue written consent. Several times, I asked the doctors to require written consent. They repeatedly refused. The entire time I worked there the Center had no written informed consent, and none that was provided to or signed by patients. [53]

[Additionally,] doctors knew that many of our former patients had stopped taking cross-sex hormones and were detransitioning. Doctors did not share this information with parents or children. [54]

The clinic's reckless approach spread to the community. Misdirection continued outside the clinic's walls. When a fifth-grade teacher emailed the clinic, concerned gender dysphoria was spreading through her class, a doctor responded the students really were transgender and "the best we can do is affirm, validate and allow for exploration." [55] These were *fifth graders*.

But over in Finland, Riittakerttu Kaltiala, their expert in gender dysphoric youth, reports:

In youth gender identity research units, it has often been observed that a small town has suddenly received a disproportionate number of referrals compared to the population.

Research has shown that all patients are from the same school or even from the same circle of friends.

"Especially for girls, sharing things with a circle of friends is really important," says Kaltiala. According to him,[†] it is common for psychiatric symptoms to spread among girls in the same hospital ward.[56]

## Scandal in London

While the St. Louis Clinic placed their young patients on the path toward medical transition, scandal consumed London's Tavistock Gender Identity Disorder Service (GIDS). As you remember from Chapter Three, GIDS saw a 4,555 percent increase in referrals in slightly over a decade.

In 2019, Marcus Evans resigned after serving as the associate clinical director of Adult and Adolescent Service at Tavistock and wrote a scathing article: "Why I Resigned from Tavistock: Trans-Identified Children Need Therapy, Not Just 'Affirmation' and Drugs." Gender care at GIDS, he wrote, is influenced by a "de facto censorship regime [that] is harming children." Parents were concerned children were "fast-tracked through GIDS without any serious psychological evaluation." One in five staff members at the clinic had "grave ethical concerns," including fears of the clinic's "failure to stand up to pressure from trans activists."[57]

In Evans's opinion, the very foundation of affirming care is unsound: "When doctors always give patients what they want (or think they want), the fallout can be disastrous, as we have seen with the opioid crisis. And there is every possibility that the inappropriate medical treatment of children with gender dysphoria may follow a similar path."[58]

Evans went further. He lamented that GIDS officials "bought into the idea that transition is a goal unto itself, separate from the wellbeing of individual children, who are now being used as pawns in an ideological campaign." "This is the opposite of responsible and caring therapeutic work, which is based on the need to re-establish respectful but loving bonds between mind and body." [59]

When Evans resigned in protest, he joined thirty-five psychologists who had left for the same reason.[60] Also in 2019, as described above, Michael Biggs exposed[61] the GIDS's cover-up of their attempt to replicate the original Dutch study on puberty blockers, because the outcomes were not positive.[62] Some members of the British government were paying attention to the scandal: Lord Moonie, a physician, sponsored an event examining GIDS,

---

† Dr. Kaltiala is a woman, but Finnish does not have male and female pronouns, so the digital translation of the article defaulted to "him."

"First Do No Harm: the Ethics of Transgender Healthcare," in the House of Lords. Accused of transphobia, Lord Moonie quit the Labour Party.

*Inventing Transgender Children and Young People,*[63] a collection of essays by clinicians, educators, parents, and detransitioners, was dedicated to "the countless individuals who daren't publicly voice their deep concerns about transgendering children"; the book demonstrated the harms perpetrated on youth by trans ideology, including the aggressive treatment approach at GIDS and the silencing of dissent.

Soon after, the UK High Court was asked to assess the ability of young people with GD to consent to puberty blockers. The woman at the center of the case was Kiera Bell, who was put on puberty blockers and hormones as a teen at GIDS, before receiving a double mastectomy at age twenty.[64] She later regretted her medicalization and said she was treated like a "guinea pig" at the gender clinic.[65]

The judges determined that suppressing puberty in gender-dysphoric young people is experimental and the first step in a trajectory that almost invariably leads to cross-sex hormones with irreversible consequences. Because of this, the Court ruled that persons under age sixteen are unlikely to be able to provide valid informed consent, as they lack the capacity to properly comprehend and evaluate the profound and lifelong impacts of these interventions.[66]

Dr. Hilary Cass,[67] former president of the Royal College of Paediatrics and Child Health, was appointed to perform an independent review of GIDS. She found serious deficiencies in provision of services including the failure to gather evidence about comorbidities or long-term outcomes. Cass described "diagnostic overshadowing": once a patient declares gender dysphoria, all other mental health issues are overshadowed. Among her conclusions:

- The evidence base for an affirmation-only model is severely lacking.
- Puberty blockers, rather than acting as a "pause button" allowing children time to explore their identity, seem to lock them into a medicalised treatment pathway.
- There is too little evidence to make any recommendations on hormone treatment.
- The best way to support young people experiencing gender distress has not been determined.[68]

Cass concluded that treatment for GD at GIDS was based on poor evidence and its model of care left young people "at considerable risk" of poor mental health. Following her report, the National Health Service announced GIDS would close, to be replaced by smaller regional hubs with a more cautious and holistic approach.

The events in Britain were a huge fiasco. I can't help but ask again, how could they have escaped the attention of doctors running the St. Louis clinic, or for that matter, any gender clinic?

While GIDS made international headlines, Reed decided to speak up:

> By spring 2020, I felt a medical and moral obligation to do something. So I spoke up in the office, and sent plenty of emails. . . . In all my years at the Washington University School of Medicine, I had received solidly positive performance reviews. But in 2021, that changed. I got a below-average mark for my "Judgment" and "Working Relationships/ Cooperative Spirit." Although I was described as "responsible, conscientious, hard-working and productive" the evaluation also noted: "At times Jamie responds poorly to direction from management with defensiveness and hostility."[69]
>
> There was a team of about eight of us, and only one other person brought up the kinds of questions I had. Anyone who raised doubts ran the risk of being called a transphobe.[70]
>
> Things came to a head at a half-day retreat in summer of 2022. In front of the team, the doctors said that my colleague and I had to stop questioning the "medicine and the science" as well as their authority. Then an administrator told us we had to "Get on board, or get out." It became clear that the purpose of the retreat was to deliver these messages to us.[71]
>
> Because the Center was unwilling to make any changes in response to my concerns, I left the Center in November 2022.[72]
>
> By the time I departed, I was certain that the way the American medical system is treating these patients is the opposite of the promise we make to "do no harm." Instead, we are permanently harming the vulnerable patients in our care.[73]

## "It Wasn't True"

Reed didn't blow the whistle at once. Going public, she said, would be "putting myself at serious personal and professional risk."[74]

Then, she saw an article quoting the Admiral and knew she must act. Reed:

The article read: "Levine, the U.S. assistant secretary for health, said that clinics are proceeding carefully and that no American children are receiving drugs or hormones for gender dysphoria who shouldn't."

I felt stunned and sickened. It wasn't true. And I know that from deep first-hand experience.

So I started writing down everything I could about my experience at the Transgender Center. [75]

I brought my concerns and documents to the attention of Missouri's attorney general. He is a Republican. I am a progressive. But the safety of children should not be a matter for our culture wars. [76]

While America embraces blockers, hormones, and surgery on demand, progressive nations in Western Europe and Scandinavia slam on the brakes. Britain planned to close GIDS in 2023.‡ Sweden restricted medical interventions for minors after "Leo's" malpractice case.

The Finland Health Authority made psychotherapy, not puberty blockers and cross-sex hormones, the first-line treatment[77] for gender dysphoria in minors. In that country, medical interventions have been limited to two centralized research clinics and are only on a "case-by-case-basis."[78]

The Norwegian Healthcare Investigation Board changed their guidelines. "The knowledge base, especially research-based knowledge for gender-affirming treatment . . . is deficient and the long-term effects are little known," the Board wrote. "This is particularly true for the teenage population."[79]

The Royal Australian and New Zealand College of Psychiatrists warned, "There is a paucity of quality evidence on the outcomes of those presenting with gender dysphoria. In particular, there is a need for better evidence in relation to outcomes for children and young people." They called for a "psychotherapy-first approach . . . before initiating hormones and changing the whole physical nature of the child."[80]

Why are teenagers in London, Stockholm, Helsinki, and Oslo protected from the experiment called "gender-affirming care" while ours in Washington, Chicago, Boston, and San Francisco are not?

Come to think of it, "experiment" may be the wrong word. I will end with more wisdom from Jamie Reed:

---

‡ As of this writing, the closure has been postponed a year.

Experiments are supposed to be carefully designed. Hypotheses are supposed to be tested ethically. The doctors I worked alongside at the Transgender Center said frequently about the treatment of our patients: "We are building the plane while we are flying it. No one should be a passenger on that kind of aircraft."[81]

# CHAPTER SEVEN

# Emma or Oliver?

Fifteen-year-old Emma is in the emergency room after slashing her arm with a razor. Her father texts me photos, and I am alarmed at the number of wounds—too many to count—and their depth: they're not the superficial scratches she made in the past with a paper clip. Emma will need many stitches, but thankfully she did not hit her radial artery that courses just under the skin of her wrist. If she had, Chris might have contacted me from the morgue.

Emma's short life has been filled with adversity. Her mother committed suicide when she was six, and Emma has not had a positive female role model. A speech defect has led to extreme shyness. She has no siblings or family nearby, and her father works long hours.

For Emma, making friends was always a challenge. Most kids just couldn't understand what she said. She was in speech therapy for a few years. In seventh grade things worsened, Emma was bullied throughout the year. She had some friends but struggled with her changing body and was not adequately prepared for her period.

During lockdowns, Emma isolated in her room. Her real-life social contacts dwindled, and she made a few online friends instead. She was terrified of COVID and refused to leave home for days at a time. While Emma had never expressed any problem with being a girl, at the start of ninth grade, she cut her hair and began wearing baggy, androgenous clothing. Her grades fell.

When Emma told Chris she was omnisexual, then transgender, he was stunned. His gut said, *No, she's not transgender, there's something else going on*, and he contacted me.

I met with Chris to gather a history on Emma and the family. He impressed me as a loving and devoted father who was struggling on his own to raise a daughter with multiple challenges. Emma had been in therapy twice before—after his wife's death and during the bullying at school. He emphasized that he fully supported everything LGBT and he'd support Emma if she really was lesbian or transgender, but he believed it was premature to make those decisions. First, he told me, she needs help dealing with all her hardships past and present. She needs to handle stress better, like herself, make friends, experience a romance, grow up more. He hoped I'd agree because he couldn't trust a therapist who'd automatically accept Emma's self-diagnosis.

At our first meeting, Emma told me she first heard about being transgender at school, but it wasn't until she met her online friends that she really started to think about it. They identified as trans or non-binary, and they all loved Ty Turner and others on YouTube, TikTok, and Twitter. She described to me what was essentially binge-watching YouTube videos of girls on testosterone celebrating their deeper voices and growth of facial and body hair, and for some, the removal of their breasts. Emma said she identifies as trans because she wants her periods to stop and for her chest to be flat. She wants people to look at her and think, "That's a guy." If only those things could happen, she told me, she'd feel so good.

Emma admitted that since being bullied in seventh grade, she rarely spoke with anyone at school; to this day she becomes sweaty and shaky at the very thought of it. Hanging out on Discord is much easier because her speech defect is a non-issue.

She was lonely, sad, and worried; she avoided mirrors, cried frequently, had irritability, poor concentration and motivation, didn't enjoy anything, and was without much hope that things would improve unless she was able to live as a boy.

Emma complained that her father refused to call her the name she'd picked, Oliver, and to use the pronouns he/him. She'd heard there are parents who refuse to accept their child's gender identity, but she was surprised, when she came out to him, to discover he was one of them, because he'd always been caring and responsive to her needs. Now she saw him as bigoted and disrespectful, and their relationship was often hostile. A few times she called him transphobic. Emma was easily overwhelmed by her strong emotions and worked hard to avoid them; she became distraught when Chris "misgendered" her and her friends or voiced opinions with which she disagreed. On several occasions she felt an urge to harm herself, Emma told me, but she did not want to die.

I agreed with Chris: Emma latched on to the idea that becoming Oliver will relieve her emotional struggles. She requires therapy to explore what's really going on, why she's fleeing her femininity, and to treat her trauma, poor self-regard, and symptoms of anxiety and depression.

Considering her symptoms and family history, I placed Emma on an antidepressant, taught her some skills to use when overwhelmed, and created a crisis plan to follow if she felt the urge to harm herself. I explained that I'm the type of therapist that sees gender as only one part of the large, complex tapestry that's Emma, and that we will examine, together, the entire tapestry in order to understand her. People are complicated, I told her, and gender is related to deep issues that take time to understand. Until then, I would not affirm Oliver, because that places her on a specific path that may not be right for her and, once on it, can be hard to leave. I was optimistic that as we got to know each other and she was able to share her experiences and feelings and learn how to cope sadness and frustration, she'd feel better. I would also work with her father, I said, so that he could understand her better.

Chris arranged to restart speech therapy and nutrition counseling. Emma learned about communicating her feelings and skills for coping with intense emotions. Her access to the Internet was limited and her social media monitored.

With time I learned that Emma had been molested by an older male cousin, and that she'd been exposed to misogynistic pornography.

With medication, psychotherapy, speech therapy, and parent support, Emma slowly began to feel better. Chris got better at listening and communicating with his daughter. For example, he was able to tell Emma that her rejection of the name he and her mother had carefully picked was painful for him. While she hoped he'd eventually give in and call her Oliver, she was able to accept his position.

Chris learned about gender dysphoria and joined a parent support group. He established boundaries about names, pronouns, hair, and clothing with which they could both live. He made changes at work, allowing him to be home when Emma returned from school; they bonded while preparing and having dinner, and on a road trip to visit some cousins. For her birthday, they went to the pet store and bought a lizard.

The three of us were working well together, and Chris and I were hopeful. Emma looked forward to speaking with me every week, and trust was building. I hoped I could be the strong feminine role model she never had.

After six months, Emma showed improvement. Her mood was better, and she was more motivated and able to focus. Chris took her out to celebrate an improved report card. She began to speak in class and joined an after-school photography club. While she still identified as a boy and was called Oliver by her friends, she no longer obsessed about her breasts and periods, and she was able to agree to disagree with her father about gender-related issues, at least for the time being.

Then, out of the blue, Emma discovered the girls who had bullied her in middle school wrote cruel, humiliating posts about her on social media. Home alone and overwhelmed by distress, Emma slashed her arm.

The emergency room doctor wanted to admit Emma to the psychiatric unit, but Chris was unsure: he was concerned the hospital staff would immediately zero in on Emma's gender identity. He told me the ER forms asked for her gender, preferred name, and pronouns. Chris wondered: when they learn he was still calling her Emma, would they paint him as unsupportive, or worse? After all he'd done to strengthen their bond and address Emma's challenges, he was terrified the hospital would place a wedge between them. That's when he texted me the photos and wanted to speak.

I wanted to know more about what happened, specifically if Emma's cutting was a genuine suicide attempt, and why she didn't follow our crisis plan. But I was not able to evaluate her or play a significant part in her care, because I was not on the staff of the hospital.

But I knew that Chris's worries were justified: the moment Emma walked through the hospital doors,[1] she would become Oliver.

## "The Hospitals Produce the ROGD"

A nurse working in a psychiatric unit for adolescents in New England emailed me:

> I'm having a hard time, I feel I'm doing something wrong with the kids.
> The biggest issue here is identity. 50–70 percent of them are queer or trans,
> the vast majority are girls, they all have depression and suicidal ideation and
> are on meds. 50 percent have SIB.[*]

---

* "SIB"—self-injurious behavior.

When I admit a patient, I go to the ambulance bay and the patient is on a stretcher. I have to introduce myself with my pronouns and ask the patient their pronouns. That's the first thing I'm supposed to do! It just feels wrong.

There's a checklist of questions. I'm supposed to ask them: what's your sexual orientation, what's your gender identity? I preface it with, "I know these questions are really weird, but. . ." It feels terrible to ask these things. Sometimes they don't even understand what I'm talking about!

She told me, *I asked one girl, why do you think you are trans? She said, "I hate getting my period."*

I asked her if binders were given to the hospitalized girls? *Yes, if the girl asks for one, and she's not suicidal,† the doctor writes an order.*

All the other RNs wear "we support trans rights" buttons. My nurse manager says to make sure to use preferred pronouns in charting, but it will say in the chart not to share [gender information] with parents, even if the patient is thirteen. It's wrong. It makes me so mad! I want this stuff to stop!

I'm aware of the hazards posed by adolescent psychiatric units from speaking[2] with Alex Capo, the executive director of Charlton School, a small therapeutic program for teens in upstate New York. He described an "explosion" of ROGD patients at his facility that began around 2019. Ninety percent of them arrived directly from the hospital, and many had self-injurious behaviors.

"The hospitals," he told me, "Produce the ROGD; they promote and encourage" the new identities. "For sixty percent of [patients], the onset was in the hospital. That's where it first surfaced." He also noted the powerful peer culture on adolescent units, and the "live daughter or dead son" mantra staff repeat with parents.

Upon admission of their child to Charlton parents said affirmation was mandatory, or their kids' self-injury will continue. "So we went with affirming, with staff tripping over each other to not misgender."

But staff did not see improvement in their young patients. After a while, Alex told me, "We decided we are hurting kids." They discovered Stella O'Malley, an Irish psychotherapist and founder of Genspect[3]—an organization calling for a slower and more nuanced approach to treating gender confused youth—and invited her to train Charlton staff.

---

† The binder could be used for self-strangulation.

"We got educated," Alex said, "and decided, let's not play this game anymore."

When patients arrived, staff would explain, "We are not affirming, we go with birth names here." In each case, Alex told me, their opposite sex identity faded, whereas students who had been affirmed at Charlton and graduated, they remain trans-identified.

According to Alex, treatment at Charlton now "draws from biopsychosocial models and uses an exploratory approach as opposed to an affirming model." His staff use a guide created by the Gender Exploratory Therapy Association (GETA)—a group of clinicians including O'Malley, who advocate for exploratory psychotherapy before patients embark on irreversible medical treatment.

Yes, I knew what was in store for Emma in the hospital, but now I was on the phone with Chris, and a decision had to be made. His anguish was evident—all he wanted was for Emma to be safe and get help, but it felt like a lose-lose situation.

Unfortunately, there was no choice. I explained that Emma's serious self-injury required hospital admission for evaluation and stabilization. Her physical safety was our priority, and even though the hospital was far from perfect, it was safer than home. If he refused admission, I told him, social services would probably be called. I arranged for a lawyer (also the parent of a gender-questioning child who's been hospitalized) to advise him on navigating the predicament, and Emma was admitted to the adolescent psychiatric unit.

Everyone agreed Emma was suffering and needed help, but what kind of help? "Affirm" her as Oliver, or explore why she's fleeing Emma? Give her a binder, or figure out why she hates her breasts? Start puberty blockers, or explain that all teens have discomfort with their bodies?

Emma or Oliver? Which is her authentic, real self? Which identity will lead to despair, which to health and wellness?

And most critical: which approach protects Emma from suicide?

Those are the questions at the center of a heated debate taking place in medical journals and courts of law, but you haven't heard about it because the media regurgitate the Castro consensus.

The governing council of the American Psychological Association, in a formal resolution about gender dysphoria, categorized any approach other than prompt affirmation of Oliver to be unethical and dangerous.[4]

The US federal policy of the current administration endorses early gender-affirming care, that is, prompt affirming of Oliver, as crucial to Emma's overall health and well-being.[5]

A report prepared for the Substance Abuse and Mental Health Services Administration (SAMHSA) claims:

> No research indicates that gender identity change efforts are effective in altering gender identity. Research indicates that these efforts can cause significant harm, including suicide attempts and other negative behavioral health outcomes.[6]

All these authorities and many more tell us Emma's male self-perception overrides the "female" she was "assigned" at birth. Her male gender identity is simply a variant of normal development, they claim. *There is no more Emma, only Oliver*, and Chris and I—indeed everyone in Oliver's life—must give him space to forge his path. Even if he's only three years old, we are instructed, only Oliver can make decisions about pronouns or "aligning" his body with his mind. Our job is to respect, understand, and support Oliver. We must delete our memory of him as a girl and scrap our expectation that one day Emma will be a woman. If we don't, we're at best misinformed and at worst dangerous.

They want you to believe the issue has been thoroughly studied, closely examined, and there's a consensus, one voice in unison: *Oliver not Emma.* Even the POTUS told parents like Chris, "*. . . affirming your child's identity is one of the most powerful things you can do to keep them safe and healthy.*"[7]

That's why, as I explained, the moment Emma enters the hospital she becomes Oliver. With or without Chris's agreement. Staff will call her Oliver, "he" and "him" exclusively, instead of Emma "she" and "her," what they call her "birth-assigned name and gender."[8]

Hospital staff are trained in how their gender-affirming speech creates a "welcoming and safe place" and warned of the dire consequences of failing to do so:

> Once a patient tells you their name and gender it is important to continue using them. Refusing to acknowledge their gender identity and choice of language harms the therapeutic relationship, is discriminatory, and insults the patient. Furthermore, this may add to any trauma they have already experienced and possibly foster increased thoughts of suicide and self-harm.[9]

For example, a nurse may write in Emma's chart, a legal document, "Oliver is having a hard day. He's preoccupied with his breasts and hips and dreading his period."

I'm going to explain this once again because it is difficult to absorb.

Health professionals, MDs and PhDs and others, who went to school for many years and have lots of diplomas on their walls, are telling kids like Emma that yes, it's possible to have a mismatch between your brains and bodies. Yes, you might be both male and female, neither male nor female, or some combination of male and female. Yes, in fact, all that is normal, it just means you don't conform to society's rigid norms, you're defying traditional roles, you're marching to the beat of a different drummer.[10] Your discomfort with your growing breasts or erections, it all makes sense: your bodies are mistakes!

This is gender-"affirming" care: and we are told ad nauseam that it saves lives.[11] Never mind that "gender" is an ephemeral concept without empirical evidence supporting its existence. "Oliver" is nothing but a persona in Emma's mind, quite possibly a temporary one, and affirming him requires denying the objective reality of Emma. Nevertheless, healthcare professionals are instructed GAC is medically necessary, evidence based, and lifesaving. Any other approach, we are told, is unsupportive, judgmental, does not appreciate the child, and fails to promote acceptance and inclusion of all children.[12]

I am joined by many other clinicians in believing that Emma's body is just fine, without need for "alignment"—it's her trauma and psychic wounds that demand attention. Some of us support legislation protecting minors like Emma from disfiguring and sterilizing medical interventions. For speaking out, we are maligned. We are called ignorant, noninclusive, "dinosaurs," and of course, transphobic.

To the Admiral, "anti-trans" doctors like me are preying on people's fears, and that leads to darkness and hate:

> I like to quote that sage Yoda from Star Wars. You know, "fear is the path that leads to the dark side. Fear leads to anger. Anger leads to hate. Hate leads to suffering." I think that people fear what they don't understand.[13]

Do you hear this? To the second-most senior medical official in this country, my views about helping teens like Emma, which are shared by some of the giants in this field, lead to fear, anger, and suffering.

## "Mom, What Am I"?

As discussed earlier, Jason Rafferty, a pediatrician and child psychiatrist,[14] is the lead author of the American Academy of Pediatricians' (AAP) policy statement‡ on Transgender and Gender-Diverse Adolescents.[15] In the statement, published in the prestigious journal *Pediatrics*, Rafferty regurgitates the Articles of Faith, conflating sex and gender along the way: sex is a label "assigned" at birth, gender identity is fluid and "may be male, female, somewhere in between, a combination of both or neither." He warns against "binary notions of gender" and implies that any approach outside of affirming Oliver is unsupportive and judgmental, lacking understanding and appreciation of Emma's "gender experience," and more likely to result in *more* mental health issues.

Rafferty's views are not supported by the evidence. Nevertheless, he wants doctors like myself to promptly place Emma on the trans assembly line.

My medical training included an unspoken commandment. It wasn't explicitly stated, it was absorbed by osmosis: "Thou shalt trust the AMA, the CDC, the Dept of HHS, the American Psychiatric Association, and the American Academy of Child and Adolescent Psychiatry. Thou shalt turn to them and other medical authorities for clinical guidance, because they speak Truth."

But now the medical establishment is demanding I go against all I know about human biology, child development, and psychotherapy. They instruct me to endorse Emma's irrational rejection of her sexed body. They expect me to stand by and watch as she constructs her own reality and to recognize that reality as valid.

But I know that emotionally healthy people live in reality, no matter how painful it may be, and that it's my job as a doctor to represent that reality. When parents, teachers, and doctors fail to represent reality to children and youth, they do a terrible disservice.

For example, in the first season of the TLC reality series *I am Jazz*, Jazz's mother, Jeannette, describes an instance when as a very young child, Jazz (then Jared) asked her, *Mom, what am I?*—meaning, her son asked, Am I a girl or a boy?

Jeannette says she answered, *Well what do you feel like?* Jared answered, of course, that he felt like a girl. And it seems like that was that.

‡ NOTE: The first page of this "policy statement" has the following disclaimer: "The guidance in this statement does not indicate an exclusive course of treatment or serve as a standard of medical care. Variations, taking into account individual circumstances, may be appropriate."

I want to acknowledge the very challenging position of all parents with a child with severe gender dysphoria. But in this case, the mom's response was incorrect. The proper answer would have been, *You are a boy who feels like a girl right now. Your feelings can change, but your sex cannot.*

Returning to Chris, he and many parents instinctively know the born-in-the-wrong-body notion is rubbish, and that's why, when it comes to gender, so many no longer trust the medical system. They know their kids better than anyone else and know they are not the opposite sex; rather, to the distressed young person it's a way of coping with their autism, depression, or anxiety. It's also a way to gain acceptance of peers. Parents know that pills and injections and operations are not the answer.

Chris is certainly not having any of it, no matter what the medical authorities and the president tell him. He's right to hesitate before placing his daughter in the hospital, which, as he saw in the ER, seems like a mouthpiece for trans ideology. The hospital will crystallize Oliver in Emma's mind, instead of focusing on the cyber-bullying, emotional dysregulation, and other issues that led to her self-injury. We know from decades of research that a secure bond with Chris is perhaps the single most critical factor predicting Emma's future flourishing;[16] the bond with her father must be strengthened, not undermined with charges of bias and transphobia.

I have another concern I didn't mention to Chris: the other patients on the unit. I imagine all the troubled teens with nose rings and blue hair who identify as who-knows-what. Days before, I came across an article quoting adolescent psychiatrist Riittakerttu Kaltiala, Finland's expert on gender dysphoric youth, as mentioned in the previous chapter (emphasis mine):

*"Especially for girls, sharing things with a circle of friends is really import-ant," says Kaltiala. According to him, it is common for psychiatric symptoms to spread among girls in the same hospital ward.*[17]

Will Emma leave the hospital with her boy identity more concretized than before? Will one of the other girls tell her how to buy T online, or suggest she leave home and seek refuge with a glitter family or in an LGBT shelter?

I know those things are likely, but I also know, considering the severity of her self-harm, we had no choice. I feel outraged that my profession is so entrenched in the trans crusade Articles of Faith, so angry that Chris must deal not only with his disturbed daughter, but with a system stacked against their long-term interests; upon admitting her to the hospital, he should feel relief she'll begin to heal, not anxiety that she'll get worse.

*We should all be on the same team helping Emma,* I reflect, *this is madness!* For a long time that night, sleep evades me.

❄ ❄ ❄

With the memory of Emma's bloody arm haunting him, Chris will meet with the treatment team. They will very likely explain that his unconditional acceptance of Oliver is—you guessed it—medically necessary, even lifesaving. *You must validate and support your son,* the doctors and social workers will soberly tell him, implying that any other approach with Emma is *invalidating* and *unsupportive* and could lead to disaster.

Chris may be asked, as many parents have told me they were, *Which do you prefer—a live son, or a dead daughter?*

He must be prepared to hear frightening statistics, for example: more than half of transgender youth seriously consider attempting suicide;[18] 41 percent of all transgender and gender nonconforming youth attempt suicide;[19] transgender youth attempt suicide nearly six times more than non-LGBTQ youth.[20]

Those statistics are certainly cause for concern, but how accurate are they, and should they guide treatment decisions? Does Chris really have only two choices, a live Oliver or a dead Emma?

More and more parents find themselves emotionally manipulated by experts with the transition-or-death narrative. They're led to believe that only by denying their parental instincts will their child survive.

Of course, any risk of suicide demands attention and assessment. However, there's no evidence the affirm-or-suicide mantra is true. While it is accurate that the suicidality of gender-distressed adolescents and young adults is higher than the general population, it is similar to those with other mental health conditions.[21]

Michael Biggs reported[22] that at London's GIDS, over eleven years and among about 15,000 patients (including the waiting list) there were four suicides. That represented an estimated annual suicide rate of 13 per 100,000, making them very rare events.

Here's the most important nugget: two of the suicides were of individuals on the waiting list, presumably not getting treatment, but the other were of patients in treatment, being "affirmed" in counseling and possibly receiving blockers and opposite sex hormones.[23] These data contradict claims of an epidemic of suicide in gender distressed youth, and the trope of "transition or die."

When Finland's expert Kaltiala was asked about the claim that trans youth have an increased risk of suicide and therefore urgently need treatment and support, she stated, "It's purposeful disinformation, the spreading of which is irresponsible."[24]

Here's how I suggested Chris present his preferences for Emma's care to the hospital apparatchiks. I told him to bring someone supportive to the meeting, even if that person doesn't say a word. He needed someone there on his side, even via virtual connection, like another parent of a gender kid he met in a parent support group.

Try to remain calm, I told him, Remember the staff are probably decent people following the guidance of those they trust. They don't realize they've been misinformed. They haven't thought as deeply about the issue as you have. If you get emotional its ok—your strong feelings are understandable—she's your precious child!

**Dr. A:**   Hello Chris, I am Dr. A, Oliver's psychiatrist, my pronouns are they/them. This is Xander, Oliver's social worker, his pronouns are ze/zir.

**Chris:**   Hello, good to meet you. I appreciate all you are doing for Emma.

**Dr. A:**   "Emma?" Oh yes, we heard you use Oliver's birth-assigned name and pronouns.

**Chris:**   Actually, I don't want to get off on the wrong foot, but my wife and I picked the name Emma months before she was born, and we thought about it for a long time. It was not "assigned" at birth. That makes it sound arbitrary and thoughtless, and it wasn't those things at all.

I want to start off saying I know you mean well. I'm not here to argue but to let you know where I stand as Emma's parent. And I also have some requests.

Yes, I call my daughter Emma. She wants me to call her "Oliver," and I know that in the hospital you do that, but I don't believe it's in her best interest.

**Xander:**   Chris, you may mean well, but an affirming approach is best for your son's mental health. It might even be lifesaving. That means using his preferred name and pronouns.

**Chris:**   I'm glad you realize that I mean well, because I have always been devoted to Emma, I've considered that my most important job since the day we found out we were pregnant. And I have no plans to stop now.

My daughter has experienced different traumas and challenges, and I have always done my best to make sure her mental health issues are addressed. May I ask why you believe my acting as if she's a boy is best for her mental health?

**Dr. A:** Chris, it's not about acting. Gender identity is real. Oliver is real.

**Chris:** I know you genuinely believe that. And Emma does too. But I'll tell you, since this whole thing started, I've been digging deep into gender, and I have to say, I can't wrap my head around the idea that Emma can pick from dozens of gender identities, and change it on a dime, construct her own reality, and hers is the only reality that counts. Hard science like biology and genetics says she's been female since the moment of conception and will remain female forever. That makes no sense to me.

Emma can never be a boy, only a synthetic version of a boy. I don't understand how you call that "real." I don't agree that everyone makes their own gender reality and we all must accept it, or else. I believe there's one reality.

**Dr. A:** Chris, you're confusing gender with sex.

**Chris:** No, I know the difference: Emma's sex is hardwired and cannot be changed. Her gender is how she feels at the moment or wants others to see her. Those are the correct definitions, right?

**Xander:** Yes.

**Chris:** We were talking about acting and what's real. Emma is female and can never be a boy. It's not doing her any kindness to act like she can just construct her own reality. Reality is fixed. If she denies that, she's going to pay a price. It could be a very high price. And I want to protect her from that. That's what I believe and there are many who agree with me.

**Xander:** Chris, there's no debate about this. There's a consensus, every major medical organization agrees.

**Chris:** I've heard that, but I believe it's not as clear cut as you may think. Please hear me out. Ever since my daughter told me she is transgender I've been reading everything I can, listening to podcasts and interviews with doctors, therapists, and parents, and I discovered—maybe you're not aware—there's a fierce debate about the best way to help these kids.

I'm not a doctor or a therapist, but I know that treatment of transgender kids is controversial. I thought we might disagree today, so I put together some articles that you probably haven't seen. Here they are [see Appendix Two], I'm asking that you please look at them. They are by highly respected professionals such as Dr. Stephen Levine at Case Western Reserve University, he has been caring for transgender people for fifty years. There's also an article by Kenneth Zucker who for decades ran one of the only clinics in the world for children with gender dysphoria and has seen 2,000 kids. They both argue that social transition is an intervention with consequences. They are highly qualified voices who are silenced by the authorities you trust.

**Xander:** I've heard of them, and they are outliers.

**Chris:** Also included in the articles are the statements by medical authorities in Britain, Sweden, Norway, and Finland announcing they have studied all the data carefully and there's a severe lack of research on kids like Emma, and it is unknown whether affirming them has any long-term benefit.

**Dr. A:** In this hospital we follow WPATH's Standard of Care.

**Chris:** Oh yes, I know about WPATH. Their Standards of Care are highly controversial. Did you know over 2,000 health professionals signed a declaration[25] saying they're unethical and damaging?

Listen, I'm not trying to be difficult. I just want the best for Emma and want you to understand there isn't a consensus about how to help her, there's a debate.

This hospital follows WPATH, but those countries I just mentioned reject WPATH. And that's the point: there's controversy not consensus.

**Xander:** But Chris, Oliver is saying this is who he is, his authentic self, and he needs your validation. He is really hurting from your lack of support. Studies show he'll be less depressed and feel better about himself if you support him.

**Chris:** Please stop saying I don't support Emma. With respect, you don't even know us. The opposite is true. I don't want to get angry; I want this meeting to be productive. Please stop saying that.

Like many teenagers, Emma must learn how to deal with frustration and disappointment when things don't go her way. That includes me continuing to call her Emma.

Emma doesn't know who she is. Last year she begged me to wear padded bras and get a naval ring. Now she says she's a boy. She's trying different identities.

I'll do anything for Emma, but I draw the line at denying the truth. I won't lie to her and say she's a boy, even though it would put a smile on her face for a while. That's not a kindness. That leads her down a path towards medicalization, and that's dangerous.

I know there are some studies that show short term improvement if I—as you say—"validate" her, but I know they're not the gold standard of studies which are randomized and controlled. But in any case, I have her lifelong health and happiness in mind, not the short term, and there are no studies that indicate the long-term results are positive.

You've shared some very scary statistics about suicide, and it feels to me like you're saying if I don't accept Emma is my son, she could very well kill herself. I don't know if you have kids, Dr. A and Xander, but if you do, I'm sure you understand how hard it is to even say those words.

I have learned that suicide is a complicated subject and people don't kill themselves for just one reason,[26] for example, because their father won't affirm their new identity.

**Dr. A:** It is true, suicide is complicated.

**Chris:** I looked up the suicide rates for girls Emma's age. Thankfully it's extremely rare for girls her age to kill themselves. Out of 100,000 girls her age, around 5 will commit suicide. Of course, every suicide is a tragedy, but the risk for Emma is extremely low.

I also learned that suicide attempts may be unrelated to a real intent to die. It may be a manipulation, a cry for help or, as I suspect with Emma's, a way to cope with overwhelming distress.

You just met Emma so there's a lot you don't know about her. My daughter has had many challenges. Since she was little, Emma was very anxious around people because of her speech. She had trouble making friends. My wife committed suicide. Emma was sexually abused, and she's been bullied. Sadly, there hasn't been any mother substitute in her life because my family lives far away and both her grandmothers passed. I think you'll agree that's a lot for a fifteen-year-old. And this was all before she had any gender dysphoria whatsoever.

I know there's evidence that kids like Emma are more vulnerable than the general teen population to suicidal thoughts, self-harm, and suicide, but it is unclear how significant a role their transgender identity plays, if any.

She's already at risk due to my wife's suicide,[27] having an anxiety disorder, being bullied, and possibly being lesbian or bisexual.[28] All those things increase her risk for suicide, so it's incorrect to put it all on my not accepting her boy identity.[29] You shouldn't do that.

And there's no evidence that allowing her to "transition" will decrease her suicide risk.

In the material I've given you there's an article[30] by Dr. Michael Biggs summarizing research at the world's largest clinic for kids like Emma. Over eleven years, the annual suicide rate was thirteen suicides out of 100,000 youth, which is a whole lot lower than those statistics you threw at me.

And please hear this, it's important. There was no difference in the suicide rate of those who had received treatment and those that were on the waiting list for treatment.

**Dr. A:** Well, you certainly have done a lot of research, I'll give you that much. But as I keep saying, your position goes against the guidelines of every major medical organization . . .

**Chris:** Yes, I know. Dr. A and Xander, I want to say this again. I know you mean well. I'm not here to argue but to let you know where I stand as Emma's parent. I think you genuinely believe if I don't affirm Emma as Oliver her mental health will plummet. I see it differently. I hope you'll think about what I said and review the literature I've given you with an open mind.

In the meantime, my daughter must stay with you for stabilization and adjustment of her meds. I can't control what name and pronouns you and your staff use with her. But I want to be clear: I don't want anyone on your staff bringing up transgender ideology with Emma, thereby encouraging her on a path towards risky medical interventions. That includes gender dysphoria, binders, hormone blockers, cross sex hormones, and surgery.

If Emma brings up those topics staff should refer her to her out-patient therapist or myself.

If I learn that any of your staff volunteered those topics for discussion, I will hold you responsible for any negative consequences that result.

Finally, I am a loving and responsible parent, and Emma's secure bond with me protects her against suicide. I expect that bond to be honored during her hospital stay. If I learn that your staff undermines my parental authority or says something disparaging about me, I will hold you responsible for any negative consequences that result.

\* \* \*

There's a lot here, to be sure. I encouraged Chris to practice making these points with a friend before going to the meeting.

I advised him to bring notes, and to keep returning to his main points: he knows Emma best and is devoted to her; she needs treatment for emotional disturbances that predated gender dysphoria; there is no consensus about treatment of kids like Emma; there is no evidence that affirmation helps in the long term or decreases her risk of suicide.

You're probably wondering, what happened to the nurse from the psych unit? You won't be surprised that a few months later she wrote,

> I spoke with management about my concerns but was basically told "this is how we are handling these issues. If you can't accept it this might not be the job for you."
>
> So I resigned as a nurse at that adolescent inpatient facility. I could not tolerate what was happening and being promoted with the teens there.

Pay attention, everyone, this is how it works. There are a few rare individuals, like the nurse above, who speak up and question the pro-affirmation narrative, but their concerns are dismissed by the higher-ups. What can she do? She's one person against Big Brother. She has a conscience and can't go to work each day, harm people, go home and have dinner as usual. So she quits, and you know who's left?

Dr. A, Xander, the nurse manager, and the nurses wearing the "trans rights" buttons—that's who's left. They do as they're told, go home, and have dinner, as usual. No questions, no doubts. No lost sleep over the Emmas in their care. That's the disturbing truth, and the reason you must be prepared.

# CHAPTER EIGHT

# Educators' Dangerous Ideas

Heather, from Santa Barbara, came to me with a history of severe mental illness. You may ask, what makes mental illness severe? I'm not speaking of a girl who cuts herself after a breakup. When I describe Heather as having "severe mental illness," it's because she was so intent on ending her life that she'd tried to drown, hang, and immolate herself.

During one of her multiple psychiatric hospitalizations, Heather befriended a girl who identified as a boy. Their relationship became so intense that staff considered it unhealthy and separated them. Soon after, Heather announced she was "Harry," "they/them." Regarding that decision, she told me a year later that she'd thought, "I think I'll try it. It will make me happy."

Hospital staff rubber-stamped her male identity, adding gender dysphoria to her long list of diagnoses.

Also long was Heather's list of medications: Tegretol, a mood stabilizer; Risperdal, an anti-psychotic; Celexa, an antidepressant; Trazodone for sleep; and Benadryl as needed up to four times a day for acute anxiety. Heather was fifteen.

Her parents disagreed with the hospital; they considered "Harry" to be another manifestation of her mental illness. They saw her as suffering primarily from features of borderline personality, a disorder characterized by instability in emotions, relationships, and identity.

But hospital staff continued to call their daughter "Harry." Heather was discharged to an out-of-state residential treatment center (RTC) where she remained for six months. The treatment center, like the therapeutic program mentioned in Chapter Six, used only birth names and correct pronouns. Heather attended frequent individual, group, and family therapy sessions. The "Harry" persona slowly faded. Heather went back home as Heather, on one medication, ready to return to school.

Her parents were clear with the principal that should Heather request it, the school was under no condition to affirm a male identity. They put their wishes in writing more than once. The director of the RTC, and Heather's therapist there, spoke with the principal and explained that social affirmation was contraindicated. Heather now had a local non-affirming therapist and psychiatrist, and everyone was on board—or so her parents thought.

Two months into the school year, another mom from the school casually mentioned that "Harry" was using the boy's bathroom. The principal pointed to district policy instructing schools to respect students' wishes. Even after explicit written instructions from parents and mental health professionals, the school had secretly facilitated Heather's social transition. Her parents put their foot down, but the school wouldn't budge. Only following my letter detailing how social transition may harm Heather, coupled with a cease-and-desist letter from attorneys, did the school cave.

## A Child Is Not a Miniature Adult

I began fighting transgender ideology in schools years ago. In 2013, I traveled to Sacramento to testify[1] against Senate Bill 48, [2] legislation mandating instruction in "the cultural and racial diversity of our society" starting in kindergarten. The bill seemed reasonable: who doesn't want their child to learn about the contributions of Americans of diverse races? But included in California's list of "diversity" was transgenderism.

In my testimony, I pointed out what was once common sense: "The authors of this bill . . . have ignored the fundamental principles of child development. Children process and integrate information and experiences differently than adults. There are facts that a child cannot easily assimilate because he simply lacks to the tools to do so.

"A child is not a miniature adult," I reminded legislators. That's why we have movie ratings and computers filters. I continued:

> This Bill mandates the introduction of ideas into the classroom without considering the capacity of the students to absorb them. For example, transgenderism—the idea that nature made a mistake, and a person is trapped in the wrong body. The idea that a person might ask a doctor to remove a

normal body part. These are difficult concepts for adults to comprehend, let alone children.

Please tell me, how does one explain to first graders in an age-appropriate way, the idea of a person coming to a doctor and asking for critical body parts to be removed? There is no age-appropriate way that that can be done.

This Bill ignores the principles of normal child development which are that at around age three a boy knows that he is a boy. He identifies himself as a boy. That's called gender identity. By age four, the boy should know that he will grow up and become a man. That's called gender stability. By six, seven at the latest, a child, say a boy, should know that he cannot become a girl even if he wears a dress—that's called gender permanence.

If this Bill becomes law these principles go out the window. Children will learn that gender permanence does not exist. They'll be led to believe a woman can turn into a man and a man into a woman.

It is our responsibility to protect children as best we can from exposure to facts and experiences that they are not equipped to handle. . . . Certainly, we can teach children the importance of respect and tolerance in a manner that is consistent with child development and biological truth.

I thought my proposal was a no-brainer, but the California legislature passed the bill, opening the door to increasingly aggressive indoctrination of students like Heather.

Does your children's school follow the model legislated by California's Senate Bill 48? If so, "diversity" refers not only to race, ethnicity, and sex, but to transgender-identifying individuals. Therefore, if you don't accept your child's opposite sex identity, you're no better than a racist. Your home is unsafe, and your child might be better off with a different family.

A Wisconsin high school displayed a sign: "If Your Parents Aren't Accepting of Your Identity I'm Your Mom Now."[3] In deep-red Oklahoma, a tattooed eighth-grade teacher with a unique hair style posted a video announcing, "If your parents don't accept you for who you are, f*ck them. I'm your parents now."[4]

Another teacher proudly posted a video criticizing the "right wing idea of parents' rights." Sporting a nose ring and rainbow glasses, the teacher declared parents' rights as "literally just fascism. . . . Parents and caregivers who reject their children's gender identities are not taking care of their children."[5]

Tell that to Heather's parents. The pain and sacrifice they endured trying to help her could fill several chapters. No matter. To this teacher,

Heather's mother and father "are not taking care of" her, and their legal rights are "fascism."

In this book I'm talking about dangerous ideas. The dangerous idea of educators is: we know better than you what's best for your kids.

## At the Library

Students—especially young ones—look up to their teachers. Teachers know everything and are never mistaken. When classrooms are decorated with trans posters, rainbow flags, and slogans,[6] it shapes students' attitudes.

One California teacher packed up the American flag in her classroom; it made her feel uncomfortable. After a student asked to which flag he should pledge allegiance, she suggested the gay pride and trans flag.[7]

When an elementary school teacher displays a "pride library" in her class, with rainbow banners and books about changing pronouns,[8] students perceive her wishes, what she hopes they'll believe.

Speaking of books, entire sections of school libraries feature transgender content. The Los Angeles Unified School District received "an enormous donation of LGBTQIA-themed books" from Open Books (previously called Gender nation), an organization that celebrates transgender identities in children.[9]

We've already talked about one book on LA school shelves—likely in your school library too: *I am Jazz.*

*I am Jazz*[10] was published in 2014; you met the author in Chapter Three. Jazz explains, *I have a girl brain but a boy body. This is called transgender. I was born this way!* From a medical perspective, that's nonsense. But your child is innocent and trusting.

Your four-year-old will believe her teacher when she states with certainty, "The only way to really know if someone is a boy or a girl is to ask them!"[11]

Haim Ginott, a famed child psychologist, said, "Children are like wet cement. Whatever falls on them makes an impression." Parents, everything your child sees and hears shapes her little heart, mind, and soul. Activist "educators" know that. From the youngest age, children absorb beliefs about transgenderism in their classrooms, their books, from the Disney Channel, even from their Legos.[12]

The bombardment of falsehoods without opportunity to question is called indoctrination. Lies are not presented as theory, but as unquestionable truths: Jazz *was* born in the wrong body. The doctors *did* make a mistake in identifying Jazz as a boy. Therefore, Jazz's body *must* be "aligned" with drugs and surgeries.

Listening to *I am Jazz* in preschool, your son is led to believe "boy" and "girl" are random designations and could very well be incorrect. I remind you that this is an Article of Faith. The idea will be repeated endless times. No one should be surprised, then, that he might wonder, maybe I'm a girl too? Maybe my sister is a boy? My mom a man?

A 2022 poll found only 18 percent of those over 65 believe "gender is an identity that is distinct from a person's biological sex." That number rose to 27 percent for 45-to 64-year-olds, 46 percent for those between 30 and 44 years old, and a whopping 61 percent for 18-to-29-year-olds![13]

Trust me, those numbers are only going up. The researchers didn't question anyone under eighteen, but I bet up to 90 percent of grade schoolers think sex has no bearing on gender.

Why? Because they're more familiar with *I am Jazz* than with *The Cat in the Hat*. And because of teachers like the one in North Carolina who taught her preschoolers about colors using flashcards that depicted a pregnant "man."[14] *Preschool*. That's three-to-four-year-olds being taught that men can have babies.

## The Danger of Social Transition

We've discussed trans ideology's spread through websites, social media, and peer groups, but schools are perhaps most influential. Students not only respect teachers, they give schools the best hours of their day—when their alertness and possibility for engagement are at their peak.

Social transition is the public adoption of a new gender identity, including some or all of the following: a new name and pronouns; altering one's presentation such as clothing, hairstyle, make-up, etc.; use of opposite sex facilities like bathrooms and lockers rooms. It may also include chest binding or genital tucking.

Social transition is sometimes called social affirmation—an Orwellian term if there ever was one, because what it affirms is your child's rejection of their body, their material reality. With social "affirmation," you and other adults endorse the child's belief he or she is in the wrong body. But there is no such thing. Affirming a falsehood is not a loving gesture, especially when it leads to harm.

For Heather, social transitioning meant living a double life. At home she was Heather. At school she was "Harry." Her mother called *her* down to dinner. Her teacher called on *them* to answer a question. For an emotionally disturbed girl seeking to escape her biological reality, living out different personalities was destabilizing. But the school did it anyway.

Most parents think affirmation is the decent thing to do, and I can already hear their objections: *"What's the harm of new names and pronouns? Kids go through phases. It's not like medical transitioning—social transition is completely reversible."*

"Affirmation" has a positive connotation, and when ideologues chose that word it was a strategic move. Affirming your child seem kind and loving. Instead of distressed, she's comfortable. She's happy. But it's not kind or loving to validate an untruth.

Adults have a responsibility to represent reality. The reality is your daughter's sex was established at conception.

If you fail to convey that truth—and if your daughter's school allows her to secretly adopt a new persona—she could be moving in a perilous direction.

Some studies show social transition improves short-term mental health, others do not.[15] How about the *long-term* impact of social affirmation on teens like Heather, with (ROGD)? We don't know.

We do know this: with the younger kids, supporting an opposite-sex identity makes it more likely the child will remain dysphoric.

A Dutch study found "affective cross-gender identification and a social role transition" were "associated with the persistence of childhood [gender dysphoria]."[16]

Dr. Kenneth Zucker agreed: "Social transition of prepubertal children will increase dramatically the rate of gender dysphoria persistence."[17]

*Pediatrics* reported: Of children who were six to seven years old when they socially transitioned, by the age of eleven to twelve, 97.5 percent remained transgender-identified or "nonbinary."[18]

In case you're still wondering what that is, I will remind you of my fifteen-year-old patient's definition: "It basically means, I haven't figured this sh*t out yet."

Might Jazz have desisted? It's certainly possible. Remember, by young adulthood 61–88 percent of early-onset kids, depending on the study, cease wanting to be the other sex. But almost every child who socially transitions continues to reject their sex.

Social transition is a big deal; it's not a simple kindness or show of respect.

If you validate your son's girl identity, you agree that his body is wrong, and should be rejected. You confirm the disconnect between his mind and his physical reality. You agree he knows best who he is, and what he needs, and you inform everyone else in his life to follow suit: change how they speak, change how *they think*.

Putting aside whether any of that is sensible, think of the impact on your son. He feels he's a girl, and you agree! He wants to run the show, and you're stepping aside.

*I'm listened to. I'm special. I'm getting so much attention at home and school. Adults are making big changes for me.* He's never felt so empowered. You've turbocharged his self-esteem. Of course it feels good, at least temporarily.

Consider also the possibility that your son's social affirmation may affect the wiring of his brain. You heard me right. Neuroplasticity is the well-established phenomenon in which thinking, behavior, and experience alter brain microstructure.[19] Each time your son hears his new name and pronouns it's a learning experience that creates a memory. We all know repetition is key to learning. We know as well that the brain is constantly rewiring—its structure is changing—in response to life experiences.

Back to Heather, from a plasticity perspective, each instance of being called "Harry" and "they/them" is another learning experience for her brain.

That's one reason Heather's parents objected to "Harry," and I supported them. The new name and pronouns concretize her false beliefs, perhaps even on a cellular level.

Haim Ginott was right: Kids' brains are like wet cement, and over time that cement hardens. If your son is told yes, he is a boy and uses a male name, pronouns, and clothes, that changes how he thinks of himself.

I wonder, when my professional organization, the American Academy of Child and Adolescent Psychiatry (AACAP), advises parents to "Use the name and gender pronouns (e.g., 'he/she/they') your child prefers,"[20] do they give any thought to these legitimate questions?

There's another issue to consider. What if after one or two years, or more, your son starts to doubt: he's not sure about his girl identity after all. Now he has a dilemma. Yes, he had been so sure. His parents, teachers, friends, therapist, principal, and even the lunch lady went through the trouble of accepting his new identity, and getting used to his new name and pronouns. Everyone was careful not to misgender or "deadname" him. There were many phone calls, appointments, and meetings. He got to use the girls' bathroom. Maybe it caused conflict within the family, between you and your spouse, siblings, or grandparents. You went through a lot, all for him, because he was so sure.

How do he make a U-turn after all that? Even an adult would need lots of confidence and courage.

## Iatrogenic Persistence

Dr. Zucker calls social transition a psychosocial intervention "with the likely consequence of subsequent (lifelong) biomedical treatments. . . (gender-affirming hormonal treatment and surgery)." He argues it's an intervention often conducted by schools and other institutions unqualified to implement such a course of treatment. [21]

In 2014, the American Psychological Association (APA) warned: "[P]remature labeling of gender identity should be avoided" and "early social transition . . . should be approached with caution to avoid foreclosing this stage of (trans)gender identity development." They added that social transition might be "challenging to reverse" even if the person is no longer gender dysphoric. [22]

Dr. Hilary Cass, whom you read about in Chapter Six, allows for social transition in some cases. But in her investigative report of GIDS she warned that social transition "is not a neutral act" but an "active intervention" because of the profound impact it has on a child psychology. [23]

Still think that social transitioning is "no big deal"—that Heather's parents overreacted? Here's Dr. Stephen Levine's opinion: [24]

> With rare exceptions, educators do not have the professional training and experience necessary to guide children and parents through the difficult and **potentially life-altering decisions** surrounding social transition to a transgender identity . . . [emphasis added]
>
> Social transition of pre-pubertal children is a major, experimental, and controversial psychotherapeutic intervention that substantially changes outcomes . . .
>
> . . . studies conducted before the widespread use of social transition for young children reported desistance rates in the range of 80–98 percent, a more recent study reported that fewer than 20 percent of boys who engaged in a partial or complete social transition before puberty had desisted when surveyed at age fifteen or older . . .
>
> Some vocal practitioners of prompt affirmation and social transition even claim that essentially no children who come to their clinics exhibiting gender dysphoria or cross-gender identification desist in that identification and return to a gender identity consistent with their biological sex.

Dr. Levine was referencing a 2022 study by pro-affirmation researcher Kristina Olson, who inadvertently confirmed 98 percent of gender-dysphoric children affirmed at an early age remain transgender after five years.[25]

## "Rehoming" Your Child

Is your child leading a double life, a boy under your roof, a girl at school? Do peers and teachers call him by a girl's name and pronouns? Perhaps he wears a dress and lipstick in his geometry class?

You may want to check.

The daughter of January and Jeffrey Littlejohn in Tallahassee, Florida, became gender confused during the pandemic. When her school reopened, officials asked her gender preference without her parents' permission. When January called the school about it, they were tight-lipped. They said by law they couldn't share what they had discussed in secret with the thirteen-year-old unless her daughter consented.[26]

Only later did the Littlejohns discover their daughter had signed a "gender non-conforming student support plan" with the school's vice principle, guidance counselor, and a social worker. The plan included questions about which bathroom their daughter wanted to use, which sex she wanted to room with on overnight trips, and, most damaging, how the school should refer to her when they speak to her parents.

These adults—at least one of whom was a stranger—were conducting a psychosocial intervention on a young girl without her parents' consent. The Littlejohns discovered the district policy stated, "parents are not to be informed when their children announce a transgender identity with school personnel."[27]

Parents in Massachusetts sued middle-school teachers, alleging they were secretly urging their children to socially transition. The teachers were "intentionally concealing that information" from the parents. The school district asserts that students "may decide to discuss their gender identity openly and may decide when, with whom, and how much to share private information."[28]

One teacher in that Massachusetts school—Bonnie Manchester—thought it was wrong to keep what she knew from parents. She told one of the dads that his sixth-grade daughter changed her name and pronouns at school. For that, Manchester was fired.[29]

California teacher Jessica Tapia faced a similar crisis. She asked her district, "Are you asking me to lie to parents [about their child]?" The district answered, "Yes, it's the law." Jessica refused to lie if a student came out as trans and refused to allow boys in the girls' locker room. She too was fired.[30]

These aren't isolated instances in deep-blue localities. Undermining parents is built into the education system. Consider the case of Amy Cannava, a school psychologist in Virginia. She fought against a proposed Virginia policy requiring schools inform parents when their child starts to present as the opposite sex.

"You have to sometimes break rules to do good for kids," she said on a podcast, later adding in another episode, "I recognize that parental consent is a big deal, but when I'm doing anything LGBT, I don't worry about that. . . . Let's be honest, it's an electronic permission slip. You type in a parent's name and I'm like, 'Oh, that parent signed consent.' There's no actual signature."[31]

On a private message board for the organization Pride Liberation Project, Cannava was featured as a point of contact for kids who face "familial rejection": "in the event of you needing to leave your home, we can provide you with emergency housing from a supportive, Queer friendly adult."[32]

You might be familiar with the term "rehome," meaning to find a new home—typically in reference to a pet. The word is now applied to children. As a child psychiatrist, I am aware there are homes that are unsafe and rare instances in which children must live elsewhere. But we have to examine this closely, because if you choose to keep calling your gender-dysphoric son or daughter their given names, Amy Cannava and others probably consider that "familial rejection." The group offers to pick him or her up "within one or two days" and take them to "a kind and affirming home."

Cannava is the chair of the National Association of School Psychologists' (NASP) LGBTQI2-S Committee, a prominent position in an influential professional organization.

NASP is in the bag for hiding your child's new identity from you. Their guidelines instruct school psychologists to "maintain confidentiality of the student's birth sex, gender identity, and gender expression by keeping identifying records separate and limiting unnecessary disclosure, doing so only with the explicit assent of the student."[33]

NASP is only one of numerous professional associations shaping school policies and training school personnel that have been captured by gender activists.

The National Association of Secondary School Principals (NASSP) calls for schools to allow social transition—including cross-sex dressing and use of opposite sex locker rooms, restrooms, and overnight facilities.[34] If parents wonder what's going on, NASSP threatens "disclosure of [transgender status] to other school staff or parents could violate the school's obligations under FERPA* or constitutional privacy protections."[35]

Do you see what I mean? School staff believe they know better than you what's good for your child.

The American School Counselor Association (ASCA) recommends using special markers to note when a student uses a new name unbeknownst to parents. "If students have not disclosed their gender identity to a parent or guardian," the group says, "their chosen/affirmed name should be noted as 'preferred name' in the system." Meanwhile, "the right to privacy and prohibition of disclosing student's gender identity extends to students' parents/guardians."[36]

In the face of legislation to restrict trans indoctrination and require parental notification of a child's gender identity, the former president and current ethics chairman of ASCA, Carolyn Stone, told members at their annual 2022 conference to "learn the rules so you know how to break them."[37] Yes, I'm quoting the chair of ethics!

How about the National Education Association? "Privacy and confidentiality are critically important for transgender students who do not have supportive families . . . so it is important to have a plan in place to help avoid any mistakes or slip-ups."[38]

The Department of Education? Schools should maintain "the confidentiality of a student's birth name or sex assigned at birth if the student wishes to keep this information private."[39]

The National Association of Social Workers? "Let [transgender kids] decide when to come out and to whom. . . . Do not disclose the identity of young people who are LGBTQI2-S without their permission."[40]

I hope you understand. All these powerful groups believe you don't have a right to know your teen daughter is changing in the boys' locker room, and that if you have an issue with that, maybe it's time to "rehome" her.

## Glistening Classrooms

Think of all these groups as satellites of a mothership called GLSEN—pronounced "glisten"—formerly the Gay, Lesbian & Straight Education Network. They've been laying siege to our educational system since 1990. If there's a single organization responsible for transforming your child's

---

* For more information on FERPA, please see Appendix Three.

teacher, principal, and guidance counselor into gender warriors, and filling your child's classroom with trans symbols, books, and flags, it's GLSEN.

In their own words, GLSEN "strives to dismantle all identity-based oppressions"[41] in K-12 public and private schools. We're talking about a large operation here. Among many other activities, GLSEN provides teacher training, lesson plans, school policy guides, "inclusive" curriculum, and Gender and Sexuality Alliance (GSA) clubs in schools nationwide. They collaborate with associations that accredit private and public schools and maintain a public policy office in Washington.

A priority is recruiting students. This is done through GSA clubs and teacher indoctrination, of course, but also through school programs—always clothed in the language of respect, civil rights, and freedom.

As GLSEN explains to students on their website, the purpose of programs such as "Day of Silence" and "Solidarity Week" is "to give you the tools that you need to urge your school to address and help end anti-LGBTQ+ bullying and help build a school community around solidarity and respect for all."

"Respect for all," sure, unless your daughter prefers to "pledge allegiance to the flag of the United States of America, and to the Republic for which it stands." Then she's a hate-filled fascist transphobe. Do you really think anyone is going to sit with her in the lunchroom?

GLSEN instructs[42] all school staff to immediately, upon her request, affirm your daughter's boy identity by using her new name and pronouns. This mandate extends to her peers.

GLSEN doesn't fool around:

> Having a policy that clearly affirms a student's right to use the name and pronouns that are consistent with their gender identity is essential for the health and safety of the student. While mistakes happen, it is important for staff, faculty, and peers to make every effort to correct mistakes, ensure they are not repeated, and address any intentional misuse of a student's name or pronouns.[43]

They're instructing schools that "misgendering" and "deadnaming" should not be tolerated as per the Articles of Faith.

GLSEN's edict includes your daughter's right—without your permission or knowledge—to use the boys' restrooms, locker rooms, and changing facilities and to participate in all boys' physical education, athletics, and other extracurricular activities. All she needs to do is say the word.

Here's how GLSEN instructs your child's school to keep you in the dark:[44]

> Some transgender and nonbinary students may not yet be out to their parents or guardians. . . . It is essential to have open communication and plans established with the student to go over potential circumstances. For instance, mail may be sent home with a student's prior and/or legal name, which may not be their affirmed name. If a student is not yet out to their parent(s)/guardian(s), using their prior name in correspondence may be the desirable course of action, although they use a different name amongst peers and educators in school. Educators and staff should work closely with the student to determine what changes are necessary, and where, to ensure their safety and well-being.

Now you understand, don't you? What happened at Heather's school, to the Littlejohns, to teachers Bonnie Manchester in Massachusetts and Jessica Tapia in California. The same thing is happening all over the country, and I consider it grooming.

Grooming is emotional and psychological manipulation in order to exploit someone at a later point in time. Often grooming is sexual, but it doesn't have to be.

The grooming that's taking place in schools is ideological. GLSEN seeks to convert your children and add them to their ranks of believers. After thirty years, it's a well-oiled and well-funded process.

A final note to parents about GLSEN. Their website features a special function: hitting the "escape" button three times takes you to the Google homepage. That's for your kids to secretly ingest their content and, when you walk in, to exit quickly.

## Erosion of the Parent-Child Bond

When gender evangelists drive a wedge between you and your child, it harms both of you. Dr. Erica Anderson, the first transgender president of USPATH—a regional affiliate of WPATH—said this about secret social transitions: "It's well established that one of the most important factors in helping gender-questioning children is family support. So to deliberately deprive a child of support at a time potentially when they most need it is, I think, a serious error in judgment."[45]

Studies—one of them involving 90,000 American teens[46]—are unequivocal: Teenagers with strong emotional bonds to their parents fare better. A child must be attached to those responsible for her. Attachment is based, in part, on trust and honesty. When a school facilitates a student's "social affirmation" in the absence of parental consent, it encourages secrecy, distrust, and a "double life." This is unhealthy, will increase tension and conflict in the home, and may precipitate emotional struggles.

If your daughter has different identities at school and at home, she—using the black-and-white thinking of her immature mind—may decide school, not home, fulfills her need for love, understanding, and support; school, not home, nurtures and protects her; school is "safe" and home "unsafe." With rare exceptions, these are dangerous untruths. They erode her attachment to you and threaten her development, and the path to healthy adulthood.

When school staff think they know better than you and drive a wedge into your family, the results can be catastrophic.

They were for Sage Lilly.[47]

The start of Sage's story is sadly familiar to me. Sage had depression, anxiety, and a history of early trauma—the loss of both parents followed by six foster home placements. When she was two, Sage was adopted by her paternal grandparents.

She began ninth grade and reported to her grandmother, Michelle, that all the kids were "bi and trans and emo and gay and goth."[48] Sage soon declared herself a boy at school, "Draco." She wore boys' clothes and used the boys' bathroom. She requested the school not inform her parents, and they obliged. They did this knowing Sage had just been hospitalized for depression and was on psychiatric medication.

Her parents remained in the dark until one day Sage told Michelle, "The boys are following me, they're touching me, they're shoving me, they're threatening me with rape and violence."[49]

One day, the school called Michelle to pick up Sage because she was distraught. Sage admitted that she was identifying as a boy at school and that she had been told by the counselor she could use the boys' bathroom.

Michelle: "She had been jacked up against the wall by a group of boys in the boys' bathroom and threatened with violence. Later I learned there was a rape too. She was trying to hold back tears. . . . I told her she could stay home from school, and we would figure out what to do."

But Sage disappeared that night.
Michelle:

> She actually thought she was meeting—I guess the counselor gave her transgender sites—and she thought she was meeting a sixteen-year-old kid to go skateboarding and it turned out to be a sex trafficker who groomed her online.
>
> Nine days later, the FBI found her in Baltimore, Maryland. She had survived cruel abusive rapes, lost her virginity to multiple vile men and then taken to DC and Maryland, and these men drugged and raped her and transported her to live with their family. That's a code word for sex traffickers to let the guy know that they're seasoning a new kid . . .

There's a lot more to Sage's saga that you'll read in the next chapter. Suffice to say she and her grandparents went through a hellish ordeal, and it all began with her secret social transition at school, and her turning to transgender "support" sites. Whether the school counselor or someone else at school directed Sage to those sites is not clear.

You must be vigilant and proactive regarding schools. Appendix Three outlines how to accomplish both. You must also be prepared to fight as Heather's parents did with a cease-and-desist order. Don't forget—you have the fundamental right, according to the Supreme Court, to control the upbringing and education of your children.[50]

One of my patient's parents wrote to me about the Catch-22 of asserting her preferences at school. From her seasoned perspective, it is a lose-lose- situation:

> One of the big hurdles of this issue is the complexity of the legal, medical, and psychological framework that most people and parents can't comprehend . . . until their kid is on the chopping block. Once you are in this mess, you have to deliberately but gently diffuse the bomb, and battling the school will only paint you as transphobic and pit the child against the parent further.

In my survey of 500 parents, many voiced regrets about the schools their child attended or still attends. I urge parents to remove their children from public school if possible. Home school is best, but not every family can do that. Whatever school you decide on, please, scrutinize it and know your rights.

## The Stroop Effect

When a young person demands the use of an opposite-sex name and pronouns, or some variation thereof, it does not occur in a vacuum. Their social transition impacts everyone they know, especially their peers.

Sara Stockton is a therapist who once wrote letters in support of hormones and surgeries for youth. Then the dangers of gender ideology hit home:

". . . my child, he's ten . . . and he was explaining to me about his friend who transitioned. . . his first question, of course, was 'did this child grow a vagina over the summer? . . . can I grow a vagina over the summer? How do I know I'm not next?' And my son asked me, 'well, how do I know if I'm a boy?' And I was just like, this is scary, and it is disorienting our children."[51]

Yes, it certainly is disorienting, just as I predicted ten years ago in my Sacramento testimony. And to a child with underlying vulnerabilities their peer's transformation can be destabilizing. To her credit, Stockton is now an outspoken critic of the affirming care she once supported.

Consider also that following a student's declaration, for example, a boy announcing "she/her" pronouns, the school compels the use of those pronouns. Is this the simple matter it's made out to be? A sign of decency and respect of others like not cutting in line?

Thanks to a parent, I recently learned about a phenomenon called the Stroop effect,[52] and it needs to be considered in any conversation about social transition.

The Stroop effect demonstrates that brain function is impacted when presented with a mismatched or incongruent stimulus. For example, it's quicker and easier to read "red" if the word appears in red rather than in another color. If "red" appears in green, it takes longer to read, and there is a higher likelihood of error. This has been tested and proven repeatedly.

We do not understand the neurological mechanisms for the Stroop effect, but it's fair to ask, what effect might it have on the brains of anyone trying to use wrong pronouns, but of youth in particular? Their friend was a boy, then one day he is a "girl," and they must override their brain's perceived mismatch and call him "her"—or else.

This has to be particularly hard for children whose brains are developing, for the elderly and for anyone with preexisting cognitive processing issues.

Sage's grandfather, for example. You'll soon hear Michelle describe the custody hearing at which the grandpa who was in his seventies kept forgetting to use Sage's boy name and use the male pronouns. The judge was livid and threatened to throw him out of the courtroom, but it was due to the Stroop effect: the incongruence of having to call his granddaughter "he" and use a name incongruent with who she was nearly impossible. Even though he was trying to be compliant for the sake of a favorable hearing, he kept slipping back into the congruence his brain knew and understood.

Finally, consider that students are told the identities of their peers are private: what happens at school stays at school. Your daughter isn't supposed to tell you she shares a bathroom with boys. That's an enormous secret and, as the incidents of assault by boys in girls' bathrooms attest[53], potentially a treacherous one.

In this chapter you've learned of the catastrophes that may result when educators think they know better than you. Next, we look at Child Protective Services and courts of law. They have dangerous ideas, too.

# CHAPTER NINE

# Lawyers' Dangerous Idea

I walked into the Starbucks in St. Paul and saw Hank—he was exactly as I'd expected. A few weeks earlier he'd posted a comment on the PITT Substack (Parents with Inconvenient Truths about Trans) about the ordeal he went through with his daughter, and I was intrigued. He was eager to meet and share his story.

Hank sat there in jeans and a plaid flannel shirt, three large office storage boxes on the floor, overstuffed with files—his daughter's medical and legal records he wanted me to see.

Hank, a car mechanic, was the definition of salt of the earth. He didn't mince words; he wore his heart and his Christian faith on his sleeve. What you see is what you get.

As I carefully filed through the documents, Hank began his story.

Olivia is a teenager now, but the troubles started much earlier when she was only four. Her mother was always out-of-the box. Still, everyone was shocked when she ran off, in love with a man in Panama she'd met online. One day she was home with Hank and Olivia, the next day she wasn't.

Olivia was never the same. She blamed herself, no matter how many times her dad, therapists, and eventually her loving stepmom and stepbrother said it wasn't her fault. She was emotionally disturbed and didn't fit in at school.

In sixth grade a bully told her to kill herself, and she started cutting.

That began a string of hospital visits, nine over the next four years. I read through the many evaluations and daily notes by psychiatrists, psychologists, and social workers. I didn't have to read much to know that

Olivia suffered from significant mental illness. She had persistent severe depression and self-loathing and an eating disorder. She also lacerated herself from head to toe.

Hank handed me a sheet, part of the intake from one of Olivia's early hospitalizations. I gazed at the body diagram illustrating innumerable lacerations, up and down each arm, thigh, and leg, on her chest and belly. Into her flesh she'd carved "die," "whore," and other words a child shouldn't know.

"She looked like a cutting board," Hank said. I have seen an awful lot in my forty years of psychiatry, but that diagram was shocking. Olivia was twelve years old at the time.

The records indicated Olivia had hallucinations—voices told her to kill and starve herself. "The voices bully me all day long," she told staff, "I don't deserve to live." I read how she overdosed on pills and planned to hang herself from a tree. Aside from an eating disorder, depression, and anxiety, Olivia's diagnoses included psychotic disorder, emerging borderline personality disorder, and schizophrenia.

During her third hospitalization, she developed a crush on another patient, an older girl who identified as a boy. Olivia never had issues with gender, but she soon announced her new name, "Maddox."

"I don't want to be a woman like my mom," she told Hank. He and his wife did not accept her boy identity, and Olivia had a tantrum. Hank told her, "You can't become a boy, it's impossible. We must figure all this out." But Olivia became militant.

Back at the hospital, the staff were on board with "Maddox," and—you guessed it—Hank and his wife were in trouble. "Dad and stepmom are unsupportive," one psychologist wrote. "They are ultra-Christian and do not accept Maddox as their son. They continue to use his birth name." Being the straight arrow that he is, Hank told therapists Olivia is a girl and would always be his daughter no matter what. The issue, he ventured to suggest, wasn't her gender—it was the abandonment by her mother. Why was nobody asking her about that? Why was everyone fixated on names and pronouns?

## An Investigation

Hank and his family were already going through hell. With his bold defiance of the Articles of Faith he did not fathom the abyss into which he was about to descend.

For failing to accept "Maddox," for his constant "deadnaming" and "misgendering," Hank was reported by the hospital social worker to Child

Protection Services (CPS). The allegations were emotional abuse and physical and emotional neglect. An investigation was opened.

Hank had been fighting to save his daughter from herself. Now he had another battle. CPS showed up at his door demanding to interview his stepson. Hank refused. Then they discovered he attends a Bible-believing church. "It was a big problem for them," Hank told me. "They gave me 'edicts'—they told me I must think about how my beliefs affect others."

It sounded unlikely to me; perhaps Hank was exaggerating?

He was not. I found a document from the State of Minnesota Superior Court, Juvenile Matters, called "Specific Steps." It stated Hank and his wife were

> ordered to . . . take part in counseling and make progress toward the following goals: Explore how your own past and present values and beliefs impact the way you function and how you interact with others, and learn and utilize new parenting techniques related to parenting a teenager with mental health and gender identity issues.

The State declared Hank was the problem: "Explore your values and beliefs?" "Learn new parenting techniques?" Their message was clear: if you want to hold onto your child, you better forget about your Bible and your Church, buddy, and toe the line.

Sure, Olivia was psychotic, hearing voices, carving up her body, starving herself, overdosing, and looking for a tree from which to hang herself. Even while taking four psychiatric medications, she was so unstable as to require hospitalization every few months. Her mental illness was severe and her connection to reality tenuous.

It didn't matter. Everyone involved with Olivia's care at the hospitals and at CPS were devotees of the Articles of Faith: *GENDER IDENTITY is sacred. Thou shall honor the self-diagnosis of children.*

As I listened to Hank, and read more and more of Olivia's hospital and legal records, I was dumbfounded.

In one note, a therapist asked Olivia about her gender identity: "It depends on the day," she replied. What about her sexual orientation? "One day it's one thing and the next day it's something else." Yes, Olivia's gender and sexual identities certainly were, as they say, "fluid." In plain language, she was one mixed-up girl.

Again, it didn't matter. She'd claimed at one point to be a boy, and for the hospital staff, that was that. The issue for them, it seems, was Hank wasn't an "ally." CPS left a note on his door: "You are to blame that Maddox is not getting better because you did not affirm him."

Olivia continued to go in and out of hospitals. Hank and his wife wouldn't budge on the gender issue. A friend advised him to lawyer up, but it wasn't easy. Nobody wanted to touch such a hot potato. He eventually located and hired a courageous one.

Hank handed me another document from the State. This one showed CPS made allegations in juvenile court that Olivia is "neglected and uncared for." She was "being denied proper care and attention," and she lived "under conditions injurious to her well-being."

You're probably wondering, what in the world? OK, she was called Olivia at home, not Maddox, but "neglected and uncared for"? "conditions injurious to her well-being"? Really?

I'll explain.

Not long ago, lawyers in Hank's state had an idea: reinterpret "abuse" and "neglect." Being steeped in ideology, they believed gender identity to be the permanent authentic self, and any response to "coming out" aside from immediate validation could lead to suicide. According to the reinterpretation, Hank's insistence on calling his daughter Olivia was emotionally abusive. And his rejection of "affirming care" was medical neglect. That's how CPS could make those outrageous allegations—because of the reinterpretations.

## Allegations Substantiated

One day when Olivia was fourteen and being discharged from the hospital, Hank arrived to take her home. But he learned it wasn't going to happen; the hospital couldn't discharge "Maddox" to him, because family court was placing Olivia in foster care.

Hank showed me another document from CPS: "NOTIFICATION OF INVESTIGATION RESULTS."

The charges of emotional abuse and neglect were substantiated. On the next page was the statement "I disagree with the findings that I have abused or neglected a child," and next to it a box where Hank had placed a big "X."

Hank continued the story. Olivia was put in foster care with two gay men. With this Hank stopped and peered at me quizzically. "Two *men*?" he asked. To this day he couldn't understand the decision by CPS. "But she needed a healthy woman in her life!" he told me, shaking his head.

Hank was not provided with an address or phone number for his daughter. He told me how he and his lawyer disputed the investigation results, and

| Child's Name | Allegation | Disposition |
|---|---|---|
| ███████ | Physical Neglect | Unsubstantiated |
| ███████ | Emotional Abuse | Substantiated |
| ███████ | Emotional Neglect | Substantiated |
| | (Select One) | (Select One) |
| | (Select One) | (Select One) |
| | (Select One) | (Select One) |

how he fought to see Olivia. There were countless motions and hearings, but Hank didn't give up. He wrote his state representatives and Health and Human Services.

In the midst of the Kafkaesque ordeal, Hank made a discovery. "I kept getting EOBs* from my health insurance with laboratory charges for Olivia. I wondered, is something wrong? Why does she need so much bloodwork? My lawyer discovered they'd put my daughter on hormones. I was completely against hormones, and my attorney made that clear to the court. But the men Olivia lived with advocated for blockers and testosterone, and they were authorized by a CPS medical panel."

I knew before our meeting that Hank's story was going to be rough to hear. But with each passing minute it was getting more hideous.

"This went on for a few years," Hank explained. "I was unable to see Olivia and she wouldn't accept mail or gifts from us. She cut herself off—even her cousins and grandparents. My insurance was paying for the testosterone, and I didn't want to have anything to do with it. If I continued the fight, CPS would force me into therapy and interrogate me and my family. I was also worried I could lose my estate if I die, because the State could take my money for all her treatments. I have another child to care for.

"We had no contact for two and a half years and she was almost eighteen. I couldn't take it anymore. So I relinquished my parental rights."

---

* Explanation of Benefits

I spoke to Hank's lawyer about the case. "CPS is dangerous," she told me. "Parents need to know they have a right to representation from the first moment of contact."

## Lawyers' Dangerous Ideas

In medical school I learned about child abuse and neglect, and later on, as a doctor in a busy New York City emergency room, I came across such cases. For example, once I saw a child in need of an urgent blood transfusion, but her parents wouldn't permit it on religious grounds. Another time I had a thirteen-year-old with a mouth full of rotten teeth: he'd never been to the dentist. There were kids who kept showing up with poorly explained black eyes, burns, and broken bones. In these cases and others, following consultation with the hospital social worker, I sometimes reported my suspicions of neglect or abuse to CPS. That was my professional obligation, and that's what I did.

I know CPS serves an important role when families must be investigated, and in those rare instances when a child must be removed from their home. But parents calling their child by their given name is emotional abuse? And refusing interventions that validate their child's impossible identity is medical neglect?

No. Absolutely not.

Lawyers' new interpretations mean parents like Hank are in the same category as the parents I met who never took their kid to a dentist or refused a life-saving blood transfusion. That's preposterous.

Hank's position, grounded in reality, was the one every responsible adult must take. Olivia was a girl, and that would never change. To endorse her false belief was not a kindness. If Hank was guilty of anything, it was the crime of having common sense and speaking the truth fearlessly.

The number of cases in which courts adopt the reinterpretations and decide against parents like Hank who oppose their child's social transition and medicalization is rising. In Arizona, parents who insisted their daughter is a girl lost custody.[1] In Dallas, a judge awarded full custody to an "affirming" mom, ordering the father he must consent to her decisions regarding medical interventions.[2] In Indiana, a court removed a minor from his parents' custody because they refused to accept his female identity.[3]

In California, an affirming mother received full custody while the nonaffirming father was banned from seeing or even speaking to his son. After being grilled on his views about transgenderism, the father learned the judge, Joni Hiromoto, had affirmed her own child.[4]

Hiromoto claims to have queried whether she needed to recuse herself, but I suspect that she was less than forthright about her ability to be impartial, especially in light of the fact that she presented a continuing education course in which she basically stated that the parent who will support the child's delusion is always the more fit parent. She shared her panel with one of the most prolific transgender activists, attorney Asaf Orr, a lead author of the HRC's *Schools in Transition: A Guide for Supporting Transgender Students in K-12* that counsels teachers that in a custody battle, they should testify on behalf of the parent who will support transition.

## "The Best Interest of the Child"
California Assembly Member Lori Wilson, who also transitioned her daughter, and Senator Scott Wiener, a childless gay man who authored SB 48 to teach transgenderism starting in kindergarten, discussed previously, coauthored AB 957, a bill to codify what's already happening in family court rooms. This bill will tip the scale in custody and visitation battles.

It states that courts should "strongly consider" that affirmation is in the best interest of the child, especially when faced with a "nonconsenting parent" who objects to the minor's gender identity.⁵ With a super majority of Democrats, the bill has already passed the Assembly and has little impediments to become the law, a law that will spread to other states, including red ones.

The acceptance of a child's self-diagnosis and the immediate use of preferred names and pronouns are Articles of Faith. It is not up for debate. Having read this far, you understand that so-called social affirmation is a controversial psychosocial intervention for which evidence of long-term benefit is lacking. There is evidence, however, that it may solidify a child's false identity, increasing the likelihood of risky medical interventions. Nevertheless, social affirmation is being legislated as the soundest approach for every child.

The legislation will lead to more demonization of dissenting parents (usually fathers), more destruction of parent-child bonds, and more disfigurement and sterilization of young people.

Yet proponents talk about "the best interest of the child." I don't think so.

If AB 957 passes, the state of California will be warning parents they better lie, or else. They better lie to their child, lie to the world, and ultimately lie to themselves. It may already be too late, but I hope there are still some who will heed Jordan Peterson's wisdom:

"The way that totalitarian states develop is that people give up their right to be, to exist, with their own thoughts. They lie. The individuals sacrifice their own souls to the dictates of the state. . . . You falsify your being bit by bit."[6]

So beware, parents, if you refuse to go along with your child's new persona and fail to provide her with "affirming" care. In other words, if you won't "sacrifice your soul," you may be found guilty of emotional abuse and medical neglect. A judge could then "rehome" your child.

If that isn't horrifying, I don't know what is.

## Back to Sage's Story

You remember Sage—her school permitted her secret social transition when she was fourteen. She then met a sex trafficker posing as a sixteen-year-old boy on a trans "support site." We left her story when she was saved by the FBI after nine days of sexual abuse.

Sage's grandparents drove all night to pick her up and bring her home—the backseat of the car filled with blankets and stuffed animals. Eager to see Sage after such a harrowing separation, they discovered she'd been assigned an attorney and could not return home without a hearing.

Her grandmother, Michele, described the Maryland court scene:[7]

> Sage comes up on a huge Zoom screen. She looks tiny and broken, and I cry out, "I love you, Sage." Sage says, "I love you too, Nana."
>
> The public defender, Issa Khan, quickly takes over and points the finger at us for calling her "Sage." "She's a *he* and *his* name is Draco not 'Sage'" . . . we are floored. . .
>
> The attorney proceeds to advise the judge that we are emotionally and physically abusive parents and that we aren't using the right name and pronouns . . .
>
> We were willing to use any name and pronouns. I just wanted her . . . back home. . . . But my husband, he's seventy-three. He was overcome with tears. He kept forgetting [to use male pronouns], so the judge got so upset and exasperated he had the bailiff take him out of the courtroom. I am crying and pleading for my daughter to be sent home so she can receive treatment for the trauma she endured. Judge Kershaw told me if I said trauma one more time, he would throw me out too. . . . So we had to leave without her . . .

For two months Khan tried to prove Michelle and her husband were abusive, even bringing in school counselors to testify against them. During that time Sage was housed in—can you guess?—a home for disturbed teen boys, where she was, yes, assaulted again.

Listen closely: had Sage's school prohibited social transitioning instead of encouraging it, if the boy's bathroom was off-limits to her, if the school had shared and not concealed her gender struggles with her parents, if the words "abuse" and "neglect" were still interpreted in a reasonable manner, this nightmare, this dreadful horror (none of these words seem adequate) would not have happened. It was entirely preventable.

Sage told her math teacher she was going to run away, and the teacher gave her a backpack. Sage disappeared for months. Michelle dived into Sage's social media, and her daughter was finally located locked away in a room in Texas, trafficked again.

There's even more to this story, about attorney Khan and Judge Kershaw, enough to fill an entire book, maybe two. You can look up the details yourself—no one should ever suffer what poor Sage and her parents endured.[8]

Cleared of charges and with effective legal representation, Michelle and her husband finally brought Sage home. She'd been gone almost a year. Reflecting on her past confusion, she told her grandmother, "I never was a boy. Everybody was doing it, I just wanted to have friends."[9]

Sound familiar? Sage had early trauma and comorbidities, and her peers were all LGBT, emo, and goth. Seeking acceptance, she became "Draco." Yup—another case of ROGD.

I'm going to be generous here and assume all the people whose actions led to catastrophe had good intentions. I'm pretty sure Sage's school counselor, her lawyer Issa Khan, and Judge Kershow never heard of Lisa Littman, the Dutch Protocol, or GIDS. They're unaware that the few studies we have on kids like Sage are poor quality, there's no consensus on how to help them, and some experts oppose new names and pronouns. They only know one thing: parents like Sage's are abusive and drive their kids to suicide. Hence their mighty effort to prevent her return home.

I'm not saying everyone at every school, or every judge, lawyer, and CPS agent is entrenched in radical gender ideology. I'm saying some are, and you must be prepared.

Will the CPS agent at your door or the judge deciding your case see things as you do? Will they help your troubled child, or endanger him? Or are they activists with medicalized children of their own, fervent devotees of the Articles of Faith, following the Castro consensus, trusting the affirmation lobby?

In the legal system, it's Russian roulette. Maybe the judge or CPS agent will be reasonable, they may compromise and permit use of a child's nickname or the first syllable of her new name—parents sometimes come up with creative solutions to the name issue.

I want to recognize that social work agencies also have among their ranks individuals who truly protect children and families.

Brette in Illinois had an unexpected visit from a social worker after she posted a celebratory message about her daughter's desistance. Brette's post became the target of harassment by a radical group who sicced the DCFS on her, claiming her daughter Anna was being abused. Thankfully, after meeting Anna and being shown the social media evidence, the social worker confirmed it wasn't Anna who was being abused. Instead, she counseled Brette to file a police report.

Brette:

> I'm lucky I had one [Department of Child and Family Services social worker] that I showed her my tweet and the messages I had, and she was just like—I'm scared for YOU actually. . . . I think you guys are in danger but you're not the cause of the danger and she was the one who actually made me file a police report.[10]

Like I said, it's Russian roulette. One thing is sure, never go it alone. As parents, you have rights, including the right to forbid a CPS agent from entering your home and questioning you without legal counsel [see Appendix Four].

## Yaeli's Story

Sixteen-year-old Yaeli Galdamez was bullied at her Los Angeles school and suffered from anxiety and depression. She learned about being transgender from a school counselor, an LGBT group, and the mother of a trans-identified girl, a.k.a. a "glitter mom." Glitter moms are usually LGBT or have an LGBT child; they imagine themselves saviors of children from homes less rainbow-friendly than theirs.[11]

Soon Yaeli informed her mom, Abigail, that her name was "Andrew." Her mother considered the new identity a symptom of her emotional issues. She didn't agree with a new name and pronouns, and she certainly wouldn't permit hormones.

One day, Abigail and Yaeli got into a fight over an iPad,[12] and Yaeli, aided by the glitter mom, ran away. She was lured by the promise that anyone older than twelve can dictate their own medical care once in the California foster system.[13]

And so began another dreadful saga of a disturbed adolescent, indoctrinated to believe she's in the wrong body, that fleeing biology is the sole solution, and that anyone in her way is transphobic. And yet another epic failure of the educational, social services, medical, and legal institutions charged with protecting her.

Abigail searched for hours and found Yaeli, who then claimed she'd been physically abused by her mom; she'd been coached to lie by her "allies." When her claims were unsubstantiated, Yaeli asserted she was emotionally abused because her mother didn't affirm "Andrew." Using the new interpretation, the court agreed and removed Yaeli from Abigail's home.[14]

She tried her best to get her daughter back, going to court every month.[15] Desperate to keep a connection, Abigail played by the rules. She used her daughter's chosen names, even as they changed. She was visited regularly by members of the trans-advocacy group, RISE.[16] One of them encouraged her to "have a funeral for your daughter and adopt your son." Abigail said they told her not to talk about God with Yaeli: "They told me if you do that, you'll never see your daughter."[17]

While the legal wrangling continued, Yaeli, age sixteen, was brought to the gender clinic at Children's Hospital Los Angeles and given testosterone. Abigail, an immigrant with English as a second language, did not stand a chance against the well-funded gender center, the lawyers trying to make their names as civil rights heroes and the judges who were trained that Yaeli's male identity was real and immutable.

RISE convinced the court that Yaeli needed testosterone and to be saved from her family. Abigail lost custody.[18]

For three years, Yaeli moved from facility to facility, sleeping on floors and struggling with mental and physical anguish. By the time she turned nineteen, after three years of testosterone, her mental health had not improved.[19] It didn't turn out as Yaeli had been promised: life as a boy didn't free her from pain.

This was one instance in which rejecting biology was literally a dead-end. One day, Yaeli walked down to the railroad tracks, knelt between the cold metal rails, and removed herself from this world.[20]

When Abigail showed up, the police urged her to look away. Her daughter's body had to be picked up in pieces off the tracks and in a tree.[21]

Instead of acknowledging that transition fails to resolve suicidality, the cruel media spin was that Abigail abandoned Yaeli. If only she'd supported her daughter's gender journey, they want you to think, Yaeli would have been fine. Only followers of the Articles of Faith believe such garbage.

## Sage's Law

For a brief time, it appeared something positive might emerge from Sage's year in purgatory. Virginia's Child Protection Act,[22] nicknamed "Sage's Law," was proposed to protect kids like her in three ways. It required schools to notify parents if their child asserts a gender different from his or her sex; it prevented school counselors from withholding or encouraging minors to withhold information about a child's gender identity; and it asserted that raising a child according to his or her biological sex may not be construed as abuse.[23]

Sage's Law was passed by the Republican-controlled State House but defeated in the Senate Education and Health Committee on a 9–6 vote, with all Democrats voting against the bill and all Republicans voting for it.[24]

Michelle testified in support of the bill. Sadly, some legislators ignored her wise words:

> We love our children more than any counselor, judge, or teacher. They have no business teaching our children what gender they are and certainly no business teaching them to keep secrets from their parents. Let us parents do our job. we know our children better than you do.[25]

❋    ❋    ❋

After four hours, Hank and I were both weary. It would take me time to absorb everything I'd seen and heard, I told him. As we stood in the parking lot, he returned to what was for him the most mysterious element of the entire saga: the State placing Olivia with two gay men. He shook his head, incredulous: "But she needed a healthy woman in her life!"

I told Hank he was right. He was a car mechanic, but he had more wisdom than all the doctors and social workers put together.

As we said our good-byes, Hank pressed me, "Please, doctor, tell my story. Describe what they did to us. I want the world to know."

I promised him I would, and so I have.

# CHAPTER TEN

# Mourning the Living

In the fall of 2021, I offered to give some educational sessions for parents of ROGD kids. By then I'd talked to maybe one hundred parents and read a few dozen testimonies on PITT. Each one's horror story was worse than the next, and many felt lost, with nowhere to turn. My heart ached for them, and I wanted to do something.

I ran the idea by AC—her adult son has lived as a woman for a few years. AC lives in South Carolina and is one of the warriors in this battle: she organized and led Zoom meetings for parents of ROGD kids. Parents came from private or secret Facebook groups, and from other parent organizations, national and international. Most provided only first names or initials.

Joining one of those groups was not an easy process: there was a rigorous vetting system. First, parents had to complete a lengthy questionnaire about themselves and their child. Then they waited weeks for a response. Then one of the leaders of the group emailed with more questions. That was followed by more waiting, and then questions by phone.

The waiting was an additional stress for already-overwhelmed parents desperate for help and connection, but the organizations were, and still are, swamped. The vetting ended with a Zoom, after which approval to join was given, or not.

Why the secrecy and robust vetting? Because parents feared being fired or their children removed by CPS. And many don't want their gender-distressed child to learn they belong to a "transphobic" group.

AC said there are thousands of parents in these groups and the numbers were growing daily. She wanted me to know that while the focus was on girls, there were many boys, as well. She told me that parents, especially those whose kids had announced a new identity recently, needed basic information because they'd been ambushed, were ignorant about gender ideology, and were lost.

I made a list of things I thought parents needed to know. But the day prior to the event, I changed my plan. It happened during a parent group that I'd joined as an observer, in order to listen and learn.

The first questions were what you'd expect. Should we call our son by his girl name and female pronouns? How do we explain what's happened to his younger sibling? What about grandma?

Then a mom spoke up whom I'll never forget. She was seated on a sofa next to her husband. "Yesterday our son told us he's our daughter," she told the group. "How should I be feeling?"

*How should I be feeling*—that was her question. I noted her lack of emotion and wide, intense eyes. Her husband offered nothing, his face blank. Lots of blinking. "I just don't know how I should be feeling," she said again matter-of-factly.

I understood at once: she was asking how to feel because she didn't feel anything. She was numb. Someone asked a question, another made suggestions, but the mom and dad continued to look bewildered.

*This is trauma*, I thought. *Theirs are the faces of trauma, like those of people who return home after a tornado and find rubble.*

I recalled the many parents who'd contacted me over the previous year. They were all distraught, some were falling apart. I would comment on their distress, but without fail the discussion returned to the child. As I watched and listened to the couple on my screen, it hit me: we're focused on the kids and overlooking the parents' off-the-charts traumatic stress.

Of course, therapists working with this population, and journalists reporting on the catastrophe, were aware of parents' anguish. But no one had recognized parents were victims of actual trauma and their symptoms were serious, even debilitating. Not only that, but unlike a car accident or hurricane, where trauma is due to a single event, the ordeals these parents face are ongoing, typically lasting years.

I decided, before talking about their kids, I need to talk with parents about themselves.

There was a good turnout; about fifty people were on my screen. Word had gotten around, and many parents, some new to the world of ROGD and others not so new, signed up. I was nervous but knew what I must say.

It went something like this:

"I know you're expecting me to talk about your kids—you have lots of questions. Your child is struggling with an issue you don't understand, there's some conflict at home, and you want guidance. You can't stop worrying about your child—what to do, what to say, what about school, internet, new friends,—it's consuming, I know.

"But I'm not going to speak about your kids today, today I am speaking about you.

"From what I am seeing in my office and in parent groups and reading in PITT, you parents are traumatized and it's time we start talking about it."

I explained that trauma results from deeply disturbing events such as experiencing or witnessing a serious injury, or the threat of serious injury, to oneself or another person. This doesn't mean only earthquakes or mass shootings: the injury can be psychological, as well. The event causes feelings of fear, helplessness, or horror that persist. It also affects one's thoughts and behaviors.

"We need to talk about the many traumas you have experienced.

"Your son announced he's your daughter. Your daughter announced she's your son. You couldn't absorb it. It was preposterous, how could your child believe it? Your very smart, even brilliant, child who excels in math, physics, and robotics. How are these words coming out of her? Yet there he was telling you his girl's name. And he is insisting he always felt this way. How could my child be transgender? And the school's in on it? We're the only ones in the dark? She asked to go to a gender clinic. He asked for medicine to stop puberty.

"The conversation kept replaying in your head. You didn't sleep that night. Well of course you didn't: you'd just been hit by a nuclear bomb.

"To begin, it's shocking to learn your child has embraced the impossible. He genuinely believes he's in the wrong body. He's not living in reality—that's alarming! She must be under the influence of others, but who? Will she transform into someone you don't recognize? Will she lose her beautiful soprano voice? Her breasts? Will she become sterile? Will your family be destroyed?

"Will you have to choose between estrangement and agreeing with your child's delusion? That's a Sophie's Choice no parent should face.

"You feel helpless: your child is headed down a dangerous path, maybe he or she is far down it already, and what can you do when the whole world is applauding? To whom can you turn?

"You called her school. Yes, they use the new name. It's been a few months, they say: your daughter wasn't ready for you to know. She is free to use the boy's facilities, they inform you, including locker rooms.

"Another sleepless night: Your daughter changes her clothes in the boys' locker room, and you're supposed to sleep?

"Then came the appointment. The gender specialist called your daughter by her made-up name instead of the one you carefully chose when you were pregnant or adopting her.

"At the end of the session, the therapist said you must accept your daughter's boy identity and her development should be stopped. It's safe and reversible, she reassured you.

"You weren't so sure. What about her anxiety and eating disorder? Couldn't that be related? She was bullied. Her sister was sexually assaulted. Aren't those things relevant?

"You suggested a slower process and more caution. You insisted: we know our child! There's more going on here.

"Then, in a condescending manner, and maybe with your child in the room, she replied that *their* physical development and periods are causing *them* distress, and puberty blockers will help. In fact, it's already late. 'There's a consensus among professionals,' she explained. 'Affirmation saves lives.' She spoke with authority and confidence.

"Then the heaviest blow. 'If you're not supportive, if you are not an ally,' she warned, '*they* might commit suicide.'

"You are stunned. The specialist is saying *you're* the problem. Not your child's wacky beliefs. Not her anxiety and social media addiction. Everything would be okay, she's telling you, your child would be smiling right now, if only you were on board. We can deal with the gender issue, not a problem. You, mom and dad, are the problem.

"You searched for an expert, you took your child to see her, and she endorsed the lie! Then she belittled you, dismissed your concerns, undermined your authority, and weakened the bond with your child.

"She's known your family for entire forty-five minutes, and she calls you 'unsupportive?' Wow. Just wow.

"You'd like to know, were you also 'unsupportive' when you quit your job and stayed on bed rest for three months so she wouldn't be premature? When you kept nursing, because it was best for her, when your nipples were cracked and bleeding? When you were up with him night after night trying to sooth him from colic? When you turned down your dream job because it required travel? Were you not an ally when you slept next to her in a hospital chair for three nights when her appendix burst? When you confronted the parents of a bully on the bus? When you both took second jobs to pay for therapy and tutoring? And on and on, countless instances of devotion and self-sacrifice, who can remember them all? And now the expert says you're 'unsupportive.'

"You're shocked and horrified. You want to vomit—again, for good reasons.

"At home you googled the medications and learned about osteoporosis and vaginal atrophy. You found pictures of girls your daughter's age with fresh scars across their now-flat chests. You discovered surgeons eager to harm her advertising with memes and emojis on Tik-Tok.

"Maybe it was at this point you had your first full-blown panic attack. Or maybe it was the next day when you told your sister and she agreed with the therapist, or the following week when you found a binder in your daughter's bedroom.

"Sleep, laughter, and concentration were distant memories. You felt numb and detached. You're avoiding people. Your child's announcement kept playing in your head; you imagined her in the boy's bathroom; the therapist's words rang in your ears; those ghastly mastectomy scars flash in front of your eyes.

"Parents, listen to me. That is trauma. What you are going through has a name. Let's recognize it right now.

"Fear. Horror. Helplessness. The hallmark features of trauma.

"Let's not forget triggers. They suddenly remind you of your trauma and cause distress, fear, or disorientation. A trigger can be anything—an object, memory, or smell; a holiday or an angry voice; a time of year or day.

"Of course, I already knew the everyday items and occurrences you can't escape: Rainbows. Flags. Words beginning with "trans." Planned Parenthood and ACLU ads in your social media feed. You have a strong reaction that's seems out of proportion because you are reliving your trauma." (As I was speaking the parent chat was on fire.)

> *Anytime I see a rainbow now . . . even if it is a beautiful photo, I get a knot in my stomach*
>
> *It feels like there are no walls or perimeters around this, its a never ending flood of feelings. no boundaries*

I was curious about the unusual triggers that no one would imagine. I wanted to get a sense of what it's like to walk in your shoes on a regular day. After the

## Parents' Trauma-Induced Terror Moments
### Aka Triggers

Seeing his name on old mail we receive

The young men's clothing aisle

Hearing her younger sisters say he/him

Photos of friends' grandchildren

Seeing her with a beard and hearing her deep voice

Baby clothing

The word "journey"

Young couples with their child, my heart aches to return to those innocent years

Recipes, my son was a foodie

My phone – all the shock from him has been by text

The word "trans" – transformation, Trans Canada highway, transit...

Other people's normal kids.

The song Sweet Caroline.

Not being able to speak my truth

The words "pronoun" and "ally".

Grocery stores

Christmas cards

DEI trainings

The clothing I was wearing when he made the announcement

Walking through Target

Happy children like mine once was.

Photos of myself when I was so happy before this all began.

Putting my head on the pillow at night.

Zoom sessions, AC took my query to three groups: Parents of ROGD Boys, a Secret FB group for parents of ROGD children and young adults, and a WhatsApp group of Moms.

The poignant responses came flooding in, and I wish I could list them all. (See Triggers list above with just a few of them.)

One came from "A Mom from the USA":

*Can we be honest here? I hate to call them "triggers." They are so much more than that. I prefer "trauma-induced terror moments."*

I agree with "Mom from the USA"; "trigger" is overused; your description is superior, and I will use it from now on.

Terror moments can be so awful they may lead to avoidance of places, people, or situations. This can further seep the pleasure from your lives. But it may be necessary to survive. From the chat:

*I feel like I am always under siege. Battle mode 24/7*

*There is a cloud over all fun times and holidays. Nothing is the same. I have to pretend to be OK in order to not wreck my connection with my kids. Its a constant stress.*

*We have lost the simple joy of watching the results of our hard work raising our kid. We are denied the fruits of our labor. . . . The joy is sucked away.*

Many parents who seek my help have never talked to a psychiatrist before. They may have gone through cancer, divorce, financial losses, and other terrible things. But this is the first time, they tell me, they ever made an appointment with a psychiatrist to talk and maybe get medication. They tell me their child's gender confusion is the most difficult thing they've ever been through. Crying all day. Panicked, hopeless, avoiding people, hardly functioning. All because of what's happening with their child.

I continued with the parents:

"Okay, so you're traumatized. But there's something else that needs to be said. There's another layer to this.

"Normally my profession rushes to promptly identify and help victims of trauma. Whether it be due to abuse, sexual assault, natural disasters, mass shootings, 9/11, racism, discrimination—the large mental health associations advocate for services. And that's the case especially when the victims are members of a marginalized population.

"But who's advocating for you? Where's the awareness campaign, the media coverage, the support groups, the ads on buses and subways, the 800 numbers to call?"

*Its so hard to talk to anyone about it nobody understands they act like I'm crazy so I have to keep in inside*

"You know better than I—there are none.* Unlike other victims, your trauma is not only unacknowledged, you're to blame! And that's why you found one another online and have these underground, secret meetings.

"Marginalized? There's no one more marginalized than parents who won't accept their child's opposite-sex persona. Marginalized would be a step up—at least you're noticed; but you parents of ROGD kids are not even on the paper.

"I am recognizing each of you right now. I am recognizing your trauma and suffering.

"You should not be underground, huddled together in secrecy like outcasts, using fake names. It's the proponents of this destructive social movement, and the gender medical establishment, that's disfiguring and sterilizing kids that should be ashamed and hiding, not you.

"And I want to say—and it's very important you hear me say this—that the medical profession, my profession, has betrayed you. You have a right to all you are feeling, and you have a right to be recognized and validated. The entire mental health profession—psychology, social work, counseling—was captured by radical ideologues years ago, and you and your families are paying the price.

"The doctors are wrong, your gut is right. Your son will always be your son. Your daughter will always be your daughter. To say differently is inane. And to place blame on you, parents who representing reality, is shameful.

"Too many of my colleagues believe that denying biology is part of normal development, and if parents and society would just accept that, it would be all rainbows and unicorns for youth. Doctors at Johns Hopkins tell you to embrace your child's 'evolving sense of self.' They either believe it or they are intimidated into silence.

"We failed you. It's a painful reality and hard for me to say, but it's the truth.

"In this whole gender fiasco, parents are bad, toxic, unsafe bigots if they dare to question an irrational belief system with no scientific foundation. The therapists undermine your parenting and swoop in and want to save your kids from you. They see themselves as saviors and you're the toxic

---

* This was prior to GENSPECT and the documentaries that included interviews with parents.

unsafe parents. The same goes for the pediatricians and endocrinologists who prescribe the hormones. And the surgeons? Sinister.

"I know that many of you feel you're at odds with the whole world: your child, family members, friends, schools, doctors, therapists, politicians, the media, the culture. On how many fronts can one person fight?

"One mom recently told me, 'Sometimes I wish my son had cancer. At least I'd get sympathy and understanding. The whole world would be there for me.' It didn't surprise me, and I'm sure it doesn't surprise you."

Again, from the chat:

> *5 years of holding my breath. I'd take cancer or addiction at this point, any day*

> *I am numb and there is little pleasure in anything. I have no trust in anything or anybody and I am bewildered every day by the madness that has taken over my son.*

"The point of today is for you to hear all these things from me, a doctor. I want to acknowledge your trauma and suffering and to say I am sorry. I am so sorry all this is happening to you and that you have been betrayed. You deserve to be recognized and supported as much as the victims of hurricanes and mass shootings."

I stopped for a drink of water and scrolled through the grid of participants. Why, I wondered, did so many parents turn off their cameras? I assumed because of a bad hair day, or they were in the kitchen or bathroom.

I asked AC about it afterward, and she told me their cameras were off because they were crying. From the chat:

> *I thought I'd cried all my tears out, but what you said, your validation, it opened the faucet.*

> *i didn't think i had any more tears to cry till today*

> *I can't even have the camera on. tears flowing from her first sentence to us.*

> *That's why I turned mine off.*

> *I cry harder for this than I did when I lost my mother and father. The sounds that emanate from me are primal.*

Despite the tears—or perhaps because of them—there was an outpouring of gratitude for my talk. I had hit a chord. So I went to work on the next one.

※　※　※

I decided to talk about the weeping.

"What are tears about? Different emotions can cause crying, but most commonly they are due to sadness. Sadness is due to the loss of someone or something to which you are attached: a person, a home, a job, a dream. One's health, independence, or finances can be lost. When the loss is great, it may lead to grief. Grief can be a heavy burden."

> *I have been on and off suicidal for a full year.*

"Many of you are grieving and carrying a burden, whether others realize it or not. It's vital for you to name, acknowledge, and understand your grief, otherwise you can't begin to heal.

"There is simple grief and complex grief. With simple grief you feel sad, you miss the person, you are preoccupied with your loss, but no more than that. It hurts, but you can say good-bye and move forward.

"With complicated grief there are emotions like guilt, regret, and anger. How could she have done this to me? Am I to blame? Could I have prevented it? What if I'd done something different? What if, what if?

"Parents of children who have or are going through medical transition face loss that is ambiguous: your child is still alive, but he's transformed. The loss is of the child you once knew—their personality and their appearance. Some changes are final such as double mastectomies, but others are not. The ongoing uncertainty can be torture. This is what you face. There's also hope: every day there are more desistors and detransitioners—maybe yours will join their ranks! You have hope, but you also want to live in reality. That's the challenge: to live in reality, but hold on to hope.

"This is what you face, and I can't think of a grief more complicated than yours.

"I feel honored you parents have shared with me the losses you've endure because your child fell into the grips of gender ideology. While every situation is unique, I think most of you grieve in varying degrees many of the same losses.

"Every loss has primary and secondary elements.[1] A primary loss, for example, is the death of a spouse, and secondary losses might be

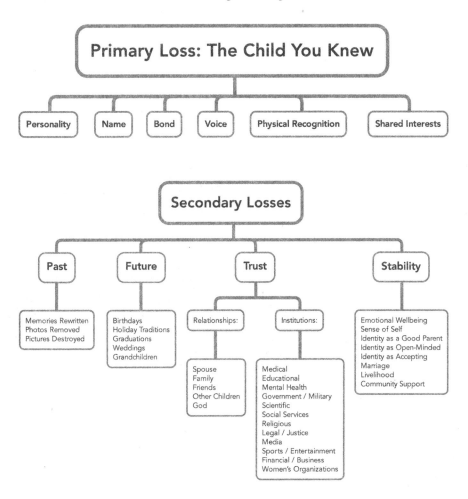

financial security and retirement dreams. Secondary losses can be highly personal, such as loss of faith, and they can compound the grief of the primary loss.

"The primary loss is the child you once knew.

"Let's start at the beginning: her name. You probably chose it before she entered this world. You deliberated before picking it, knowing it was a momentous decision. You may have celebrated her naming with family and friends—it was a meaningful rite of passage. And the countless times you repeated it to get his attention, call her to come, comfort her, call her for a meal, inscribe it on a cake. . . . Now, she says, that name is 'dead.' It's a knife in your heart.

"Such a simple thing, a name. Such a huge, painful loss.

"You lost a relationship. Your previously easy-going, compliant, affectionate son became moody, hostile, and distant. You once played music together, and Scrabble. Now he seems alien to you. You've lost the lovely connection you once had.

"Your daughter's long, beautiful hair and soprano voice—gone.

"Those primary losses are just the start. We have to look as well at ancillary, or secondary losses."

"For example, the past has been erased. Your child rewrote it to fit his beliefs: 'I never liked those swim trunks. I was miserable on that vacation. In that birthday video I was only acting like I was happy.'

"Cherished memories are stained by the narrative. He might insist you remove and delete all the old photos of him. He knows his life history better than you."

Mothers have asked me, why did I give up a career for motherhood, if this is the result? I stayed home all those years, for what?

Parents describe their loss of trust in institutions. The educational and medical systems, the media, their candidates and political parties, feminist organizations, the LGBTQ community, their families and friends, and sometimes, sadly, their spouses. Betrayed by all of them. They either pushed the ideology that entrapped their child or went MIA during their dark hours of need.

From the chat:

> *I'm not sure if/when I can forgive my family for abandoning me in my greatest time of need.*

> *I don't think there's anyone on our side. Everyone keeps telling me I just need to accept it. Even friends and family say it. Nobody can understand this unless they go through it.*

Social services have taken children away from parents grounded in reality. Regarding businesses, one mom told me: "We are assaulted visually with flags and unicorns when we walk in, and women's restrooms and changing areas are no longer safe."

Some parents have been betrayed by the justice and legal systems who rule against parents who are reality-based, removing their children, e.g., Olivia, Yaeli, Sage, and so many others.

Parents feel betrayed by churches, who are either ideologically captured or simply unsupportive of parents. And they feel abandoned by God, for allowing their families to descend into hell.

A future that was assumed has been thrown into question: holiday celebrations with the whole family, trips, a wedding, grandchildren.

Parents fear their child will not attend their grandparents' funerals.

They lose their identities as liberal, progressive, tolerant individuals. They cease seeing themselves as good parents. They are ashamed. They lose their sense of self.

It's difficult to overstate the magnitude of these losses. It's impossible to measure the burden. What parents describe is a loss of one's bearing. The crumbling of what they always assumed to be true.

These losses go to the core of a person's being: who they are, what they believe, who they can trust. They are profoundly shaken.

*It's the feeling that the floor has fallen out beneath you and you just keep falling. Endless terror.*

"Parents, when I consider your immense trauma and grief, I have to conclude that we don't yet have a term in psychiatry that encompasses it all.

"Normally, grief is recognized and socially sanctioned. There is support. There are rituals. There are cards, announcements, flowers, and food sent to your house. But sometimes grief is not acknowledged. Dr. Kenneth Doka,[2] a bereavement expert, coined the term *disenfranchised grief.* When something that is your right is taken away, you are disenfranchised.

"Dr. Doka gives as examples of disenfranchised grief an early miscarriage or the death of an ex-spouse. Most people may assume they weren't difficult losses for you. 'You'll get pregnant again,' 'he was your ex, big deal.' You might be suffering mightily from the losses, but there's little or no acknowledgment."

*Its so hard to talk to anyone about it nobody understands they act like I'm crazy so I have to keep it inside*

"Like your trauma, your grief is disenfranchised. There's no recognition, so you are isolated without support. You're driven underground, living double lives, using fake names, but you've done nothing wrong—it should be the gender evangelists, therapists, and doctors who should be hiding.

"Parents, you are grieving, you have a multitude of losses. They must be named and recognized. Others may trivialize your grief or even blame you for it. They might say you brought it on yourselves. I know this is done by family members, trusted friends, and doctors. I cannot imagine how that feels—another trauma on top of all the others."

*Never before in my long life have I felt less understood about anything than I do about this issue.*

*I have such trust issues now. Major feelings of abandonment.*

"In psychiatry we know that emotional contact is essential for health. Isolation is an enormous stressor and can lead to physical illnesses.

"Parents, I've talked to expressed their distrust of and rage toward the medical system to the degree of avoiding doctors altogether. One mom told me her husband was devastated to discover a trusted therapist was secretly affirming his daughter. He had not been in the best health before it all began, she told me. He stopped going to doctors and died of a heart attack.

"My message to you: honor your reality. You are entitled to your grief. It's legitimate even if you're the only person who recognizes it. Don't disenfranchise yourselves!"

# CHAPTER ELEVEN

# Euphemisms*

*"I had beautiful breasts. Now they're in the incinerator. Thank you, modern medicine."*

—Chloe Cole

Beverly from Oregon emails me: "Urgent need help with ROGD daughter please answer ASAP." She tells me that not only did discover a breast binder in her fifteen-year-old's bedroom, but that her daughter's best friend and main influence, sixteen-year-old Mia, just had "top surgery" as part of her own male identification process. Beverly is beside herself. "Do doctors really do that?" she asks incredulously. "They sure do," I reply.

As I write this, there are 45,375 girls† seeking donations on GoFundMe to pay for what gender surgeons call a "masculinized chest."

"Top surgery" is a euphemism, of course: what they're talking about is breast amputation, a bilateral mastectomy. Why the vague, bland language? To normalize the atrocity. *Nothing to see here folks, just an eighth grader having her healthy breasts sliced off. Just "top surgery."*

Mind you, these are the same people who insist that five-year-olds use anatomically accurate terms, not childish nicknames, for their genitals. They soberly instruct us to teach the words "scrotum" and "vulva" to kindergarteners. But the imprecise, trivial-sounding "top surgery"—that language is fine.

---

* Based on https://www.city-journal.org/moral-atrocity-top-surgery.
† In March 2023, but subsequently GoFundMe does not allow searching for total number of campaigns.

And don't tell me these operations are only done on adults. In a study[2] of 68 patients who underwent the procedure at Children's Hospital Los Angeles, almost half were girls between thirteen and seventeen, and that was way back in 2016. A letter[3] from plastic surgeons at Vanderbilt University School of Medicine published in the journal *JAMA Pediatrics* reported between 2016 and 2019, the annual number of "gender-affirming chest surgeries" increased by 389 percent, likely a significant underestimate, because it included only surgeries performed in hospitals. Many of these procedures take place outside of hospitals in surgery centers owned by plastic surgeons. The letter documented that 77 percent of patients used private insurance or were self-pay, and the average cost was $30,000.

Kaiser Permanente Oakland performed seventy top surgeries in 2019 on teenagers ages thirteen to eighteen, up from five in 2013. "I can't honestly think of another field where the volume has exploded like that," said Dr. Karen Yokoo, a retired plastic surgeon at the hospital.[4]

Why do girls and young women dream of going under the knife and waking up with flat chests, and sometimes, to save a few bucks, without nipples?[5] They have mental health problems, a traumatic past, family issues, or maybe just intense teenage angst and erroneously believe my colleagues who claim removing body parts will bring them relief.

As an intern in pediatrics, when a patient needed a medical procedure, I was required to obtain informed consent from the parents or guardian. I was obligated to explain, accurately and comprehensively, the risks—both immediate and long-term—of the procedure. I wonder: when surgeons perform mastectomies on minors like Mia, how accurate and comprehensive are the consents?

Even if valid arguments exist for surgical solutions to emotional distress, the outcomes of mastectomies for Mia and the 45,000 girls on GoFundMe are highly uncertain. Yes, there exist individuals who, decades after breast removal for gender distress, claim to have no regret. I believe them, but first of all, they underwent surgery in adulthood; decades ago, "top surgery" was not performed on minors. Second, as you will see, the best studies we have indicate that overall, even the women having surgery as adults are not doing well. Mia and many of the GoFundMe girls are minors, an unstudied group. We have no long-term data whatsoever on them. We have no idea how they're going to fare even five years after surgery, let alone twenty.

## Zero percent regret rate?

Proponents of gender-affirming care for minors such as the Admiral at HHS call the treatments "crucial" and "medically necessary," but there is no evidence to support those claims. Mia's mother was almost certainly told that mastectomies for minors with gender dysphoria are evidence-based treatment, supported by well-documented standards of care. Again, that is not the case.

When proponents say they have evidence of benefit, to what do they refer? They are citing studies that are, to put it bluntly, poor. They have a small numbers of subjects, no control groups, a self-selection bias, high dropout rates, and short follow-ups.

One example is the study mentioned above from the pediatric gender clinic at Children's Hospital Los Angeles, claiming only one patient experienced "occasional" feelings of regret. Johanna Olson-Kennedy, an adolescent medicine specialist at Children's Hospital Los Angeles, and leader in pediatric gender transitioning, told the *New York Times*, "There's very few things in the world that have a zero percent regret rate. And chest surgery, clinically, I've experienced that" (i.e., she has seen zero regret following mastectomies).

The doctor didn't seem concerned that 30 percent of patients could not be contacted or declined to participate. Why would a patient fail to return to a clinic? There are lots of possibilities.

Maybe she moved. Maybe she dislikes the doctor. Maybe she's disappointed with the results but wants to avoid an unpleasant conversation. Maybe she's furious with the doctor and staff and never wants to see them again. Maybe she's in a psychiatric hospital or in prison. Maybe she's dead.

Dr. Olson-Kennedy ignores what we hear from those who describe their regret: it appears to take on average eight or more years[6] to develop and admit. Most patients in Dr. Olson-Kennedy's study were surveyed less than two years after their surgeries.

"Zero percent regret rate?" I think you're speaking too soon, Dr. Olsen-Kennedy. I think you're misleading girls and their parents. I think you are leading them toward harm.

There is only one high-quality long-term study following gender surgeries, and it's from Sweden, where a database exists that includes each instance of medical and mental health care provided from birth to death to each of the almost fourteen million people in its medical system. It also includes all suicides.

Use of that database removes "confounding variables" that plague other methods of collecting information. The Swedish database provides more reliable answers to questions that everyone—especially the "gender-affirming" medical establishment in our country—should be asking, such as: what is the long-term relative risk of suicide in women who have been given testosterone and surgery, when compared to women of the same age and demographic?

The Swedish research, published in 2011, is not perfect, but it's the best we have.[7] It found that ten years after sex reassignment, women living as men had increased mortality from many causes, especially suicide. They were forty times more likely to die from suicide than women in the general population matched for age and other demographics.

The authors concluded: ". . . surgery and hormonal therapy . . . is apparently not sufficient to remedy the high rates of [mental illness] and mortality found among transsexual persons. . . . Our findings suggest that sex reassignment, although alleviating gender dysphoria, may not suffice as treatment for transsexualism. . ."

Another Swedish study also failed to demonstrate improved mental health following surgery. But this is noteworthy: the authors claimed the opposite—an example of how GAC proponents misrepresent their findings.

An October 2019 publication[8] concluded that while "gender-affirming" hormones did not lead to improved mental health, "gender-affirming" surgeries like mastectomies did. If correct, that would have been a significant finding. They measured three parameters following surgery in men and women:

1. Visits for anxiety or mood disorder
2. Prescriptions for antidepressant or antianxiety medication
3. Hospitalizations following suicide attempts

They found that [italicized by this author]:

> Compared with the general population, individuals with a gender incongruence diagnosis were about *six times as likely* to have had a mood and anxiety disorder health care visit, *more than three times as likely* to have received prescriptions for antidepressants and anxiolytics,‡ and *more than six times as likely* to have been hospitalized after a suicide attempt . . .

---

‡ Antianxiety medications

Obviously, that doesn't sound good, but they also found that the numbers decreased with time—fewer appointments, prescriptions, and hospitalizations following suicide attempts. They concluded that the decrease "lends support . . . to provide gender-affirming surgeries to transgender individuals who seek them."

But the study had severe shortcomings: no numbers on psychiatric hospitalizations for reasons other than suicide attempts, no control subjects, a limited one-year time frame, retrospective design, and major loss to follow up.

The most conspicuous and concerning of the shortcomings was the omission of suicides. You read that right: the authors' goal was to examine mental health outcomes; the study was titled "Reduction in mental health treatment utilization among transgender individuals after gender-affirming surgeries," but they excluded suicides! With the information accessible in the Swedish database, leaving out suicide data was glaring.

The month after its publication, I joined pediatric endocrinologist Michael Laidlaw, family medicine physician Andre Van Mol, and Prof. Paul McHugh of Johns Hopkins in a letter[9] to the *American Journal of Psychiatry*. We submitted that the study lacked the evidence to support its conclusion supporting gender-affirmation surgery.

It took ten months for the study authors and AJP to publicly respond to our criticism. Finally, in August of 2020, the editor in chief reported[10] the receipt of six letters in addition to ours questioning the study's statistical analyses and conclusions. *AJP* sent the study and letters to a statistical reviewer, and based on the reviewer's findings, it issued a major correction: there was, after all, "no advantage to surgery" for gender dysphoria regarding appointments for mood and anxiety, prescriptions for antidepressants and anxiolytics, and hospitalizations following suicide attempts.

So there you have it, a study showing *no long-term benefit* from surgery was touted as *providing evidence of long-term benefit* from surgery. You know the rest: the utterly unsubstantiated conclusion had already been publicized near and far:

United Press (UPI): "Gender Reassignment Surgery brings Mental Health Benefits Study Shows"[11]

ABC News: "Transgender surgery linked with better long-term mental health, study shows"[12]

NBC News: "Sex-Reassignment Surgery yields long term mental health benefits"[13]

The LGBT site Out.com: "Study: Trans People with Access to Surgery Have Better Mental Health"

Yale University: "Mental Health Outcomes Improve Transgender Individuals After Surgery"[14]

American Psychiatric Association: "Study Finds Long-Term Mental Health Benefits of Gender-Affirming Surgery for Transgender Individuals"[15]

WebMD, the popular news site for physicians: "Gender Reassignment Surgery Benefits Mental Health"[16]

Do you understand? This is another John Money scenario: faulty research, unsubstantiated conclusions, aggressive publicity, wide acceptance, and the gender affirmation lobby declares, "The science is settled."

It's the same old story. How many heard the truth about David Reimer in 1999? How many heard in 2020, almost a year after publication, that the "surgery helps mental health" conclusion had been corrected/retracted?

The answer is very few. And by that time, the unsubstantiated conclusions are baked into the system and into the minds and hearts of unsuspecting doctors, educators, politicians, parents—nearly everyone.

The only accurate conclusion to draw—and this is the conclusion reached by authorities in a growing number of countries—is that mastectomies on minors such as Mia are experimental. There is no high-quality evidence they benefit in the long run, but there is evidence of harm. Sweden, Norway, Finland, and Britain all say girls like Mia need in-depth psychotherapy, not a surgeon's scalpel.

But in the US, it's full steam ahead.

For Mia's mom's consent to be valid, those facts needed to be acknowledged. Bottom line: the surgeon had an obligation to explain to Mia's mother that performing a mastectomy on her daughter is highly controversial.

## "I do not have a minimum age in my practice."

If the girls on GoFundMe manage to reach their goals, the funds may end up in the coffers of Sidhbh Gallagher, a Miami surgeon whose patients find her on TikTok. Gallagher's unique approach to marketing was covered in a *New York Times* article.[17] Until recently, she posted bubbly videos of gleeful clients recovering from what she called "teetus deletus." On one video she brags, "I have yeeted 100s of unwanted teets." On another she laments, "Just realized I only get to Yeet 4 Teets next week."

Gallagher, who admits to removing the breasts of girls as young as fourteen,[18] seems to have pivoted away from her odious ads about yeeting teets, perhaps due to a 2022 complaint filed with the Federal Trade Commission for allegedly engaging in aggressive and deceptive marketing to minors.

On the other hand, it could be a result of a testament posted on multiple platforms ("warning: graphic medical images") by one of Gallagher's patients who claims she nearly died before a second surgeon removed "over half a foot of dead, rotting tissue" from the incision site on her chest. Not to be deterred, Gallagher has a new persona. She is now "The VagicianMD" on social media, peddling castration and vaginoplasties to her 253,000 followers.

Dr. Giancarlo McEvenue at Toronto's McLean Clinic in is another popular surgeon. His Instagram shows him in surgical scrubs and a Santa hat. Caption: "For all you good boys, Dr. McEvenue is not bringing gifts, he's taking them away!" [smiley emojis] In each hand is a pail labeled "breast tissue." The doctor is masked, but his eyes are beaming.

Another choice would be Dr. Scott Mosser in San Francisco, who self-describes as "super committed to gender surgery":

> At the Gender Confirmation Center . . . we try to live with our values thirty to forty years in the future . . . that puts us in a mindset of *extreme affirmation,* because affirming at that time is a foregone conclusion. This is a time in the future when gender is just a thing, nobody makes a big deal out of it. . . . I do not have a minimum age in my practice . . . with parental consent, someone could even do a consult with me at age ten, eleven or twelve.[19]

I'm often asked how so many people can embrace gender madness, what's behind it? They don't mean the well-meaning people who blindly trust authority, but the brains and money behind the movement.

Dr. Mosser's statements demonstrate two motives. First is a vision of radical social reform. An ardent adherent of the Articles of Faith, he envisions a society in which "nobody makes a big deal out of" the disfigurement and sterilization of children. He's so certain of that ideal, it cannot come too soon. The other factor, of course, is money. Mosser claims to have performed 2,000 mastectomies.

Mosser was a WPATH SOC-8 committee member for the chapters on surgery and adolescence. Is that not a conflict of interest? With the guidelines removing all age restrictions§ for "chest masculinization," his business must be booming.

---

§ So long as a child has reached Tanner Stage 2 of puberty, which in some cases occurs by age nine.

Do surgeons like Gallagher, McEvenue, and Mosser get to know patients like Mia before cutting them open? Are they curious to learn why a young girl loathes herself to the degree that she goes under the knife? Do they inquire about her history of autism or how peers shamed her in elementary school when she began to develop? How about the sexual assault by her cousin?

Anxiety and depression are highly prevalent in girls and women seeking "top surgery."[20] Laura Becker, a vocal detransitioner who describes with brilliant insight the role played by her autism and complex PTSD in adopting a transgender identity, was suicidal on the day of her double mastectomy and told her surgeon as much.[21]

But proponents of GAC argue that delving into a transgender-identifying women's mental health is "gatekeeping"—an abomination according to the Articles of Faith. Removing her breasts is a human right, they say, to "align her body with her identity." WPATH SOC-8 encourages a mental health evaluation but doesn't make it mandatory. The crusaders want the troubled girls in the driver's seat.

## The Joy of Binding

Girls such as Mia typically get mastectomies following years of binding. A binder is a thick spandex and nylon undergarment whose purpose is to flatten breasts. The research about these devices is scant, but in one large hospital gender clinic, almost 95 percent of girls wore them.[22]

Children's Hospital Los Angeles tells parents:

> A flat chest can affirm an individual's identity and allow them and their gender identity to be correctly perceived in public . . . binding can provide a new level of confidence, energy, comfort, and joy that positively enhances their self-esteem and identity.[23]

"Joy?" More on that later.

You and I know that every girl feels awkward or worse with breast development and menstruation, especially if she's earlier than her peers. We need to normalize those feelings and provide reassurance. The embarrassment, the self-consciousness, the unwanted attention—all girls feel the same way to varying degrees. But your daughter is led to believe if she feels any discomfort whatsoever with her developing body, she may be "gender nonconforming," "gender variant," or "trans"; she should try a binder and see if she likes the results.

What if your daughter needs binder shopping advice?

As one undercover mom discovered,[24] she can hop on to the chatroom or anonymous online forum "TrevorSpace" for LGBT youth hosted by the well-funded and influential Trevor Project. The Trevor Project, I remind you, is where AAP refers your child on its healthychildren.org site ("powered by pediatricians. Trusted by parents. from the American Academy of Pediatrics").[25] When your child signs on to Trevor Project, just as the GLSEN webpage, he's reminded of the quick exit feature ("Press the ESC button three times to quickly leave our site") in case you show up unexpectedly.

"I have been looking for a binder," one girl asks, "but I have no clue where to get one. Does anyone know where I could get a reliable binder?"

An adult user replied with a list of brands, adding, "I really recommend TransTape."

Another adult wrote: "If it's your first time I started with TomboyX compression tops."

What if your daughter can't afford a binder?

Point of Pride, a transgender nonprofit based in Eugene, OR, ships binders free to girls thirteen and over.[26] Your daughter is reassured their "packaging is discreet."

What if your daughter doesn't want you to know, like this girl in a Trevor Project chat:

> I know the way people usually do this is by ordering it to a friend's house..., but I don't have anyone to do that with. . . . I have money and know where I want to get it from and all that. I just need a means of getting it.

Another user suggested she have the binder sent to a post office where she could pick it up without her parents' knowledge.

Or maybe she can just get one at school. One thirteen-year-old in Maine was given one by her school's social worker, who encouraged her to keep it a secret.[27]

As you might expect, smashing your breasts for eight to ten hours daily has consequences. Some problems begin soon while others emerge years later. One study[28] of nearly 1,300 girls found 89 percent experienced at least one negative effect, such as back pain, overheating, chest pain, and shortness of breath. Nearly 40 percent experienced "severe pain," and in 20 percent the binder limited their daily activities. Doesn't sound like "joy" to me.

## Chloe: Permanent Damage

Chloe Cole had mastectomies at age fifteen and described her experience with binding on Jordan Peterson's podcast.[29] When I watched, I didn't see joy, I saw trauma and grief. I saw Dr. Peterson choke up. I don't know how any decent person could watch and listen to Chloe and not feel sorrow for her, and rage at those responsible for her misery.

I'm grateful to Chloe for being as open as she was because she taught me something. For some girls, perhaps for your daughter, binding can act like a gateway drug: it introduces them to what appears to be a temporary and harmless flattening of their curves but leads to their permanent disfigurement with or without amputation.

Chloe Cole on the Dr. Jordan B. Peterson podcast:

> . . . I was two or three years on testosterone and—I'd been binding for roughly the same amount of time. My breasts had lost their shape they didn't look like they used to before, they didn't really have, you know, they didn't, they didn't, to me, it just looked strange.
>
> And I actually started developing more insecurities with my body as I went through my transition, you know, like I had like these masculine features pop up, but it was also on a female body and there was like an incongruence between different features on my body, and especially my breasts.
>
> Like it was this masculine looking body with quite a bit of muscle and yet these things were there, and they weren't really in the best shape, and—it became a source of insecurity for me, and you know I thought that even if I wanted to . . . my chest would never be the same again. [edited slightly by author]

We must listen closely to Chloe. She is telling us two to three years of binding made her breasts look strange. Although she was binding and taking testosterone to supposedly "align" her body with her identity and get relief from her dysphoria, her dysphoria increased, especially about her misshapen breasts. Even if she wanted to return to living as a girl, she realized, they would never look the same.

> And so, there was not really any point in keeping it [i.e., her chest, her breasts].
>
> And before I went under, before I went under the knife, they did tell me that I was going to lose my ability to breast feed, but it was like, I'm going to be a man and men don't do that.
>
> I also wasn't really thinking at all about being a parent at all because (sigh) I was—I was a kid.

How can anyone read this and not weep? Yes, Chloe, you were just a kid.

"The common practice of breast binding severely impacts the quality of breast skin," reported a group of plastic surgeons from Belgium.[30] They noted decreased skin elasticity, resulting in ptosis, or sagging of breasts, typically seen in older women. Chloe was fifteen when her breasts were removed.

You want to save your daughter from this nightmare. Do not permit her to bind. It is dangerous and can have permanent consequences. If you discover she has one, tell her you have researched these devices and discovered they can harm her. Your job as a parent is to protect her, and you do not permit her to harm herself. You will allow a sports bra, so long as it fits properly. She needs to hand the binder over. Just as you would take away razors for cutting, you must confiscate the binder.

## I Made a Brash Decision

Countless young women have shared their grief over their lost breasts. They ask doctors, "How could you experiment on us? Why didn't you look deeper and help us with our real issues?" I wish I could share all their voices.

In addition to regret about their mastectomies, many also describe how, once on the "affirming" path to surgery, they were unable to turn back.

Like I've said, it's an assembly line.

Here's a young woman describing how she silenced her doubts because she'd been on the path to surgery for years:[31]

> I began to doubt my transition. . . . It started as an occasional passing thought, but it only grew in frequency. To silence this, I created a "mental wall" or "block" to keep me from considering this train of thought any further. It was too painful to consider detransitioning. Besides, I'd been waiting for top surgery for years and didn't want to cancel it now.
>
> So, I went through with it.
>
> When I saw my bandaged chest, I could feel that something was off. But it wasn't until I returned for my "top surgery reveal" days later that I realised I'd made a terrible mistake. The gruesome nature of the scarring dragged my awareness out of my head and back into physical reality. The bruises and swelling were mortifying, and my dysphoric focus was shifted from my chest to my wide hips. This surgery was supposed to cure my dysphoria. Why did it make me feel worse?

Kiera Bell, you read about her in an earlier chapter, identified as a man between the age of sixteen and twenty. She had a bilateral mastectomy and then detransitioned. This is what she told the British High Court: ". . . only recently . . . I have started to think about having children and if that is ever a possibility, I have to live with the fact that I will not be able to breastfeed my children. . . I made a brash decision . . . trying to find confidence and happiness . . . now the rest of my life will be negatively affected."[32]

In a letter to the attorney general, seven detransitioners, six of whom regret their mastectomies, wrote:

> Many of us were young teenagers when we decided, on the direction of medical "experts," to pursue irreversible hormone treatments and surgeries to bring our bodies into closer alignment with what we thought was our true "gender identity." Many of us had extensive histories of mental illness. Many of us had experienced significant childhood trauma. But all of this was ignored because we uttered the word "gender."
>
> Some of us have chosen to speak out publicly about the harm that "gender-affirming care" has caused us. But most detransitioners choose to remain silent or anonymous, because unlike the joyful and supportive communities that welcome all who transition, no such loving community awaits us. Instead, we are routinely harassed and browbeaten into silence for being an inconvenience to popular narratives around "gender." But our growing population is becoming impossible to ignore, and others have started amplifying our suppressed voices by denouncing the uncontrolled medical experiments being performed on children in hospitals in the name of "gender-affirming care.[33]

But those women are brushed off by the gender medical establishment. Listen to Johanna Olson-Kennedy from Children's Hospital Los Angeles a rabidly affirming pediatrician who believes there should be no minimum age for a double mastectomy. What if a girl regrets it? Olson-Kennedy says: "If you want breasts at a later point in your life, you can go and get them."[34]

Coming from a medical doctor who knows well the difference between breast tissue and silicon, the statement is odious.

Will Mia regret her mastectomies? There's no way to know. She's only sixteen, her brain is immature, and her identity is evolving. In the next decade, she will go through many more changes—and one of them, I hope, will be reacceptance of her female biology. I doubt Mia's surgeon advised her mother to consider the possibility, but it is real.

Mia may follow the same path as Daisy Chadra, a young woman who lived as a man for five years and had her breasts "amputated" (her word). What she lost is irreplaceable, but Daisy's back at peace with her female biology. In fact, she and her husband have a baby.

By the way, Daisy has said that just a few years ago she was 100 percent certain, 100 percent sure, that she'd be trans forever. Now she wishes she could nurse.

There appear to be thousands like Daisy who regret the medical and surgical interventions they believed would solve their emotional problems. Transgender activists claim they are rare, but reddit.com's detransitioners' site alone, as of this writing, has 47,300 members. If Mia someday joins their growing ranks, she may experience her flat, scarred chest as a loss.

And what if she decides, like Daisy, to have a child? In getting informed consent, the surgeon was obligated to raise that possibility and discuss the consequences of Mia's breast removal—not only to her daughter, but also to her grandchildren. Because in this case, organ removal may have negative consequences for the next generation.

## Breasts Are Not Disposable Sex Objects

Girls like Mia, Chloe, and Daisy who bind their breasts and go under the knife are not new to me—I've known about them for years. But I will never get used to the photos girls post; each time I see another one, with jagged scars across her chest, I'm sickened.

Maybe it's because I'm a mother and grandmother. Or because I know the science of nursing and maternal-child bonding. Perhaps it's related to my bilateral mastectomies for cancer.

*These are young girls struggling with their mental health.* Many have yet to experience the pleasure their bodies can give them; none can fathom motherhood—of that I am certain. To rob them of the pleasures and functions their breasts might provide is abhorrent and criminal.

Why would a girl consider her breasts only sex objects to be leered at, despicable and disposable? Because of our culture, obviously, but also because of her education.

For example, back when Mia was learning her ABCs, she was taught the planet is a delicate ecosystem. She shouldn't take clean air and natural resources for granted, she learned. The concept was enforced throughout her curriculum and over the years. She took it to heart and is now an avid recycler; her concerns about global warming keep her up at night.

Unfortunately, no one ever told her that *she is a delicate ecosystem*, especially her female physiology, including her breasts. If she'd been aware of their wonderful, complex functions, perhaps she'd have paused before damaging them by binding, and losing them by amputation.

When she signed on the dotted line, Mia's mother agreed to deprive her daughter and grandchildren of the opportunity to nurse. At the moment, it may have seemed irrelevant; after all, as Chloe thought at the time: *I'm a boy, boys don't nurse.*

But a few months after her mastectomies, she was in a psychology class and heard about psychologist Harry Harlow's experiment using rhesus monkeys.

The experiment showed that the bond between mother and child was much more critical to the development of the child's brain than had been known. "It occurred to me that I'd never be able to breastfeed my baby," she said.[35] She was sixteen.

Julie, twenty-seven, also underwent a mastectomy and then detransitioned. "I have this intense rage in me over the harm that was done to me," said Julie,[36] who didn't want to be identified out of fear of backlash from activists.

She called her treatment a "collaborative idiocy"—drawing together her parents, therapists, and doctors. "It took a goddamn village."

Laura Becker wrote a letter to her surgeon, Dr. Clifford King, from the offices of Top Surgery Midwest in Madison, Wisconsin, to inform him she "100 percent regrets the operation" and has detransitioned and is now living as a female with no functioning breasts.

Laura writes she "was fresh out of an inpatient psychiatric ward for suicidal ideation when I desperately made my appointment with Dr. King to try and heal my depression through altering my body with surgery."

Laura writes she "openly discussed being suicidal with Dr. King during our consultation and feeling suicidal on the day of the actual surgery." She adds:

> I was twenty, developmentally immature, mentally ill, suicidal, had PTSD, and not in a rational state of consciousness, yet the mental health system failed to provide its due service, and Dr. King and other cosmetic surgeons hungrily leapt at the opportunity for fresh meat to profit from operating on, in this unchecked, wild west market for "gender medicine."[37]

I submit for mastectomy consent to be informed, Mia and her mother had to be aware of the increasing numbers of "trans men" who revert to living as women, regret their breast surgery, and grasp the full impact of what was taken from them. And just as a kidney donor must understand the organ to be excised filters the blood and produces urine, they must learn that breasts provide the best available nourishment to infants, and that nursing is central to mother-infant bonding.

## Mommy Is Here

In general terms, for informed consent to be valid, the patient (or their guardian) must know the benefits and risks, both short- and long-term, of the procedure and must have the mental capacity to make rational decisions. The consent must also be voluntary free of threat or coercion.

Stephen Levine and coauthors have written extensively about the myriad ethical concerns of the informed consent model of care often used for "gender-affirming" interventions. In that model, mental health evaluations are not needed, and consent is sometimes obtained following surprisingly brief evaluations. They call that model "the antithesis of true informed consent . . . patients consenting to treatment do not have an accurate understanding of the risks, benefits, and alternatives."[38]

Regarding Mia, I focus here on a specific element of informed consent: knowing the long-term risk. Specifically, the risk that she may wish one day to breastfeed and will have lost that ability.

The surgeon is obligated to explain that her breasts provide the best-known nourishment for babies, and that nursing is central to mother-infant bonding.¶

How might a surgeon accomplish that? Maybe with a series of videos that walk her through the science and allow her to imagine herself as a mother, even if it seems inconceivable to her now. Because people change, and she may change.

The video could begin with Harlow's experiment, mentioned above. It could then describe how, as she approached birth, Mia's body would create the superfood called colostrum: her baby's first meal. Colostrum is thick, sweet, and the perfect temperature. Rich in nutrients, it is also a vaccine, laxative, immune booster, and anti-inflammatory agent.

When placed on her abdomen following delivery, her newborn would slowly crawl toward her breast and begin to suckle.[39] How would he find his way? With his strong sense of smell,[40] he'd be attracted to the familiar scent of her nipples.[41]

---

¶ I acknowledge that some mothers are unable to nurse or have other reasons to use formula and do not imply their bonding is impaired. Nursing, however, is the ideal.

Wait—how could he know the odor of his mother's nipples? He'd recognize it from before he was born: it would smell like the amniotic fluid[42] in which he was immersed for months. It would be familiar and calming. It would say, *Mommy is here.* With a few drops on a cotton pad placed by his tiny nose, he'd cry less when separated from her.[43]

Think about it: a newborn is jolted into an unfamiliar, harsh reality of bright lights, loud noises, cold, hunger, and pain. Any reminder of the idyllic existence he left behind must be heavenly. We all know the power of scent. When her baby would nurse with his nostrils against her nipple, he'd inhale the scent of that perfect world.

With nursing, she and her baby would have functioned as one unit. Upon seeing, hearing, or even thinking of him, her milk would have come down, causing a feeling of fullness. She'd need to nurse, *now.* Her baby's sucking would relieve the uncomfortable pressure in her breasts and stimulate the release of oxytocin, a powerful hormone that would help her relax and bond with her child.

Her baby would get a hefty dose of oxytocin too, both his own and from her milk, and he'd get it while feeling and hearing her heartbeat, as he did in the womb. It would have been a positive feedback loop: oxytocin surge, milk letdown, nurse, oxytocin surge. Repeat indefinitely until fully satisfied or asleep. If it sounds magical, trust me, it is.

No bottle, pacifier, plush toy, bouncer, swing, rocker, sound machine, mobile, light show, or vibrating mat will soothe an unhappy baby like nursing.

Her breasts and milk composition would have adapted to her baby's needs. If the baby would have a fever, her breasts would cool down; if his temperature would have dropped, her breasts would warm up. This remarkable process is called "thermal synchrony."[44] If the baby got sick, the number of white cells in her milk would rise to fight the infection.[45]

Breast milk provides lasting health benefits for both mother and child and is considered the gold standard by pediatricians[46] and the World Health Organization.[47]

Nursing would help her uterus to return to its normal size. Breastfeeding, especially at night, would increase levels of prolactin, a hormone that would enhance her milk supply and make her feel relaxed and sleepy, so even if the baby wakes up hungry at night, she can usually rest well. Nursing will suppress her ovulation and menstruation, preventing a new pregnancy and allowing her to focus on her child.

And with that the video would end.

Of course, the miracles of mother-child bonding, and the many other wonders of her female biology, are utterly foreign to Mia. Her sexuality education focused on her right to engage in oral, anal, and vaginal intercourse; to access contraception and abortions without parental consent; to reject her body and identify as a boy. Pregnancy? Nursing? You've got to be kidding.

And that's what got us here, to over 45,000 girls on GoFundMe, instead of inspiring awe for their biology, they were indoctrinated to flee it—how many will end up regretting their choices, like Chloe and Daisy?

Maybe nursing mothers should come speak to girls, moms such as these who told me:

> Nursing is our special quiet time together. I know I must stop everything and meet his needs. Only I can do this. Some moms will prop up a bottle, leave the baby, and go do something else—that's so sad. I look at how he has grown, his chubby, delicious arms and cheeks, and I know all that came from me. (CH)
>
> I was recovering from a difficult birth. Yet every time I put my baby to my breast to nourish her brain and body with my gift of liquid love, the pain, the new mom anxiety, the exhaustion, all evaporated. As my child nurses, our breath and heartbeats align, and we enter a place of deep serenity beyond the touch of time. (EW)

Some of you are rolling your eyes, but consider what your daughter learns in school right now: at five, that she may have a boy's brain;[48] at nine, to enjoy drag shows;[49] at eleven, the wonders of "Ten Years on Testosterone."[50] And in some high schools, your daughters will have access to contraception, including the "day after pill," and STD testing right down the hall, for free, without your knowledge.[51]

Parents concerned that girls' learning about nursing constitutes an offensive microaggression can opt their daughter out. And no, boys who identify as girls are not invited. Sorry, Jazz, and all "transwomen" out there: you may have curves and glittery make-up, but you'll never know those natural female wonders.

What's missing from girls' lives is a sense of awe for their biology. Sure, the Earth is a delicate ecosystem and treasure to be cared for and respected, but so are they. From where do they get that message? Certainly not at school, not in sex ed or anywhere else.

It's in your hands. You must reach your girls before the sex ed and gender activists do with their Articles of Faith and euphemisms.

Euphemisms are dangerous. Remember, it's not "top" or "chest" surgery, it's the amputation of a girl's healthy breasts. The gender medical establishment wants you to get used to the idea and to be blind to the evil. At all costs, do not allow it.

# CHAPTER TWELVE

# Surgeons' Dangerous Idea

How do you make a vagina?

Ask Jake, he has one.

Actually, he *used to* have one; the surgeon constructed it from his penis and scrotum. Six months later, Jake realized he's a man, and could never be a woman with a bona fide vagina, so he stopped the upkeep of his faux vagina, and it pretty much closed up.

Now Jake has neither a penis nor a "vagina," but he will need to inject testosterone into his thigh every week for the rest of his life. The gender-affirming industry, projected to rake in $1.5 billion by 2026,[1] has recruited another lifelong patient.

Before his first appointment, Jake, from Hawaii, completed my office forms. For the medical history portion, where patients typically list their allergies and appendectomies, he wrote three words: *I am mutilated.*

*They sliced my penis and made a vagina with it,* Jake told me. *I had doubts that morning, I wondered, is this the answer? Is this what I need? I thought of canceling the operation, but they said, "You're gonna be ok."*

Surgeons refer to "gender-affirming" procedures such as vaginoplasties and phalloplasties as genital "reconstruction." Again, in order to *affirm*, they must *deny* biological reality. And there's no "reconstructing" anything. Jake never had female genitalia. And the surgeons can only attempt, using primitive procedures, to mimic the real thing.

I acknowledge from the outset that these surgeries may help some people, but we lack robust long-term evidence that they are a majority.

And there is no way to identify those people, pre-op, with any degree of certainty. There is no long-term follow-up whatsoever of surgeries performed on young people with ROGD.

It's important for you to know the details of Jake's "affirming" surgery, as well as those performed on young women. One day it could be your child who believes, like he did, that their emotional struggles will be cured in a few hours on an operating table. I want him or her to avoid a catastrophe.

Brace yourselves, what's ahead is dreadful.

In the months leading up to Jake's surgery, his pubic hair was eliminated by electrolysis. On the operating table, his testicles were removed and his scrotal skin fashioned into "labia." His penis was flayed, inverted, and used to create a "vaginal vault." Some use the term "neovagina" for this structure; I prefer faux vagina, because "neo" means "new" or "modified," and what Jake's surgeon constructed was neither a new or modified vagina; it's something altogether different, trust me.

Back to the OR. The sensitive nerves and tissue from the tip of Jake's penis became a "clitoris." His urethra, the tube through which he eliminates urine, was shortened, and relocated.

Jake was twenty years old when he climbed on the operating table. But for a boy whose puberty was blocked at a young age, such as Jazz Jennings, a vaginoplasty is much more complicated. As explained, the penis will remain child-size ("micro-penis") because it was never exposed to the testosterone surge of puberty. There will be insufficient tissue to create a faux vagina, and the surgeons will have to harvest it from elsewhere. This gets extremely complicated; Jazz needed to go under the knife three additional times following the original surgery.

The body does not recognize a faux vagina; instead, it perceives it as an open wound. The body's natural reaction to a wound is to close it. Therefore, patients who have vaginoplasties must conscientiously dilate the new structure—a tedious process—so it remains patent, or open.

One patient described it this way on Twitter:[2]

> Having a vagina is super hard!
>
> Dilations??? Awful!!! Why do I have to feel that my anus is about to disintegrate?? Why does the labia have to burn so much every time I dilate? And every 6 f-king hours every day???? Madness!! Absolute madness!! I want to cry!![3]

## Trouble Down Under

A major issue following genital surgeries is that urination may be compromised. Not for days or weeks, but for months or years.

This is true for vaginoplasties as well as phalloplasties, during which a flap of skin from the forearm is used to create what advocates call a neophallus, but I will call a faux phallus. The surgeon rolls the skin together and attaches it to the groin. It's a complex process that typically requires multiple surgeries, including those for urethral lengthening. Additional procedures including implants are needed to be able to have an "erection."

On TikTok, Ashton shares the struggle of not being able to urinate without a catheter, following surgery to construct a faux phallus. Ashton's experience with urethral failure necessitated a urethroplasty, which involved taking tissue from her inner cheek lining to construct a new urethra:

*It's been almost six months since I've had phalloplasty, and the past six months have been an absolute ride and they have been six of the hardest months that I've ever been through.* [4]

Normally, a patient may have multiple catheters placed temporarily,[5] but Ashton ended up having a catheter for over seven months, until the next surgery to fix a blockage:

> I got what's called a stricture or a fistula. . . . I need something now called urethroplasty, which means a complete rebuild of my urethra, which means I've been having a suprapubic tube, which is a catheter, in place for about seven months.
>
> And they have to change it every month, so I've gotten it changed just about seven times now. It's very uncomfortable when they're changing it. . .
>
> Having another eighteen months of surgery ahead of me is definitely not something that I really want to do.[6]

Skin from the forearm was used to create Ashton's "penis," leaving Ashton with numbness due to nerve destruction:

*I did extensive physical therapy trying to see if we could get some feeling back into it, but according to the surgeon, there were nerves that were taken out of that arm . . . and I do not have any feeling in it whatsoever.*[7]

The goal of phalloplasty is to "stand to pee," but many ultimately cannot pee at all:

> It was so amazing to finally to be able to stand up to use the bathroom. It was really, really neat. And then I woke up the next day and I went to . . . take

my morning pee and all of a sudden I'm pushing and I'm pushing and I'm pushing and nothing is coming out.

And it is absolutely terrifying for, all of a sudden, a bodily function that has worked your entire life no longer works. I was terrified.[8]

Ashton spoke of "luckily" being able to rely on the suprapubic tube—another back-up catheter that remained "in case this [blockage] happened, because there's such a big chance of this happening."[9]

Ashton warns viewers, "When you get bottom surgery for F to M, there is a huge chance, the margins are like 14 to 60-something percent that this is going to happen to you. It's either called a stricture or a fistula."[10]

Documenter Exulansic, who "studies trans ideology as a group of religious movements threatening our civil and disability rights,"[11] keenly observes, "So, it sounds like this person was told that the risk of this happening would be somewhere between 14 percent and 69 percent. . . . How is anyone supposed to make a reasonable decision based on those odds?"[12]

Unfortunately for Ashton, prolonged use of a catheter has not surprisingly led to more complications:

I have been fighting off infection after infection. My body doesn't like it.[13]

One of the few long-term studies examined the urologic complications of trans surgery up to six years. They found that almost three-quarters of patients cited feeling intermediately to strongly bothered by their bladder symptoms.[14] These issues included overactive bladder, stress urinary incontinence, a reduced urinary flow, and meatal stenosis. In English that means feeling like you need to urinate all the time, incontinence, a weak stream, and a narrowed opening. These debilitating complications can last for years.

Remember, we are speaking of men and women who had perfectly normal plumbing prior to surgery. They weren't running to urinate every fifteen minutes, they weren't leaking. As healthy young people, they did their business and forgot about it. Were they counseled about the risks of surgeries? More than a few say they were not.

Ritchie, another detrans man who had a vaginoplasty, described his post-surgery torment in a Twitter thread:

No one told me any of what I'm going to tell you now.

No one told me that the base area of your penis is left, it can't be removed—meaning [you're] left with a literal stump inside that twitches.

I have no sensation in my crotch region at all.

Then there's the act of going to the toilet. It takes me about 10 minutes to empty my bladder, it's extremely slow, painful and because it dribbles no matter how much i relax, it will then just go all over that entire area, leaving me soake[d].

So after cleaning myself up, I will find moments later that my underwear is wet—no matter how much I wiped, it slowly drips out for the best part of an hour. I never knew at 35 I ran the risk [of] smelling like piss everywhere I went.[15]

## As Simple as Chewing Gum

I want the reader to remember that Jake, Ashton, and Ritchie's pain and suffering were 100 percent avoidable. But they fell prey to the zealous affirmation of the gender medical establishment. My patient Jake told me:

I was abused by my baseball coach, that's why I had dysphoria, it was the sexual trauma, I couldn't look at my genitals. I had tried to kill myself a few times . . . I was diagnosed with bipolar and hospitalized twice, I [overdosed] twice and tried to drown in a lake near my house. . .

I was confused and I fell victim to the gender thing . . . the clinic pushed it on me over and over that I am trans. The therapist asked, why haven't you changed your name yet? He pushed transition and I was put in the express lane. They put me on [estrogen and spironolactone]. They didn't look at my mental health history.

It was rushed. . . . I only met with the surgeon once for maybe twenty minutes . . . I was not in a stable place of mind . . . I was on three psych meds. They said it would improve my mental health. I trusted them.

Jake thought he had found a solution to his suffering. He trusted his physicians and his social worker and signed on the dotted line. Now his life trajectory has been irrevocably altered:

I have UTIs frequently, I see dark clots when I use the bathroom.

I've been gravely wronged. I wish I could go back in time and undo it. . .

I lost my manhood. I can't be a father. I told them several times I want that. They didn't speak with me about sperm preservation. . .

Where do I go from here? How do I move forward?

Beyond mutilation of his genitals and urinary incontinence, Jake suffers from frequent pain, infection, bleeding, and concerns about his sexual function. Jake's complaints are not unusual; he has lots of company: at one post-vaginoplasty clinic, over half of the patients reported pain, over a third had sexual function concerns, and 42 percent were experiencing "vaginal" bleeding.[16]

Why the frequent infections? They're due to hair growing in Jake's faux vagina.

Wait, what?

Well, in spite of Jake's many painful electrolysis sessions, so painful he required local anesthesia, some follicles must have persisted, and they grew hair in their new location. Not good: the presence of hair can lead to infection, pus, and a putrid odor. As you might imagine, it's very hard to permanently remove hair growing deep inside the faux vagina.

At forty-two years old, Scott Newgent has been to hell and back, following her* phalloplasty. Her mission now is to protect children from the gender industry.[17] She writes:

> I endured medical complication after medical complication. . . . I lost every-thing I'd ever worked for: home, car, savings, career, wife, medical insurance, and most importantly my faith in myself and God. In a battle to survive, I went from ER to ER, trying to solve a mystery of why my health was failing.
>
> I learned firsthand the truth about how dangerous and perilous medi-cal transition really is. I learned the hard way that if you get sick because of transgender health, you will witness physicians throwing their hands up and saying one of two things: 1) "transgender health is experimental, and I don't know what's wrong" or 2) "you need to go back to the physicians who hurt you in the first place."
>
> My medical complications have included seven surgeries, a pulmonary embolism, an induced stress heart attack, sepsis, a 17-month recurring infection, 16 rounds of antibiotics, three weeks of daily IV antibiotics, arm reconstructive surgery, lung, heart and bladder damage, insomnia, hallucinations, PTSD, $1 million in medical expenses, and loss of home, car, career and marriage. All this, and yet I cannot sue the surgeon responsible—in part because there is no structured, tested or widely accepted baseline for transgender health care.[18]

---

* Scott told me she's fine with feminine pronouns.

In order to "empower" the transgender identifying patient, gender-affirming care eliminates gatekeeping. Patients are left with a rosy depiction of the outcomes of these primitive surgeries. Scott writes:

> When you start to medically transition, you are told a Disney version akin to watching toddlers skip through the daisies; imagine watching the sun set and leaning back against a tree and sipping iced tea. This is the image that was painted for me. At 42, even I wasn't able to decipher what the complications were as the medical and mental health industry made transition seem as simple as chewing gum. Each time I asked a question, my concerns were skimmed over, making me feel insignificant and childish. Now I was middle-aged and a successful business sales executive. If I was intimidated, children and adolescents don't stand a chance.[19]

Take note, everybody: Scott was a successful middle-aged business executive, Yet, she was intimidated by the gender surgeon. This chapter arms you with facts you need to know should you, or someone you love, consult with a gender surgeon. You're not insignificant, and your concerns are real. Don't allow them to be dismissed.

Shape Shifter, a vocal male-to-female detransitioner whose YouTube channel's byline is "Survivor of experimental transgender health care," has said, "The surgeries are not where they should be. They're not as safe as they're sold, I was sold a sex reassignment surgery. I'm still male . . . I never became female . . . that's the reality.[20]

## What do the data say?

Remember Ashton, who needed continuous catheterizations following phalloplasty? That and other issues are commonplace among recipients of affirming surgeries:

- **infection:** the skin near the incision and the urethra are common areas for infection; prolonged catheterization is required, increasing one's risk of serious infection
- **partial phallic loss:** if the faux penis does not maintain adequate blood flow, it cannot survive
- **stricture:** inadequate blood flow can cause scar tissue to form. This may slow or block the release of urine.
- **fistula:** an abnormal connection between the urinary tract and a nearby organ, like the bowel, or to the body surface

A 2022 phalloplasty systematic review and meta-analysis (a type of study known for its high quality of evidence)[21] of 1,731 patients revealed the following staggering outcomes: an overall complication rate of more than three-quarters of patients; almost a third experienced urethral fistula; and a quarter experienced urethral stricture.

The authors conclude that the evidence for patients getting the outcomes promised is "weak."

A large 2022 review[22] of phalloplasty including eleven studies found that nearly a third developed a serious complication, namely, stricture or fistula. Meanwhile, the medical establishment and the media continue to portray these surgeries as improving the lives of individuals with gender distress.

Sexual function was addressed in a crucial follow-up study, mentioned previously, by the Dutch—the first long-term study we have. Although only male-to-female patients were included, they found that over three-quarters had problems with libido; slightly more than two-thirds experienced failure to orgasm. And 71 percent experienced pain during sex.[23]

A 2018 survey of those who had undergone male-to-female surgery concluded that the majority experienced orgasms more intensely after surgery.[24] But the response rate was less than half; how can we conclude anything at all when so few responded?

One question addressed overall sex life satisfaction.† On a scale from 0 ("very dissatisfied") to 10 ("very satisfied"), less than 8 percent said they were very satisfied.

Far from glowing results.

Now let's look at another of the very few long-term studies, which followed patients for thirteen years.[25] The authors conclude that the available studies suffer from many limitations: a lack of control populations, high dropout rates, and very few that describe the surgical outcomes in detail.

In other words, the data supporting phalloplasties and vaginoplasties are low-quality. Yet the gender-affirming industry advocates their benefits. Surgeons welcome patients like Jake, Ritchie, and Scott with open arms. That is, until they complain about the appearance of their genitals or return to the office with appalling complications: feces exiting from the wrong orifice; nerve damage impeding sexual intimacy; chronic bleeding, oozing or infections . . . you get the picture.

---

† In order to gather information on patients' general satisfaction with their sex lives, they were asked to place themselves on a Likert scale ranging from 0 ("very dissatisfied") to 10 ("very satisfied"). Nearly a quarter of participants either selected scores from 0 to 3 (n=29; 24.4%), from 4 to 6 (n=30;25.2%), or from 7 to 10 (n = 29; 24.4%) or refused to answer (n = 31; 26.1%).

While thankfully rare, deaths from "affirming" surgeries do occur. The one from the Dutch study discussed earlier was reported in 2016:[26] An eighteen-year-old thought he was getting a "vagina" but in the process was infected with a type of E. coli commonly known as flesh-eating bacteria. He developed septic shock and organ failure. And he was put through this, as I keep reminding you, even though evidence of lasting benefit from the surgery was lacking. His death was 100 percent avoidable.

Shape Shifter describes how when complications emerge—which they inevitably do for over one third of patients—physicians run the other way:

> Nobody wants to touch other surgeon's work because they don't want to attach their name to a complicated case . . . because every time you go in there is more scar tissues, more complications.[27]

Even worse, the blame is placed on the patient, not the procedure:

> They don't really tell you that the body treats you as a wound and tries to close up—yes constantly trying to close up [the neovagina]. So, I got a revision . . . a few months later I was back on [the] operating table and I got blamed at the time that [I] didn't dilate enough even though I was religiously dilating . . . they kept on blaming me for not dilating enough.[28]

A patient starts out with one problem—dysphoria—and ends up with a multitude of problems. Unlike gender dysphoria, the new iatrogenic issues could be permanent, or require additional surgeries.

One example is women's excruciating orgasms following testosterone. Aydian Dowling describes in a YouTube video, "The ALMOST Every Day Vlog Ep. 06":

> . . . it literally feels like someone takes two knives and shoves them into [the pelvic region] and twists and turns them and that goes on for about anywhere from maybe a minute . . . to six, seven minutes it's very disruptive to the sexual experience it makes me kind of at certain points feel like I don't necessarily want to engage sexually because it's extremely painful. . .[29]

Like so many complications stemming from affirmative care, the agonizing orgasms were unexpected, and Aydian, who's heard the same complaint from others, wants to publicize the problem. Not only is it incredibly

painful, causing her to seek a hysterectomy—which may lead to other medical issues—but it seems the professionals aren't talking about it.

Once again, where is the informed consent? Aydian estimated that about
eight in ten women on testosterone are affected by this debilitating issue and
that physicians recommend a hysterectomy—major surgery with possible
complications—as a solution. Why aren't women warned? Aydian's estimate
isn't far off base—in a study of almost 490 participants, 72 percent reported
pelvic cramping following the initiation of testosterone. The authors declare
that "further research . . . is warranted" given the pelvic floor musculature
is sensitive to androgens such as testosterone.[30]

Upon being prescribed a hysterectomy to help with the iatrogenic pain
patients experience, are they made aware of the additional risks of *that* procedure: bladder injury, urinary tract infections, and overactive bladder? What
about the cardiovascular risks[31]—increased strokes and heart attacks—
among women undergoing hysterectomy at young ages for "benign" reasons
(i.e., not cancer)?

It boggles the brain.

In a YouTube video, Joey Maiza describes iatrogenic bladder issues following a hysterectomy performed years ago:

*I have . . . issues with my bladder which I found out was also related to my
hysterectomy that I had many years ago because now my bladder dropped. . .*[32]

Moving beyond the complications of elective hysterectomies, will these
women one day regret being unable to carry and give birth to a child?

Let's return to the first long-term follow-up study mentioned previously, which came from the Dutch.[33] Like so much of gender-affirming
research, this study had an unimpressive response rate of fewer than half of
participants, which leads to biases and omissions of adverse outcomes. The
study found that over half of those surveyed wanted to have kids, a number
expected to grow as more participants reached their mid to late thirties. At
ages twelve to fifteen, none of the subjects wanted to preserve fertility.

This is a travesty, a life-altering reality that can never be undone. Yet,
as mentioned in Chapter Five, gender-affirming pediatric endocrinologist
Daniel Metzger of British Columbia Children's Hospital casually remarked
during a meeting shared on YouTube,

> Some of the Dutch researchers . . . gave some data about young adults who
> had transitioned and reproductive regret. Like, regret. And, it's there. And I
> don't think any of that surprises us . . . most of the kids are nowhere in any
> kind of a brain space to really, really talk about it in a serious way.

That's always bothered me, but, you know, we still want the kids to be happy . . . happier in the moment, right?[34]

Here we have a physician, a professional bound by medical ethical principles including *beneficence* and *nonmaleficence* who is endorsing the notion that making a minor "happier in the moment" trounces the future devastation caused by sterilization of a minor who cannot fathom the lifelong consequences of their decisions.

Looking at the totality of egregious issues through a wide lens, one can't help but wonder what happened to the Hippocratic Oath taken by the "gender-affirming" physicians who once promised to "Do no harm"?

## Ignoring the Red Flags

"What I really needed was therapy, not surgery," Shape Shifter said on TikTok.[35] He's right. He had a history of untreated trauma and abuse. But affirming care told Shape Shifter to "align" his body with his mind, so he focused on hair and make-up, breasts, and "vagina." After all the operations, he's still in emotional pain, but added to it is a laundry list of medical woes.

Some look back incredulously at how the medical professionals failed to carefully and holistically examine their histories.

Shape Shifter:

> I was drinking the Kool-Aid for years and I was convinced that I was an actual woman . . . and I felt like this will help me and help my depression anxiety . . . but somehow mental health professionals ignored all the signs and all the other mental health issues I had that I discovered later on. . .
>
> . . .the truth is it didn't take away any of my issues and I got even more depressed after the surgery because . . . the surgery is sold incorrectly as something that will solve your issues.[36]

Ritchie:

> During transition, I was obsessive and deeply unwell, I cannot believe they were allowed to do this to me, even after all the red flags.

Shape Shifter and Ritchie are far from alone in realizing their mental health issues were the driving force behind their insatiable desire to transition. A 2022 Reddit (r/detrans) Demographic Survey[37] revealed that 82 percent of detransitioners "realized gender dysphoria was related to other issues," including mental health. Slightly more than 40 percent of natal females and 32 percent of natal males in one detransitioners' survey endorsed the statement, "I discovered that my gender dysphoria was caused by something specific (ex, trauma, abuse, mental health condition)."[38] With time, many of these individuals find themselves no longer fleeing who they are.

When underlying problems aren't addressed, they will resurface sooner or later. Az Hakeem, distinguished psychiatrist in the United Kingdom who works with transgender-identifying individuals both before and after surgery, writes: "Whilst such surgery may offer help to some patients . . . what about the unfortunate patients for whom surgery does not provide a resolution to their serious internal conflict?"[39]

Dr. Hakeem calls sex reassignment surgery—now called gender-affirming surgery—"mechanical transformations." I like that.

For eight years, Dr. Elif Gurisik ran a weekly psychotherapy group for dissatisfied post-operative patients. Many felt a great deal of anger and resentment for being allowed to undergo a process that they now regarded as leaving them mutilated and neither male nor female.

The group was considered very successful in preventing suicide among these individuals living helplessly and hopelessly with regret. Although groups such as hers are incredibly rare—The Portman Clinic was a lone player[40]—patient regret is not rare, despite what we're told. The affirming industry insists that regret is around 1 percent. Fortunately, we have experts like Dr. Hakeem who in 2021 informed us otherwise:

> The public are often told that relative regret is extremely low. But this of course is a complete fiction. There are no follow-up studies, no one knows what the regret rate actually is and this low rate results from the lack of any information being collected. The patients I saw did not officially exist in any gender identity clinics' books.[41]

D'Angelo et al. (2021) in a Letter to the Editor[42] addressed the research examining regret: ". . . these studies may understate true regret rates due to overly stringent definitions of regret (i.e., requiring an official application for reversal of the legal gender status), very high rates of participant loss to follow-up (22 to 63 percent), and an unexplored relationship between regret and high rates of post-transition suicide."

It's generally accepted that regret may take about eight to ten years to manifest.[43] For people like Jake, Ritchie, and Shape Shifter, regret surfaced much earlier. Studies that claim regret is extremely low—like so much of the research discussed here—are often poorly conducted. They may fail to follow patients long enough, or follow an entirely different group of patients—not the current ROGD cohort that is the focus of this book.

More from Dr. Hakeem:

> . . . 26 percent of my patients are post-operative regretters. . . . These people were all non-existent data. No one had followed them up from the gender clinic since they had been given their sex changes. . . . Many of them were too embarrassed to admit that they regretted their decision having persuaded the Doctors and Psychiatrists and gender clinic to give them what they wanted and felt they needed. Many of them were living in a post-operative role which they now felt to be fraudulent but from which they felt there was no return.

We have no way of knowing how many transitioners live with regret, and how many are genuinely satisfied. Although we don't yet have high-quality research, we do have the 47,300 people who have joined the Reddit thread r/detrans. And Lisa Littman's 2020 study that found "76 percent of respondents did not inform their clinicians . . ."[44] More research on detransitioners is critically needed.

## WPATH

How in God's name are these atrocities taking place? Simple. The surgeons who carved up Jake, Ritchie, Shape Shifter, Scott, and others—leaving them infertile and disfigured—can justify their work: They provide gender-affirming care; they "follow WPATH's standards of care."

What is WPATH? Read carefully, parents, you need to know.

WPATH is the "World Professional Association for Transgender Health"—sounds impressive, right? Like a group of doctors with stethoscopes and pocket protectors, conducting research, examining evidence, and carefully formulating guidelines for clinicians? It may once have been, but no longer.

WPATH is an NGO formed in 1979. They promote their standards of care (SOC) as the model of best practice, the gold standard. Many, if not most, US hospitals, clinics, and private physicians and therapists base their practices on WPATH's SOC.

How close to a gold standard are they? An independent, peer-reviewed analysis in 2021[45] gave them a quality score of zero out of six.

WPATH presents its approach to patients, parents, and providers as the only valid, evidence-based option, yet its recommendations have been formally rejected by Sweden, Finland, Norway, and Britain and questioned by medical groups in France, Australia, and New Zealand. Although WPATH guidance advises hospitals, clinicians and even courts, WPATH itself suffers from identity confusion: while presenting as an unbiased science-based medical group, it is in truth an advocacy organization run by activists who have an unwavering goal of affirmation at all costs. Ideology colors its recommendations, which have fallen prey to affirmative bias and rest upon research that's inherently flawed or very low-quality.

Dr. Marci Bowers, current president of WPATH, performed Jazz's castration and vaginoplasty.

I remember watching the episode of *I am Jazz* during which Jazz and parents consult with Dr. Bowers for first time. Jazz is so excited about getting a "vagina," but after examining Jazz, Dr. Bowers explains that as a consequence of the puberty blockers started at age eleven, Jazz's penis is very small, and there isn't enough tissue to construct a "vagina."

My heart dropped, Oh, no . . . if only, years ago, they'd let this child be, Jazz would likely now be a feminine, perhaps gay, boy. Instead, Jazz's physical, emotional, sexual, and cognitive development were chemically interrupted, Jazz is infertile, probably can't orgasm, and has been led to believe surgery can create female genitalia. Now Dr. Bowers is saying . . . What?!

In the episode, the famous gender surgeon tells Jazz and parents that the solution, the only way to now construct a "vagina," is to borrow tissue from Jazz's colon. That caught my attention. I want to hear this. I may be a psychiatrist, but I remember my histology, and the lining of the colon is altogether different from the lining of the vagina.

For one thing, I recall the colon lining has cells that produce mucus to ease the passage of fecal material. Now, that's not going to be at all like the mucus produced by the cervix or vagina. Forgive me, I don't know what colonic mucus smells like, but okay.

So tissue from Jazz's colon was used to help construct a "vagina," despite evidence that many of these Frankenstein sigmoid colon-derived "vaginas" are chronically inflamed, swollen, and sensitive . . . not exactly what you want, especially during intercourse.[46]

Did Jazz truly understand the hazards ahead? One episode filmed Jazz saying, "When I was two years old, I had a dream of the good fairy coming to change my penis into a vagina, and today that's finally happening, and I feel like, you know, Dr. Marci Bowers is the good fairy, and now my dream is coming true."[47]

But Jazz's dream quickly morphed into a nightmare after complications led to multiple trips to the OR.

Jess Ting, a surgeon who joined Dr. Bowers in the operating room, admitted in one clip that this was going to be an unusual surgery.

"Taking Jazz on as a patient for surgery, we knew it was going to be a one-of-a-kind surgery," Ting explained. "We don't have the experience of having said we've done fifty of these. I was just not expecting her to have a complication as severe as what she did have." [48]

Okay, time out a second. I realize that "affirming" genital surgeries were developed years ago to help patients with severe dysphoria who begged for relief. The outcomes weren't great, but the point is those patients were middle-aged adults. We are speaking of much younger people here, and of more complicated procedures.

Jazz, placed on the gender transition expressway at age five, underwent "one-of-a-kind" surgery at seventeen.

Let me tell you something. When you have an operation, you don't want it to be "one-of-a-kind." That's the last thing you want. You want, if possible, to be one of millions who had the surgery; you want your surgeon to have performed the procedure hundreds or thousands of times.

You surely don't want your surgeons squabbling during the operation about what the next step should be, as happened with Ting and Bowers.

Listening to Jake, Ashton, Jazz, and so many others, sometimes it seems these surgeries are yet another example of doctors saying: "I have an idea. Let's do this to patients and see what happens."

In fact, I just learned that surgeons have a new and improved solution for the micro-penis in patients such as Jazz: construct a "vagina" using tilapia skin.

Yes, the fish.

I admit to being impressed by surgeons coming up with creative solutions to vexing surgical dilemmas. Still, I wonder, is there a point at which they say: "Sorry, we cannot do this?"

I learned from Michael Biggs's 2022 exposé [49] of the Dutch Protocol that concerns for patients like Jazz were raised at a conference all the way back in 2005. A 2008 article by the Dutch pioneers recognized "the genital tissue available for vaginoplasty may be less than optimal" [50] and that more invasive and complicated procedures would be needed. That's exactly what Dr. Bowers was talking about in that disturbing episode.

Were Jazz and parents made aware of that risk when blockers were started in 2011? Were Jazz's medical and surgical interventions examples of the "evidence-based care" promised by WPATH's SOC in its mission statement?[51]

How could they be, when we *do not yet have the evidence* for these complicated surgeries in a patient whose puberty was blocked at an early age? As whistleblower Jamie Reed recalls the doctors at the Transgender Center at St. Louis Children's Hospital saying,[52] "We are building the plane while we are flying it." Pretty scary. Yet patients and their parents will not realize this upon boarding. Nor will they likely come across WPATH's disclaimers that in adults the empirical evidence available is "limited" and does not include randomized controlled trials or long-term longitudinal research.[53]

Pay attention—the disclaimer is *just for the adults*! There's even less data available for the youngest patients. Don't worry, though, WPATH assures us that "Longitudinal studies are currently underway . . ."[54]

Does this admission that studies are in progress absolve WPATH? Of course not. We're not crash-testing cars here. But let's imagine for a moment that we were. How would you feel if the car you had just purchased came with the following disclaimer:

*The testing on these brakes is "limited," and there's no long-term research on their safety. But studies are currently underway.*

If you're the parent of a boy for whom puberty suppression has been recommended, you need to know that out of forty-nine patients who started blockers in early-to-mid puberty, 71 percent lacked sufficient tissue for construction of a "vagina" and required, like Jazz, the grafting of part of the intestine.[55]

## Passionate Convictions, Dangerous Intolerance

Dr. Stephen Levine was a member of WPATH for twenty-five years. He served as the chairman of the International Standards of Care Committee that issued the fifth version of the Standards of Care. Dr. Levine writes in an expert report:

> The Standards of Care (SOC) document is the product of an effort to be balanced, but it is not politically neutral. WPATH aspires to be both a scientific organization and an advocacy group for the transgendered. These aspirations sometimes conflict. The limitations of the Standards of Care, however, are not primarily political. They are caused by the lack of rigorous research in the field, which allows room for passionate convictions on how to care for the transgendered.[56]

Dr. Levine also comments on WPATH's dangerous intolerance for diversity of thought:

> WPATH claims to speak for the medical profession; however, it does not welcome skepticism and therefore, deviates from the philosophical core of medical science.[57]
>
> Skepticism as to the benefits of sex reassignment surgery to patients, and strong alternate views, are not well tolerated in discussions within the organization or their educational outreach programs. Such views have been known to be shouted down and effectively silenced by the large numbers of nonprofessional adults who attend the organization's biennial meetings. Two groups of individuals that I regularly work with have attended recent and separate WPATH continuing education sessions. There, questions about alternative approaches were quickly dismissed with "There are none. This is how it is done." Such a response does not accurately reflect what is known, what is unknown, and the diversity of clinical approaches in this complex field.[58]

Dr. Levine recounted to me[59] an incident that happened at a 1997 WPATH meeting. He gave a talk on the risks or consequences of public and private cross-dressing and socially presenting oneself as a woman on wives and children. But in the audience were middle-aged men dressed as women. Dr. Levine felt pressured not to trigger them into guilt, shame, or rage. "It certainly does not encourage a free exchange of ideas. Having these stakeholders in the audience inhibits both the speaker, the speaker's speech, and colleagues' responses to the talk. Booing during a presentation is not exactly profession decorum."

I asked Dr. Levine if there was a defining incident that led to his resignation from WPATH following twenty-five years and after holding several senior positions.

He said yes, in 2001 he was chairman of the eight-member group charged with developing the fifth Standards of Care. The committee had decided to maintain the SOC-4's requirement of two letters of support from mental health providers prior to hormonal interventions, and another two prior to surgeries.

Dr. Levine presented the SOC-5 to the executive committee of WPATH that included former WPATH president Richard Green,[60] who was incidentally a colleague of John Money's. "When Green saw we recommended two letters from psychotherapists for hormones," Dr. Levine told me, "he said no. Two letters is too conservative, treatment must be more accessible."

All eight members of the group that came up with these recommendations were in agreement about the two letters. However, Green only wanted one letter. He at once appointed a new committee to write the SOC-6 requiring only one letter for hormones; and later SOC-7 would dispense with a letter altogether, claiming the letters are "gatekeeping," which was considered wrong.

Dr. Levine resigned. Green's actions were a clear signal to him that WPATH's objective was no longer recognizable, nor was it ethical. Their goal had become to affirm everyone and eliminate all barriers to care.

In an expert report for a case before the Southern District Court of West Virginia,[61] Dr. Levine wrote:

> I resigned my membership in 2002 due to my regretful conclusion that the organization and its recommendations had become dominated by politics and ideology, rather than by scientific process, as it was years earlier.[62]

All this is troubling considering the lifelong ramifications of the medical interventions WPATH endorses. Its claims of "consensus" among professionals couldn't be more misleading.

As Lisa MacRichard reported in the Canadian Gender Report at the 2017 USPATH/WPATH conference, activists protested and shut down a session with Dr. Kenneth Zucker, who endorsed a cautious approach to treating children with gender dysphoria.[63]

An example of a nonprofessional activist given a prominent position in WPATH is Susie Green, a mom who helped her son get on puberty blockers at age twelve and undergo sex reassignment surgery in Thailand at age sixteen.

Could we have anyone more ardent than the mom of a gender-dysphoric child who underwent complete sex reassignment? Despite her lack of professional training in any related field, she contributed to SOC-8's chapter on adolescents. How many physicians and judges are aware that WPATH is run by the transgender community and its allies? How many parents?

# SOC-8

According to the latest 2022 WPATH Standards of Care—eighth edition (SOC-8),[64] *affirmation* is the only solution for gender dysphoria. Health professionals should instruct minors on breast binding and penis tucking, concerned parents are deemed a threat, and former measures of precaution have been denounced. For WPATH, it's all about patient autonomy—blockers, hormones, and surgery on demand. Respect for patient autonomy became the primary ethical principle to follow.

Until WPATH's SOC-7, counseling was recommended, but according to SOC-8, counseling should "never be mandated." Another feature of this latest version is the removal of age restrictions. Indeed, WPATH SOC-8 is the embodiment of the Articles of Faith.

What does this mean for vulnerable populations needing protection?

Clinical psychologist Dr. Erica Anderson is a member of the American Psychological Association's committee that developed guidelines for transgender care. Anderson was also the first man living as a woman to serve as president of the US Professional Association for Transgender Health (USPATH) before stepping down in 2021. Like Stephen Levine, Anderson resigned from WPATH due to concerns about SOC-8. In an interview, Dr. Anderson said:

> What I want always is individualized evaluation and a comprehensive bio-psychosocial evaluation. . . . For professional people, whether they're medical or mental-health [specialists], to say, "Just accept what the kid says and then make your decisions accordingly" ignores the long history we have of issues in child and adolescent development, and it is a disservice to the patient.
>
> How many patients present for diabetes and just go to their doctor and say, "I'm diabetic, so give me insulin." And the doctor says, "Oh, okay, you say so. It's true."[65]

As my patient Jake stated in disbelief, "I thought there was a system in place [to evaluate people] . . . there's no system in place! They're just allowing people to self-destruct."

There's much more in SOC-8 that you must know about, but I'll focus on the most troubling—if that's even the right word.

The Standards of Care introduced a new sexual orientation: an individual who is "assigned male at birth (AMAB) and wish[es] to eliminate masculine physical features, masculine genitals, or genital functioning."[66]

I wish it weren't so, but in WPATH's latest SOC, a chapter is dedicated to eunuchs. Boys and men seeking castration are now under the ever-widening "gender-nonconforming" umbrella. They identify as people without testicles, so castration affirms their identity. No doubt they too have the right to demand and receive surgery of their choice, at any age and with any co-occurring psychiatric ills, without the interference of "gatekeepers."

WPATHs 2022 conference kicked off with a keynote from the Admiral: "Our task quite simply is to educate the public in the United States and throughout the world. . . . We have the power to expand the boundaries of science and of public understanding."[67]

Admiral, does "expanding the boundaries of science and of public understanding" include passing off as normal and good the castration of minors?

In response to SOC-8's alarming contents, a group called *Beyond WPATH* started a petition that has over 2,000 signatories as of this writing. It declares, "As mental health professionals, public health, scientists, and allied organizations and individuals, we have grave concerns about the damaging physical and mental health impacts of the current Standards of Care released by WPATH. We hold that WPATH has discredited itself."[68]

One hundred and nineteen doctors signed off on SOC-8, advocating for your son's right to autonomy in deciding to have his genitals removed. Next time you hear someone invoke the authority of WPATH, I hope you remember that.

## Trans is old. Nullo is new.

Some affirming surgeons are ready and willing to perform whatever fits a patient's fleeting fancy: phalloplasties, vaginoplasties, bilateral mastectomies, and hysterectomies; castration and "eunuch affirmation surgeries"; or even "genital nullification," leaving patients with no genitals at all. One affirming surgery clinic's website states:

> Genital nullification, Nullo, or Eunuch procedures involve removing all external genitalia to create a smooth transition from the abdomen to the groin. In some cases, this involves shortening the urethra. For patients born with a uterus, a hysterectomy is required prior to any genital nullification procedure. Your specific goals can be discussed with one of our surgeons to develop a plan that works for you. [69]

That last line means that if you want a penis *and* a vagina, that's okay too. Just tell us what you want, we create custom-made genitals.

There have always been deeply disturbed people in the world, that's nothing new. What is new is their brazenness, and our willingness to prescribe what Alison Clayton calls "dangerous medicine"[70] to satisfy their appetites.

Understand this: once the gender ideologues achieve one goal, without hesitation they move to the next. Now the monstrous "bottom surgeries" have been normalized, as if they're not sterilizing, savage procedures with too many debilitating complications, pain, and woes to count. But before you know it, they're normalizing eunuchs and "nullo" surgeries, creating bodies that appear neither male nor female . . .

We can't get used to all this.

It's just "gender-affirming surgery," nothing to see here—that's the goal, so they can go further to the next deviant thing, and the next.

Too many believe this is all about compassion, respect, and rights. That's a cover. The goal has always been the breakdown of norms. To push the limits further and further. How does the endpoint look? That's the point—there is no endpoint. *The thrill is in pushing beyond the acceptable.*

But consider the casualties. Imagine the life of Ritchie, who was mentioned earlier:

> I dream often that I have both sets of genitals, in the dream I'm distressed I have both, Why both, I think? I tell myself to wake up because I know it's just a dream.
>
> And I awaken into a living nightmare.
>
> In those moments of amnesia, as I would wake, I would reach down to my crotch area, expecting something that was there for three decades, and it's not.

The surgeons that maimed and disfigured Ritchie and so many others were not only *allowed* to do it; they were *encouraged to do so.* They placed the patient in the driver's seat, no matter how mentally ill; no matter how young.

A text from Jake: He overdosed and was admitted to a psych unit. *I am so tired of it all,* he writes. *I am not a man or a woman. I don't see a way forward.*

The answer to *How do you make a vagina* is simple: *You don't.* The best surgeon in the world can't make a vagina. Only God can make a vagina. And the sooner everyone recognizes that truth, the better.

# CHAPTER THIRTEEN

# Lasagna Surprise[*]

It's a normal Tuesday night, your family is enjoying lasagna and talking about whatever. There's a lull in the conversation, and your fourteen-year-old daughter announces: "Mom, Dad, I have something important to tell you. You may not be happy, but everyone knows about it except you and it's time. I'm pansexual and transgender. I'm not Sophia, I'm Oscar. And my pronouns are they/them. Also, I need to go on puberty blockers, so you need to make an appointment for me at a gender clinic."

She sounds confident, rehearsed. Your older daughter looks on with approval; this clearly isn't news to her. Your husband's face is frozen. You're both at a loss, stunned. Your younger son asks, "What's pansexual?"

Welcome to the club in which you never dreamt you'd be members: parents of kids who out of the blue, without any prior discomfort with being a boy or girl, announce an opposite-sex identity, or a "non-binary" one—neither male or female.

Of course, you're stunned. Of course, you're speechless. What does all this even mean?

I speak with parents like you all the time. Parents from all over the US, and from places like Spain, Scotland, and Israel. Parents write me in distress: they feel they are losing their child. Everyone tells them to fall in line, accept their new reality. Even if they don't know English and are using a translation app, their panic comes through. They plead with me to meet their child; they're ready to get on a plane and fly across the world.

---

[*] Adapted with permission from Episode 34, Erin Brewer and Maria Keffler (2022), *Commonsense Care: Parenting Gender-Confused Kids with Truth & Love*, Advocates Protecting Children.

Here's what I tell them: They don't have to give in, and they don't have to lose their child. I explain to those parents what I've been saying to you: What they're being told by their pediatricians, gender therapists, guidance counselors, the APA, Joe Biden, and the Admiral—that the only effective treatment is giving their child what he or she demands, that there's a medical consensus—isn't true. There's no consensus, and there's no high-quality evidence that living life as the opposite sex provides long-term improvement in mental health. There are clear data, however, demonstrating that a high price is paid physically and emotionally for the process called medical "transition."

There is another option in dealing with a young person. I can't provide the results of long-term studies, because the current group of patients is new and distinct from previous ones, and no one knows how things will look ten or fifteen years down the line. But from my own practice and from speaking to other therapists and detransitioners, from reading and watching online accounts, and—perhaps most of all—from my common sense and experience as a psychiatrist, I am confident many young people can be guided to accept themselves and off the path toward experimental medical treatments that might end in sterility and mental health decline.

## Reacting to the Announcement

In this chapter you'll find one example of a child's first discussion with a parent about their new identity. I hope you'll be spared this conversation, but I want you to be prepared for the possibility.

I emphasize that it's one example, because it may not be the right one for you. Each family is unique; you may feel a different approach is necessary, and that is fine. I have spoken with parents who "broke all the rules" and saw a positive outcome. Whichever path you take, I hope you will find at least portions of this chapter valuable.

This is not a comprehensive guide to parenting a child or young adult with GD. There are numerous resources for that; my favorite is *Desist, Detrans, & Detox: Getting Your Child Out of the Gender Cult* by Maria Keffler.[1] My purpose here is to highlight some aspects of parenting that are particularly relevant.

Expect to be challenged in a new way. If IVF and the terrible twos were hard, at least you had the understanding and support of family, friends, and doctors. With ROGD, you may feel you're fighting the whole world. Not only do they not support and sympathize, they think you're the problem. You're standing in the way of your child's well-being. You're an obstacle to his getting life-saving medical care. You are transphobic. You are making your kid's suicide more likely. Your home isn't safe. You probably have people in your life who are that misinformed and whose beliefs are that extreme. This may be the most difficult ordeal you've ever faced, and it may take a terrific toll on you, so you must give some priority to self-care.

Having a gender-questioning child impacts each family member. By being attentive to *your* needs, you help them all, especially the confused child, because his or her healing will be facilitated by a solid connection with you. You are the other half of the equation. It's sometimes hard to believe based on their behavior, but your child yearns for attachment to you.

I am not saying it's a poor connection that necessarily caused the gender crisis. I'm saying it's complicated, people are complicated, it's not a linear process, and there are multiple factors. I am saying that a strong connection is a real plus, because your kid has been drawn into a world that seeks to disrupt your family bonds. The stronger your bonds, the greater the chance of success.

As a backdrop, I remind you that from the moment you learned you were expecting or adopting, you were focused on the safety and well-being of your child. That was your job, and it's the most important job you'll ever have. That doesn't change now.

When your child tells you about a new identity, it's a landmark conversation. He or she needs you to be fully present—this is not the time to wash dishes or scroll through emails. If your child makes their announcement by text or email, that may be a plus, as you're given some time to process the news. Let him or her know you appreciate it, but the subject is too important to discuss electronically. You want to speak about it in person.

Don't rush the conversation. The one below is lengthy and might be spread over a number of sit-downs. It's altogether possible that either you or your child cannot tolerate the drawn-out exchange described below. Again, every family is different—you may have a very brief initial talk, then not touch on it for months. Try to be patient; it's a process—a marathon, not a sprint.

Keep in mind:

- Your child has probably been anxious about this conversation. This is not easy for her or him.
- Let your child do the talking. Calm listening does not mean agreement.

- "You are not alone, we are in this together" and "I love you"—convey support often, not with these exact words necessarily, but in your own way.
- Now is a time to gather information, not to argue—no matter how much you disagree.
- Take the opportunity to plant seeds, knowing they may lie dormant for years before sprouting.
- You are the adult, the voice of reason and empathy. When in doubt what to say, either say nothing, or return to your wish to understand your child.
- *Not the words you speak, but the emotional tone with which they are spoken, makes the deepest impression on your child.*

As you navigate this road with your child, you will make mistakes. You are in a foreign country, you don't know the language, and you have no GPS. How can you not make some wrong turns? Forgive yourself; they won't be your first mistakes in parenting, and they won't be your last. You are not perfect, you have your own issues and worries, your good moments and bad—welcome to humanity!

### Be present and listen.

**Sophia:** There's something I need to tell you. I know you're probably not going to like it, but this is really important to me. I realize that I'm not a girl, I'm a boy. My name is Oscar and you need to start calling me he/him. That's me now. You probably even know, if you know anything about me, that I'm really a boy. It's pretty obvious to all my friends. My teachers have totally accepted it. And they just said that I should tell you about it. Oh, and I've been using the boys' bathroom and locker room at school and now it's time for you to accept me as your son.

**Parent:** Wow, honey. Okay. Um, this is a lot for me. What I'm hearing is that you don't believe you're a girl, you believe you're really a boy.

I encourage you to stay calm, as much as possible. You can freak out later. It will not be easy, but you must focus on your child and the exchange you are having—it's a whopper. Now is the time for you to demonstrate emotional control. You'll be glad you did. This is difficult for your child, she is worried about your response. Trust me, she wants your approval, even if she doesn't act like it. She may expect your reaction to be negative.

This is not the time to blurt out: "Are you insane? Are you kidding me, where did you hear this?" You may be thinking those things, nothing wrong with that, but keep them to yourself.

Does that mean you're not being genuine? It means you're walking a tightrope, trying to balance authenticity with emotional regulation, because the focus must be on your child's emotions right now, not yours. Considering the disturbing things that may come out of your child's mouth, this is no easy task.

But ideally, now is a time for listening and reassurance: "I am right here with you, and I want to understand."

**Sophia:**    I really am a boy, and I need you to get it. I have been feeling bad for so long, I didn't know why and then my friends showed me this website, and it explains everything. It is like it was written about how I have been feeling.

**Parent:**    OK, please be patient with me, I want to understand—you are saying you really are a boy, not a girl. . . . I am so sorry that you have been feeling badly for so long. There is a website that seems like it was written about how you feel? Okay, please tell me more about this.

Notice the parent does not rephrase or change the content of the child's statements. Instead, she reflects exact wording, giving the child the opportunity to hear her own words. This is called reflective listening. It slows a conversation down to allow for a deeper understanding of concepts that may be confusing not only to you, but to your child.

**Sophia:**    There's not that much to say. I'm a boy, and you need to accept that.

**Parent:**    Okay. You want us to consider you a boy, and you are behaving and you're living as a boy at school and other places.

**Sophia:**    Yeah. Because they know I'm a boy, and you're the last people really who don't know. And it's important for you to know.

**Parent:**    Okay. Hmmm. But when you were born it was clear you were a girl —

**Sophia:** Girl was assigned to me. The doctors assigned that gender to me based on my genitals. But my genitals don't define me as a boy or a girl. It's all about how I feel. And I know I'm a boy.

**Parent:** Okay. I just want to understand this. This may take me some time, so I hope you can be patient with me. I can't help but wonder, how do you know what it feels like to be a boy?

**Sophia:** Well, I just am one. It's not really about even feelings. I just know I am.

You will hear many answers like that. "I just know," or "it just is." It means your child has no meaningful response. But this is not the time to point that out. Store the information for future use.

**Parent:** I really want to understand this because I see how important it is to you. If it's important to you, it's important to me. In my understanding, sex is based on chromosomes and whether a person reproduces with eggs or sperm.

This is gentle challenging, and it can go a long way. Present your understanding but remain the listener, engaged and learning. While validating her feelings (there are no wrong feelings), you can gently challenge her beliefs, which certainly may be wrong. It's unlikely she'll agree with you now, but you are planting seeds.

**Sophia:** Well, they've just shown that, like, gender is really what defines us. You know, a lot of people get confused by this. So I'm not surprised—especially because you went to school so long ago—that you don't understand how science has changed. It's really all about, like, the doctors—they look at you and they just sort of assign you based on your genitals. That's all they look at, and genitals definitely don't define me because it's possible to be a boy and have a vagina or to be a girl and have a penis.

**Parent:** Ok one minute. I want to understand the "assigned" thing. Can you explain that? First of all, we knew you were a girl from an ultrasound that was done months before you were born.

**Sophia:** That's sex, not gender. They're two different things!

**Parent:** So then what do doctors assign at birth?

**Sophia:** [Silence. . .]

**Parent:**     I must admit I don't understand how an identity can be at odds with a person's body— I mean, I'm short, can I identify as tall? I have brown eyes, can I identify as blue-eyed? I don't understand, maybe it's just me.

**Sophia:**     Oh, I knew you wouldn't understand—forget it.

**Parent:**     Well, honey, I see you're frustrated with me. I know we are not on the same page right now, but I hope you don't think we have to give up. It's nice to be on the same page with the people you love and agree about everything, but as you get older you realize that's not realistic, that's only on Netflix.

Here is a chance to model for your child that people can disagree, even about big things, and still have a loving connection. Show her you are able to handle differing opinions and you're never going to say, "forget it." Even if there is conflict, you won't abandon her.

Try to notice moments of frustration or "giving up." Of course, this is hard to do when you're having your own internal reactions. Your child's frustration or anger with you is due to her own anxiety that she wishes to avoid at all costs. Trust me, even though she appears 100 percent certain, she has doubts. When you express your doubts, they are difficult for her to hear. She wants to be certain, your doubts threaten her certainty. By hanging in there with her when she's frustrated or perhaps angry, you demonstrate you love her, period, you can tolerate her struggles, and you won't walk away.

Children and teens (especially those on the autistic spectrum) tend to use what's called black-and-white thinking. There are only two options, black or white, all or nothing. It's usually not an accurate assessment of reality.

"You either get it or you don't."

"If I get a bad grade, I'm stupid."

"If one person was mean to me at school, my whole day was horrible."

"If you don't give me what I want right now, you don't love me."

Black-and-white thinking is easy, considering the gray is more complicated. It means acknowledging nuance and uncertainty.

Gender ideology relies on all-or-nothing thinking. It separates people into good and bad. You accept and affirm blindly, or you are transphobic. You're an ally and safe, or toxic and unsafe.

## Stereotypes

**Sophia:** I don't know, I just feel something's wrong with me, and I think it's because I am really a boy.

**Parent:** Can you tell me what feels wrong to you? What would be better if you were a boy?

**Sophia:** I have felt this way all my life, but I was so scared to tell anybody about it. I knew from the time that I was little and I liked playing with those Tonka trucks. You remember? I loved those Tonka trucks. They were so much fun, but I knew if I told people that I was actually a boy, they would think I was crazy. So I never told anybody.

**Parent:** Well, it's interesting because that really is a stereotype, isn't it? It's sort of a stereotype that boys like to play with Tonka trucks. And that girls like to play with dolls.

**Sophia:** I know. it's so hard. I have some friends, you know, and they were assigned male at birth and they're girls and, like, it's so hard because they just want to wear some make-up. They just want to wear cute dresses. I shared some of my make-up with some of my friends because their parents wouldn't buy it for them. And they're just so much happier now that they're able to really be themselves. And it's so sad that society is so mean that if they want to, you know, be their true selves as girls, that they get discriminated against. So, being transgender is so simple really, it's just when you've been assigned one sex and you know that you're the opposite sex. You're making it too hard, I think.

**Parent:** I'm trying to understand, I really am. But how do you know that you're the opposite sex, when you've never been the opposite sex? And hang on just a minute for your answer because I'm thinking about my own experience. I've never lived life from anybody else's perspective but my own. I've only lived it as my female self. I've never lived it as Sophia . . .

**Sophia:** Oscar. Can you please not misgender me?

**Parent:** Okay. I hear you and we'll talk about it in a minute. I've never lived as you. I've never lived it as your dad. I've never experienced life from any perspective but my own. So how would I know what it feels like to be you? How would I know what it feels like to be a man? How can you know what it feels like to be somebody other than you?

**Sophia:**     (shrugs her shoulder) I don't know, whatever.

Parent, you've planted a seed of doubt regarding "knowing" you are the opposite sex. Leave it alone for now. You will have other chances to return to it and to plant other seeds of doubt. There are many nonsensical teachings in the belief system to which your child has fallen prey. Some of my favorites: if gender is fluid through the lifespan, why make irreversible changes? Why are detransitioners ignored, even demonized? Is gender only fluid in one direction? How can a condition require drastic medical interventions, but not be a disorder? Can you think of another circumstance calling for lifelong prescription medications and major surgery that has no medical diagnosis?

**Parent:**     Ok, is it ok to go back to the trucks?

**Sophia:**     I guess so.

**Parent:**     I can't help but think of your Aunt Liz, she's a mechanical engineer, I don't even think she owns a dress. She has always been passionate about being a strong, independent woman. I think she would even be offended if we said she might be a man. Growing up, she had short hair, she loved fishing and chasing frogs and making sure she could climb higher than any other kid in the neighborhood, especially the boys. But that didn't make her any less of a girl. And she loves your cousins and being a mom. What if when she was your age someone told her she was a boy and she had transitioned and never had kids?

**Sophia:**     I don't know, I guess I never thought about Aunt Liz when she was a kid . . . but she should've been able to do whatever she wanted.

**Parent:**     I agree! But I don't think anyone should suggest she's not a girl. If she was a student today, would friends at school suggest she change her pronouns or her name?

**Sophia:**     Well . . . maybe. It would depend on how she felt.

**Parent:**     But honey, feelings change.

   What I don't get is if someone told Aunt Liz that she was a boy because she liked short hair and catching frogs or climbing trees and she became convinced of that . . . well then, she may have taken a path a long time ago that she may regret today.

**Sophia:**    I don't know. . .

**Parent:**    It's okay honey. You see, I think this is more complicated than you may think. We will figure it out together as we both learn more.

**Sophia:**    What about shopping for boy's clothes? And I want a haircut.

**Parent:**    I hear you. We will figure that out too. Give me some time here, this is a lot to absorb all at once.

Adolescence and young adulthood are times of trying different modes of being and of presenting oneself. Modeling people he or she admires, your child will appropriate pieces of their identities: hairstyle, make-up, outfits. I know it frightens you. One option, of course, is androgenous styles. But clothing and hair can become a major point of contention, and you may wisely decide to "pick your battles"—better your daughter gets a buzz cut than wear a binder. Tell yourself, "She is trying on being a boy." And remember, she's uncertain but wants to appear certain. Don't be misled.

### Statistics, Studies, Suicide

If your child wants to talk about statistics and percentages, that's fine, but don't let it distract you from your goal. Your goal is to listen and to stay curious. Your child may bring up studies because she wants to convince you and, more importantly, convince herself. This conversation is not about numbers, statistics, or research, and it's not about winning an argument. This is not the time to run to google and prove her wrong—that will push her away. You're on the same team. Express interest, compliment her for doing so much research.

**Sophia:**    Mom, it's amazing how many transgender people kill themselves. It's so hard. And that's why I hope you can accept that I'm your son.

**Parent:**    I can see that you're really having a hard time with this, and I'm sorry. I don't want you to be in pain. Tell me more about all the suicides.

**Sophia:**    Oh yeah, it's like 50 percent of us end up attempting suicide. Because it's so hard being transgender in a world that is transphobic.

**Parent:**    Fifty percent? That's terrible! I have to find out more about that. What's most important to me right now is you—do you feel that badly, I mean, are you thinking of hurting yourself?

**Sophia:**    No, I wouldn't do that, don't worry, but . . . what's really bothering me, Mom, and this is OMG so awkward . . . no never mind. I can't.

| | |
|---|---|
| **Parent:** | Oh honey, I'm sorry this is so hard. But I hope you can tell me. I really want to know what's on your mind. I want to understand, maybe I can even help. |
| **Sophia:** | Well, I just hate my body. I can't even tell you how much I hate it. Like my chest is getting big and the boys are looking and I hate it, Mom. I hate it so much. |
| **Parent:** | Oh yes, I understand! I remember that. I developed earlier than my friends. It was awful. |
| **Sophia:** | I hate it. And I wasn't going to tell you, but I've been using an ACE bandage to make my chest flat like a boy. I want them cut off. I hate them. |

This is difficult to hear, a punch in the gut. You counted her fingers and toes over and over when she was born, and now she loathes her body to such an alarming degree! Take a deep breath, she is not going to the operating room tomorrow. Sharing these feelings with you is a positive thing. This is what you want. A minute ago, she feared sharing her distress. Now is an opportunity to acknowledge it was hard for her and you are so glad she did.

| | |
|---|---|
| **Parent:** | Oh gosh, that sounds horrible. I believe you and thank you for telling me. We have to talk more about the ACE bandage; maybe I can take you to get a sports bra. You probably feel like you're the only one going through this. But you're not. |
| **Sophia:** | How did you get through all of it? The chest, the periods, and all of a sudden the guys are looking. I just hate it. I just want to go back to when I was a little kid. |
| **Parent:** | I understand. I want to say, and I hope you believe me, your feelings are temporary. They really are. The discomfort is so temporary, and it's part of puberty and it's normal and everybody feels it to some degree and wants to escape it. It is so normal wanting to do anything to make it stop. |
| | But it doesn't mean you're not a girl. It means you're going through a hard time. There are ways to get through it. There are ways to feel better. But sometimes in life, stuff happens, and you just have to suck it up and say, "Well, I'm going to be a mess for a while until I get through this." |

Your job is to be there through the many challenges she will experience, not to take them away. In fact, that can do more harm than good. Life is full of struggle. There will be many storms. She must learn to cope with negative emotions like distress, shame, and uncertainty. You are by her side right now, not eliminating the difficulty, but helping her through it. In the process, she will gain the confidence to tolerate future hardships.

### You Are Not Transphobic

**Sophia:**  So you're going to call me Oscar, right? And he/him?

**Parent:**  We are not making any decisions right now. I know you want this to happen at once, but this is the first time I am hearing about all this, and I need to do a lot of research and thinking.

**Sophia:**  What? But it's just a name and pronouns! What's the big deal?

**Parent:**  I know this isn't what you wanted to hear and you're disappointed.

**Sophia:**  Why? Why won't you just call me Oscar? Everyone does!

**Parent:**  I'll try to explain. First, I want to tell you something fascinating I read recently about names.

When people are in the later stages of dementia, they may forget absolutely everything, they don't recognize their spouse or children, but they respond to their name.[2] So a name is a very deep thing.

The other thing I want you to know is when your dad and I discovered we were pregnant with you, we began to think of possible boy and girl names, but nothing felt right. Then, as you know, your grandmother suddenly died. We were in shock; it was very hard. She was the kindest, most generous, loving person I ever knew. We stopped thinking about names for a while because we were grieving. We just loved her so much, and suddenly she was gone.

Then we found out we were having a girl—you! And immediately we both knew, even without talking about it, we were certain: we'd give you her name. When we made that decision, it was like holding on to a part of her. The grief was a bit lighter. And at your official baby-naming, we sensed she was smiling down at us.

Your name is not random. For us, it is filled with meaning.

I know you're going through a hard time and it's probably difficult to step outside of yourself and think of us. But I am asking you to do that. Your name has a history. It has memories and significance. It's not something we will erase.

**Sophia:** OK, but when you picked that name you didn't know I was a boy. And when you keep saying I was a girl and calling me a girl name, that's transphobic.

At this point you can stop the conversation momentarily because name-calling is not okay.

**Parent:** Calling me names is disrespectful, and that's not allowed in our family. Please don't do that.

If I was transphobic it would mean I fear transgender people. I do not.

What I fear is the harm that may come to if you go down a path that might lead to medical interventions. I fear that going down this path will close doors for you that you may regret, like Aunt Liz would have closed doors.

I want the best future that you can have, healthy and happy and fulfilled. I want you to have as few doctor's appointments as possible. It's awfully unfair for you to call me "transphobic."

**Sophia:** Well, ok, but if you really loved me and my authentic self, then you would totally affirm me.

**Parent:** I do love you, and wonder how you can doubt that for a second. But I believe this is more complicated than you think, and that there are more solutions than the one that you now want so much.

**Sophia:** That's right, there is one solution, it's not complicated at all. I am Oscar and I don't know why you're being like this, you were always so supportive of LGBTQ+.

**Parent:** It sounds like you believe loving someone means agreeing with everything they want. Remember we just spoke about that?

**Sophia:** Yeah, I guess so.

**Parent:** Getting back to your name, I want to remind you that all of us have strong feelings about one thing or another, and that includes me and your dad. We have strong feelings about the name we picked for you. It's important for you to step away from your strong feelings about being called Oscar, if only momentarily, and respect our strong feelings. To do that is a sign of maturity. It's also a sign of love.

You know, I'm wondering, what if might change your mind about this at some point?

**Sophia:**   I'm not going to change my mind. That would be silly. I mean, I've thought about this. It's not like I just thought of this yesterday. I've felt like this my whole life and I'm not going to change my mind. I've researched it. I've talked to a lot of people and all the people in my after-school club that I go to are like, "This is definitely the right path." And so, there's no way I'm going to, like—

I know you worry because sometimes I'm kind of impulsive, but this time I've researched this. I've really researched it.

**Parent:**   Do you know of anybody who's changed their mind about transitioning?

**Sophia:**   No. I know there's some videos out. There are some detrans people who pretended to be trans and then were like, "Oh, I made a mistake." But they weren't really trans, obviously, because they didn't stick with it. So just because somebody else makes a bad choice, doesn't mean it's a bad choice for me.

**Parent:**   I'm going to tell you something you never knew about me, but when I was 18, I almost got married. I was in love.

**Sophia:**   WHAT??

**Parent:**   I thought he's the one—I was absolutely in love with him. And he wanted to get married. We were at college, but we were like, "Oh, we can totally make this work. I was about to marry him and before it happened, I found out I was not the only girl he was seeing. I was heartbroken. I cried for weeks. But I look back on that and I think, "Wow, I'm really glad I found out. . ."

**Sophia:**   That happened to a friend of mine. She was going out with this guy and he was all she'd talk about. And then she found out he had a whole bunch of other girlfriends.

**Parent:**   Oh, that must have been painful.

**Sophia:**   It was. I guess sometimes bad things happen.

A moment like this, when you are both genuine, sharing, and on the same page, is special. It diffuses the earlier tension. Savor it.

**Parent:**   You can say that again, bad things happen. But there's a lesson here. You can want something so much, right? And then realize later: "Wow. Even though I wanted that, it would've been bad for me."

This is my concern about what you're telling me about being a boy. I'm saying, hold on, this is huge—probably the biggest decision you will make in your life—and big decisions need to be deeply considered.

You planted a seed when you described the big mistake you nearly made. If you almost made a huge error in judgment, she's probably capable of that as well. . .

**Sophia:**   Actually there's something else I want to tell you.
**Parent:**   Sure!
**Sophia:**   Well, I have a boyfriend.
**Parent:**   Oh, really? Tell me more. Who is he?
**Sophia:**   His name is Saturn. He's in my class and he's so cool. He was assigned female at birth but he's non-binary. We are gay.

Your daughter is telling you she's in a relationship with another girl and they consider themselves gay guys. You'd think she was joking, but she's dead serious.

You hear this, and you cannot wrap your brain around it. Well of course you can't!—it's fiction, delusional, fantasy. Unfortunately, your daughter has fallen into it. There will be times you understandably want to grab her shoulders and shake some sense into her for regurgitating these idiotic beliefs. But you will restrain yourself.

A mother told me that when her son insisted he's not attracted to guys and in the next sentence said how happy he is with his "girlfriend," six-foot strapping young man on estrogen, she bit her tongue so hard it bled. She knew if she reacted in the moment, with her strong emotions, it would threaten their connection. And connection is what it's all about. Even when you think you're losing your mind.

**Parent:**   That sounds interesting! How long have you been an item?
**Sophia:**   Only a week, but he's totally cool.
**Parent:**   I'm so glad you told me, because I want to know what's going on in your life. Getting back to your new identity, do you see it as a very big decision?
**Sophia:**   Yes.
**Parent:**   I'm glad you realize that. I'm proud of you for seeing that.
**Sophia:**   So you're not going to call me Oscar?

**Parent:**     No. because that would be taking the first step onto a path that's full of unknowns. And it might be hard to get off. But I promise you, we are going to fully research everything. We are going to find out what the experts are saying and if there's a debate about any of this.

   And as your dad and I study this and talk about this with you, I hope you'll be open to hearing what we have to say without throwing slurs at us—calling us transphobic for asking questions. That's really unfair. When you throw something this big at us, we're going to have questions and it's not transphobic to ask questions.

**Sophia:**     It's hard because everybody at school says, "If your parents really love you, then they'll go ahead and they'll support you." And some kids, they even get parties when they come out, their parents are really excited about it. But that kinda of stinks, because you're not really excited and you're not really supporting me in this.

**Parent:**     Let's look at the word "support." You said, "If I loved you, I would agree to this." And I take exception to that because always saying "yes" isn't love. If that was love, you could hire someone whose job would be to always agree with you and give you whatever you want at the moment. Is that love? Love is more complicated than that, trust me.

**Sophia:**     Well, I'm going to give you all the research and I know you'll be like, "Okay, this is definitely what's going to be best for Oscar." Then you'll go ahead and follow the recommendations of all the experts?

**Parent:**     I'll read the research, both what you give me and what I find. But it's going to take time, it's going to be a process. I'm not going online for an hour and then deciding on my position. This is a big thing with huge consequences.

**Sophia:**     Well, I have so much to share with you. I'm super excited for you to read it because I think it's going to blow your mind. You're going to be like, "Wow, this, this is so different from what I learned in school, like so much has progressed since then." So I'm super excited for you to read it.

**Parent:**     I'm excited too. Thank you for trusting me with all this personal information. I'm sorry that I didn't respond the way you wish that I had. But I love you. And that will never change.

I can't say how this will pan out for your family. You may be lucky, like the parents of my patient Rosa—she did a 180 from her boy identity in about six months. Or maybe your kid will be like Charlie, he realized after a few years that it was okay to have feminine qualities and be vastly different from his father and brothers: he could be himself without becoming a girl—as if that's even possible.

You may be in for a lengthy ordeal that lasts years and includes psychiatric hospitalizations and struggles with therapists, family, and schools. Your mental health may take a major hit. Your marriage may falter. You may need legal representation. And yes, your child may end up with a new voice and a flat chest, someone you don't recognize, with your dreams for grandchildren destroyed. That's possible, too.

You may have a few battles ahead, or a full-out war, I can't say. But I can tell you one thing for sure—lasagna will never taste the same.

# Conclusion

James is sporting a scruffy beard. Sarah wears skirts and doesn't care about pronouns. Taylor wants to talk about college, not testosterone.

These small changes—all seen or reported to me recently by patients or their parents—are big.

In this book I've described monumental struggles and grief, but I want you to know there's hope. Young people and their families such as those you've read about can be helped with therapy.

They can slow their pace on the assembly line that leads to harm; some even step off. They can accept, even enjoy, their bodies. It's far from guaranteed and not always an easy road, but it's possible.

How do I treat my gender-distressed patients?* The same way I treat any other: with respect, empathy, curiosity, honesty, and with their lifelong happiness and well-being foremost in my mind.

I begin with, *Tell me about yourself,* I say. *I want to know who you are.*

My patients have been led to believe they face a simple issue with a simple solution. I explain that isn't so. They are, like all people, a huge, complex tapestry, of which gender occupies just a small corner. The entire tapestry interests me, not only the one corner.

We'll talk about gender, of course, but instead of automatic affirmation, we will look deeper.

We will try to determine what living as the opposite sex accomplishes. How will it make life better or easier? Is the new identity about becoming someone new, or fleeing who they are? Granted, some of my questions may make them uncomfortable, but this is the biggest decision of their lives, and it deserves a close, careful look.

---

\* Thank you, Dr. Stephen Levine, for supervision, in which you generously shared your knowledge and wisdom regarding these patients.

I look at my patient's family. Is there conflict in her home, an ill parent or sibling? I determine if she has a psychiatric condition such as anxiety, depression, OCD, ADD, psychosis, or if she's on the autism spectrum or has some other form of neurodiversity.

Is there a history of adoption, trauma, or abuse? Social awkwardness or bullying? Attraction to the same sex? Is the trans identity a way of exploring themselves separate from their family, a normal task of adolescence, taken to an extreme?

There may be stereotypical beliefs about men and women that are mistaken. He may think he's not "manly" and won't find love or acceptance as he is. Maybe she or someone she loves was harmed, she feels helpless against male aggression, and for that reason seeks to flee femininity. Perhaps he or she fears growing up.

The point is: being "trans" is a solution—a coping mechanism—but to which problem? That's the mystery we will solve together.

One of my primary responsibilities is education. I am older and wiser, and that benefits my patients. One line that's effective with know-it-all adolescents: "You're sixteen? I'm 116." Over my decades of practice, I learned many things, one of which is that people change. A Bernie supporter turns around and votes Republican. Couples once madly in love, certain about marriage, now at each other's throats. A woman couldn't have been more certain about aborting, twenty years later she's childless and rethinking that decision.

*People change.* I tell my patients. *You're going to change, too.*

Another wisdom I share is that being human means struggling. It means living with limitations and weaknesses. You're not the first person to hate your body, feel disconnected from your parents, and lack a place of belonging. You're not the first human being to experience confusion, pain, and loneliness.

Under some circumstances I might share a hardship of my own. Even more important is to reveal difficulties to a patient, at the moment. In doing so, she or he learns I have tough moments too, but they can be managed.

For example, if I fear a patient's response, I might say: "I must tell you something, but I have mixed feelings about it, because of how you may react." The patient learns I too have fear of conflict; I feel unsure just like she does. I've demonstrated how I tolerate those emotions.

A patient needs to feel safe and understood. It's in that trusting and honest space between us that healing begins.

I try to model thoughtfulness, humility, and especially compassion. We must have compassion for ourselves and others—including our parents. They too are human, with limitations and struggles. They're doing, or did, the best they could, and it wasn't *all* bad.

Ultimately, the choice is theirs, I tell my patients, their identity is in their hands. At the same time, whether they're requesting new pronouns or surgery, there are risks. I'm obligated to point out what they are doing has massive implications. What will their lives be like in ten, twenty, fifty years? There may be a high price to pay.

I remind patients that as a physician, I have a profound appreciation for the body's wisdom. They may think they have all the information they need, they may be convinced they're knowledgeable about social and medical interventions, but I know they don't and they're not. From new names to mastectomies and vaginoplasties, they must understand the risks and the controversy.

If I neglect to delineate those risks and the current debate, I'm not doing my job. What if he or she comes back crying, *Look what I've done to myself, why didn't you warn me?* Speaking of risks, that's one *I* am unwilling to take.

I strongly encourage gender-distressed patients to at some point read detransitioners' stories or watch their videos. When patients are unwilling to do so, or unable to hear about the dangers of medicalizing, or if they claim to be unconcerned and confident, those are red flags. All of us have some degree of doubt when we face major decisions. Every decision has plusses and minuses. To be confident and wrong is dangerous.

It's also my job to gently challenge and plant seeds, as I described in "Lasagna Surprise." Being from an older generation, I ask my young patients to define the new language and explain their beliefs. I am curious, I want to learn from them. If their definitions or explanations don't satisfy me, I'll say so.

*The goal is to recognize everyone is a mosaic of male and female. Honor the mosaic and leave the body alone.* And to parents: You must respect your child's mosaic, too. He or she may not match your ideas about masculinity and feminity.

Below are examples of patients with ROGD whose dysphoria diminished or resolved altogether with therapy. At the risk of presenting a simplistic portrayal of a highly complex and lengthy process, I focus on one or two themes of their therapies. These portrayals are composites of several patients, and identifying details have been changed.

## James

Nineteen-year-old James was from Austin, Texas. For the past year he'd been using a gender-neutral name, they/them pronouns, shaving his chest, arms, and legs, and wearing nail polish. He told me "I want to go on estrogen so I can cry."

The idea of being perceived as a girl felt comforting to James. He reported feeling happy with his smooth, hairless body and experiencing less pressure to meet cultural expectations. Being attracted to women, he imagined himself in a future lesbian relationship.

What soon became clear was in the variations of men that James knew, he never saw himself. James was always small, underweight, and quiet. He hated sports, was ridiculed by boys in his class, and felt more comfortable with girls. His fondest memories were the hours spent caring for his pet rabbit and playing the flute. An older neighbor had sexually molested James, but he had never told anyone.

James's mother had a chronic illness. When she was well enough, she was preoccupied with her business and not so much with her family. His father was more available, but he was unpredictable and prone to angry outbursts. James was repulsed by his father's coarse behavior: cursing, passing gas, and walking around in his underwear. His older brothers were physically competitive and boisterous. No one in the family was unkind, but James acutely sensed his "otherness" and was lonely throughout his childhood.

James entered puberty late. In high school he felt estranged from his peers who already shaved and were sexually active. His academic success did little to quash the certainty he could never meet the expectations of family and peers.

James and I spent many hours examining his childhood, the sexual abuse, and especially his rejection by peers and experience of a "mismatch" with his brothers' and father's masculinity. He would insist, "I don't want to become a hairy old man."

I pointed out that being crude is a human, not male, quality—women can be vulgar, too. We spoke about the wide range of masculinity, and my belief that he could find his place in it. He was, like all of us, a mosaic of femininity and masculinity, and altering his body to resemble that of a girl wasn't necessary to be refined, emotionally expressive, and compassionate.[1]

I taught him about the dangers of taking estrogen, including the impact on his sexual function and fertility. I wondered about his assumption of easily finding romance amongst lesbians and suggested instead that medicalizing would restrict his number of potential partners. He learned some skills for coping with distress.

My patient slowly understood that as a child, he had associated masculinity with his father's "Neanderthal" habits and body hair, leading to the rejection of both in a sweeping denial of manhood.

A turning point came while describing his emotional isolation in childhood and James began to cry. I said I was sorry he went through such hardship; it's optimal when parents are persistently tuned in to their children, but often that's not the case. I told him I wished I'd been there to ease his way. He was exhibiting strength by permitting himself to cry with me, not weakness, I said, and there are many women who are attracted to men who are kind, caring, and emotionally expressive. He can be loved just the way he is.

James's preoccupation with his body hair diminished. He took up a new hobby—rock climbing—and his strength and muscle mass increased. He reported moments of distress related to the changes, especially if others noticed. He coped by saying to himself, "I am who I am," and "Being a man means getting comfortable with the uncomfortable."

I encouraged him to identify more ways he could leave his comfort zone. He hadn't shaved his arms or legs for months but tolerated the dysphoria of wearing a tank top. One day, he appeared in my office with a scruffy beard.

He confessed he'd bought into a stereotype and his ideas about masculinity weren't based in reality. He was a man, just different from the one who'd raised him.

James returned to using his given name and male pronouns. When asked how it felt, he said, "So natural, like stepping into a pair of old shoes."

## Sarah

Sarah was from Portland, Oregon. A few months earlier, she picked the name "Malcolm" and "they/them" pronouns. Sarah planned to go on testosterone and have "top surgery" when she turned sixteen. She flattened her breasts with a binder all day and believed a lower voice and facial hair would improve her life, although she couldn't say exactly how. With the informed consent model of care in her state, she could get what she wanted without parental approval.

During our first meeting, Sarah's self-loathing was on full display. "I hate my wide hips and large chest. I don't make eye contact, and people notice that. I'm different, I have odd habits. I'm a mess, basically."

I asked Sarah what she *does* like about herself. A long pause followed, then a timid smile, the only smile I saw on her that day: "I love to sing. And I think I have a pretty good voice."

*She loves to sing,* I thought to myself, *and she wants testosterone. Oh God.*

There was so much I wanted to warn Sarah about, but the clock was ticking. Sarah would turn sixteen in fourteen months—would that be enough time for her to realize hormones and surgery are not the answer? Or will she walk into a Planned Parenthood on her birthday and get her first injection of "T"?

Prior to seeing me, Sarah's parents restricted her Internet use, successfully averting a meltdown by presenting Sarah with a new companion and time-consuming distraction: a puppy. In therapy we spoke of her years of difficulty fitting in with other girls. Their manner of relating was a black box to her—incomprehensible. They rejected Sarah, so she hung out with boys, but that only lasted until puberty hit—and it hit her early and fast. She was subjected to stares and comments not only from peers but from grown men, including an uncle. She needed a bra in fifth grade, and her periods started in sixth.

Sarah's thinking about her identity was black and white. If she felt so miserable in her girl's body, she must be a boy.

She had frequent insomnia, her days were filled with worry, and she met criteria for high-functioning autism. Melatonin improved her sleep. I taught her ways to tolerate negative feelings. Cognitive behavioral therapy—observing and then revising her thoughts, feelings, and actions—alleviated her distress a bit, but not enough. After a few months I added medication targeting her anxiety and obsessive angst about her appearance. She soon reported feeling calmer, and her parents confirmed the improvement.

I always ask patients what is the best and worst thing that ever happened to them. For Sarah, the worst thing was the night of the mass shooting at the Pulse club in Orlando. She overheard her father's homophobic comments and became convinced he'd never accept her.

This led to a discussion of her interest in girls, something she'd never shared with anyone. Sarah was unsure if her feelings were romantic—sexual attraction was another black box for her. But there was someone in her church choir with whom she wished to spend more time.

Sarah was a star in the choir. She loved singing so much that she'd switch her restrictive binder for a sports bra. Her extended family attended her performances, in which she always had a solo. Choir was her opportunity to shine. I saw an opportunity as well—to teach her about testosterone.

Sarah's anxiety skyrocketed when presented with information that challenged her rigid beliefs about gender identity. We discussed how black-and-white, all-or-nothing thinking felt safe, while gray, representing nuance and uncertainty, felt perilous. I explained that the plans she had to medicalize would be the most consequential decision of her life and she owed it to herself to know the risks entailed.

We reached an agreement: at each session, Sarah would learn about one effect of testosterone while we kept tabs on her anxiety. If it got close to a distressing level, she could use her coping skills.

The start was bumpy, but Sarah was gradually able to listen. We went slowly. She learned testosterone is FDA-approved only for use in men with medical conditions.[2] Sarah hadn't realized the lowering of her voice would happen so quickly—within a few months, and that she might experience hoarseness and other vocal issues. She was convinced a lower voice would give her more self-confidence but hadn't fully considered its impact on singing and participation in choir.

She'd also not taken into account testosterone's potential impact on her emotions and libido. Now that she was coping better with stress, she didn't want to risk developing the anger and aggression sometimes seen when girls take testosterone. And Sarah wanted companionship, not sex. To be in a state of arousal, distracted many times a day by thoughts and images, was not appealing.

After a few months Sarah tolerated a degree of uncertainty about medical intervention. I was proud of her ability to venture into gray areas. She agreed to move on to facts about breast binding. Again, there were risks of which she hadn't been aware. Our conversations also touched on brain development and the banning in some countries of medical interventions for minors.

We were also talking about her autism, the years of social ostracism and bullying, and the shame of her developing body. I explained that sometimes, especially in childhood, we lack the capacity to experience powerful emotions. The feelings can't be processed. In response, the mind might place the emotions into the body, or the attitude toward the body.

Sarah's body was feminized early. Her mother prepared her for the changes but couldn't prevent the harassment and stares. Sarah "held" her agony in those parts of herself that were unwanted. But even if her breasts were removed, I explained, the agony would find another home in her body, and that would continue until the agony itself was felt and shared with me. That's why we needed to keep talking about her past. Now that she was older, her ability to feel those overwhelming emotions was higher. Feeling them in a place of support and understanding would remove the body's burden.

Sarah agreed to watch some videos of detransitioners, and I suggested Helena Kirschner, due to her horrific reaction to testosterone, and Laura Becker, who is autistic. I told Sarah's parents that her nascent same-sex attraction and certainty of her father's rejection could be elements in the genesis of her boy identity.

Sarah's friendship with the girl in choir blossomed, and to her surprise, her parents were accepting. Even better: her girlfriend liked her just the way she was. That was wonderful news and an opportunity to discuss the pleasures of the body. Testosterone and mastectomies could negatively impact those pleasures for the rest of her life.

She turned sixteen and announced she wouldn't be making any decisions about hormones until much later when her brain was fully mature. Sarah still likes to be called Malcolm, but she's also wearing skirts and doesn't really care about pronouns. She knows that identity is an evolving process, she's still figuring hers out, and that's ok. Regarding "top surgery," she now thinks a reduction would be enough.

## Taylor

I heard Taylor's story from her mother, Ann. Taylor languished in a Chinese orphanage for the first eighteen months of her life prior to adoption by Ann and her husband, who live outside Chicago. Taylor's early trauma was severe; now sixteen years old, she always had difficulty with trust, attachment, and self-esteem.

Taylor developed ROGD and tried to buy testosterone online. Her first three therapists were affirming, and her mental health deteriorated: deep depression, self-injury, an overdose. Ann was beside herself watching her daughter struggle. Through research and parent groups she became convinced Taylor was in a cult. Ann told me, "Nothing was helping, and I needed to do something, anything. My hair was on fire."

Through the parents' grapevine, she heard some families saw positive results after consulting with cult experts. On a Zoom call, Ann and her husband's suspicions were validated: he too saw gender ideology as a cult, comparing it to ISIS.

They hired his team to conduct an evaluation of Taylor, followed by an intervention. It would be like the intervention Ann's brother had arranged for his addict son a year earlier.

The rest of the story could fill another book. Taylor is now home-schooled, has been removed from the influence of peers and Internet, and has an exploratory therapist. Her mental health is stable. During a summer in China (suggested by the cult expert), Taylor's interest in her heritage was sparked. She's learning Mandarin and has identified the top colleges offering degrees in Chinese studies. Therapy has helped Taylor realize her early trauma and long-standing identity challenges led to her gender confusion.

Ann and her husband feel more positive about Taylor's future, but like all parents have told me, there's always a lingering concern. "I still sleep with one eye open," Ann told me.

Arranging an intervention, switching schools or homeschooling, moving the entire family out of state, refusing to pay for college, an extended visit to another country—parents call these last resorts to remove their child from an environment that reinforces their gender beliefs "nuclear options," and I firmly believe it's wise to have one up their sleeves, just in case.

With a nuclear option, parents feel stronger and more confident. The child also sees her parents' massive efforts and will, we hope, appreciate them one day.

A psychologist with a struggling daughter whose therapist was pushing testosterone picked up and moved to the former USSR, where she had family ties:

> It helps that the local language, which my daughter is quickly absorbing and starting to speak, is devoid of gendered grammatical markers. I think she is relieved to not have to ask or answer questions about "preferred pronouns" and such. Here, no one is compelled to participate in a mass delusion that requires thought control and speech policing. They had more than enough of that during seven long decades under Soviet rule. . . . I grow more hopeful every day that removing her from a culture that would pathologize normal developmental struggles and push costly and irreversible medical treatments, will enable and reinforce long-term remission of gender dysphoria and trans ideation from her life.[3]

Two years later, the mom wrote me:

> Now 19 years old, she is fully desisted, identifies as a woman . . . and is work-
> ing hard to rebuild her life. She does not want to talk about her descent into
> the gender abyss except to say that it was a very dark time in her life.

Parents, you must consider which sacrifices you'd make to save your child.
One father responded to my survey: "What if a child molester moved in
next door? What if your water supply was poisoned?"

✳   ✳   ✳

I am pleased James, Sarah, Taylor, and others have moved toward acceptance of their sex and away from unnecessary medical interventions. If
they'd been automatically affirmed and placed on the assembly line, their
core emotional issues would have gone unaddressed. They may have felt
happy with their altered bodies, but for how long? It's a roll of the dice.

When I said earlier my approach to transgender-identifying patients
is just like with any other patient, I omitted a salient point. There is one
huge difference. After their brief weekly sessions, my patients return to their
friends, schools, and social media—a world bound to the Articles of Faith.

It's daunting, to say the least, to build a connection with heavily indoctrinated patients. They've heard over and over there's one answer to their
predicament—transition. They cannot tolerate the doubts I plant.

The hurdle may be insurmountable. Zoe was an eleventh grader attending a Boston school where tuition was higher than the median yearly house-
hold income. Her mother informed me that in middle school, Zoe and her
friends all declared themselves LGBT, they just hadn't decided which letter.

Once I tried to inform Zoe that due to safety concerns, a minor like
herself living in Sweden or Finland would not have access to puberty blockers. She placed her hands over her ears and hollered: "Don't tell me about
trans kids who can't get medical care! Don't you know fifty percent of us
try to commit suicide?"

To her accusation of being transphobic, I responded "I'm anti-suffering,
not anti-trans." I could almost sense her friends and influencers in the room
with us, scowling at me. She refused to meet again.

In my many years as a physician, I've had patients with severe schizophrenia, untreatable cancer, and other serious conditions. No one ever fired

me. Do you see why I said fighting dangerous ideas has been harder than fighting dangerous diseases?

When the young person has pledged allegiance to the Articles of Faith, the challenge facing parents and therapists is brutal. Parents who've yet to face the predicament, please listen to the five hundred mothers and fathers of ROGD kids who responded to my survey [see Appendix Seven: Responses to Parent Survey].

Many of them say flat-out: they are living in hell, and they want to warn and teach you before you're in their shoes. They are reaching out to save you from the impossible position they're in—a child announcing, in order for me to stay in this family, you must support my self-harm.

These are the parents who, when they catch a glimpse of you at a park or mall holding the hands of your toddler or school-age sons and daughters who are still attached to you, still trusting you, feel a stab in their hearts: If only you knew what may be ahead.

If they could, they'd get on a megaphone and shout:

1. Discuss gender with your child early.
2. Get out of public schools.
3. Get your child off the Internet.
4. Know who your child's talking to—at school, online, everywhere.
5. No social media, smart phones, GSA meetings, gender clinics.
6. Love without affirming. No names, pronouns, binders.
7. Validate feelings, not beliefs.
8. Be vigilant.
9. Don't think it's not happening in your area, because it is.

To all that I would add: your child is a sponge, ready to absorb whatever comes his way. He is a work in progress, and you are his scaffolding, providing support and structure. If you don't provide a belief system, a compass, or some meaningful foundation from which to understand the world, identify truth and lies, and know right and wrong, trust me—others are waiting eagerly to do just that. Before you know it, your child is a pawn, a foot soldier in a foreign crusade of dark and dangerous ideas, and you're the toxic parent with a home that's unsafe.

You want your children to know that unfortunately, they can't automatically trust what they hear at school and elsewhere. What they are taught can harm them. You want the source of their beliefs and values to be your home.

They must become critical thinkers and bring questions to you. If you don't know the answers, you say: I don't know, but I will find out. This is easier said than done, of course. Consider it an ideal toward which to strive; the closer you can get, the better.

## You Don't Need a PhD

Casey (not his real name) was a patient at the Washington University Transgender Center at St. Louis Children's Hospital exposed by Jamie Reed. He had blockers inserted under his skin when he was 14 with promises it would relieve his dysphoria; instead, he gained thirty pounds, his mental health took a dive, and he ended up in a psychiatric unit.

Of note is how Casey described his discovery at age thirteen through friends and online that "transgenderism was a thing." His response was, "Holy crap! You can do that?"

Soon he declared he was "gender fluid," meaning that his gender changed daily. After about six months, Casey says, "I decided that I was a fully transgender girl."[4]

When your children first hear about being born in the wrong body and other dogma, I want him to say, "Holy crap! That's impossible, makes no sense, and is incredibly dangerous." But for your children to have that wisdom, you must teach them what you learned in these pages. You don't need a PhD; all you need is common sense.

Tell your children, *Biology matters*. Sex is not "assigned" at birth, it's hardly a hit-or-miss process. Male and female are determined at conception and cannot be changed.

"Gender identity" rests on the belief that who you are is separate from physical reality. Sure, you can believe in it, like many believe in a soul that's independent of a body. Just know it's without scientific foundation.

Explain that each of the 70 trillion cells making up their brains, hearts, lungs, skin, kidneys, and immune systems is stamped "XX—female" or "XY—male." The information on their chromosomes is like the carefully written code in their computers. It is unchangeable and necessary for proper function.

Teach them that like the Earth, their bodies are delicate ecologic systems to be honored and preserved. High-dose estrogen in a boy and testosterone in a girl clash with the instructions in each cell. It's a war against themselves, and they'll pay a price.

A girl cannot have a boy's brain, nor can hormones and surgery turn her into a boy. Yes, hormones will masculinize a girl and feminize a boy, but the result is a synthetic persona, not the real thing, and maintaining it will require a lifetime of drugs.

These are the indisputable truths your children have a right to hear, and you an obligation to convey.

If you know a pregnant or new mom, expose your child to that wonder. Let her or him hold a new baby and look at his tiny fingers and toes. You are planting seeds.

Tell your kids being on the Internet unsupervised is like driving them to the most crime-ridden part of town and leaving them there to go in and out of strangers' homes. Smart phones are like plutonium in their pockets. Nope—not gonna happen on your watch [see Appendix Six, "Guide to Internet Accountability Tools"].

Tell your teens that in medicine, good intentions have sometimes led to calamity. Not long ago, doctors devised a treatment for people with severe mental illness: drive an ice pick through their skulls and into their brains. It took time to recognize the harm done; in the meantime, they were awarded a Nobel prize. Now lobotomies are one of the darkest chapters in modern medicine. There were other medical calamities—Tuskegee, thalidomide. Discuss them over dinner, how the doctors were so certain. Suggest your son or daughter write a report for their history or social studies class. Those were man-made catastrophes; so are puberty blockers, cross-sex hormones, and surgeries for minors.

Speaking of dark chapters in medicine, your child needs to know about John Money and the Reimer twins. Depending on her age, you can both watch and discuss the interviews with David and his mother on YouTube. There were countless other casualties of Money's fraudulent research. It took decades for it all to unfold. In the meantime, Money basked in the limelight.

By now you've heard this a million times, but please explain to your kids that there's no consensus. What they're being told is medically necessary and lifesaving is a matter of fierce debate in the medical community. There is no scientific foundation for the claim that "transition" is beneficial in the long term, but there is evidence of harm. Look at the banning of "affirming" care for minors in other countries; their medical authorities have said: psychotherapy first!

Challenge your teen: why hasn't he heard any of this before? Why is this information missing from his school, his sex ed classes, the websites of PP and gender clinics, HRC, the Trevor Project. Why doesn't her school invite detransitioners to share their experiences and views? Isn't the deliberate exclusion of facts and opinions wrong? It's something he should think about.

Your children know bullying is not okay. Point out bullying galore in the world of gender: debate squashed, dissenters punished, detransitioners vilified. You might also wonder aloud with your older teen or young adult about terms such as "cisgender." Why was it created? Do we also need a word for people who accept their eye color? As you learned from detransitioner Helena in Chapter Three, it's all about creating categories that divide us. If you're "trans," you're a powerless victim; if you're "cis," you're a privileged oppressor. Are Jennifer Pritzker (net worth $1.3 billion), Martine Rothblatt (net worth $580 million), and the Admiral powerless victims? It's worthwhile trying to have that discussion, if it can be kept civil, with your child.

It's way past time to expose the malfeasance of professional associations, including but not limited to those mentioned below.[†]

To the leadership of the American Psychiatric Association, the American Academy of Child and Adolescent Psychiatry, the American Psychological Association, and the American Academy of Pediatricians:

You have truly lost your way. You permitted a small group of activist bullies to take control. You veered away from science and became mouthpieces for a destructive ideology. You abandoned your mission, and your members have broken their vows to do no harm.

You know that adolescents yearn to consolidate their identity and stabilize their sense of self. Why do you promote beliefs that do the opposite? Why do you place children in harm's way?

You churn out lies clothed in the language of compassion and civil rights. You take advantage of the trust of your naive members and an unsuspecting public. Your publications censor opposing views, and debate is silenced at your meetings. This is not medicine; shame on you.

To fight against stigma and for insurance coverage is honorable, but psychiatric diagnoses must be based on evidence, not compassion. Why was there no referendum before making the seismic shift of normalizing disembodiment? The DSM decision was a blunder with far-reaching consequences.

A special note to WPATH:

Your gig is up. Thank you for being so bold in your new "Standards of Care." In your opinion no one is too young or mentally unstable to access disfiguring and sterilizing "treatments." Now the world knows for what you

---

† As a physician, I'll focus on the medical groups.

stand, and it's certainly not evidence-based medicine or the health and well-being of youths.

A special thanks for your chapter introducing what you call a new sexual orientation—castrated boys, a.k.a. eunuchs. This is deviance plain and simple. Thank you for being transparent.

In the documentary *What Is a Woman?*, your president, Marci Bowers, called clinicians like myself "dinosaurs." Thank you, Dr. Bowers, for your words—they are telling. You wish for my position, based on biological reality, to become extinct. It's not going to happen.

As I write these final paragraphs, the emails from family members of ROGD kids don't stop. One mom after another reached out for help, along with some dads, grandparents, and siblings. A mom tells me estrogen caused her son to develop brain tumors, but doctors continue to prescribe it. An Army Colonel who fought Jihadis for fifteen years writes that when his transgender-identifying daughter goes on a rant, "she sounds like the true believers we captured on the battlefield." A young woman who refuses to call her sister her brother writes, "I can't adequately express the type of grief this is, and it bleeds into every aspect of life."

A urologist alerts me to research showing an increased risk of prostate cancer in men living as women.[5]

A librarian informs me of these new titles: *Bye, Bye, Binary* (Ages 0–4), *The Rainbow Parade* (Ages 2–5), *True You: A Gender Journey* (Ages 4–8), and *Me and My Dysphoria Monster* (Ages 5–8).[6]

A lawyer wants advice on a case involving a family, in which not one, not two, but three girls identify as boys.

A college student writes, "I was a psych major but felt frustrated and silenced by my peers and teachers, so I switched to engineering. What about us students who have to deal with troubled and oppressive peers? Who stands up for us?"

The subject line from one mom: "HELP! My daughter is having surgery in 2 days!"

I learn that Senate Bill 5599 allows Washington State to legally hide runaway children from their non-affirming parents,[7] and about drag summer camps for children as young as seven.[8]

Calls for censoring scientific research persist. In response to one published study[9] there were demands it be retracted, and for the journal's editor, Kenneth Zucker, to be sanctioned. Why the tumult? It's because the research supported the ROGD hypothesis. Within twenty-four hours, a petition supporting Zucker had 1,100 signatures.[10]

How will it end?

A lesson is provided by the Hebrew words for truth and falsehood—*emet* and *sheker*. The letters of *emet* all stand on a flat base or two legs, but each letter of *sheker* is precariously balanced on a single leg or the vertex of an angle.[11] The letters of *emet* are the first, middle, and last letters of the alphabet. The letters of *sheker* are side-by-side at the alphabet's end.

Truth, *emet*:

Falsehood, *sheker*:

The Talmud, written over 1,500 years ago, explains: Truth stands secure and fixed, falsehoods totter and eventually collapse. Falsehoods are easily found; truth requires a search.[12]

As I said in the first pages of this book, my most difficult fight has not been against dangerous diseases, but against dangerous ideas. I have laid out the history of dangerous ideas upon which gender ideology's Articles of Faith are based. John Money's idea: deny biology. Psychiatry's idea: normalize a disorder. The Dutch idea: block puberty. Educators' idea: we know better than you. Lawyers' idea: your home isn't safe. Surgeons' idea: you name it, we'll do it.

All of it lacks foundation and cannot persist indefinitely. It will fall to pieces, and Mother Nature will prevail; she always does. In the meantime, you must guard your precious family. Now that you're at the end of this book, you understand the enemy. You have ammunition. You have a war plan.

I'll finish by saying, don't take this the wrong way, but I don't want to see you in my office. I'd rather not speak to you from your basement or bathroom. I hope to spare you a "lasagna surprise."

If I save just one family, it will have been worth it.

# Biology 101

## Colin Wright, PhD[*]

In its 2018 policy statement,[1] "Ensuring Comprehensive Care and Support for Transgender and Gender Diverse Children and Adolescents," the American Academy of Pediatrics recommends *The Gender Book*[2] as a resource to understand core concepts.

I urge parents to check out a chart found on that site under the "anatomy" tab.[3] A person wearing surgical scrubs, a white coat, and a stethoscope points to a chart whose take-home message is that male and female are not real categories. Instead, they are arbitrary labels, two ends of a spectrum.

An arrow extends over eight different depictions of genitalia; at one end are genitalia that are described as "smaller and more internal," at the other end "larger and more external." These extremes, according to the chart, represent "dyadic female" and "dyadic male." The other types of genitalia between those two are indicated to be "intersex—about 1 in 100 births."

The chart communicates that while there are some people who fall neatly in the category of male or female, there is also a vast spectrum of so-called intersex individuals between those poles.

But these depictions of sex are scientifically inaccurate and rooted in fundamental misunderstandings about biology.

---

[*] Dr. Colin Wright is an evolutionary biologist, Manhattan Institute Fellow, and Academic Advisor for the Society for Evidence-based Gender Medicine.

The main issue with this chart and others like it is that it incorrectly portrays the sex of individuals as spanning a continuous gradient when it is in fact binary, or "dyadic." While genital anatomy in humans can exhibit significant variation, a person's genitals do not ultimately define the sex of humans, or any other species for that matter. Rather, the sex of an individual has everything to do with the type of sex cell (i.e., sperm versus egg) that their primary sex organs (i.e., testes versus ovaries) produce. Because there are only two types of sex cells, there are only two sexes, and therefore, sex is not a spectrum.

What *does* exist on somewhat of a spectrum are what we refer to as "secondary sex characteristics," which are the traits that males and females acquire during puberty. In females, these include (among others) the development of breasts, wider hips, and a tendency for fat to store around the hips and buttocks. In males, these traits include deeper voices, taller average height, facial hair, broader shoulders, increased musculature, etc. While puberty produces different traits for males and females, enough variation exists in each trait that there is some degree of overlap: some males have higher voices than some women, and some women are taller than some men, for instance. But while these secondary sex characteristics are what most people might envision when they think about men and women socially, these traits do not actually define a person's (or any animal's) sex. Rather, these traits develop as a *consequence* of one's sex due to differences in the hormones produced during puberty.

Further, the idea that the overall size of a person's genitals determines their relative degree of maleness or femaleness, as this chart suggests, is both false and socially regressive. Taken to its logical conclusion, this means that males with smaller penises are somehow *less male* than males with larger penises, and that females with larger and "more external" labia and clitorises are *less female* than women with smaller and "more internal" genital anatomy.

The chart also falsely states that the prevalence of so-called "intersex" conditions is 1 in 100 births, or 1 percent. Another false statistic commonly asserted is that 1.7 percent of people are intersex, or that intersex people are "as common as red hair." But these estimates are based on a single 2000 review paper[4] that should have never passed peer review.

In 2002, a physician named Leonard Sax pointed out[5] that the review's 1.7 percent statistic included many conditions that could not be considered "intersex" in any clinically relevant sense. Indeed, the conditions making up the large majority of the review's 1.7 percent figure *do not result in any sexual ambiguity whatsoever.* According to Sax:

> [T]his [1.7 percent] figure includes conditions which most clinicians do not recognize as intersex, such as Klinefelter syndrome, Turner syndrome, and late-onset adrenal hyperplasia. If the term intersex is to retain any meaning, the term should be restricted to those conditions in which chromosomal sex is inconsistent with phenotypic sex, or in which the phenotype is not classifiable as either male or female.

When the conditions that do not result in the appearance of sex ambiguity were removed, the review's 1.7 percent figure drops nearly 100-fold to 0.018 percent, or less than about 1 in 5,500 individuals.

In summary, the chart at the website TheGenderBook.com falsely portrays biological sex as a "spectrum" where people aren't either male or female, but rather exist somewhere along a smooth gradient of maleness and femaleness that is determined by genital size and how internal/external they appear. Further, it inflates the true prevalence of intersex conditions by over fifty times its true rate in order to portray sex as less binary or dyadic.

The goal of the chart is to convince people that biological sex is so complex and arbitrarily defined that we should abandon "male" and "female" categories altogether in favor of letting people define themselves according to their subjective "gender identity." This is not science by any stretch of the imagination—it's pseudoscience pushed by activists to further a political agenda.

# Key Scientific Papers

## Lauren H. Schwartz, MD

## Social Transition

1.  Zucker, Kenneth J. "Debate: Different strokes for different folks." *Child and adolescent mental health* 25 1 (2020): 36–37.
    Social transition of younger children is not only a psychosocial treatment, but may be iatrogenic (therapist/doctor unintendedly induces symptoms or complications with specific treatment) given the rate of desistance otherwise (reported rates of desistance up to 97% without intervention).

2.  Sievert, E. D., Schweizer, K., Barkmann, C., Fahrenkrug, S., & Becker-Hebly, I. (2021). "Not social transition status, but peer relations and family functioning predict psychological functioning in a German clinical sample of children with Gender Dysphoria." *Clinical child psychology and psychiatry*, 26(1), 79–95. https://doi.org/10.1177/1359104520964530.
    Demonstrates that current research does not support the assumption that social transition benefits gender dysphoric youth.

3.  Singh D, Bradley SJ, & Zucker KJ (2021). "A Follow-Up Study of Boys with Gender Identity Disorder." *Frontiers in Psychiatry* 12:632784. doi: 10.3389/fpsyt.2021.632784.
    Desistance is outcome for majority of children (only 12% persisted in this study) if they are not transitioned early (socially or otherwise).

4. Wong, W. I., van der Miesen, A. I. R., Li, T. G. F., MacMullin, L. N., & VanderLaan, D. P. (2019). "Childhood social gender transition and psychosocial well-being: A comparison to cisgender gender-variant children." *Clinical Practice in Pediatric Psychology*, 7(3), 241–253. https://doi.org/10.1037/cpp0000295.

Psychological challenges appear to be similar whether a gender variant child has socially transitioned or not.

5. Kristina R. Olson, Lily Durwood, Rachel Horton, Natalie M. Gallagher, & Aaron Devor. "Gender Identity 5 Years After Social Transition." *Pediatrics* August 2022; 150 (2): e2021056082. 10.1542/peds.2021-056082.

Demonstrated early transition led to persistence as trans 5 years later in over 97%; authors argue that despite being in stark contrast to all previous research, this was confirmation that detransition/desisting is rare. However, this study reiterates significant concern for iatrogenic effect caused by Social Transition.

6. Morandini, J.S., Kelly, A., de Graaf, N.M., et al. "Is Social Gender Transition Associated with Mental Health Status in Children and Adolescents with Gender Dysphoria?" *Archive of Sexual Behavior* 52, 1045–1060 (2023). https://doi.org/10.1007/s10508-023-02588-5.

Whether or not a child socially transitioned was not associated with mood, anxiety, or suicide attempts; study "failed to find superior well-being in socially transitioned young people."

## Suicide vs. Reported Suicidality and Self-Report Surveys

Biggs, M. "Suicide by Clinic-Referred Transgender Adolescents in the United Kingdom." *Archive f Sexual Behavior* 51, 685–690 (2022). https://doi.org/10.1007/s10508-022-02287-7.

Discusses exceptionally low rate of suicide, complex, unreliable nature of self-report, especially in young children. 15,000 children referred to GIDS Clinic in England from 2010-2020, 4 completed suicide (2 in treatment, 2 on waitlist).

## Informed Consent and Gender-Affirming Care for Minors

1. Levine, S. B., Abbruzzese, E., & Mason, J. W. (2022a). "Reconsidering informed consent for trans-identified children, adolescents, and young adults." *Journal of Sex & Marital Therapy*, 48(7), 706–727. doi:10.1080/0092623X.2022.2046221.

"Beliefs about gender-affirmative care need to be separated from the established facts so that proper informed consent process can occur prepare parents and patients for the difficult choices that they must make."

2. Levine, S. B., Abbruzzese, E., & Mason, J. W. (2022b). "What are we doing to these children? Response to Drescher, Clayton, and Balon Commentaries on Levine et al., 2022." *Journal of Sex & Marital Therapy*. Advance online publication. doi:10.1080/0092623X.2022.2136117.

3. Levine S. B. "Informed Consent for Transgendered Patients." *Journal of Sex & Marital Therapy* 2019;45(3):218-229. doi: 10.1080/0092623X.2018.1518885. Epub 2018 Dec 22. PMID: 30582402. Informed consent, which requires consent to future risks, is not possible in children.

## Overstated certainty of benefits/Lack of transparency regarding risks in Gender-Affirming Care

1. Clayton, A. "Gender-Affirming Treatment of Gender Dysphoria in Youth: A Perfect Storm Environment for the Placebo Effect—The Implications for Research and Clinical Practice." *Archive of Sexual Behavior* 52, 483–494 (2023). https://doi.org/10.1007/s10508-022-02472-8.

2. Biggs, M. (2022). "The Dutch protocol for Juvenile transsexuals: Origins and evidence." *Journal of Sex & Marital Therapy*. Advance online publication. doi:10.1080/0092623X.2022.212123.

3. Biggs, M. (2020). "Gender dysphoria and psychological functioning in adolescents treated with GnRHa: Comparing Dutch and English prospective studies." *Archives of Sexual Behavior*, 49(7), 2231–2236. doi:10.1007/s10508-020-01764-1.

4. Biggs, M. (2021). "Revisiting the effect of GnRH analogue treatment on bone mineral density in young adolescents with gender dysphoria." *Journal of Pediatric Endocrinology and Metabolism*, 34(7), 937–939. doi:10.1515/ jpem-2021-0180.

5. Biggs, M. (2023). "The Dutch Protocol for Juvenile Transsexuals: Origins and Evidence." *Journal of Sex and Marital Therapy*, 49:4, 348368, DOI: 10.1080/0092623X.2022.2121238.
International standard of care for gender dysphoric youth is based on untrue assumptions (reversibility), little to no evidence of benefits, lack of long-term follow-up studies, and poorly reported to omitted permanent, negative outcomes.

6.  J. Cohn (2022) "Some Limitations of 'Challenges in the Care of Transgender and Gender-Diverse Youth: An Endocrinologist's View.'" *Journal of Sex & Marital Therapy*, DOI: 10.1080/0092623X.2022.2160396.

7.  E. Abbruzzese, Stephen B. Levine, & Julia W. Mason (2023) "The Myth of "Reliable Research" in Pediatric Gender Medicine: A critical evaluation of the Dutch Studies—and research that has followed." *Journal of Sex & Marital Therapy*, DOI: 10.1080/0092623X.2022.2150346.

8.  Levine, S.B. "Reflections on the Clinician's Role with Individuals Who Self-identify as Transgender." *Archive of Sexual Behavior* 50, 3527–3536 (2021). https://doi.org/10.1007/s10508-021-02142-1.

9.  Zucker, K. J. (2019). "Adolescents with gender dysphoria: Reflections on some contemporary clinical and research issues." *Archives of Sexual Behavior*, 48, 1983-1992.
    Addresses suicidality discourse among providers treating gender distress, the recent increase in referrals to gender clinics and inversion of ratio of male:female referrals over last several years, ROGD diagnosis and treatment.

10. Block J. (2023). "Gender dysphoria in young people is rising—and so is professional disagreement." *BMJ*; 380: p382 doi:10.1136/bmj.p382.
    Discussion of lack of evidence in support of affirming treatments, social, medical and rush to affirm without psychological support.

11. Littman, L. (2021). "Individuals treated for gender dysphoria with medical and/or surgical transition who subsequently detransitioned: A survey of 100 detransitioners." *Archives of Sexual Behavior*, 50(8), 3353–3369. doi:10.1007/s10508-021-02163-w.
    Research regarding ROGD and intervening too early with affirming care; risk of "iatrogenically derailing the development of youth who would otherwise grow up to be LGB nontransgender adults."

12. James M. Cantor (2020). "Transgender and Gender Diverse Children and Adolescents: Fact-Checking of AAP Policy." *Journal of Sex & Marital Therapy*, 46:4, 307-313, DOI: 10.1080/0092623X.2019.1698481.

## Rapid Onset Gender Dysphoria

1.  Littman, L. (2018). "Parent reports of adolescents and young adults perceived to show signs of a rapid onset of gender dysphoria." PLOS ONE, 13(8), e0202330. doi:10.1371/journal.pone.0202330.

2.  Hutchinson, A., Midgen, M., & Spiliadis, A. (2020). "In support of research into rapid-onset gender dysphoria." *Archives of Sexual Behavior*, 49(1), 79-80.

## Comprehensive Guide to Exploratory Care

Ayad S., D'Angelo R., Kenny D., Levine S., Marchiano L., & O'Malley S. (2022). "A Clinical Guide for Therapists Working with Gender-Questioning Youth." https://www.genderexploratory.com/wp-content/uploads/2022/12/GETA_ClinicalGuide_2022.pdf. Sponsored by Gender Exploratory Therapy Association (GETA) and Society for Evidence-Based Gender Medicine (SEGM).

## International Rejection of Medicalization of Minors

**England:** https://cass.independent-review.uk/nice-evidence-reviews/

**Finland:** https://segm.org/sites/default/files/Finnish_Guidelines_2020_Minors_Unofficial%20Translation.pdf

**Sweden:** https://www.sbu.se/342

**Norway:** https://tidsskriftet.no/en/2019/04/debatt/gender-variance-medical-treatment-and-our-responsibility

# APPENDIX THREE

# Dealing with Schools

## Vernadette Broyles and Joel Thornton[*]

## Child & Parental Rights Campaign[†]

## What are your rights as a parent/guardian?

This is a critical question that in recent years has been seriously challenged by school officials. Since COVID-19, we have learned there is much going on in our public schools that is driven by ideological agendas that do not have the best interest of our children in mind.

As a parent you have constitutionally guaranteed rights to oversee your child's education, upbringing, and medical / mental health decision making.

It is important to remember that federal and state laws and local school district policies or guidelines cannot infringe upon constitutional rights. Therefore, the right you have as a parent to control the educational, upbringing, and health-related decisions for your child cannot be simply denied.

The Supreme Court of the United States has been clear on a parent's right to control the education, upbringing, and healthcare of their child. You do not have the right to decide on the curriculum used, but in many states you have the right to opt your child out of questionable instruction on topics such as sex education and gender identity that advance this ideology.

---

[*] Copyright listed with CPRC.
[†] Published by permission of the Child & Parental Rights Campaign, Inc.

Social affirmation of a minor is a significant mental health intervention with potentially life-altering consequences. It, therefore, should not be done in school without your knowledge and express permission. Many school officials, however, assert they have the right to make these decisions based solely on a child's assertion and do not need parental permission or even knowledge. Nothing could be further from the truth.

You should put school officials on notice that you do not give permission for them to transition your child or to give your child any instruction, information, or counseling on these matters. Then you should monitor the activities of teachers and administrators to ensure that they are honoring your rights and instructions concerning your child.

You should always remain pleasant but firm in dealing with school administrators. Clarity and diplomacy will get you the same results and make it easier to deal with problems in the future as you assert your parental rights.

## Title IX and the Federal Government

Title IX of the 1972 Education Amendments prohibits discrimination in the educational setting on the basis of "sex." However, the US Department of Education is advising school officials that Title IX includes nondiscrimination based on gender identity and sexual orientation. This is causing tremendous confusion as to what the law requires in school districts around the country.

The Biden Administration has proposed new Title IX regulations that, if adopted, would expand the definition of discrimination to include gender identity and sexual orientation. These changes have not yet been made and would likely ultimately be struck down in the courts. Nevertheless, many local school districts believe that pursuant to Title IX schools have a mandate to affirm a child's gender identity without parental consent, causing parents to have to assert their parental rights against this inappropriate expansion of the school's authority.

## Asserting your parental rights concerning your child with your school

You need to resolve your own identity as your child's primary decision maker. No one knows and loves your child as you do. It is your responsibility and yours alone.

If your child has expressed any confusion concerning his or her sex, you should immediately cut off the influences contributing to their confusion and seek the assistance of a mental health professional who shares your beliefs and understanding of biological reality.

As parents you are the ones in charge of the educational and medical/mental health decisions for your minor child. This means that you can choose whether your child goes to public school or private school or is homeschooled. It means that you have the right, in many states, to opt your child out of objectionable classes like sex education that promote gender identity ideology.

It also means that you are the only ones who can determine what is best for your child's health. Gender dysphoria seldom occurs in a vacuum, and it is your decision how your child is to be treated, not school officials.

- ## Know what is going on at school.

It is your responsibility to know what is going on at school. Read the documents that are being sent home. Attend meetings with teachers. If possible, volunteer at the school. Ask your child about what is happening at the school.

Do not be afraid to call and set up a meeting with the principal of your child's school to discuss things that concern you related to this issue. Ask what is being taught in classes or programs concerning "transgenderism" or gender identity in school. Inquire about the school policies or practices concerning this issue, such as name and pronoun use, bathroom access, overnight accommodations during field trips, and sports teams. Most importantly, ask when and how parents will be notified if their child expresses distress with their sex or asked to be treated as something other than their sex.

- ## Educate your school central office and building level leaders with accurate information regarding gender identity ideology and its impacts on children.

Do not assume that the information school officials have is accurate. Most often school officials have been given incorrect and ideologically driven information concerning "transgender" identities in children and adolescents by education unions and advocacy groups. Because of an excessive concern over liability and threats from advocacy groups, the school attorneys often give school leaders skewed information, as well.

You should take the opportunity to educate your school principal, vice-principal, and counselor and your school district leaders with accurate information concerning the transgender phenomenon and its serious repercussions in children and adolescents. An excellent resource for this purpose is *Navigating the Transgender Landscape, School Resource Guide"* and on websites listed below.

## • Communicate to your school administrators your parental instructions, opt-outs, and family's beliefs in writing.

When you are discussing your parental instructions with teachers and administrators on matters related to gender identity, you should follow all verbal communications with written instructions so that there is no confusion as to what your parental wishes are concerning your child and whether school officials were made aware.

If you have real cause for concern, you should consider sending your school leaders a letter communicating your parental instructions concerning issues related to gender identity and your child at school. Some important information to include are:

- You demand to be immediately notified if your child requests to be treated as something other than his/her biological sex, including using different sexed names or pronouns, or facilities.
- You do not consent to any manner of your child being socially transitioning at school.
- You do not consent to your child receiving instruction or information concerning transgender identities or gender identity ideology.
- You do not consent to your child meeting with any teachers, counselors, or other school officials or third parties regarding gender identity issues, or to be referred to any counselor, medical or mental health professional, or social worker, including School Based Health Clinics ("SBHC"), without your express written consent.
- Request that you be given *prior written notice* and that your child be given alternative academic instruction during any presentation or instruction on gender identity.

If appropriate, your letter should put the school on notice that such matters are directly contrary to your family's faith (in addition to being medically controversial) and that exposing your child to these materials, gatherings, or meetings violates your family's sincerely held religious beliefs.

If the school district interprets Title IX to require affirmation of a child's asserted gender identity, in your letter you should note that your constitutionally protected parental rights to direct the upbringing, education, and medical/mental care of your child cannot be superseded by Title IX or any other federal statute.

Finally, your letter should request that this notification be placed in your child's permanent file and be provided to all adults instructing or interacting with your child during the school year.

- ## Contact an attorney if you have cause to believe there might be an issue.

Do not be afraid to seek legal advice if you believe your rights are being violated. The point of your communications is to place the school on notice should serious violations affecting your child's well-being occur and it becomes necessary to consider filing a lawsuit. It does not always take a lawsuit to resolve issues, but it often takes an attorney getting engaged to show school officials that you are serious about defending your right to protect your child.

## Applying for Section 504 of the Rehabilitation Act of 1973 or the IDEA (Individuals with Disabilities Education Act) status can help you protect your child.

Children with gender identity issues often have other underlying issues that need special attention. Therefore, it is important for you to do everything you can to get them the extra help they need, while protecting them from errant school officials.

Section 504 ("Sec. 504")[1] and the IDEA[2] are federal laws that require public school districts to accommodate unique needs of qualified students so that they have access to a free, appropriate public education. The nature of disability status means that your child will be getting more attention than children who do not have a Sec. 504 accommodation plan or are not protected by the IDEA. It also means there is a written plan about how school officials are going to work with your child to hold school officials more accountable.

These federal laws create a higher standard of care that school officials must observe when dealing with these children. All of this can work to your advantage, because school officials and activists often believe that the only issue they should be concerned about is gender confusion. A 504 plan or Individualized Education Program (IEP) developed pursuant to the IDEA means that school officials are on notice of other potential health or learning issues that impact major life activities of your child, and they cannot ignore them.

The need to accommodate children who have been identified as needing particular accommodations, or specialized instruction and programming, is engrained in school officials. The school district administration and staff are legally responsible to adhere to and implement all components of a Sec. 504 Accommodation Plan or an IEP under the IDEA. If your child qualifies under either of these Acts, this is likely the best way to set it up so that you have more control over the educational plans, services, and interactions with your child. It is also very much an underutilized area of parental control in matters affecting their child's education.

Thus, you can use Sec. 504's Accommodation Plan or the IDEA's IEP processes to require additional student assistance, services, and programming; improve parent-school communications; create structure and accountability; and place school officials on notice that other issues are involved and not merely gender confusion. If you believe your child may qualify under Sec. 504 or the IDEA, you should seek review and advice from an attorney experienced in disability rights.

## Information is power — How to get information from school officials concerning your child.

The Family Educational Rights and Privacy Act (FERPA) is the federal law that sets forth basic privacy requirements and access protocols for personally identifiable information contained in educational records created or maintained by public K-12 school districts.

There are exceptions, however, to what constitutes educational records. An important exception is records kept in the sole possession of the creator (administrator, teacher, or counselor) and used only as a personal memory aid, and are not accessible or revealed to any other person. This can include lesson plans or private notes kept by a teacher or counselor.[3]

Another exception includes test instruments or question booklets that do not contain the student's name or other personally identifiable information.[4] Also, some courts and administrative tribunals have found that emails that briefly reference a child, but are used only as a communication tool and were not maintained as part of the student's records, are not FERPA records.[5]

### • The rights of students and parents are covered.

Both parents are accorded full rights of access to a student's records under FERPA, even if divorced, unless the school district has been provided with a court order, statute, or legal document that specifically revokes a parent's rights.[6]

When a student reaches the age of majority or enrolls in a post-secondary institution, the rights afforded to parents under FERPA transfer to the student.[7] This includes Individuals with Disabilities Education Act (IDEA)-eligible students, unless a court has determined the student to be incompetent.[8]

A District must comply with requests to access a student's educational records without unnecessary delay and no later than forty-five days after the request is made.[9]

## • There are limitations on access to records.

Parents can only obtain information about their child. So, if a record contains information about more than one student, it must be redacted before the parents can obtain access, parental consent must be obtained from all other parents, or the parent can be allowed to access to only the portion of the record relating to their child.[10]

## • Enforcement of FERPA is done through the US Department of Education (DOE).

The ultimate enforcement action against a school district is termination of all federal financial assistance, where the DOE is unable to secure compliance by voluntary means.[11]

Parents or eligible students can file written complaints regarding alleged violations of FERPA with the Family Policy Compliance Office (FPCO) at:

Family Policy Compliance Office
U.S. Department of Education
400 Maryland Avenue, S.W.
Washington, DC 20202-4605

The complaint must state specific facts giving reasonable cause that a violation has occurred. Complaints must be submitted within 180 days after the date of the violation or the date on which the complainant knew or should have known of the violation.[12]

School districts must be notified in writing of the complaint and are also asked to submit a written response.[13] The FPCO will issue written findings after allowing the parties to submit additional information and argue their case.[14] There is no right to a hearing for the school district, and the FPCO's decision is final.[15]

If the District is found in violation, FPCO's findings will include the steps required for compliance and provide a reasonable timeline for the school district to comply. If a school district fails to comply, the Department of Education can withhold further payments of federal assistance, issue a cease-and-desist order, or terminate eligibility to receive federal funding.[16]

## Filing Open Records Requests—getting information about your school district

The way to get a broad set of information, including relevant policies, practices, and directives in place at your school, what clubs are in your school, and getting system wide information is through submitting Open Records Requests.

These requests must be made in writing. There is usually a place on the district's website that directs where to file your requests. You must be very specific about what you are requesting. And you typically will be required to pay for the cost of preparing the records requested.

Nevertheless, Open Records Requests are a very useful tool to get written information about policies, practices, and activities at your school and within your district, which have been used effectively by parents and their allies.

## How do you assert your parental rights at the district level?

There is strength in numbers, and courage begets courage. So it's important to gather the support of other like-minded parents. For meetings not involving your child's private concerns, it would be helpful to come to a meeting with the principal or school superintendent with several other parents. In private meetings concerning your child, the support of other parents arms you with the knowledge that you have others standing with you.

## Advocating with the school district's Board of Education

Attending school board meetings is another way to assert your rights as a parent. Remember, you always want to be conversational and pleasant. Whenever possible, bring supportive parents with you to the meeting. As few as five to ten people at a board meeting with a shared concern is often enough to get the board's attention.

Take the time they allot for public comments and go on record with your concerns. You should request to know which practices are being implemented, communicate parental concerns, and make a record.

Keep in mind that it may be the school board's attorney that is behind the resistance you are seeing from the board. It is good to have meetings with individual board members who may be sympathetic to your issues to educate them with accurate information on the transgender issue, find out how you can support them, and help them bring these issues to the attention of the full board.

## Resources

Navigating The Transgender Landscape, School Resource Guide [https:// backup.childparentrights.org/product/navigating-the-transgender-landscape -free-download/]

Sample Parental Notice concerning your child and issues related to Gender Identity Ideology
[https://docs.google.com/document/d/1IECbkuP4QZ20ZOdfrF3DtILl-MGqO2Leq/edit]

Sample Open Records Request
[https://docs.google.com/document/d/1XaNGapRov2dP2GazQy-wzMFh-7p61AZFF/edit]

# Dealing with Child Protective Services

## Vernadette Broyles, Ernie Trakas, and Joel Thornton[*]
## Child & Parental Rights Campaign[†]

There is a trend that is weaponizing Child Protective Services against loving and fit parents who seek to uphold biological reality when their child experiences gender confusion.

Child Protective Services may be called by different names in different states, such as Department of Children and Family Services, Department of Child Safety, or something similar. Their mandate is basically the same—the protection of children whose parents abuse them or who are not able to take care of them or provide for their essential needs. We will, therefore, refer to these government agencies, regardless of what they are called in a particular state, more generally as Child Protective Services (CPS).

Where there are concerns that a parent has been abusive or neglectful, CPS may seek authority to remove a child from the parents' custody and require the parents to go to Juvenile Court to have the child released back into their custody. In many instances, CPS is able to help families get the services they need, such as assisting families with addiction issues or parenting classes to help parents better care for their children. In normal circumstances, this is a good thing.

When it comes to issues of gender identity, however, CPS has been weaponized for use in the culture war. School officials, or others, might threaten to refer parents to CPS because they do not believe that their child should be affirmed as something other than their biological sex, such as being called by the name or pronouns of the opposite sex or allowed to room with members of the opposite sex. Activists are encouraging school officials to refer parents who wish to uphold biological reality to CPS by claiming that such parents are creating an "unsafe home."

So, it is important that parents be prepared to deal effectively with CPS. Parents are right to be alarmed if CPS becomes involved because of the power they wield. They often come to your home, and they can be very heavy-handed. In response, you should always be polite and respectful to CPS officials and to police officers. But it is important you know your rights and know how to effectively assert them each step of the way.

## Recognize the early signs of possible CPS involvement.

The first indication you have that CPS may be getting involved might come from your child's school or a mental health provider. If school officials or one of your child's providers mentions that this might be a time to get CPS involved, then you should begin preparing for that eventuality.

It could be that your child is asked if they feel safe around you. Or school officials might ask if your child ever feels like harming themselves because you do not "affirm" their asserted identity. Any number of questions along those lines should cause you to suspect that school officials may be considering reporting you to CPS. School officials are mandatory reporters for child abuse and neglect. Many activists consider refusing to "affirm" a child's new gender identity (upholding biological reality) to be a form of child abuse or neglect. Do not be caught unaware.

## • Stay one step ahead – the first goal is to not let it get into Juvenile Court.

Parents must be proactive. First, parents need to get on the same page. It's important you agree on the proper response to school and CPS officials. If your child reports that he or she has been asked questions like the ones above, then it is better to be prepared than surprised. You should begin having discussions with school officials to let them know that you have done your research on gender dysphoria and are prepared to protect your child and your parental rights.

Make sure school officials know that gender issues are mental health issues and you have the sole authority to make those decisions for your child. Give them information that supports your decision to uphold biological reality with your child. Let them know you are engaging a mental health professional to help your child and, if necessary, that you are in the process of retaining an attorney. Let school officials and CPS officials see that you are prepared to protect your family.

## • Remove your child from the toxic environment.

Do not hesitate to remove your child from the toxic environment contributing to their gender confusion.

If the school where your child attends has personnel who are aggressive in their promotion of gender identities and ideology to your child, then you should very seriously consider finding a new learning environment for your child. In many states, parents have the ability to move a child to a school other than the one assigned by their district or to use a portion of their tax dollars to pay for alternatives. You should immediately begin to investigate these options.

If the environment in all the public schools available to your child are the same, then you should seriously consider private school, homeschooling your child, online, or a hybrid school, or some of the other educational options that developed during Covid, at minimum until your child has matured and come to once again fully embrace their body and sex. While private school or homeschooling may be a financial challenge, the funds you will expend to fight CPS, restore your child's health, and mend your shattered family will far outweigh it.

## • Find the right lawyer before CPS gets involved.

You should also immediately begin looking for a good lawyer who will support your family's value system. It is better to have a lawyer ready to defend you and not need that lawyer than it is to need that lawyer and not have one ready. CPS handles families with lawyers differently from how they handle families without lawyers. It will force CPS to take their time and make sure they are not violating your rights from the start.

Your first interactions with CPS should include your lawyer. Your lawyer should be capable of defending your right to make all health-related decisions for your child. Your lawyer should have a workable understanding of the care that you are providing, the reasons for your decision making, and the need to treat all the mental health issues your child might have and not just the gender issues.

## What to do when CPS gets involved

The first time you hear from CPS is often when they show up at your door. Just because they are there does not mean there is going to be an investigation. Cases are often screened out at the very beginning, which helps to keep their caseloads down. So, it would be wise of you to give them a good reason not to open a case against you.

CPS caseworkers can at times be aggressive and insist that they have the right to enter your home. They are often willing to intimidate you, using your fear against you. Do not panic and try not to be afraid. CPS is a government agency, and that means they can only enter your house with a warrant, an invitation, or if they reasonably believe someone in the house is in imminent danger.

Meet them at your door. Step out of the house and close the door behind you. Do not worry about your neighbors being able to see you—worry more about protecting your family. Be polite and let them know you understand their work is important; however, you are taking care of your child's needs. Make it plain from the start that they do not get access to your child or your home merely by showing up at your house.

If they have a document signed by a judge, tell them that you will cooperate with them after you speak with your lawyer. Set an appointment for them to come back when your lawyer can be present and insist that this is the only way they are going to talk to you or your child. They may become upset, and if you need to calm them down, let them speak to your lawyer on your phone.

It is also important that CPS understand you are doing everything you can to take care of your child's health needs. Let them know that you have found (or are actively seeking) a mental health counselor to provide care for your child. This helps you document, on the front end, that you are doing everything you can to meet your child's needs, and that takes away one of their strongest weapons against you—the accusation that you are not willing or able to meet your child's needs.

### • Is there a police officer with them?

At times CPS will have a police officer with them. This increases the intimidation and causes most parents to think they have no choice but to let them in their house. The law does not change because a police officer is at your door. They still have to have a warrant specifically allowing them to enter your house.

You do everything the same if there is a police officer present. You step out and close the door. Make sure your child is inside the house. You are happy to set up an appointment when your lawyer can be present.

## • Understanding your Fourth Amendment rights

In these situations, the Fourth Amendment is an important part of your civil rights that is worth restating here:

*The right of the people to be secure in their persons, houses, papers, and effects, against unreasonable searches and seizures, shall not be violated, and no warrants shall issue, but upon probable cause, supported by oath or affirmation, and particularly describing the place to be searched, and the persons or things to be seized.*

Even police officers do not have an automatic right to search you, your house, or your child without probable cause. This means that they cannot demand to be let into your house or interview your child without a warrant or without showing that someone in the house is in immediate danger. The police and CPS can wait for your lawyer to arrive. Or they can schedule a time to return so that you are properly represented.

Politely insist that you are not surrendering your Fourth Amendment rights and that they are not allowed in your house. Once you have waived this right, it is difficult to get it back. That is why it is best that you do not let CPS workers, even with police officers with them, into your house without a warrant. Anything they discover while inside, if you have granted them permission, can be used against you in the investigation. While it may be difficult to say, a polite and insistent "I am not comfortable with you entering my home without a warrant" should be enough.

If they still are convinced your child is in immediate danger, there is the potential that they may seek a warrant signed off on by a judge. If this happens, politely insist that you want to speak with your lawyer before they execute the warrant. They may insist that they have right to enter. Again, politely insist that you merely want to consult with your lawyer by telephone before you agree to allow them to execute the warrant.

If they have a warrant signed off on by a judge, then you have no choice but to ultimately let them do whatever the warrant permits. Read the warrant carefully to make sure they are not doing more than the judge has given them permission to do.

## • What to do when CPS comes to the medical or mental health facility where your child is

If your child is admitted to a medical or mental health facility due to a crisis, know that many facilities will be pushing affirmation. Immediately ask to speak with the psychiatrist and social workers involved at the facility. It is critical that they understand you are caring, involved parents. Develop a positive relationship with the healthcare workers caring for your child, knowing that you have authority over the treatment of your child.

If you do not already have one, you need to quickly locate and retain a mental health professional who will work with you and help you remove your child from the facility to outpatient care as quickly as possible. The goal is to remove your child from the facility without CPS involvement and to regain physical control of your child.

This may take some time. If you attempt to remove your child too quickly while your child is still psychiatrically unstable or actively threatening suicide, your attempts may trigger a call to CPS. So do not panic, but rather attempt to work directly with the medical personnel and enlist the direct involvement of your family's mental health professional to advocate for you.

Your child may have been coached by a counselor or teacher or by the Internet to claim that they will kill themselves if they are not affirmed in their new identity. This is a tenuous situation that requires great care. This claim empowers mental health professionals, many of whom have been trained to believe that affirmation is what is needed. So, use wisdom. Avoid getting into an argument about affirmation. Rather, seek to demonstrate that you understand the gravity and dynamics of the situation and that you have engaged competent mental health professionals (perhaps both a psychiatrist and a therapist) to assist you to do what is best for your child on an outpatient basis.

If CPS comes to the facility where your child has been admitted, you must immediately engage your lawyer. It is critical that you show CPS your engagement and willingness to work reasonably with them. Again, use great wisdom and, without compromising your family's belief system, work to avoid getting into a fight over affirmation. Focus, instead, on showing you

252 Lost in Trans Nation

are willing and able to provide the medical and mental healthcare needed to address the various issues that led to this crisis in your family in a holistic way on an outpatient basis.

## • What to do when CPS starts an investigation

If an investigation is opened, it is important for you to cooperate. If you do not cooperate, CPS will be more convinced that you are hiding something. Cooperating does not mean that you give them everything they ask for. It means that you answer their questions, with your lawyer present, and you provide them with proof for the statements you are making to them and of the care you are providing your child.

## • Cooperate, but do not concede.

This is a fine line. CPS has a lot of power, so you do not want to offend the worker with whom you are dealing. You need to cooperate with reasonable requests. You do not, however, need to concede your parental authority to them. If they ask you to do something that you believe is not in your child's best interest, then tell them you are uncomfortable with their request.

Many investigations end early on. Some of that depends on your getting along with the case worker, making them feel comfortable with you as a parent, and the proactive steps you are taking to address your child's needs. Do not be afraid to show them your parenting skills. Address their concerns. Outright hostility will only backfire on you. Support your insistence on your right to be making these decisions, and that these decisions are in the best interests of your child, with a clear understanding of what your rights are.

## • Insist on your First Amendment religion exercise and free speech rights.

If you have a sincerely held faith that guides your decisions concerning your children, do not be afraid to let CPS know. Don't give in to the temptation to compromise your faith and secularize your interaction with CPS. There are constitutional rights that protect your sincerely held beliefs. The state does not have the authority to deny the exercise of your religious beliefs concerning your children unless they can prove that you are harming your child.

The First Amendment also grants you and your family free speech rights to not be coerced into saying things that conflict with your faith or your sincerely held beliefs. So long as you are caring for your children's needs, do not be intimidated to surrender any of your First Amendment rights to adopt the dictates of gender identity ideology for your family.

- ## Do not let your child be questioned without you and/or your attorney being present.

Often CPS will want to question your child without you in the room. You should politely insist that because they are a minor you are not waiving your right to be present during their questioning. You should insist that you or your family's attorney must be present for any communication with your child.

CPS may insist that they have a right and a need to question the child without you present, but you should not give in, especially in the investigation stage in the absence of a warrant when no documents have been filed with the Juvenile Court.

## What to do when CPS takes you to court

In order for CPS to take custody or control of your children, they must have a court order. This means that you will need to defend your parental rights in Juvenile (or Family) Court. Should CPS take emergency custody of your child or if they seek to force you to take certain actions in order to retain custody of your child, the court is required to hold a hearing within the first few days.

This initial hearing is difficult to win, but it helps set the stage for the rest of the interactions in Juvenile Court. It is important that you have an attorney for this first hearing, even though one is generally not required.

CPS is required to show that your child is suffering a "dependency," meaning that you are causing, or allowing, your child to suffer harm or that you are unable or unwilling to provide for your child's needs. To do that CPS must present witnesses and evidence that prove their case in court.

The court will appoint a Guardian Ad Litem (GAL) for your child. This is a person, most often a lawyer, who is tasked with representing your child's "best interests" during the court process. You should work hard to establish a positive relationship with the GAL, and even seek to educate them with accurate literature on gender dysphoria, as the judges will listen carefully to their recommendations.

You should have an attorney for all of these hearings. Your attorney should be prepared to present witnesses, and very likely even an expert witness (such as a medical or mental health professional or a parenting expert), and other evidence that shows you are a fit parent that is making appropriate decisions and providing appropriate care in the best interest of your child according to the Juvenile Code of your state.

## • Defending your parental rights in court

Hearings in Juvenile Court tend to be less formal than most court hearings. Do not be taken off guard by that. Your child's well-being and your ability to raise him or her in accordance with your beliefs and what you know is in their best interests are at stake.

Many of these hearings will not have formal witnesses but will involve updates from CPS officials and their attorneys. Your lawyer should raise all of your objections at each hearing. Constitutional claims are not generally brought in this court, so your attorney should be prepared to lay a solid foundation for why these rights matter at this stage in case you wish to raise these issues on an appeal or in a subsequent civil rights lawsuit.

Do not sit back and assume the system will protect you. You must aggressively defend your parental rights in court. The Juvenile Court judge may be inclined to defer to CPS because the judge deals with them and their lawyers on a daily basis. They are also used to seeing dysfunctional families. However, just because you believe in biology reality or hold a faith-informed position contrary to CPS concerning your child's gender confusion does not make you an unfit parent. If you and your attorney can show you are loving parents willing and able to make decisions that are in the best interests of your child, then you stand a strong chance of prevailing.

## • Defending your relationship with your child in court

It will be the responsibility of you and your lawyer to defend your relationship with your child in court. Be sure to paint a picture that shows you are invested in what you believe is best for your child. Your lawyer should be armed with cases and research that explain the rights you are claiming and rationale for your decision to seek therapeutic care that upholds both biological reality and your family's sincerely held beliefs so that the court is not confused.

It will also be important throughout the process that you remain in frequent and affectionate contact with your child. Do your best to minimize conflict on the gender issue without compromising what you know to be true. Often that may mean agreeing to disagree on certain things. Never lose site of the fact that you love and know your child better than any CPS worker. Make it your goal, and that of your attorney, to show to the judge that this is the case.

# Finding a Therapist

## Lauren H. Schwartz, MD

*Every child and family seeking psychotherapy deserves to be treated with respect, dignity, and care that encompasses the entirety of who they are, today and every day to come.*

## Assessing Your Child's Needs

- Every child who expresses gender curiosity or confusion is not necessarily in immediate need of therapy.
- Consider co-occurring factors that may contribute to your child's distress.
- Examples of co-occurring challenges in children and adolescents include depression, anxiety, ADHD, PTSD, learning and processing differences, and autism.
- Consider influences such as social media, school organizations, clubs, friend groups, etc.

## Finding a Therapist

Finding a therapist who will be a good fit for your child and family can be a daunting task. You may be tempted to rush through the vetting process, but thoughtful consideration will provide the best results. Bad therapy can be more harmful than no immediate therapy, especially during child and adolescent development, so take your time.

Begin by searching for a therapist that is adequately trained, credentialed*, and utilizes well-established therapy techniques. You don't have to be an expert, but it is helpful to be familiar with types of therapy that are widely accepted among mental health professionals. Examples include psychodynamic, supportive, cognitive-behavioral, and family systems. All well-established therapeutic methods are comprehensive, developmentally appropriate, are not rushed, and will not guarantee a specific outcome. Gender Exploratory Therapy Association† provides useful information and resources for parents seeking care for their gender curious, questioning, or distressed child. Their site includes a directory of therapists from all over the world.

## Vetting a Therapist

At least one pre-treatment session with a potential therapist is strongly encouraged, and you may decide to meet more than once before your child begins therapy. This will help you identify a therapist whot works best with your child and compare therapists if needed. You can ask your child's therapist or potential therapist questions at any time. Outside of confidentiality issues, if a therapist is hesitant to answer your questions, this should be cause for concern.

Examples of questions to consider:

- What is your understanding of gender distress, dysphoria, or confusion, and how much experience do you have working with those issues?
- Which therapy techniques or methods do you use? Do you utilize an affirming or exploratory approach when working with gender distress? Are you familiar with the Gender Exploratory Therapy Association's guidelines?
- When and how often do you meet and communicate with parents/ families?
- To whom do you refer if psychiatric, neurological, or medical care is needed?

---

* https://www.nami.org/About-Mental-Illness/Treatments/Types-of-Mental-Health-Professionals
† https://genderexploratory.com/

- Do you feel medical intervention is ever warranted for a child experiencing gender distress? If so, can you expand on this?
- Are you familiar with distress related to detransitioning?
- What is your policy regarding safety, confidentiality, and minors?
- Do you have children of your own? (Parenting is the hardest job in the world. It can be reassuring to know the therapist can relate to your distress when your child is struggling.)

## Beyond The "Affirmative Model"

A therapist or "gender clinic" that advertises affirmative care raises a multitude of red flags. Examples include:

- Affirming care has evolved to narrowly focus on gender distress, ignoring your child's developmental, neuropsychological, medical, family, social, or trauma experiences. *This is not comprehensive, psychological care nor does it affirm your child's well-being.*
- Affirming care often prioritizes transition as the desired treatment outcome. *There is a growing body of evidence that gender-affirmative approaches encourage children toward irreversible decisions, medical and otherwise.‡*
- Gender-affirmative approaches have evolved to mean taking your child's complaints, intrusive thoughts, or all-or-nothing thinking at face value. *In all well-established therapeutic models, this is considered harmful; it ignores the complexity of gender and sexuality in the context of healthy child and adolescent development.*
- The risk of suicide is used to justify medical and surgical treatment. *This is not only unfounded, it also promotes emotional manipulation and a rush to permanent medical interventions when your child is most vulnerable.*

In summary, any distress in childhood that does warrant intervention, related to gender or otherwise, requires a comprehensive, individualized, developmentally appropriate approach that explores all contributing psychological, social, familial, biological, historical, and developmental aspects

---

‡ https://www.transgendertrend.com/current-evidence/

of the child. Gender-affirming care abandons these well-established thera-peutic principles.

*Dr. Lauren Schwartz is a psychiatrist and psychotherapist in private practice in Oklahoma. She is Board Certified in Psychiatry by the American Board of Psychiatry and Neurology and is a fellow of the American Psychiatric Association.*

# Guide to Internet Accountability Tools

## By a Concerned Citizen

As a parent, you'd like to protect your child from being exposed to harmful or inappropriate content.

The following resource was created to help you navigate the world of parental controls and Internet-free devices and to guide you toward the most effective tech tools to monitor your child's digital activity and minimize their exposure to predators, cyber bullying, and explicit or addictive sites, apps, or language. Parental controls also have capabilities to manage and control which websites and apps can be accessed, purchased, or downloaded, and when, as well as other perks, essentially giving you the ability to oversee your child's Internet usage.

There are several ways to limit the Internet on your child's devices.

## Built-In Parental Controls

Many products and platforms you already use have features or paid add-ons designed to monitor and restrict your child's Internet access.

- Some routers, such as Gryphon, and Internet Service Providers, such as Comcast, Sprint, AT&T, Verizon, Charter/Spectrum, and others, provide parental control tools. Note: While router blockers typically work only when your child's devices are connected to your home Internet, you can find exceptions. Gryphon Premium, for example, comes with the Homebound app that routes traffic back to the Gryphon server even when your child's device is connected to mobile data or outside Wi-Fi.

- Amazon Prime, Netflix, Hulu, Google Play, and Disney+ offer one or more of the following to help limit your child's viewing experience to kid-appropriate content: a children's profile, content restrictions, and a PIN to access certain content.
- Carriers such as AT&T, Verizon, T-Mobile, and others also have parental control add-on options. Note: Check with your carrier to ensure all features remain in full effect even when your child switches to Wi-Fi.
- Internet browsers such as Bing, Google, and DuckDuckGo, apps such as Instagram, TikTok, Facebook, and YouTube, and even Apple and Android devices allow you to filter out adult content or block or limit specific features, websites, or apps.

*Despite their convenience, a tech-savvy child can bypass many built-in parental controls by using another product or login to access the Internet uninterrupted. Therefore, using a combination of parental controls is often recommended. As well, built-in parental controls typically aren't preset and generally need to be consciously turned on.*

## Third-Party Parental Controls on Devices
Third-party parental controls are designed to protect your child while they surf the Internet. They come in all shapes and sizes with a wide array of features.

A few easy-to-manage, full-featured parental control systems include:

### Qustodio
Qustodio enables you to:

- Block websites, apps, and certain words:
  - Qustodio automatically blocks access to websites matching a list of ten problematic categories.
  - You can further refine the filtering process by blocking specific inappropriate sites, apps, or words.
  - You can also choose to "allow", "block" or "receive alerts" when your child tries to access content from a list of predetermined categories.

- Monitor your child's Internet usage:
  - Qustodio has a dashboard that details your child's Internet activity, including their browsing history (websites, apps, and social media activity), YouTube views, and screen time usage.
  - You can see who your child calls and texts, read their personal text messages, and set a list of blocked numbers.
  - You'll receive a report of their activities on a daily, weekly, and monthly basis, thus informing you if they've tried to enter blocked sites or are in trouble.

- Manage your child's screen time:
  - You can set limits on your child's screen time from the dashboard.
  - Using the Pause button, you can "pause" Internet access on your child's registered devices at any given time, and your child will be unable to access the Internet on any devices using Qustodio.

- Track devices:
  - Qustodio has a GPS location tracker. You can even save the locations your child visits most often and receive notifications when they've arrived or departed from those locations.
  - For Android users, Qustodio also has a panic button. If activated, you'll automatically receive an alert regarding your child's whereabouts.

Qustodio is available for Windows, Mac, Chromebook, Android, iPhone, iPad, and Kindle. While Qustodio offers a free plan with basic features for a single device, its subscription-based premium service allows families to make use of additional features, such as the location tracking service, calls and texts monitoring, and application management.

### Aura Parental Controls (Powered by Circle)

Aura enables you to:

- Block, limit, or restrict websites and apps:
  - Aura allows you to select websites, apps, games, and streaming services that you want to completely block, limit, or restrict by using the content Internet Filter feature.
  - You can further customize what your child sees online and filter content by category or by individual website/app/platform.

- While Aura comes with default settings by age, you can modify the settings to change access on individual apps or categories to "allow" or "not allow" for each child.

- Monitor usage:
  - Aura allows you to see which apps and websites your child tried to access.

- Manage screen time:
  - You can manage and set limits on the amount of time your child can use specific websites and apps.
  - You can also "pause" the Internet with a single tap using the Pause the Internet® feature. When the Internet is paused, devices can't get online at all.

- Provides antivirus and other online safety protections:
  - Aura also comes with other online safety features and family identity fraud protection for your entire family. This includes Child SSN monitoring and Dark Web monitoring to detect breaches, Antivirus to secure your devices from malware, VPN and Privacy Assistant for online data privacy, and a password manager to keep accounts secure.

Aura works on Android and iOS phones and tablets, although it is not available for PCs or MACs. Aura covers an unlimited number of children and devices and has 24/7 customer support.

### Net Nanny
Net Nanny enables you to:

- Block harmful content on websites and apps:
  - Net Nanny allows you to block dangerous content in fourteen pre-created categories and create a list of "always allow" or "always block" websites and apps. Net Nanny also has a social media protection function for social media platforms.
  - Using the custom web-filter, you can further block the content categories you choose.

- o Net Nanny is capable of recognizing context, and its profanity filter uses XXX in place of expletives.
- o Net Nanny uses AI to block content, thereby enabling real-time interventions.

- Monitor your child's digital activity and screen time usage:
  - o Net Nanny allows you to track in real time your child's digital activity. You'll see an instant report of Internet searches, get updates when apps are used, receive alerts that your child may have viewed inappropriate content, and even see the blocked websites your child tried to access. You'll have access to a Family Feed too, and you can also get educational insights from other parents about websites and trending apps.

- Manage screen time:
  - o You can control how your child uses their devices by scheduling curfews for daily or weekly access to the Internet. You can also turn off the Internet on your child's devices for a fixed amount of time, for example, when allocated screen time runs out.

- Location Tracking:
  - o Net Nanny has location tracking with location history, as well as the ability to enable notifications when your child checks in at a pre-defined location.

Net Nanny works on Chromebook, Windows, and Mac computers and Android and iOS mobile devices such as smartphones and tablets. Net Nanny offers subscriptions that cover one (computers/laptops only), five, or twenty devices.

Note: Net Nanny is working on an updated version of its parental control product, with a planned release in 2023. The new version will modernize Net Nanny in terms of usability, privacy, and UI, while adding new features such as a real-time image and video threat detection solutions, placing a stronger focus on well-being support, as well as providing guidance for safe online behavior.

## Bark Premium App

Bark enables you to:

- Block websites and apps:
  - You can block access to 18 different categories of content, such as streaming platforms, gaming, adult content, and more. You can also block individual sites and apps.

- Monitor content in texts, social media platforms, and websites and receive alerts in the event Bark spots a potential danger:
  - Once you install your child's app on their devices, Bark uses advanced technology to scan text messages, emails, and over 30+ different apps and platforms for potential safety concerns like bullying, depression, online predators, and more.
  - You'll receive an alert when Barks spots a potential danger so you can check in with your child and make sure everything is okay. Bark will also provide you with a series of recommendations on how to handle the issue.
  - Since its system is based on account information, Bark monitors your child's social media regardless of device. For example, if your child logs onto Groupme on any computer, Bark will still be monitoring the content.

- Manage screen time:
  - Bark's other notable features include screen time management, such as enabling you to control when a child can access the Internet and what specifically they can access at the time, as well as the ability to set limits on apps or websites.

- Location tracking:
  - With the Bark app, you can get location alerts when your child enters and leaves pre-set locations. You can also request location check-ins when your child is out and about to ensure they arrive safely.

Despite their sophistication, third-party parental control solutions aren't foolproof. Your child can successfully circumvent some of the Internet safety protections you've installed on their devices by downloading a VPN (or by deleting the app, if the third-party solution is in the form of an app), although in such cases, you would usually receive an alert informing you that something is wrong. And that isn't all. From software glitches to inadvertently overlooking a toggle or two during setup, third party systems, while designed to be as secure as possible, are far from perfect.

Therefore, whether you're using built-in parental controls or third-party solutions, you may want to add additional layers of protection such as:*

*Keeping family devices in an area where everyone can see them:* You can gain insight into the content your child is viewing every time you pass them, and they'll know it.

*Changing passwords on password-protected devices and programs often:* The best passwords are a mix of upper-case and lower-case letters, numbers, and special characters since they're more difficult to guess.

## Internet-Free Phones

Some elements to consider when choosing a phone without Internet capabilities are:

*Design:* Will your child be happy with a flip phone or do they want something that resembles a smartphone even if it doesn't have smartphone capabilities?

*Battery Life:* Unless your child walks around with a battery pack, you'd want to ensure their phones have enough battery life to last them comfortably throughout the day.

*4G or Satellite Network:* Most major mobile carriers have already phased out 3G networks. Purchasing a 4G, 5G, or satellite phone will allow the phone to be used for a longer period of time.

*Durability:* Is the phone strong enough to withstand being dropped or tossed around?

*Cost:* Price point is something to take into consideration especially if your child isn't careful with their possessions.

Internet-free phones fall into several categories:

### Basic Phones

You can think of basic phones—often called feature phones—as old-fashioned cell phones. Basic phones use a cellular service for calling and texting. Some basic phones have data services, albeit limited, such as email or minimal web browsing.

Nokia has several basic phone options. Nokia 8110 4G is one example. A durable phone with a long battery life, it has games and a basic web browser. If limited web access concerns you, the Jitterbug flip phone, originally designed for seniors, comes without a camera or Internet access. Jethro SC490, another basic phone, has more wireless carrier options than Jitterbug while still remaining Internet-free.

Despite their convenience, the simple design of basic phones can render them unappealing to some children.

## Smartphone-Style Internet-Free Phones

### Gabb Phone

- The Gabb phone (and Gabb Phone Plus) plans have unlimited talk and text, as well as a spam blocker and 14 pre-loaded kid safe apps. The Gabb phone doesn't have Internet access, social media apps, or games. Notifications are sent to you if your child is texting or calling significantly more than the average user.
- The Gabb phone allows you to enable picture messaging and group messaging when you believe your child is ready.
- As a parent, you have the option to download the MyGabb app to enable location tracking. When purchasing a Gabb watch for your child, all contacts, preset text messages, and GPS location tracking are managed via the MyGabb app.
- If you want your child to have the ability to do more, Gabb Phone Plus has a list of third-party apps that Gabb deems safe. All of them are optional, and you must approve them before your child can download them.
- Purchasing the Gabb phone and choosing a plan are done with Gabb wireless. No contract options are available.

### Bark Phone

- The Bark Phone is an Android A13 that has Bark's parental controls built in. Plans come with unlimited talk and text, and a free case.
- The Bark Phone is designed to give you greater control over your child's digital activities. Some features include texts that can't be deleted, contact approval options that, if applied, block calls and texts from unapproved contacts on the Bark phone or on apps, a remote phone lock, and more.

- The phone is fully customizable and is designed to grow with your child. It is thus as controlled as you want it to be. You can add in or take away functionality to almost any level — your child's phone can be as locked down as a flip phone (with no Internet) or as fully operational as a regular smartphone. You can monitor content, block websites and apps, create screen time schedules, and track location with GPS.
- You can purchase your phone plan directly through Bark. No contract is required.

### Pinwheel Phone

- Pinwheel is a system that comes pre-installed on specific phones and is designed to be remotely monitored and managed from your phone or computer. It is not a cellular service. You choose the carrier and cellular plan that's right for your family. Most major carriers are compatible with at least one Pinwheel phone model, including Verizon, AT&T, T-Mobile, Mint Mobile, Red Pocket Mobile, and US Mobile.
- Pinwheel's companion app, the Caregiver Portal, has a whitelist that is comprised of a list of contacts with whom you allow your child to communicate. You can define when each contact is available, and whether or not your child and the contact can exchange images. As your child gets older, they can manage their own contacts.
- Through the Caregiver Portal, you can read your child's texts and see their call history. Texts show up even if they've been deleted from the phone. You can also track your child using a GPS locator.
- Pinwheel has no web browser, social media apps, streaming video apps, or ad-driven apps. It also doesn't have an app store on your child's device. The Caregiver Portal, however, has a library of 700+ apps, labeled with insights into what each app really allows. You can also define which apps and contacts are available at which times using the Schedule features on the companion app on your phone, as well as set up reusable permission sets of apps and contacts to be available at the same time (called "modes") to make setting up their timelines easier.
- Pinwheel has an added bonus of remote managed "to-do" lists to help your child remember their responsibilities.

- Pinwheel does not require a contract. Pinwheel phones can be purchased directly from Pinwheel's website or through Amazon.

Additional resources can be found at:
- https://internetsafety101.org/objects/5_steps_to_Mitigate_Online _Harms_During_COVID_19_-_Copyright.pdf
- https://internetsafety101.org/objects/Moble_and_Wireless_101 _-_Copyright.pdf

# Responses to International Parent Survey

## Parent-to-Parent Advice

# Ideology

"... I would advise them that no child is born in the wrong body, that sex is binary and immutable, and thoughts of a different identity are because of self-hatred and a maladaptive coping mechanism... The answer is to confront the problem, and not escape the problem by denying reality."
**—Laurie from Florida**

"... Be highly protective about online content—porn and trans ideology slips in, in so much much animé and other seemingly kid-friendly content... After our son came out and we read through his discord servers we realized that he had been coached and cheered on in this identity."
**—Josh & Katie in the PNW**

"First I suggest starting conversations early so you can head this ideology off at the start. . ."                    **—Another crying mother, Los Angeles, CA**

"... Start talking with your child before this becomes an issue. Talk about how some people might tell them that you can choose if you're a girl or a boy, but that this is a lie. Use the strongest words possible. Tell your child that surgery and drugs don't change who a person is."                    **—Lin**

"... I might suggest presenting gender ideology as a belief system that does not believe in biology and focus on the science. I would suggest emphasizing the physical reality of the body while focusing on the underlying psychological issues. I would say ... it's not possible to be born in the wrong body. . ."
**—Parents in NY**

"... It would have helped me to know that nothing in queer ideology is innocent or haphazard. Its operation is that of a sect and its purpose is to add followers. They more easily capture minors who have a condition that makes them more vulnerable, such as being on the autism spectrum. Also, those who have suffered some type of trauma such as sexual abuse, bullying, etc...."                    **—Fixyou, España**

"... Think of it as a sect from which it will be very difficult to get out, you will only succeed with love and patience and a therapist who does not affirm the idea that you were born in the wrong body."     **—SUPER MRC 72**

"Don't freak out, learn the language that they are using to understand more thoroughly. Coming from a fear-based heart only perpetuates distance, dysfunction, and gives the child a sense of gaslighting and rejection. . ."
**—Athena, Oregon, USA**

"... Responding with affirmation and medical treatments is going to turn out to be yet another dark chapter in the medical/psychology establishment's treatment of women. I predict a generation of girls will be very angry in the next 5 to 10 years."     **—Laura in California**

"I would advise ... to come in firm and clear on the ideologies that are connected to any concept that is being put forward. Prepare for pushback, be clear about empathy and compassion, support holding space for many possibilities, and you can support your kid without being silent on your beliefs. . ."     **—Kate, Metro-Boston**

"... DO NOT fall into the new name and pronouns. You can adopt the child initials or a nickname. Society is creating the problem by affirming an identity that is not real. In my opinion that fits 99 percent of cases."     **—AGA**

"... Exempt them from all sex ed in the schools... Teach that yourself and leave ideology out of it. Teach it biologically. Use the word "woman" when you talk about pregnancy! Also, the ideology wasn't being talked about in my kids' elementary school then, but it is now. . ."
**—Page, Bellingham, WA**

"...Make sure your child knows that they can't actually change sex. My younger kids were shocked to know what is actually involved in transitioning. It's not the rainbows these poor distressed kids are being promised. . ."
**—Danielle**

"... Recognize that this gender ideology is destructive nonsense. And it is everywhere in your child's life. Cherish the small number of friends and family who will be supportive and do your best to avoid toxic people who will hurt your child and encourage medical harm."     **—Claire F.**

"... I wish I had known that trans ideology existed. It was something I would have never thought to be aware of, look out for, or keep an eye on my children for signs of it. It wasn't on the list of dangers in child rearing like 'drugs are dangerous, don't talk to strangers, don't drink and drive.'"

**—Jean**

"... I recommend careful, honest, and calm but judicious questions to gently poke holes in the ideology and get your child to think beyond the mantras and thought-stopping clichés."                    **—2014 OG Mom**

"I might suggest presenting gender ideology as a belief system that does not believe in biology and focus on the science. I would suggest emphasizing the physical reality of the body while focusing on the underlying psychological issues. . ."                    **—@fullowl and husband in NY**

## Parent-to-Parent Advice
# Schools

"Do not affirm anything. Shut down the Internet. Threaten the school if they affirm. . ." **—TZ US**

"Get them out of the public school system... Get back to nature. Highlight a focus on giving to others." **—Unresolved Grief in Vancouver BC**

"Don't doubt yourself or question the past. You know your child, you are the expert, not the school, or the doctors... Keep a close eye on what is being taught at school, be involved at board level if need be. Be aware of GSA clubs and who runs them. Be familiar with state law. Be aware of school counselors and psychologists who may influence your child. (Sadly) assume everyone is affirming until you can prove otherwise, don't let your child be alone with well-meaning adults unless you know for sure they are gender skeptical." **—HBgirl**

"… Get involved in their school, make your presence known. Do not affirm anything. No name, pronouns, binders nothing!" **—Lydia**

"… I would homeschool. If that fails, take your child off social media. Remove all access to Internet. Get your child working outside with animals. Be present, Stay connected. If you're in a progressive state, like CA, move." **—Another crying mother, Los Angeles, CA**

"Pull them from school, pull the Internet, basic flip phone and keep the communication open." **—Christen Florida**

"… Exempt them from all sex ed in the schools. I used to be pro-sex ed in the schools. I was too trusting that they would do it in a reasonable way... I would try harder to homeschool. . ." **—Page, Bellingham, WA**

"… Do not allow them to attend GSA meetings—they are not for inclusion but indoctrination. . ." **—Aggie in Bklyn**

"… I wish I had put together a group of her and her peers and had them participate in positive empowering female enrichment (which is impossible to find where I live—UNLESS it involves trans issues—then you can find groups, schools, activities that all celebrate "being your true self and being brave"… I would have homeschooled her starting in grade school… I would have taken her out of school immediately and restricted her Internet use. Probably wouldn't work for all kids. . ."

—JB

"…Get involved in your child's school and educate yourself on the issues and what their policies are around trans before they hit. If you don't agree with them, stand up and fight against it for your child. Inform other parents because I don't think most of them know about this yet."

—Momdog, Southwestern US

"… I wish I had known how pervasive the ideology was in every institution: school, camps, social media, etc.…"

—Maria

"… Pull them from school if you can. Move to another state even. But whatever you do, preserve the relationship first."

—Audra

"… Draw a line with the school—if they don't comply find other education."

—Joy

"… Withdraw them from all sex education classes. Know that gender ideology is being taught in kindergarten."

—Danielle

"…Try to keep friendly contact with the school—most teachers and admin are not activists and most recognize there's something going on they are a little uncomfortable with. Some are and try to avoid engaging with them or with activist clinicians. This can lead to a child protection investigation."

—Michelle B., Canada

"…Another important piece of advice … is to remove your children from public school. This is where my children were indoctrinated from a young age. The peace of mind knowing no "trusted adults" can hurt them again is worth all the sacrifice of private Christian school & homeschool. . ."

—Erin, mother from Colorado (@erinforparentalrights)

"... I would also consider homeschooling or a religious school, even though I am not religious. . ." **—2014 OG Mom**

"... Be aware that many schools are captured and by the time the child tells the parents, they may already be fully out at school with the affirmation of the teachers. . ." **—Betty somewhere in rural red-state America where gender is surprisingly a huge issue**

"I wish I had a better understanding of the harms of DEI. I think DEI sets out with good intentions but how it's executed is very toxic. . ." **—Torie**

"... Don't be afraid to question the school and ask questions regarding the curriculum. . ." **—Ruth from Virginia**

"... Homeschool, take away all social media, move house out to the country if you have to, get your precious children as far away from this toxic ideology of pedophiles as possible. . ." **—N P from Christchurch, NZ**

"... Make it clear to the schools that you do not want your child hearing these messages and calling them out, every time, when they promote it in school. Or get your kid out of public school entirely and homeschool or send to private/Christian school." **—@SciMom22, from Niagara**

## Parent-to-Parent Advice

# Therapists

"… Only allow non-affirming professionals to be a part of any medical care. Try to treat other mental health issues best you can, but stay away from affirming therapists."      **—TZ, US**

"Don't go near the medical profession."      **—Jude in Australia**

"… find a good therapist."      **—Suzanne from Ypomoni, France**

"… Don't go to mental health system except as a last resort. Join an online forum with other non-affirming parents and get advice."      **—Anonymous in Ohio.**

"…Vet therapist—they need to have at least 30 years' experience. If they affirm get them out. No gender clinics."      **—Lydia M from CA**

"… Find a non-affirming therapist to deal with the comorbidities."      **—Flannon Shee**

"To talk openly and honestly, ask a lot of questions and get them in therapy with a non-affirming therapist."      **—Anonymous USA**

"… Find them a non-affirming counselor, this will be extremely difficult… Find detransitioners and talk to them about why they transitioned in the first place and why they went back and what health problems they have because of that. If you think it's appropriate, see if those people would be willing to talk to your child."      **—Matilda F. from Tennessee**

"… Find support—it can be challenging when an issue has been so politicized but speak out and you will find those in agreement and willing to help. Interview therapists and if your values don't line up, move on. . ."      **—Jen, Missouri**

"… Find a therapist who understands these issues, as that choice can be helpful or harmful. There are not many therapists who are trained in this area.

Be very careful before you implement life-altering drugs and medical treatments like irreversible surgeries. Your child's future is at stake."
                                                              **—Robert B, South Carolina**

"… Make sure you go to a non-affirming therapist!"        **—Daisy101**

"I wish I had known that affirmative care was the wrong thing and picked a GETA therapist. Listen, ask questions, read as many books as you can, get involved with groups and make sure they go to a therapist that will do the work to find out what is going on besides just the dysphoria."
                                                              **—ES, California**

"Be supportive but don't push transition. Look for other causes, too. Neutral therapy. Not pushing trans ideology. Act with love, but don't reinforce a false sense of gender."        **—Anonymous**

"… Don't get involved with a gender clinic or gender affirming therapist: they are blinded by ideology. . ."        **—A mum in Queensland, Australia**

"Get a non-affirming therapist to sort out other issues (depression, anxiety, socialization, borderline personality, autism) FIRST; do not affirm identity; discuss emotions/depth therapy."        **—Canada**

"…Be very careful with therapists. Most are not on your side and may try to pull your kid even further away from you by painting you as the enemy. . ."
                                                              **—KMC**

"…If they are gender non-conforming, don't let them see an affirming therapist; focus on allowing them to be whoever they want to be in their own bodies. . ."        **—Struggling South African mom**

"… Avoid affirmative therapists like the plague. Sadly, healthcare has become something to be fearful of with regards to gender."
                                                              **—Lisa, Australia**

"… The therapy sessions pushed our child further into the rabbit hole. When the trans label just wouldn't fit, our girl became suicidal. It was the affirming therapy that caused her suicidality. This was the scariest, darkest time of all our lives, and I'm certain that therapy led to it. . ."

**—Erin, mother from Colorado (@erinforparentalrights)**

"… look for a psychologist that does not work with the 'affirmative therapy.' That's what we did, and it seems it worked, my daughter is now wearing nice girly clothes and feeling better with her body."          **—A. J., Germany**

"… I should have NOT taken her to therapy because the therapists affirmed her delusion and encouraged her to 'educate' me about how she is 'really a boy.'"                              **—@SciMom22 from Niagara**

"… Find a non-affirming therapist for your child to address the underlying issues that may be complicit in his or her feelings of being different and uncomfortable in their own body. Get yourself a therapist or at least someone to have confidential conversations with about your feelings and thoughts."                              **—Cassie, South Carolina**

"… I would ask any therapist about his approach before putting my child in his hands. . ."                              **—Vater, Hamburg, Germany**

"… I'd also advise parents to avoid 'gender clinics' at all costs, and to try to get guardianship over their child when he turns 18 if s/he has any mental illness."                              **—Martha J**

"… the only thing I did well was a psychologist and a psychiatrist for me, who helped me, and the psychologist helped me get her to come, then she went to the psychiatrist, and he had success raising her self-esteem, he knew how to reason with her…"                              **—Meme**

## Parent-to-Parent Advice
# Internet and Social Media

"Get them out in nature, offline."                    **—Susanna, Virginia**

"Restrict online access while being open on the reasons why."
**—RB from Australia**

"No smartphones, no unaccompanied Internet use, preview all television shows before allowing them to watch, even if it's on a kids' network. Know who your kids are talking to online and at school."     **—Jennifer B.**

"...Keep them away from Internet as long as possible."     **—MtnGal US**

"Trust your ears and eyes. Animé is not innocent. Monitor the Internet: creepy predators are real."                    **—Jolene US**

"... Stay off social media. Get back to nature. Highlight a focus on giving to others."                    **—Unresolved Grief in Vancouver BC**

"Don't allow them Internet use until at least 16. . ."
**—Jennifer @nogenderpredtrs Washington State**

"Limited and controlled Internet access, push back against schools. Listen but do not affirm."                    **—Wilhelmina, Germany**

"Severely limit Internet access."                    **—Kathleen**

"Do the research, arm yourself with knowledge of what to look out for, and don't give smartphones to younger teens and kids. A list of sites to watch out for, and make sure they stay away from social media."
**—K squared and Loscar**

"... Restrict social media and block access to porn."     **—Rose F**

"… Would not allow the Internet without an adult to see and understand. In my case I listened to it in English and I did not understand it very much. I should never have let her listen without knowing what they were saying. . ."

**—Meme**

"… Do not let your child online unsupervised and block social media and any games that have a chat component. Make sure you have access to all accounts and passwords. There are cell phones that restrict apps and contacts if your child must have a phone. In any case, restrict time online severely early on so that restricting later won't be a shock. . ."        **—Lin**

"… And keep them off the Internet as long as possible. Keep them grounded in real-world activities. Send them to an unplugged summer camp."

**—Mary**

"No private time on the Internet. It would have helped a lot to have parent controls and serious monitoring in public areas of the house. . ."

**—Judy C USA**

"Pull them from school, pull the Internet, basic flip phone and keep the communication open."                  **—Christen, Florida**

"I would advise parents to NEVER allow their child online unsupervised, EVER. . ."                                  **—Martha J**

"… Yes, if I had had information, I would have limited and controlled the use of social networks, of her watching animé that seemed harmless to me because they were drawings, but she hid something because this hobby is shared by many kids with ROGD. . ."        **—MVRR, España**

"Take a look at your child's habits, determine where this influence is coming from (social media, friends at school), try your best to remove the influence and replace with positive activities. . ."                **—Suzanne L**

«… TIK TOK AND INSTAGRAM and their algorithms are not as harmless as they seem. Both applications can affect people's mental health. The best for their studies: a computer in the living room until the age of

18 and many books on paper. Avoid iPad... No smartphones until the age of 18. . ." **—SUPER MRC 72**

"Encourage ANY activity other than online/virtual activities." **—Amanda J.**

"I tell everyone with young children not to let their kids have cell phones or use the Internet unless the computer is for schoolwork and the computer is located in a family room or kitchen (not a private space)." **—Julie F.**

"Parental controls of any connected device are a must, more activities together." **—T.T.**

"Keep them off of technology. Monitor any and all use. Block their ability to get on private message boards. There is so much adult content out there, too much for these children to understand. . ." **—Anonymous mother in St. Louis, MO**

"Ground your kids in real life and family and downplay the importance of technology for as long as possible." **—J., Cary, NC**

". . . don't buy them a phone (let them buy their own when they're earning), severely restrict and monitor their Internet access. . ." **—LovingMum, UK**

". . . Lock down the Internet and don't provide open access to a smart-phone..." **—Australia, Victoria**

"Limit social media, look at their friend group, and try to minimize the influence as much as possible. . ." **—Tristia, UK**

## Parent-to-Parent Advice

# Parenting

"Don't get caught in the weeds of their feelings: that is subjective. Rather engage them more when the opportunities arise on the physical outcomes/ harms that cannot be philosophically argued. "          **—RB from Australia**

"Show your child unconditional love. Affirm their feelings but not the new identity. Keep them close to the family."          **—Anonymous in Philadelphia**

"Have the hard talks from the start. Draw the line in the sand and hold that line. Let them know that you understand they have these feelings, and you'll help navigate them but that feelings aren't fact. That you love them no matter what and want them to stay whole and healthy."          **—Jennifer B.**

"Do not be afraid to take decisive and strong action immediately. And do not affirm."          **—M. & S.**

"Don't doubt yourself or question the past. You know your child, you are the expert, not the school, or the doctors. Keep your child away from even subtle propaganda. . ."          **—HBgirl**

"You are up against a social mania that is burning through the culture including most of the institutions you'd like to trust. Be very serious about this, right from the start, and don't assume that easy measures will suffice. Don't compromise with it. What would you do if a pimp or drug dealer moved in next door? What would you do if it turned out that the land or water where you live is poisoned?"          **—Harry**

"It is okay to tell your child that you do not subscribe to the ideology, that you don't use the words that it prescribes, and that you will not make the decisions that are meant for him or her to make as an adult, that you won't take that from their future self."          **—Canadian Mom Fighting for my Kid**

"Don't panic… Join an online forum with other non-affirming parents and get advice."          **—Anonymous in Ohio**

"Remind your child often that they are loved and there is nothing they can do that will change that. Also, be firm and clear that any physical changes they make, from cross-sex hormones to surgeries, are a mutilation of their otherwise healthy bodies and will not help their mental health. . ." **—K.M. and the late J.M., who unfortunately passed away in the middle of the fight**

"… Have family meals as much as possible. Don't let sports, clubs, or anything else get in the way of family time. If you are parents of faith, pray for your kids daily. You will need so much wisdom and strength to navigate this new cowardly world our kids are living in."
**—A. Still Hoping in the USA**

"Listen a lot, ask thought-provoking questions. Remove them (if age appropriate) from environments where it is being reinforced. Don't speak out of fear or anger." **—Anonymous**

"Start strong in the truth. You don't have to bend your beliefs to them. Find out where these influences are coming from and try to pull them out of those relationships. Just as if they were in a cult." **—JH from Kentucky**

"Pre-emptive conversations are essential, the way many parents talked to me when I was little about drugs and alcohol. That is what we are doing with our youngest, who is only 12." **—"KD"**

"Die on the hill of reality and truth. Do not lose your integrity, do not doubt biological fact. You can never go wrong with following the path of truth in a strong but loving and kind way. Do not offend, but do not affirm. You can refuse to use pronouns and alternate names and still show love to your child. Be clear and succinct. 'I understand that you want me to use X/Y pronouns. But I'm not going to, and here's why. I love and respect you so much and feel you deserve nothing less than my honesty.'" **—Anonymous**

"Instill that your child is EXACTLY who they are supposed to be. They were not assigned anything—they are complete and whole as they were born, even with challenges or disabilities. . ." **—KLG,**
**—Mom of Desisting Daughter**

"Listen to them. Most importantly make sure there is open line of communication. This is vital. But DO NOT fall into the new name and pronouns.

You can adopt the child's initials or a nickname. Society is creating the problem by affirming an identity that is not real. In my opinion that fits 99 percent of cases."                                                   **—AGA**

"Stay calm; don't get too worked up. They are told that parents that don't immediately celebrate are the enemy. Likewise, don't agree to their demands (no binder, for example). Stay in conversation, show lots of love and attention; be firm but loving. Spend lots of time with them—lots. They need you."                                    **—Margaret in Seattle**

# Notes

## FOREWORD

1    Ellenberger, H. F. (1970). *The Discovery of the Unconscious: The History and Evolution of Dynamic Psychiatry.* Basic Books.

2    Jung, C.G. (1957). *The Undiscovered Self.* New York: Signet Books. p. 73.

3    Smith, D. J., Lapedes, A. S., de Jong, J. C., Bestebroer, T. M., Rimmelzwaan, G. F., Osterhaus, A. D., & Fouchier, R. A. (2004). Mapping the antigenic and genetic evolution of influenza virus. *Science, 305,* 371-376.

4    Gleaves, D. H. (1996). The sociocognitive model of dissociative identity disorder: A reexamination of the evidence. *Psychological Bulletin, 120,* 42-59; Piper, A., Merskey, H., & Piper, G. (1996). The persistence of folly: Critical examination of dissociative identity disorder. Part II. The defence and decline of multiple personality or dissociative identity disorder. *Canadian Journal of Psychiatry, 41,* 703-709.

5    Ellenberger, H. F. (1970). *The Discovery of the Unconscious: The History and Evolution of Dynamic Psychiatry.* Basic Books.

6    Reijnders, U. J. L., de Keijser, J., & Mokkenstorm, J. K. (2017). The Etiology of Hysteria: A Contemporary Perspective. *Journal of Nervous and Mental Disease, 205,* 691-697.

7    Whitlock, J., Eckenrode, J., & Silverman, D. (2006). Self-injurious behaviors in a college population. Pediatrics, 117, 1939-1948; Lewis, S. P., & Buchholz, A. (2011). Self-injury and suicide contagion among adolescents. *Current Opinion in Pediatrics, 23,* 635-639.

8    Stice, E. (2002). Risk and maintenance factors for eating pathology: A meta-analytic review. Psychological Bulletin, 128, 825-848; Levine, M. P., Smolak, L., & Hayden, H. (1994). The relation of sociocultural factors to eating attitudes and behaviors among middle school girls. *Journal of Early Adolescence, 14,* 471-490.

9    Woods, D. W., Flessner, C. A., Franklin, M. E., Keuthen, N. J., Goodwin, R. D., Stein, D. J., & Walther, M. R. (2006). The Trichotillomania Impact Project (TIP): Exploring phenomenology, functional impairment, and treatment utilization. *Journal of Clinical Psychiatry, 67,* 1877-1888; Keuthen, N. J., Deckersbach, T., Wilhelm, S., Hale, E., Fraim, C., Baer, L., & Jenike, M. A. (2000). Repetitive skin-picking in a student population and comparison with a sample of self-injurious skin-pickers. *Psychosomatics, 41,* 210-215.

[10]    Robertson, M. M., Eapen, V., Singer, H. S., Martino, D., Scharf, J. M., Paschou, P., & Roessner, V. (2007). Gilles de la Tourette syndrome. *Nature Reviews Disease Primers, 3*, 16097; Verdellen, C., van de Griendt, J., Hartmann, A., Murphy, T., & ESSTS Guidelines Group. (2011). European clinical guidelines for Tourette syndrome and other tic disorders. Part III: Behavioural and psychosocial interventions. *European Child & Adolescent Psychiatry, 20*, 197-207.

[11]    Women tend to score higher on measures of neuroticism, which is characterized by emotional instability, increased negative affect, and heightened sensitivity to stressors (Costa Jr., P. T., Terracciano, A., & McCrae, R. R. (2001). Gender differences in personality traits across cultures: Robust and surprising findings. Journal of Personality and Social Psychology, 81, 322-331; Schmitt, D. P., Realo, A., Voracek, M., & Allik, J. (2008). Why can't a man be more like a woman? Sex differences in Big Five personality traits across 55 cultures. *Journal of Personality and Social Psychology, 94*, 168-182. Women also suffer from higher rates of depression. This proclivity becomes more prominent during adolescence and continues into adulthood (Kessler, R. C., Berglund, P., Demler, O., Jin, R., Merikangas, K. R., & Walters, E. E. (2005). Lifetime prevalence and age-of-onset distributions of DSM-IV disorders in the National Comorbidity Survey Replication. *Archives of General Psychiatry, 62*, 593-602; Weissman, M. M., Bland, R. C., Canino, G. J., Faravelli, C., Greenwald, S., Hwu, H. G., ... Wickramaratne, P. J. (1993). Cross-national epidemiology of major depression and bipolar disorder. *JAMA Psychiatry, 270*, 2217-2224. Finally, anxiety disorders are also more prevalent among women (McLean, C. P., Asnaani, A., Litz, B. T., & Hofmann, S. G. (2011). Gender differences in anxiety disorders: Prevalence, course of illness, comorbidity, and burden of illness. *Journal of Psychiatric Research, 45*, 1027-1035; McLean, C. P., & Anderson, E. R. (2009). Brave men and timid women? A review of the gender differences in fear and anxiety. *Clinical Psychology Review, 29*, 496-505.

[12]    Dragowski, E. A., Halkitis, P. N., Grossman, A. H., & D'Augelli, A. R. (2020). Mental health of transgender and gender nonconforming youth compared with their peers. *Clinical Child and Family Psychology Review, 23*, 365-391; Reisner, S. L., Greytak, E. A., Parsons, J. T., & Ybarra, M. L. (2015). Gender minority social stress in adolescence: Disparities in adolescent bullying and substance use by gender identity. *Journal of Sex Research, 52*, 243-256.

[13]    Freud, S. (1895). *Studies on Hysteria*. Standard Edition, 2, 1-335.

[14]    Perloff, R. M. (2014). Social media effects on young women's body image concerns: Theoretical perspectives and an agenda for research. *Sex Roles, 71*, 363-377.

[15]    Jonason, P. K., & Webster, G. D. (2010). The Dirty Dozen: A concise measure of the dark triad. *Psychological Assessment, 22*, 420-432; Marshall, J. (2010). Personality disorders in the modern medical profession. *Journal of the Royal Society of Medicine, 103*, 384-387; Prasad, K., & Appelbaum, P. S. (2018). A quick and dirty screening tool to detect physicians' dark triad traits. *Academic Psychiatry, 42*, 244-247; Wisse, B., Sleebos, E., & Rus, D. (2013). Nurses' and physicians' personality traits in abusive behavior by male and female nurses. *Journal of Nursing Scholarship, 45*, 84-91; Xu, S., & Tracey, T. J. (2017). Perceived entitlement among physicians: A new construct and its relationship to psychopathy, narcissism, and work engagement. *Journal of Personality Assessment, 99*, 95-104.

16    Hankin, B. L., Young, J. F., Abela, J. R., Smolen, A., Jenness, J. L., Gulley, L. D., ... & Oppenheimer, C. W. (2015). Depression from childhood into late adolescence: Influence of gender, development, genetic susceptibility, and peer stress. *Journal of Abnormal Psychology, 124*, 803-816; Kaltiala-Heino, R., Marttunen, M., Rantanen, P., Rimpelä, M., & Rimpelä, A. (2018). Early puberty is associated with mental health problems in middle adolescence. *Social Science & Medicine, 211*, 240-247; Petersen, A. C., Crockett, L., Richards, M., & Boxer, A. (2020). A self-organization perspective on adolescent pubertal timing. *Child Development Perspectives, 14*, 171-177.

17    Coleman, E., Bockting, W., Botzer, M., Cohen-Kettenis, P., DeCuypere, G., Feldman, J., ... & Zucker, K. (2012). Standards of care for the health of transsexual, transgender, and gender-nonconforming people, version 7. *International Journal of Transgenderism, 13*, 165-232, p. 164.

18    Abbruzzese, E., Levine, S.B. & Mason, J.W. (2023). The myth of "reliable research" in pediatric gender medicine: a critical evaluation of the Dutch Studies—and research that has followed. *Journal of Sex and Marital Therapy* https://doi.org/10.1080/00926 23X.2022.2150346

19    https://www.gminsights.com/industry-analysis/sex-reassignment-surgery-market

# INTRODUCTION

1    Grossman, M. (2009). *You're Teaching My Child WHAT? A Physician Exposes the Lies of Sex Education and How They Harm Your Chil.* Regnery.

2    Grossman, op cit., 157

3    https://siecus.org/ a private organization that receives generous federal funding: https://siecus.org/wp-content/uploads/2022/05/FY22-Federal-Funding -Overview.pdf.

4    https://www.advocatesforyouth.org/issue/honest-sex-education/.

5    www.AdvocatesForYouth.org, "I think I might be transgender, now what do I do?"

6    Grossman, op. cit., 182

7    Hammond, Mel. (2022). *Body Image: How to Love Yourself, Live Life to the Fullest, and Celebrate All Kinds of Bodies.* Middleton: American Girl Publishing, p 38.

8    https://www.walmart.com/c/kp/chest-binder

9    https://www.themainewire.com/2022/12/damariscotta-maine-teacher-social -worker-gender-transition-sam-roy/

10    https://ftm-guide.com/guide-to-packing-underwear-for-transmen/

11    https://www.healthline.com/health/transgender/tucking

12    Private communication with Scott on 12/1/2022

13    https://thesafezoneproject.com/activities/genderbread-person/

14    https://www.realityslaststand.com/p/intersex-is-not-as-common-as-red

15    https://www.cs.hmc.edu/~montanez/pdfs/allen-2020-castro-consensus.pdf

16    https://www.nationalreview.com/2019/05/ray-blanchard-transgender-orthodoxy/ Kearns: Why was there a name change then? Was that to avoid the word "disorder?" Blanchard: Yes, it was primarily to make patients and also trans activists and transsexual-activist groups feel happy or that they had been listened to, but I would say that the name change probably owed more to—or owed as much to—politics as it did to any change in the science.

17     https://www.whitehouse.gov/briefing-room/statements-releases/2022/06/15/fact
       -sheet-president-biden-to-sign-historic-executive-order-advancing-lgbtqi-equality
       -during-pride-month/

## CHAPTER ONE

1      *Diane Rehm Show*, February 22, 2000; http:/www.wamu.org/programs/Dr./00/02
       /22.php.

2      Johns MM, Lowry R, Haderxhanaj LT, et al. "Trends in Violence Victimization and
       Suicide Risk by Sexual Identity Among High School Students—Youth Risk Behavior
       Survey," United States, 2015–2019. MMWR Suppl 2020;69(Suppl-1):19–27.
       DOI: http://dx.doi.org/10.15585/mmwr.su6901a3; Kidd KM, Sequeira GM,
       Douglas C, et al. "Prevalence of Gender-Diverse Youth in an Urban School District,"
       *Pediatrics.* 2021;147(6): e2020049823.

3      Di Ceglie, D., "The use of metaphors in understanding atypical gender identity
       development and its psychosocial impact," *Journal of Child Psychotherapy*, 44, (2018):
       5–28. doi:10.1080/0075417X.2018.1443151.

4      https://gids.nhs.uk/about-us/number-of-referrals/

5      https://link.springer.com/article/10.1007/s10508-022-02287-7

6      https://www.nyc.gov/site/cchr/law/legal-guidances-gender-identity-expression.page

7      He defined the word's new meaning as "the overall degree of masculinity and/or
       femininity that is privately experienced and publicly manifested . . . and that usually
       though not invariably correlates with the anatomy of the organs of reproduction."
       John Money, *Gendermaps: Social Constructionism, Feminism, and Sexosophical History*
       (New York: Continuum International Publishing Group, 1995), 19.

8      Ibid, 52

9      Colapinto, John. (2000). *As Nature Made Him: The Boy Who was Raised as a Girl.*
       New York: HarperCollins.

10     Ibid, 26–27

11     *TIME,* April 14, 1980, 72

12     Chilgren and Briggs: "On Being Explicit: Sex Education for Professionals," *SIECUS
       Report* Vol 1, No 7 May 1973.

13     Chilgren and Briggs, op. cit

14     Colapinto op. cit., 156

15     Ehrhardt, A., "John Money," *PhD Journal of Sex Research* Vol 44, No.3, (2007):
       223-224.

16     "Money gave the example of pedophilia, which is usually seen as child molestation,
       a crime, and is "never called 'a love-affair between an age-discrepant couple,'" which it
       sometimes is." Marsha Pomerantz, "Sexual Congress," Jerusalem Post, June 24, 1981,
       6; and "If I were to see the case of a boy aged ten or eleven who's intensely erotically
       attracted toward a man in his twenties or thirties, if the relationship is totally mutual,
       and the bonding is genuinely totally mutual . . . then I would not call it pathological
       in any way." Theo Sandfort, *Boys on Their Contacts with Men: A study of Sexually
       Expressed Friendships* (New York: Global Academic Publishers, 1987), 5–7.

17     "A childhood sexual experience, such as being the partner of a relative or of an older
       person, need not necessarily affect the child adversely."

18     Colapinto, op. cit., 38–39

19     Colapinto, op. cit., 50

20      Colapinto, op. cit. 54

21      Colapinto, op. cit. 65

22      Colapinto, op. cit. 68–69

23      https://www.youtube.com/watch?v=uC0zn0D_MyM

24      Christine Gorman, "A Boy Without a Penis," *TIME* magazine, March 24, 1997; Peggy T. Cohen-Kettenis, "As Nature Made Him: The boy who was raised as a girl," book review in *The New England Journal of Medicine* 342, no.19: 1457–8.

25      Colapinto, op. cit., 167

26      Colapinto, ibid.

27      Colapinto, op. cit. 170

28      Paraphrased from Colapinto, 129

29      Paraphrased from Colapinto, 212

30      https://www.youtube.com/watch?v=0Zw1EdRKocI.

31      Diamond M, Sigmundson HK. "Sex reassignment at birth. Long-term review and clinical implications." Arch Pediatr Adolesc Med. 1997 Mar; 151(3): 298-304. doi: 10.1001/archpedi.1997.02170400084015. PMID: 9080940.

32      Natalie Angier, "X 1 Y=Z," *New York Times Book Review*, February 20, 2000.

33      Ehrhardt, A. John Money, *PhD Journal of Sex Research* Vol 44, No.3, (2007) 223–224.

34      *Kinsey Institute Newsletter*, "John Money's Legacy," November 2006.

# CHAPTER TWO

1      Grossman, M. (2006). *Unprotected: A Campus Psychiatrist Reveals How Political Correctness in Her Profession Endangers Every Student*. New York: Sentinel.

2      Rufo, Christopher, A Parent's Guide to Radical Gender Theory. https://christopherrufo .com/content/uploads/2022/09/Chris-Rufo_Radical-Gender-Guide-v2.pdf

3      Joseph D. Noshpitz. (1979). *Basic handbook of child Psychiatry*, Vol Two: *Disturbances in Development*. New York: Basic Books

4      Kaplan, Harold and Sadock, Benjamin. (1989), *Comprehensive Textbook of Psychiatry*. Vol 1, 5th edition. Philadelphia: Williams & Wilkins. P. 1061–1068.

5      Kaplan and Sadock, *Comprehensive Textbook of Psychiatry*, 1063.

6      The American Academy of Child and Adolescent Psychiatry, Your Child: What Every Parent Needs to know About Childhood Development from Birth to Preadolescence, Pruitt, David, Editor (1998)

7      Bornstein, K. (1998) *My Gender Workbook: How to Become a Real Man, a Real Woman, The Real You, or Something Else Entirely*. UK: Routledge.

8      Behrman, Richard; Kliegman, Robert; Jenson, Hal B. (2000) *Textbook of Pediatrics*. Philadelphia: WB Saunders.

9      Lewis, M. (2002) *Child and Adolescent Psychiatry: A Comprehensive Textbook*. Philadelphia: Lippincott Williams & Wilkens. p. 275.

10      "I think I might be transgender, now what do I do?" Found on www.AdvocatesforYouth. org; see also Jessie Gilliam, "I'm coming out . . . I want the world to know. . . (Or do I?)" Transitions 14, no. 4 (June 2002), available online at: http://www.lgbthealth.net /downloads/research/AdvocatesforYouth.pdf.

11      https://www.plannedparenthood.org/blog/i-am-17-year-old-male-i-want-to-be-a -girl-what-to-i-do

12      http://www.scarleteen.com/article/body/genderpalooza_a_sex_gender_primer>

13      https://siecus.org/about-siecus/our-history

14    Palmer SS et al Genetic Evidence that ZFY is not the testis-determining factor *Nature* 1989; 342:937-939

15    CD: "Caring for the Transgender Student," ACHA May 31-June 4, 2005

16    American Psychological Association Office of Public Communications, 2006. "Answers to Your Questions About Transgender Individuals and Gender Identity."

17    https://www.psychiatry.org/psychiatrists/practice/dsm/frequently-asked-questions

18    American Psychological Association Office of Public Communications, 2006. "Answers to Your Questions About Transgender Individuals and Gender Identity."

19    https://transgenderinfo.be/wp-content/uploads/gender-dysphoria-Jack-Drescher.pdf

20    https://www.researchgate.net/publication/296700032_The_DSM-5_Diagnostic_Criteria_for_Gender_Dysphoria

21    https://www.researchgate.net/publication/233150866_Recommendations_for_Revision_of_the_DSM_Diagnoses_of_Gender_Identity_Disorders_Consensus_Statement_of_the_World_Professional_Association_for_Transgender_Health

22    Coleman E, Bockting W, Botzer M, et al. Standards of Care for the Health of Transsexual, Transgender, and Gender-Nonconforming People, Version 7. *International Journal of Transgenderism* 2012; 13(4): 165-232.

23    https://www.researchgate.net/publication/233106777_Opinions_About_the_DSM_Gender_Identity_Disorder_Diagnosis_Results_from_an_International_Survey_Administered_to_Organizations_Concerned_with_the_Welfare_of_Transgender_People

24    https://www.researchgate.net/publication/286602677_Psychological_warfare_Robert_L_Spitzer_and_Allen_Frances_criticize_the_DSM-5_process

25    https://www.bbc.com/news/world-us-canada-35185138 AND https://www.medscape.com/viewarticle/804378

26    https://www.scribd.com/document/17172432/Letter-to-APA-Board-of-Trustees-July-7-2009-From-Allen-Frances-and-Robert-Spitzer

27    https://www.medscape.com/viewarticle/804378

28    https://issuu.com/humanrightscampaign/docs/hrc_2014_annual_final

29    https://hrc-prod-requests.s3-us-west-2.amazonaws.com/HRC-HRCF-2021-Annual-Report.pdf

30    https://hrc-prod-requests.s3-us-west-2.amazonaws.com/HRC-990-2022.pdf

31    https://www.hrc.org/about/corporate-partners

32    https://opa.hhs.gov/sites/default/files/2022-03/gender-affirming-care-young-people-march-2022.pdf

33    https://www.hrw.org/news/2019/05/27/new-health-guidelines-propel-transgender-rights

34    https://quillette.com/2019/03/29/denying-the-neuroscience-of-sex-differences/ (archived for reference: https://archive.is/uCcgV#selection-593.0-593.153)

35    Brizendine, L. (2010) *The Male Brain: A Breakthrough Understanding of How Men and Boys Think. Harmony*, New York: Harmony.

36    Brizendine, L. (2006) *The Female Brain*, Broadway Books.

37    https://www.sciencedirect.com/science/article/pii/B9780128035061000516

38    https://orwh.od.nih.gov/about/mission-history

39    https://orwh.od.nih.gov/sites/orwh/files/docs/SexGenderInfographic_11x17_508.pdf.

40    Fiddler, M., Abdel-Rahman, B., Rappolee, D.A. & Pergament, E. Expression of SRY transcripts in preimplantation human embryos. *Am. J. med. Genet.* 55, 80–84 (1995).

41   Marianne Legato et al (2017): *Principles of Gender-Specific Medicine: Gender in the Genomic Era*, 3rd edition, Academic Press, 426.

42   Marianne Legato et al (2017): Principles of Gender-Specific Medicine: Gender in the Genomic Era, 3rd edition, Academic Press, Chapter 35

43   Eaton WW, Rose NR, Kalaydjian A, et al. Epidemiology of autoimmune diseases in Denmark. *J Autoimmun* 2007; 29(1):1-9

44   https://gendermed.org/about-gsm/

45   https://bmcnephrol.biomedcentral.com/articles/10.1186/s12882-019-1670-x.

46   Jennifer Connellan, Simon Baron-Cohen, Sally Wheelwright, Anna Batki, and Jag Ahluwalia, "Sex differences in human neonatal social perception," Infant Behavior and Development 23 (2000): 113-18

47   Svetlana Lutchmaya, Simon Baron-Cohen, "Human Sex Differences in social and non-social looking preferences, at 12 months of age," Infant Behavior and Development 25 (2002): 319-25.

48   Svetlana Lutchmaya, Simon Baron-Cohen, and Peter Raggatt, (2002) "Foetal testosterone and eye contact in 12-month-old human infants," Infant Behavior & Development 25 (2000): 327-35.

49   Jill B. Becker et al, eds., *Sex Differences in the Brain: From Genes to Behavior* (Oxford University Press, 2008).

50   D. N. Ruble, C. L. Martin, and S. A. Berenbaum, "Gender Development," in N. Eisenberg, ed., Handbook of Child Psychology 3: social, emotional, and personality development, 6th edition, 858-32 (New York: Wiley, 2006).

51   Lisa A. Serbin, et al, "Gender Stereotyping in Infancy: Visual preferences for and knowledge of gender-stereotyping in Infancy: Visual preferences for and knowledge of gender-stereotyped toys in the second year," International Journal of Behavioral Development, 25, no.1 (2001), 7-15.

52   Anne Campbell, Louisa Shirley, Charles Heywood, and Charles Cook, "Infants' visual preference for sex-congruent babies, children, toys and activities: A longitudinal study," British Journal of Developmental Psychology 18 (2000): 494.

53   https://www.washingtonpost.com/national/health-science/meet-the-gender-affirmation-surgeon-whose-waiting-list-is-three-years-long/2016/04/22/a4019f2e-f690-11e5-8b23-538270a1ca31_story.html

54   https://thenewamerican.com/nobel-prize-winning-german-biologist-multiple-genders-are-nonsense-and-unscientific/.

## CHAPTER THREE

1   https://tavistockandportman.nhs.uk/about-us/news/stories/referrals-gender-identity-development-service-gids-level-2018-19/

2   https://gids.nhs.uk/about-us/number-of-referrals/

3   https://segm.org/

4   Biggs, M. Suicide by Clinic-Referred Transgender Adolescents in the United Kingdom. *Arch Sex Behav* 51, 685–690 (2022). https://doi.org/10.1007/s10508-022-02287-7.

5   https://tavistockandportman.nhs.uk/about-us/news/stories/referrals-gender-identity-development-service-gids-level-2018-19/

6   https://gids.nhs.uk/about-us/number-of-referrals/

7   https://link.springer.com/article/10.1007/s10508-022-02287-7

8    *Nordic Journal of Psychiatry* 2020, VOL. 74, NO. 1, 40–44. https://doi.org/10.1080
     /08039488.2019.1667429

9    Johns, M. M., Lowry, R., Andrzejewski, J., Barrios, L. C., Demissie, Z., McManus,
     T., Rasberry, C. N., Robin, L., & Underwood, J. M. (2019). Transgender Identity
     and Experiences of Violence Victimization, Substance Use, Suicide Risk, and
     Sexual Risk Behaviors Among High School Students—19 States and Large Urban
     School Districts, 2017. MMWR. Morbidity and Mortality Weekly Report, 68(3),
     67–71. https://doi.org/10.15585/mmwr.mm6803a3; Kidd, K. M., Sequeira, G. M.,
     Douglas, C., Paglisotti, T., Inwards-Breland, D. J., Miller, E., & Coulter, R. W. S.
     (2021). Prevalence of Gender-Diverse Youth in an Urban School District. Pediatrics,
     147(6), e2020049823. https://doi.org/10.1542/peds.2020-049823

10   https://nces.ed.gov/fastfacts/display.asp?id=372

11   American College Health Association. (2021). American College Health Association-
     National College Health Assessment III: Undergraduate Student Reference Group
     Data Report Spring 2021. ACHA-NCHA III. https://www.acha.org/documents
     /ncha/NCHA-III_Spring-2021_Undergraduate_Reference_Group_Data
     _Report.pdf

12   https://www.npr.org/2022/01/13/1072529477/more-than-1-million-fewer
     -students-are-in-college-the-lowest-enrollment-numbers-

13   https://www.reuters.com/investigates/special-report/usa-transyouth-data/

14   https://khn.org/news/article/medical-coding-creates-barriers-to-care-for-transgender
     -patients/

15   https://www.macrotrends.net/cities/23100/pittsburgh/population

16   Kidd KM, Sequeira GM, Douglas C, Paglisotti T, Inwards-Breland DJ, Miller E,
     Coulter RWS. Prevalence of Gender-Diverse Youth in an Urban School District.
     Pediatrics. 2021 Jun;147(6):e2020049823. doi: 10.1542/peds.2020-049823. Epub
     2021 May 18. PMID: 34006616; PMCID: PMC8168604.

17   Blanchard R. Early history of the concept of autogynephilia. Archives of Sexual
     Behavior 2005; 34(4): 439-46. 10.1007/s10508-005-4343-8.

18   https://www.nytimes.com/2021/05/08/us/politics/rachel-levine-transgender.html

19   Hayley Wood , Shoko Sasaki , Susan J. Bradley , Devita Singh , Sophia Fantus,
     Allison Owen-Anderson , Alexander Di Giacomo , Jerald Bain & Kenneth J. Zucker
     (2013) Patterns of Referral to a Gender Identity Service for Children and Adolescents
     (1976–2011): Age, Sex Ratio, and Sexual Orientation, Journal of Sex & Marital
     Therapy, 39:1, 1-6, DOI:10.1080/0092623X.2012.675022

20   http://www.mental-health-today.com/gender/dsm.htm

21   James M. Cantor, "Transgender and Gender Diverse Children and Adolescents: Fact-
     Checking of AAP Policy," *Journal of Sex & Marital Therapy*, Vol. 46, No. 4, 2020),
     pp. 307–313

22   https://pubmed.ncbi.nlm.nih.gov/26754056/

23   https://www.amazon.com/10-000-Dresses-Marcus-Ewert/dp/1583228500/ref
     =asc_df_1583228500/?tag=hyprod-20&linkCode=df0&hvadid=312680791333
     &hvpos=&hvnetw=g&hvrand=16588166907787061723&hvpone=&hvtwo=
     &hvqmt=&hvdev=c&hvdvcmdl=&hvlocint=&hvlocphy=1019457&hvtargid
     =pla-464500990444&psc=1&tag=&ref=&adgrpid=62255331975&hvpone
     =&hvptwo=&hvadid=312680791333&hvpos=&hvnetw=g&hvrand

=16588166907787061723&hvqmt=&hvdev=c&hvdvcmdl=&hvlocint=&hvlocphy
=1019457&hvtargid=pla-464500990444

24 https://time.com/3486048/most-influential-teens-2014/

25 https://quillette.com/2019/03/19/an-interview-with-lisa-littman-who-coined-the
-term-rapid-onset-gender-dysphoria/

26 Littman L (2018) Rapid-onset gender dysphoria in adolescents and young adults:
A study of parental reports. PLoS ONE 13(8) :e0202330. https://doi.org/10.137
/journal.pone.0202330

27 Ibid.

28 Ibid.

29 Ibid.

30 Byne W, Bradley SJ, Coleman E, Eyler AE, Green R, Menvielle EJ, et al. Report of
the American Psychiatric Association Task Force on Treatment of Gender Identity
Disorder. *Archives of Sexual Behavior*. 2012; 41: 759–796. pmid:22736225

31 https://uncommongroundmedia.com/rogd-a-primer/

32 https://quillette.com/2019/03/19/an-interview-with-lisa-littman-who-coined-the
-term-rapid-onset-gender-dysphoria/

33 Littman L (2018) Rapid-onset gender dysphoria in adolescents and young adults:
A study of parental reports. PLoS ONE 13(8) :e0202330. https://doi.org/10.137
/journal.pone.0202330

34 Littman L (2018) Rapid-onset gender dysphoria in adolescents and young adults:
A study of parental reports. PLoS ONE 13(8) :e0202330. https://doi.org/10.137
/journal.pone.0202330 page 14

35 https://quillette.com/2019/03/19/an-interview-with-lisa-littman-who-coined-the
-term-rapid-onset-gender-dysphoria/

36 Littman L (2018) Rapid-onset gender dysphoria in adolescents and young adults:
A study of parental reports. PLoS ONE 13(8) :e0202330. https://doi.org/10.137
/journal.pone.0202330

37 Ibid.

38 Rapid-onset gender dysphoria in adolescents and young adults: A study of parental
reports. PLoS ONE 13(8) :e0202330. https://doi.org/10.137/journal.pone.0202330
page 32

39 Rapid-onset gender dysphoria in adolescents and young adults: A study of parental
reports. PLoS ONE 13(8) :e0202330. https://doi.org/10.137/journal.pone.0202330
page 5

40 https://www.youtube.com/user/partar400/featured

41 https://www.youtube.com/watch?v=TAaT0ATLb2k

42 https://quillette.com/2019/03/19/an-interview-with-lisa-littman-who-coined-the
-term-rapid-onset-gender-dysphoria/

43 Littman L (2018) Rapid-onset gender dysphoria in adolescents and young adults:
A study of parental reports. PLoS ONE 13(8) :e0202330. https://doi.org/10.137
/journal.pone.0202330

44 Ibid.

45 https://lacroicsz.substack.com/p/by-any-other-name

46 https://www-hs-fi.translate.goog/tiede/art-2000009348478.html?_x_tr_sl
=auto&_x_tr_tl=en&_x_tr_hl=en&_x_tr_pto=wapp

47    Littman L (2018) Rapid-onset gender dysphoria in adolescents and young adults: A study of parental reports. PLoS ONE 13(8) :e0202330. https://doi.org/10.137/journal.pone.0202330

48    Ibid.

49    Ibid.

50    Ibid.

## CHAPTER FOUR

1    https://uncommongroundmedia.com/rogd-a-primer/

2    https://www.jpeds.com/article/S0022-3476(21)01085-4/fulltext

3    https://www.caaps.co/rogd-statement

4    https://www.hrc.org/resources/online-communities-and-lgbtq-youth

5    From my own review of the recording of the lecture. I did not listen to the Q&A

6    https://www.wpath.org/media/cms/Documents/Public%20Policies/2018/9_Sept/WPATH%20Position%20on%20Rapid-Onset%20Gender%20Dysphoria_9-4-2018.pdf

7    https://auspath.org.au/2019/09/30/auspath-position-statement-on-rapid-onset-gender-dysphoria-rogd/

8    https://pubmed.ncbi.nlm.nih.gov/30582402/

9    Personal email April 19, 2023

10    https://www.washingtonpost.com/outlook/2021/11/24/trans-kids-therapy-psychologist/

11    https://twitter.com/jokestress/status/1447964908088283138/photo/1

12    https://quillette.com/2022/01/06/a-transgender-pioneer-explains-why-she-stepped-down-from-uspath-and-wpath/

13    https://www.youtube.com/watch?v=gOD7Nuwltf0

14    Personal communication, January 20, 2023.

15    https://publications.aap.org/pediatrics/article/142/4/e20182162/37381/Ensuring-Comprehensive-Care-and-Support-for?autologincheck=redirected

16    Laurie Higgins, "Do 66,000 Pediatricians Really Support the AAP's "Trans"-Affirmative Policy?" Illinois Family Institute; 4/5/17. Available at https://illinoisfamily.org/homosexuality/66000-pediatricians-really-support-aaps-trans-affirmative-policy/ Accessed May 11, 2023.

17    https://www.tandfonline.com/doi/full/10.1080/0092623X.2019.1698481

18    Ibid.

19    https://segm.org/AAP_silences_debate_on_gender_diverse_youth_treatments

20    https://acpeds.org/

21    https://vimeo.com/800032857

22    Ibid.

23    https://genderclinicnews.substack.com/p/gagging-the-debate

24    https://vimeo.com/800032857

25    https://genspect.org/an-open-letter-to-the-american-academy-of-pediatrics/

26    https://www.aap.org/en/community/aap-committees/

27    Personal communication, February 7, 2023.

28    https://aapca1.org/annual-leadership-forum/

29    https://vimeo.com/800032857

30    https://www.researchgate.net/publication/344703449_A_Castro_Consensus
      _Understanding_the_Role_of_Dependence_in_Consensus_Formation
31    https://www.youtube.com/watch?v=Hq8ryFVy_LM
32    https://uncommongroundmedia.com/rogd-a-primer/
33    https://www.nbcnews.com/feature/nbc-out/brown-university-criticized-over
      -removal-transgender-study-n906741
34    https://www.brown.edu/about/brown-glance
35    Moore and Brunskill-Evans (editors) 2020 *Inventing Transgender Children and Young
      People,* Cambridge Scholars Publishing p 239
36    https://news.yahoo.com/results-study-trans-teens-unchanged-214337284.html?
      guccounter=1&guce_referrer=aHR0cHM6Ly9zZWFyY2guU29tLw&guce
      _referrer_sig=AQAAADLt0vefPbueZEqOb88kBoOjDzs9BI8OfYaf06-loUW
      iIKJRGLC1YqmG7lLoUMBAVr8BtqTnqCL32UBDIGXj2yL0vhjX-Coy6
      aHYwADJGpv4ldUhdZwNvJoFKzdQK6FpolIK8gtRRcvdCnGyomZ-Ag25
      QQ663brMYQ8BTgmF2lf3
37    https://www.hrc.org/resources/online-communities-and-lgbtq-youth
38    https://www.splcenter.org/fighting-hate/extremist-files/group/american-college
      -pediatricians
39    https://www.nytimes.com/2022/06/10/science/transgender-teenagers-national
      -survey.html
40    Wiepjes CM, den Heijer M, Bremmer MA, Nota NM, de Blok CJM, Coumou BJG,
      Steensma TD. Trends in suicide death risk in transgender people: results from the
      Amsterdam Cohort of Gender Dysphoria study (1972-2017). Acta Psychiatr Scand.
      2020 Jun;141(6):486-491. doi: 10.1111/acps.13164. Epub 2020 Mar 12. PMID:
      32072611; PMCID: PMC7317390.
41    2022 AACAP meeting 10/18/22; Clinical Perspectives #11: Trans Youth: Evolving
      Gender Identities and Detransition.
42    https://segm.org/false-assumptions-gender-affirmation-minors
43    https://uncommongroundmedia.com/rogd-a-primer/
44    https://www.vice.com/en/article/xg8jq4/spotify-joe-rogan-transphobic, and https://
      www.vulture.com/2020/11/spotify-responsible-joe-rogan.html
45    https://www.foxnews.com/media/conservative-publisher-regnery-amazon
      -transgender
46    https://www.washingtonpost.com/technology/2022/06/01/amazon-trans-pride
      -month-books-protest/
47    https://www.foxnews.com/media/abigail-shrier-book-deemed-transphobic-target
      -pulls
48    https://www.thecut.com/2016/02/fight-over-trans-kids-got-a-researcher-fired.html
49    https://www.lgbtmap.org/equality-maps/conversion_therapy
50    https://www.usatoday.com/story/news/world/2021/12/09/canada-bans-conversion
      -therapy/6446262001/
51    https://www.npr.org/2021/12/09/1062720266/canada-bans-conversion-therapy
52    https://www.thecut.com/2016/02/fight-over-trans-kids-got-a-researcher-fired.html
53    https://www.psychotherapy.net/article/transgender-youth-care-science-or-beliefs
54    https://www.lgbtmap.org/equality-maps/conversion_therapy
55    https://www.hopkinsmedicine.org/health/wellness-and-prevention/tips-for-parents
      -of-lgbtq-youth

# CHAPTER FIVE

[1] https://www.thefp.com/p/i-thought-i-was-saving-trans-kids

[2] Ibid.

[3] Affidavit 6 (https://ago.mo.gov/docs/default-source/press-releases/2-07-2023-reed-affidavit---signed.pdf?sfvrsn=6a64d339_2)

[4] https://www.thefp.com/p/i-thought-i-was-saving-trans-kids

[5] Ibid.

[6] https://twitter.com/byLizAllen/status/1623943278172442625

[7] https://www.thefp.com/p/i-thought-i-was-saving-trans-kids

[8] Ibid.

[9] Ibid.

[10] Ibid.

[11] Affidavit, 21

[12] Affidavit, 82

[13] https://www.thefp.com/p/i-thought-i-was-saving-trans-kids

[14] Affidavit, 16

[15] https://www.thefp.com/p/i-thought-i-was-saving-trans-kids

[16] Affidavit, 64

[17] https://www.stlouischildrens.org/conditions-treatments/transgender-center as of 2/23

[18] https://www.thefp.com/p/i-thought-i-was-saving-trans-kids

[19] Affidavit, 59

[20] Affidavit, 22

[21] https://www.stlouischildrens.org/conditions-treatments/transgender-center accessed 4/1/23

[22] Levine SB, Solomon A (2009) Meanings and Political Implications of "Psychopathology" in a Gender Identity Clinic: Report of 10 cases. Journal of Sex and Marital Therapy 35(1): 40-57.

[23] Nordic Journal of Psychiatry, 2016 VOL. 70, NO. 4, 241–247. http://dx.doi.org/10.3109/08039488.2015.1081405

[24] https://www.tandfonline.com/toc/ipsc20/70/4

[25] Levine SB, Informed Consent for Transgender Patients, Journal of Sex and Marital Therapy, 2019;45(3):218-229. doi: 10.1080/0092623X.2018.1518885

[26] https://thebridgehead.ca/2019/09/25/world-renowned-child-psychiatrist-calls-trans-treatments-possibly-one-of-the-greatest-scandals-in-medical-history/

[27] Affidavit, 70

[28] Affidavit, 62

[29] https://www.thepublicdiscourse.com/2020/01/59422/

[30] https://www.accessdata.fda.gov/drugsatfda_docs/label/2019/020517s042,019732s044lbl.pdf

[31] Faubion SS, Kuhle CL, Shuster LT, Rocca WA. Long-term health consequences of premature or early menopause and considerations for management. Climacteric. 2015;18(4):483-91. doi: 10.3109/13697137.2015.1020484. Epub 2015 Apr 7. PMID: 25845383; PMCID: PMC4581591.

[32] https://www.ema.europa.eu/en/documents/psusa/leuprorelin-cmdh-scientific-conclusions-grounds-variation-amendments-product-information-timetable/00001844/201707_en.pdf

33    Nguyen PL, Alibhai SM, Basaria S, D'Amico AV, Kantoff PW, Keating NL, Penson DF, Rosario DJ, Tombal B, Smith MR. Adverse effects of androgen deprivation therapy and strategies to mitigate them. Eur Urol. 2015 May;67(5):825-36. doi: 10.1016/j.eururo.2014.07.010. Epub 2014 Aug 2. PMID: 25097095.

34    https://www.youtube.com/watch?v=kuwOx9YdHXY

35    https://www.bumc.bu.edu/sexualmedicine/informationsessions/restoring-sexual -function-after-luproncancer-treatment/ (This is in prostate cancer survivors, but the mechanism of action is applicable.)

36    https://eje.bioscientifica.com/view/journals/eje/155/suppl_1/1550131.xml AND https://academic.oup.com/jcem/article/104/3/686/5198654

37    https://genspect.org/swedish-documentary-stopping-the-trans-train/

38    Ibid.

39    Transbarnen: Tvärvändningen – SVT Play With English subtitles)

40    https://www.svt.se/nyheter/granskning/ug/sjukhusets-harda-sjalvkritik-efter-leos -transvard

41    https://www.youtube.com/watch?v=Ow-XwdauYr0&t=6s;  https://irislee.substack .com/p/child-suffers-serious-injury-by-puberty

42    https://segm.org/sites/default/files/English%20Translation_22.2.25-Communique -PCRA-19-Medecine-et-transidentite-genre.pdf

43    https://www.nytimes.com/2022/11/14/health/puberty-blockers-transgender.html

44    Ibid.

45    Ibid.

46    https://academic.oup.com/jcem/article/102/11/3869/4157558#99603463

47    Data taken from "Summary of Recommendations." Not every recommendation had a evidence rating applied. https://academic.oup.com/jcem/article/102/11 /3869/4157558#99603463

48    https://genderexploratory.com/wp-content/uploads/2022/12/GETA_ClinicalGuide _2022v1.1.pdf, p. 2

49    Wylie C Hembree, et al. Endocrine Treatment of Gender-Dysphoric/Gender-Incongruent Persons: An Endocrine Society Clinical Practice Guideline, *The Journal of Clinical Endocrinology & Metabolism*, Volume 102, Issue 11, 1 November 2017, Pages 3869–3903, https://doi.org/10.1210/jc.2017-01658 page 3895

50    https://www.stlouischildrens.org/conditions-treatments/transgender-center accessed 4/1/23

51    https://www.tandfonline.com/doi/full/10.1080/20502877.2022.2088048

52    https://www.bbc.com/news/health-56601386

53    https://www.bbc.com/news/health-47456938

54    @FAIRinMedicine 3/10/23

55    Pediatrics pediatrics.aappublications.org Pediatrics Vol. 135 No. 5 May 1, 2015 pp. e1366 (doi: 10.1542/peds.2015-0313A) Letter to the Editor Puberty Is Not a Disorder Den Trumbull, MD, FCP Michelle A. Cretella, MD, FCP Miriam Grossman, MD Author Affiliations

56    Linda Patia Spear, "The psychobiology of adolescence," in Kathleen Kovner Kline, Authoritative Communities: The Scientific Case for Nurturing the Whole Child (New York: Springer-Verlag, 2007). AND https://pubmed.ncbi.nlm.nih.gov/29305910/

57    Katz, A. L., Macauley, R. C., Mercurio, M. R., Moon, M. R., Okun, A. L., Opel, D. J., & Statter, M. B. (2016). Informed consent in decision-making in pediatric

practice. Committee on Bioethics. Pediatrics, 138(2), e20161484. https://doi
.org/10.1542/peds.2016-1484

58  Littman, L. (2021). Individuals Treated for Gender Dysphoria with Medical
and/or Surgical Transition Who Subsequently Detransitioned: A Survey of 100
Detransitioners. Archives of Sexual Behavior. https://doi.org/10.1007/s10508-021
-02163-w; Vandenbussche, E. (2021). Detransition-Related Needs and Support: A
Cross-Sectional Online Survey. Journal of Homosexuality, 20. https://doi.org/10.10
80/00918369.2021.1919479

59  Richards C, Maxwell J, McCune N. Use of puberty blockers for gender dysphoria:
a momentous step in the dark. Arch Dis Child. 2019 Jun;104(6):611-612. doi:
10.1136/archdischild-2018-315881. Epub 2019 Jan 17. PMID: 30655265.

60  https://www.ncbi.nlm.nih.gov/pmc/articles/PMC5333793/.

61  Littman L (2018) Rapid-onset gender dysphoria in adolescents and young adults:
A study of parental reports. PLoS ONE 13(8) :e0202330. https://doi.org/10.137
/journal.pone.0202330

62  https://www.youtube.com/watch?v=6O3MzPeomqs (timestamp 1:33:09)

63  https://www.youtube.com/watch?v=9EYdzTPaguU

64  https://www.tandfonline.com/doi/full/10.1080/0092623X.2022.2136117

65  https://www.youtube.com/watch?v=9EYdzTPaguU

66  https://www.judiciary.uk/wp-content/uploads/2020/12/Bell-v-Tavistock
-Judgment.pdf

67  http://www.barnlakarforeningen.se/2019/05/02/blf-staller-sig-bakom-smers
-skrivelse-angaende-konsdysfori/

68  Antony Latham (2022) Puberty Blockers for Children: Can They Consent?, The
New Bioethics, 28:3, 268-291, DOI: 10.1080/20502877.2022.2088048

69  https://www.childrenshospital.org/bchp/specialty/adolescent-medicine/gender
-affirming-lgbtq-care

70  https://www.stlouischildrens.org/conditions-treatments/transgender-center/puberty
-blockers

71  https://opa.hhs.gov/sites/default/files/2022-03/gender-affirming-care-young-people
-march-2022.pdf

72  Affidavit, 69

73  Affidavit, 23

74  https://pubmed.ncbi.nlm.nih.gov/33529227/

75  Susan R Davis, et al, Global Consensus Position Statement on the Use of Testosterone
Therapy for Women, The Journal of Clinical Endocrinology & Metabolism, Volume
104, Issue 10, October 2019, Pages 4660–4666, https://doi.org/10.1210/jc.2019
-01603.

76  https://lacroicsz.substack.com/p/by-any-other-name

77  Affidavit, 31

78  Affidavit, 7

79  https://www.thefp.com/p/i-thought-i-was-saving-trans-kids

80  Affidavit, 73

81  Affidavit, 76

82  https://www.thefp.com/p/i-thought-i-was-saving-trans-kids

83  https://www.thefp.com/p/i-thought-i-was-saving-trans-kids

84  Affidavit 72 and https://www.thefp.com/p/i-thought-i-was-saving-trans-kids. NOTE: This story is a single compilation with details from two sources with minor edits for clarity and to reduce repetition.

85  https://www.hopkinsmedicine.org/center-transgender-health/clinician-resources. "Quick Guide to Hormone Therapy for the PCP" to download tgd-ghat-quick-guide.pdf.

86  Children's Hospital Los Angeles: Assent to Participate in a Research Study, Trans Youth Care – Blocker Cohort. Date: 6/23/2016, IRB#: CHLA-16-00108

87  Getahun D, Nash R, Flanders WD, Baird TC, Becerra-Culqui TA, Cromwell L, Hunkeler E, Lash TL, Millman A, Quinn VP, Robinson B, Roblin D, Silverberg MJ, Safer J, Slovis J, Tangpricha V, Goodman M. Cross-sex Hormones and Acute Cardiovascular Events in Transgender Persons: A Cohort Study. Ann Intern Med. 2018 Aug 21;169(4):205-213. doi: 10.7326/M17-2785. Epub 2018 Jul 10. PMID: 29987313; PMCID: PMC6636681.

88  https://academic.oup.com/jcem/article/102/11/3869/4157558 (see table 10)

89  de Blok CJM, Wiepjes CM, Nota NM, van Engelen K, Adank MA, Dreijerink KMA, Barbé E, Konings IRHM, den Heijer M. Breast cancer risk in transgender people receiving hormone treatment: nationwide cohort study in the Netherlands. BMJ. 2019 May 14;365:l1652. doi: 10.1136/bmj.l1652. PMID: 31088823; PMCID: PMC6515308.

90  Nota NM, Wiepjes CM, de Blok CJM, Gooren LJG, Kreukels BPC, den Heijer M. Occurrence of Acute Cardiovascular Events in Transgender Individuals Receiving Hormone Therapy. Circulation. 2019 Mar 12;139(11):1461-1462. doi: 10.1161/CIRCULATIONAHA.118.038584. PMID: 30776252.

91  https://www.hopkinsmedicine.org/center-transgender-health/clinician-resources. "Quick Guide to Hormone Therapy for the PCP" to download tgd-ghat-quick-guide.pdf.

92  Motosko CC, Zakhem GA, Pomeranz MK, Hazen A. Acne: a side-effect of masculinizing hormonal therapy in transgender patients. Br J Dermatol. 2019 Jan;180(1):26-30. doi: 10.1111/bjd.17083. Epub 2018 Oct 14. PMID: 30101531.

93  Irwig MS. Cardiovascular health in transgender people. Rev Endocr Metab Disord. 2018 Sep;19(3):243-251. doi: 10.1007/s11154-018-9454-3. PMID: 30073551.

94  Rasmussen JJ, Selmer C, Frøssing S, Schou M, Faber J, Torp-Pedersen C, Gislason GH, Køber L, Hougaard DM, Cohen AS, Kistorp C. Endogenous Testosterone Levels Are Associated with Risk of Type 2 Diabetes in Women without Established Comorbidity. J Endocr Soc. 2020 May 5;4(6):bvaa050. doi: 10.1210/jendso/bvaa050. PMID: 32537541; PMCID: PMC7278278.

95  Laidlaw MK, Van Mol A, Van Meter Q, Hansen JE. Letter to the Editor From Laidlaw et al: "Erythrocytosis in a Large Cohort of Transgender Men Using Testosterone: A Long-term Follow-up Study on Prevalence, Determinants, and Exposure Years." J Clin Endocrinol Metab. 2021 Nov 19;106(12):e5275-e5276. doi: 10.1210/clinem/dgab514. PMID: 34297088.

96  https://www.webmd.com/a-to-z-guides/what-is-erythrocytosis

97  https://academic.oup.com/jcem/article/102/11/3869/4157558 (see Table 10)

98  Gurrala RR, et. al. The impact of exogenous testosterone on breast cancer risk in transmasculine individuals. Ann Plastic Surg 2023; 90: 96-105.

99  Nota NM, Wiepjes CM, de Blok CJM, Gooren LJG, Kreukels BPC, den Heijer M. Occurrence of Acute Cardiovascular Events in Transgender Individuals Receiving

Hormone Therapy. Circulation. 2019 Mar 12;139(11):1461-1462. doi: 10.1161 /CIRCULATIONAHA.118.038584. PMID: 30776252.

100    Alzahrani T, Nguyen T, Ryan A, Dwairy A, McCaffrey J, Yunus R, Forgione J, Krepp J, Nagy C, Mazhari R, Reiner J. Cardiovascular Disease Risk Factors and Myocardial Infarction in the Transgender Population. Circ Cardiovasc Qual Outcomes. 2019 Apr;12(4):e005597. doi: 10.1161/CIRCOUTCOMES.119.005597. PMID: 30950651.

101    https://www.tandfonline.com/doi/full/10.1080/15265161.2018.1557288       AND https://www.karger.com/Article/FullText/501336 AND AThe Journal of Clinical Endocrinology & Metabolism 2019; 104(3): 686-7. AND Howard E. Kulin, et al., "The Onset of Sperm Production in Pubertal Boys. Relationship to Gonadotropin Excretion," American Journal of Diseases in Children 143, no. 2 (March, 1989): 190-193,

102    https://twitter.com/Styron53/status/1631716595184672774

103    Kulin HE, Frontera MA, Demers LM, Bartholomew MJ, Lloyd TA. The onset of sperm production in pubertal boys. Relationship to gonadotropin excretion. Am J Dis Child. 1989 Feb;143(2):190-3. PMID: 2492750.

104    https://transcare.ucsf.edu/guidelines/youth

105    Children's Hospital Los Angeles: Assent to Participate in a Research Study, Trans Youth Care – Blocker Cohort. Date: 6/23/2016, IRB#: CHLA-16-00108

106    Ibid.

107    https://www.youtube.com/watch?v=kSx-3CkcGh8 (53:22)

108    https://www.lifesitenews.com/news/biden-health-chief-confirms-admins-support -for-transitioning-gender-confused-children/?utm_source=featured-news&utm _campaign=usa

109    Affidavit 79

110    Affidavit, 80

111    https://www.thefp.com/p/i-thought-i-was-saving-trans-kids

112    Affidavit, 66

113    https://www.thefp.com/p/i-thought-i-was-saving-trans-kids

114    Affidavit, 66

115    Affidavit, 81

116    Affidavit, 77

117    https://www.thefp.com/p/i-thought-i-was-saving-trans-kids

118    https://www.thefp.com/p/i-thought-i-was-saving-trans-kids

## CHAPTER SIX

1      https://www.jsm.jsexmed.org/article/S1743-6095(15)33617-1/fulltext AND https://pubmed.ncbi.nlm.nih.gov/25201798/

2      Michael Biggs (2022) The Dutch Protocol for Juvenile Transsexuals: Origins and Evidence, Journal of Sex & Marital Therapy, DOI: 10.1080/0092623X.2022.2121238 page 4

3      Delemarre-van de Waal, H. A., & Cohen-Kettenis, P. T. (2006). Clinical management of gender identity disorder in adolescents: A protocol on psychological and paediatric endocrinology aspects. *European Journal of Endocrinology*, 155(suppl_1), S131–S137. doi:10.1530/eje.1.02231

4      https://www.jsm.jsexmed.org/article/S1743-6095(15)33617-1/fulltext AND https:// pubmed.ncbi.nlm.nih.gov/25201798/

5   Michael Biggs (2022) The Dutch Protocol for Juvenile Transsexuals: Origins and Evidence, Journal of Sex & Marital Therapy, DOI: 10.1080/0092623X.2022.2121238

6   Biggs p 6

7   Tishelman, A. C., Kaufman, R., Edwards-Leeper, L., Mandel, F. H., Shumer, D. E., & Spack, N. P. (2015). Serving transgender youth: Challenges, dilemmas, and clinical examples. Professional Psychology: Research and Practice, 46, 37–45. doi:10.1037 /a0037490

8   Spack, N. P., Edwards-Leeper, L., Feldman, H. A., Leibowitz, S., Mandel, F., Diamond, D. A., & Vance, S. R. (2012). Children and adolescents with gender identity disorder referred to a pediatric medical center. Pediatrics, 129, 418–425. doi:10.1542/peds.2011-0907

9   https://www.nytimes.com/2015/06/17/nyregion/transgender-minors-gender -reassignment-surgery.html

10  Hembree, W. C., Cohen-Kettenis, P., Delemarre-van de Waal, H. A., Gooren, L. J., Meyer, W. J., Spack, N. P., Tangpricha, V., & Montori, V. M. (2009). Endocrine treatment of transsexual persons: An Endocrine Society clinical practice guideline. Journal of Clinical Endocrinology and Metabolism, 94, 3132–3154. doi:10.1210 / jc.2009-0345

11  https://www.tandfonline.com/doi/epdf/10.1080/0092623X.2022.2121238?need Access=true&role=button page 9

12  Carmichael, P., Butler, G., Masic, U., Cole, T. J., De Stavola, B. L., Davidson, S., Skageberg, E. M., Khadr, S., & Viner, R. (2021). Short-term outcomes of pubertal suppression in a selected cohort of 12 to 15 year old young people with persistent gender dysphoria in the UK. PLoS One, 16, e0243894

13  https://www.tandfonline.com/doi/full/10.1080/0092623X.2022.2150346

14  Earl, J. (2019). Innovative practice, clinical research, and the ethical advancement of medicine. The American Journal of Bioethics, 19(6), 7–18. doi:10.1080/15265161 .2019.1602175

15  https://www.tandfonline.com/doi/full/10.1080/0092623X.2022.2150346

16  Negenborn, V. L., van der Sluis, W. B., Meijerink, W. J. H. J., & Bouman, M.-B. (2017). Lethal necrotizing cellulitis caused by ESBL-producing E. coli after laparoscopic intestinal vaginoplasty. Journal of Pediatric and Adolescent Gynecology, 30, e19–e21. doi:10.1016/j.jpag.2016.09.005

17  https://www.tandfonline.com/doi/full/10.1080/0092623X.2022.2121238

18  https://www.tandfonline.com/doi/full/10.1080/0092623X.2022.2150346

19  Affidavit, 13

20  Affidavit, 14

21  https://www.voorzij.nl/category/transgenderzorg/

22  https://publications.aap.org/pediatrics/article/146/4/e2020010611/79688 /Challenges-in-Timing-Puberty-Suppression-for?autologincheck=redirected

23  https://genderexploratory.com/wp-content/uploads/2022/12/GETA _ClinicalGuide_2022v1.1.pdf

24  https://www.tandfonline.com/doi/full/10.1080/0092623X.2022.2150346

25  Smith, Y. L. S., Van Goozen, S. H. M., & Cohen-Kettenis, P. T. (2001). Adolescents with gender identity disorder who were accepted or rejected for sex reassignment surgery: A prospective follow-up study. Journal of the American Academy of Child & Adolescent Psychiatry, 40(4), 472–481. doi:10.1097/00004583-200104000-00017

26    https://www.tandfonline.com/doi/full/10.1080/0092623X.2022.2150346

27    https://academic.oup.com/jsm/advance-article/doi/10.1093/jsxmed/qdac029
      /7005631

28    Ibid.

29    https://www.thefp.com/p/top-trans-doctors-blow-the-whistle?utm_source=url

30    Affidavit, 32

31    Affidavit, 33

32    Affidavit, 35

33    https://www.thefp.com/p/i-thought-i-was-saving-trans-kids

34    Affidavit, 55

35    Affidavit, 57

36    https://www.stlouischildrens.org/conditions-treatments/transgender-center

37    Affidavit, 7

38    Affidavit, 9

39    Affidavit, 10

40    Affidavit, 12

41    Affidavit, 12

42    Affidavit, 51

43    https://www.thefp.com/p/i-thought-i-was-saving-trans-kids

44    Ibid.

45    Affidavit, 39

46    Affidavit, 38

47    Affidavit, 41

48    Affidavit, 42

49    Affidavit, 43

50    Affidavit, 44

51    Affidavit, 45

52    Affidavit, 37

53    Affidavit, 48

54    Affidavit, 53

55    https://www.breitbart.com/politics/2023/02/17/st-louis-gender-clinic-told-teachers
      -encourage-whole-5th-grade-group-be-transgender/

56    https://www-hs-fi.translate.goog/tiede/art-2000009348478.html?_x_tr
      _sl=auto&_x_tr_tl=en&_x_tr_hl=en&_x_tr_pto=wapp

57    https://quillette.com/2020/01/17/why-i-resigned-from-tavistock-trans-identified
      -children-need-therapy-not-just-affirmation-and-drugs/

58    Ibid.

59    Ibid.

60    https://www.telegraph.co.uk/news/2019/12/12/childrens-transgender-clinic-hit-35
      -resignations-three-years/

61    https://www.telegraph.co.uk/news/2019/03/07/nhs-transgender-clinic-accused
      -covering-negative-impacts-puberty/

62    https://users.ox.ac.uk/~sfos0060/Biggs_ExperimentPubertyBlockers.pdf

63    http://www.heather-brunskell-evans.co.uk/body-politics/inventing-transgender
      -children-and-young-people/

64    https://segm.org/Keira_Bell_ruling_global_repercussions

65    https://www.dailymail.co.uk/news/article-9005007/High-Court-rules-puberty
      -blockers-transgender-clinics-landmark-case.html

66  https://www.judiciary.uk/wp-content/uploads/2020/12/Bell-v-Tavistock-Judgment.pdf

67  https://segm.org/Keira_Bell_ruling_global_repercussions

68  The Cass report itself can be found here https://cass.independent-review.uk/publications/interim-report/) AND https://segm.org/Tavistock-closure-the-times AND https://segm.org/GIDS-puberty-blockers-minors-the-times-special-report

69  https://www.thefp.com/p/i-thought-i-was-saving-trans-kids

70  Ibid.

71  Ibid.

72  Affidavit, 8

73  https://www.thefp.com/p/i-thought-i-was-saving-trans-kids

74  Ibid.

75  Ibid.

76  Ibid.

77  https://palveluvalikoima.fi/en/frontpage

78  https://segm.org/Finland_deviates_from_WPATH_prioritizing_psychotherapy_no_surgery_for_minors

79  https://news.yahoo.com/norwegian-medical-watchdog-encourages-country-210209339.html

80  https://themedicalprogress.com/2021/10/07/psychiatrists-shift-stance-on-gender-dysphoria-recommend-therapy/

81  https://www.thefp.com/p/i-thought-i-was-saving-trans-kids

## CHAPTER SEVEN

1  Of course, there are probably variations depending on the location and type of hospital, academic vs. community hospital.

2  December 21, 2022

3  https://genspect.org/

4  https://www.apa.org/about/policy/resolution-gender-identity-change-efforts.pdf

5  https://opa.hhs.gov/sites/default/files/2022-03/gender-affirming-care-young-people-march-2022.pdf.

6  https://store.samhsa.gov/sites/default/files/pep22-03-12-001.pdf

7  https://www.youtube.com/watch?v=8wCjz2SIYVo

8  Acosta, W., Qayyum, Z., Turban, J.L. *et al.* Identify, Engage, Understand: Supporting Transgender Youth in an Inpatient Psychiatric Hospital. *Psychiatr Q* 90, 601–612 (2019). https://doi.org/10.1007/s11126-019-09653-0.

9  Ovens H. WTBS 13 transgender patients: how to foster a safer emergency department environment. Emergency Medicine Cases; 2017. Retrieved from https://emergencymedicinecases.com/transgender-patients-emergency-department. Accessed November 2022.

10  Menvielle, Edgardo J., et al. "To the beat of a different drummer: the gender-variant child *Contemporary Pediatrics*, vol. 22, no. 2, Feb. 2005, pp. 38+. Gale Academic OneFile, link.gale.com/apps/doc/A129967410/AONE?u=anon-7aa263cc&sid=googleScholar&xid=cfbeda43. Accessed 1 Dec. 2022.

11  https://www.columbiapsychiatry.org/news/gender-affirming-care-saves-lives

12  https://www.lifespan.org/lifespan-living/understanding-gender-identity

13   https://www.politico.com/newsletters/the-recast/2021/07/02/rachel-levine-hhs-covid-anti-trans-hate-493459

14   https://www.lifespan.org/providers/jason-r-rafferty-md-mph-edm

15   Rafferty, J. Committee on Psychosocial Aspects of Child and Family Health; Committee on Adolescence; Section on Lesbian, Gay, Bisexual, and Transgender Health and Wellness. Ensuring Comprehensive Care and Support for Transgender and Gender-Diverse Children and Adolescents. *Pediatrics* 2018;142 (4): e20182162. https://doi.org/10.1542/peds.2018-2162

16   https://www.sciencedirect.com/science/article/abs/pii/S1056499321000791?via%3Dihub. From: Social and Relational Health Risks and Common Mental Health Problems Among US Children The Mitigating Role of Family Resilience and Connection to Promote Positive Socioemotional and School-Related Outcomes.

17   https://www-hs-fi.translate.goog/tiede/art-2000009348478.html?_x_tr_sl=auto&_x_tr_tl=en&_x_tr_hl=en&_x_tr_pto=wapp.

18   https://www.thetrevorproject.org/wp-content/uploads/2021/05/The-Trevor-Project-Ntional-Survey-Results-2021.pdf

19   https://transequality.org/sites/default/files/docs/resources/NTDS_Report.pdf

20   https://hrc-prod-requests.s3-us-west-2.amazonaws.com/ProjectThrive_YRBSData_Statement_122120.pdf?mtime=20210104125112&focal=none

21   Carmichael, P. (2017). Meeting the needs of gender diverse children and young people with mental health difficulties. ACAMH Conference. https://soundcloud.com/user-664361280/dr-polly-carmichael-developments-and-dilemmas.; de Graaf, N. M., Steensma, T. D., Carmichael, P., VanderLaan, D. P., Aitken, M., Cohen-Kettenis, P. T., de Vries, A., Kreukels, B., Wasserman, L., Wood, H., & Zucker, K. J. (2022). Suicidality in clinic-referred transgender adolescents. European Child & Adolescent Psychiatry, 31(1), 67–83. https://doi.org/10.1007/s00787-020-01663-9; Levine, S. B., Abbruzzese, E., & Mason, J. M. (2022). Reconsidering informed consent for trans-identified children, adolescents, and young adults. Journal of Sex & Marital Therapy, 48(7), 706–727. https://doi.org/10.1080/0092623X.2022.204622

22   Archives of Sexual Behavior (2022) 51:685–690. https://doi.org/10.1007/s10508-022-02287-7

23   https://link.springer.com/article/10.1007/s10508-022-02287-7

24   Finland: https://www-hs-fi.translate.goog/tiede/art-2000009348478.html?_x_tr_sl=auto&_x_tr_tl=en&_x_tr_hl=en&_x_tr_pto=wapp.

25   https://beyondwpath.org/

26   https://afsp.org/what-we-ve-learned-through-research.

27   Archives of Sexual Behavior (2022) 51:685–690. https://doi.org/10.1007/s10508-022-02287-7;. https://acamh.onlinelibrary.wiley.com/doi/full/10.1111/jcpp.12560; https://acamh.onlinelibrary.wiley.com/doi/full/10.1111/j.1469-7610.2010.02298.x.

28   https://afsp.org/risk-factors-protective-factors-and-warning-signs

29   Sweden's National Board of Health and Welfare conducted a thorough analysis of existing data on adolescents with gender dysphoria and concluded, "…it is difficult to interpret suicide risk among people with gender dysphoria—other co-occurring psychiatric diagnoses may be more pronounced contributing factors to suicide that the fact that a person has gender dysphoria."

30   Biggs, M. Suicide by Clinic-Referred Transgender Adolescents in the United Kingdom. *Arch Sex Behav* 51, 685–690 (2022). https://doi.org/10.1007/s10508-022-02287-7.

## CHAPTER EIGHT

1    https://vimeo.com/53694901
2    https://leginfo.legislature.ca.gov/faces/billNavClient.xhtml?bill_id=201120120SB48
3    https://www.newsweek.com/sign-telling-identity-confused-kids-im-your-mom-now-sparks-controversy-1685713
4    https://www.theblaze.com/news/pro-lbgtq-8th-grade-teacher-f-parents-im-your-parents-now-resigns AND https://americanwirenews.com/middle-school-teacher-if-your-parents-dont-accept-you-fk-them-im-your-parents-now/?utm_source=dlvr.it&utm_medium=twitter
5    https://twitter.com/libsoftiktok/status/1625633485875453953?s=20
6    https://www.buzzfeednews.com/article/laurenstrapagiel/nevada-teacher-banned-from-showing-rainbow-flag
7    https://nypost.com/2021/08/30/ca-teacher-encouraged-students-to-pledge-gay-pride-flag-video/
8    https://twitter.com/libsoftiktok/status/1624175710272118792?s=20
9    https://www.breitbart.com/education/2022/07/11/los-angeles-unified-school-district-provides-lesson-plans-that-promote-child-transgenderism/
10   Herthel, Jessica, and Jazz Jennings. I am Jazz. Dial Books, 2014.
11   https://docs.google.com/document/d/1gV4mahx1eyJ7aXRHKbnALdPPoN2dDdT2wjvKfmyDM68/edit this google doc was a link from https://www.dcareaeducators4socialjustice.org/black-lives-matter/resources/early-childhood-elementary#lessons
12   https://www.usatoday.com/story/tech/2021/05/20/lego-announces-lgbtq-set-ahead-pride-month-everyone-awesome/5179622001/
13   https://www.nytimes.com/interactive/2022/09/16/upshot/september-2022-times-siena-poll-crosstabs.html
14   https://www.washingtontimes.com/news/2022/jun/1/north-carolina-preschool-teacher-resigns-over-flas/
15   Sievert, E. D., Schweizer, K., Barkmann, C., Fahrenkrug, S., & Becker-Hebly, I. (2020). Not social transition status, but peer relations and family functioning predict psychological functioning in a German clinical sample of children with Gender Dysphoria. Clinical Child Psychology and Psychiatry, 135910452096453. https://doi.org/10.1177/1359104520964530; Wong, W. I., van der Miesen, A. I. R., Li, T. G. F., MacMullin, L. N., & VanderLaan, D. P. (2019). Childhood social gender transition and psychosocial well-being: A comparison to cisgender gender-variant children. Clinical Practice in Pediatric Psychology, 7(3), 241–253. https://doi.org/10.1037/cpp0000295
16   https://www.sciencedirect.com/science/article/abs/pii/S0890856713001871
17   Zucker, K. J. (2019). Debate: Different strokes for different folks. Child and Adolescent Mental Health 25(1): 36-37.
18   https://publications.aap.org/pediatrics/article/150/2/e2021056082/186992/Gender-Identity-5-Years-After-Social-Transition?autologincheck=redirected
19   Gu J, Kanai R. What contributes to individual differences in brain structure? *Front Hum Neurosci* 2014;8:262.

20   https://www.aacap.org/AACAP/Families_and_Youth/Facts_for_Families/FFF
     -Guide/transgender-and-gender-diverse-youth-122.aspx

21   Zucker, K. Debate: Different strokes for different folks. Child and Adolescent Mental
     Health. Accepted for publication: 18 March 2019 (https://acamh.onlinelibrary.wiley
     .com/doi/10.1111/camh.12330)

22   W. Bockting, Ch. 24: Transgender Identity Development, in 1 American Psychological
     Association Handbook on Sexuality and Psychology, 750 (D. Tolman & L. Diamond
     eds., 2014).

23   Report can be downloaded here: https://cass.independent-review.uk/publications
     /interim-report/

24   https://www.aclu.org/wp-content/uploads/legal-documents/031_expert_affidavit
     _of_dr._stephen_levine_with_exhibit.pdf

25   https://publications.aap.org/pediatrics/article/150/2/e2021056082/186992
     /Gender-Identity-5-Years-After-Social-Transition?autologincheck=redirected

26   https://tallahasseereports.com/2021/12/02/tallahassee-mom-gender-ideology
     -almost-destroyed-my-family/

27   Ibid.

28   https://legalinsurrection.com/wp-content/uploads/2022/04/Foote-v.-Ludlow
     -School-Committee-Complaint.pdf   AND   https://thehill.com/changing-america
     /respect/equality/3270131-massachusetts-parents-file-lawsuit-against-school
     -officials-over-gender-identity-policy/

29   https://www.nytimes.com/2023/01/22/us/gender-identity-students-parents.html?re
     ferringSource=articleShare&smid=nytcore-ios-share

30   https://redstate.com/kiradavis/2023/02/10/california-teacher-fired-for-refusing-to
     -lie-to-parents-about-student-gender-identity-n701444?bcid=1861e4411b30955a5
     1b3645fbdc009861660b0ae64003b5d63136e442427683e

31   https://www.dailywire.com/news/top-national-school-psychologist-part-of-group
     -offering-to-pay-rehome-gay-kids-to-new-parents

32   https://www.dailywire.com/news/top-national-school-psychologist-part-of-group
     -offering-to-pay-rehome-gay-kids-to-new-parents

33   https://www.nasponline.org/research-and-policy/policy-priorities/position
     -statements (see pdf downloaded under the headline "Safe and Supportive Schools
     for Lesbian, Gay, Bisexual, Transgender, Questioning (LGBTQ+) Youth" and "safe
     and supportive schools for transgender and gender diverse students"

34   https://www.nassp.org/top-issues-in-education/position-statements/transgender
     -students/?utm_medium=web&utm_source=position-statement&utm
     _campaign=NASSP21ADV-0030

35   https://www.nassp.org/top-issues-in-education/position-statements/transgender
     -students/?utm_medium=web&utm_source=position-statement&utm
     _campaign=NASSP21ADV-0030

36   https://www.schoolcounselor.org/Standards-Positions/Position-Statements/ASCA
     -Position-Statements/The-School-Counselor-and-Transgender-Gender-noncon

37   https://www.youtube.com/watch?v=K9pdGiZOqpc

38   https://hrc-prod-requests.s3-us-west-2.amazonaws.com/files/assets/resources
     /Schools-In-Transition.pdf

39   https://www2.ed.gov/about/offices/list/ocr/docs/ed-factsheet-transgender-202106.pdf

40   https://www.socialworkers.org/LinkClick.aspx?fileticket=jjq0-NcZlU0%3d &portalid=0

41   https://www.glsen.org/state-and-local-policy-manager

42   https://www.glsen.org/activity/model-local-education-agency-policy-on -transgender-nonbinary-students#d

43   https://www.glsen.org/activity/model-local-education-agency-policy-on -transgender-nonbinary-students#d

44   https://www.glsen.org/activity/model-local-education-agency-policy-on-transgender -nonbinary-students#d

45   https://www.foxnews.com/us/trans-psychologist-files-brief-md-school-district -hiding-transitions-parents-terrible-idea

46   M Resnick et al (1997) Protecting Adolescents from Harm: Findings from the National Longitudinal Study on Adolescent Health JAMA Sept 1997

47   https://pitt.substack.com/p/saga-of-sage

48   Ibid.

49   https://www.youtube.com/watch?v=_t0cH6U_G2w&ab_

50   Pierce v. Society of Sisters, 268 US 510 (1925); Troxel v. Granville, 530 US 57, 66 (2000) ("As our case law has developed, the custodial aren't has a constitutional right to determine, without undue interference by the state, how to best raise, nurture, and educate the child."0 see also Wisconsin v. Yoder, 406 US 205, 233 (1972)

51   https://www.youtube.com/watch?v=pCH-bUFR3WM&t=5317s

52   Stroop J. R. (1935). Studies of interference in serial verbal reactions. *J. Exp. Psychol.* 18 643–662. 10.1037/h0054651

53   https://www.newsweek.com/loudoun-county-teen-put-under-electronic-monitoring -before-transgender-bathroom-assault-1638787

# CHAPTER NINE

1   https://nypost.com/2022/02/26/dad-lost-custody-after-questioning-sons -transgender-identity/

2   https://thetexan.news/texas-supreme-court-to-review-james-younger-custody-case -after-mother-took-children-to-california/#:~:text=In%20August%20 2021%2C%20Dallas%20County,Georgulas%20full%20custody%20of%20James.

3   https://public.courts.in.gov/Decisions/api/Document/Opinion?Id=43s ECCBSPUXV-GW6EVq-1kPFe78ZcDjIZ2Z02dJj4PJm2Zg4xeJxo-NI 9b8cRe8U0

4   https://nypost.com/2022/02/26/dad-lost-custody-after-questioning-sons -transgender-identity/

5   https://trackbill.com/bill/california-assembly-bill-957-family-law-gender -identity/2367575/

6   https://www.instagram.com/reel/Cly-tiDu9HU/

7   https://www.youtube.com/watch?v=_t0cH6U_G2w

8   https://pitt.substack.com/p/the-governments-war-on-our-children;  https://pitt.substack .com/p/saga-of-sage?utm_source=%2Fsearch%2Fsage&utm_medium=reader2  ; https://www.youtube.com/watch?v=_t0cH6U_G2w

9   https://thefederalist.com/2023/01/19/virginia-teen-sex-trafficked-twice-after -school-hides-gender-identity-from-her-parents/

10   https://www.youtube.com/watch?v=oaBYyvh6Z0w

11      https://www.washingtonexaminer.com/news/mother-of-transgender-teenager-los
        -angeles-county-killed-my-daughter
12      https://pitt.substack.com/p/remembering-yaeli
13      https://www.nbcsandiego.com/news/local/california-law-affirms-gender-related
        -care-for-foster-youth/171832/ AND https://pitt.substack.com/p/remembering-yaeli
14      https://pitt.substack.com/p/remembering-yaeli
15      https://www.washingtonexaminer.com/news/mother-of-transgender-teenager-los
        -angeles-county-killed-my-daughter
16      https://rise.lalgbtcenter.org/
17      https://pitt.substack.com/p/remembering-yaeli
18      Ibid.
19      Ibid.
20      Ibid.
21      https://pitt.substack.com/p/remembering-yaeli AND https://www.heritage.org/gender
        /event/protecting-our-children-how-radical-gender-ideology-taking-over-public
        -schools-harming
22      https://www.nbc12.com/2023/01/19/legislation-over-gender-pronouns-identity
        -notifications-heads-virginia-general-assembly/
23      https://thefederalist.com/2023/01/19/virginia-teen-sex-trafficked-twice-after
        -school-hides-gender-identity-from-her-parents/
24      https://www.washingtontimes.com/news/2023/feb/16/democrats-kill-virginia-bill
        -banning-schools-hidin/
25      https://www.nbc12.com/2023/01/19/legislation-over-gender-pronouns-identity
        -notifications-heads-virginia-general-assembly/

## CHAPTER TEN

1       Adapted from www.whatsyourgrief.com
2       http://drkendoka.com/

## CHAPTER ELEVEN

1       JAMA Pediatr. 2018;172(5):431-436. doi:10.1001/jamapediatrics.2017.5440
2       JAMA Pediatr. 2018;172(5):431-436. doi:10.1001/jamapediatrics.2017.5440
3       Citing: Das RK, Perdikis G, Al Kassis S, Drolet BC. Gender-Affirming Chest
        Reconstruction Among Transgender and Gender-Diverse Adolescents in the US
        From 2016 to 2019. JAMA Pediatr. Published online October 17, 2022. doi:10.1001
        /jamapediatrics.2022.3595
4       https://www.nytimes.com/2022/09/26/health/top-surgery-transgender-teenagers
        .html
5       https://www.genderconfirmation.com/no-nipple-grafts-ftm-top-surgery/
6       Dhejne C, Öberg K, Arver S, et al. An analysis of all applications for sex reassignment
        surgery in Sweden, 1960–2010: prevalence, incidence, and regrets. Arch Sex Behav.
        2014;43:1535–1545. Wiepjes CM, Nota NM, de Blok CJM, et al. The Amsterdam
        cohort of gender dysphoria study (1972–2015): Trends in prevalence, treatment, and
        regrets. J Sex Med. 2018;15:582–590.
7       https://journals.plos.org/plosone/article?id=10.1371/journal.pone.0016885

8   Bränström R, Pachankis JE: Reduction in mental health treatment utilization among transgender individuals after gender-affirming surgeries: a total population study. *Am J Psychiatry* 2020; 177:727–734. https://doi.org/10.1176/appi.ajp.2019.19010080

9   Am J Psychiatry 2020; 177:765–766; doi: 10.1176/appi.ajp.2020.19111130

10   https://ajp.psychiatryonline.org/doi/10.1176/appi.ajp.2020.20060803

11   https://www.upi.com/Health_News/2019/10/08/Gender-reassignment-surgery-brings-mental-health-benefits-study-shows/9801570504167/

12   https://abcnews.go.com/Health/transgender-surgery-linked-long-term-mental-health-study/story?id=66125676

13   https://www.nbcnews.com/feature/nbc-out/sex-reassignment-surgery-yields-long-term-mental-health-benefits-study-n1079911

14   https://wgss.yale.edu/news/mental-health-outcomes-improve-transgender-individuals-after-surgery-study-finds

15   https://www.psychiatry.org/news-room/news-releases/study-finds-long-term-mental-health-benefits-of-ge

16   https://www.webmd.com/sex/news/20191009/gender-reassignment-surgery-benefits-mental-health

17   https://www.nytimes.com/2022/09/26/health/top-surgery-transgender-teenagers.html

18   Ibid.

19   @realchrisrufo May 17, 2022 4:56

20   Plast. Reconstr. Surg. 146: 1376, 2020.

21   https://truthinbetween.substack.com/p/ep-58-transition-and-de-transition#details

22   https://www.nytimes.com/2019/05/31/well/transgender-teens-binders.html

23   https://www.chla.org/sites/default/files/atoms/files/Binding_English%20parent.pdf

24   https://nypost.com/2022/09/01/mom-discovers-depravity-in-trevor-projects-trans-chat-room/

25   https://www.healthychildren.org/English/ages-stages/gradeschool/Pages/Support-Resources-for-Families-of-Gender-Diverse-Youth.aspx?_ga=2.29348284.1416039863.1678933218-2133834036.1678933218&_gl=1*tpiele*_ga*MjEzMzgzNDAzNi4xNjc4OTMzMjE4*_ga_FD9D3XZVQQ*MTY3ODkzMzIxOC4xLjEuMTY3ODkzMzgyNS4wLjAuMA..

26   https://www.pointofpride.org/free-chest-binders#about-the-program

27   https://www.themainewire.com/2022/12/damariscotta-maine-teacher-social-worker-gender-transition-sam-roy/

28   Transgender Health Volume 3.1, 2018 DOI: 10.1089/trgh.2018.0017

29   https://www.youtube.com/watch?v=6O3MzPeomqs

30   http://www.hbrs.no/wp-content/uploads/2019/02/chest-wall-contouring-surgery-in-female-to-male-transsexuals-a-new-algorithm-2008.pdf

31   https://twitter.com/amelieprobably/status/1549751562779639808?s=20&t=kEERJ1CI5Y2sSOrwyfucTQ

32   Bell, K. (2020). British High Court Case No: CO/60/2020 Bell v Tavistock (01/12/2020). Retrieved from https://www.judiciary.uk

33   https://www.realityslaststand.com/p/detransitioners-respond-a-letter

34   https://www.youtube.com/watch?v=5Y6espcXPJk

35   https://www.thefp.com/p/the-testosterone-hangover

36   https://www.thefp.com/p/the-testosterone-hangover

37    https://funkypsyche.substack.com/p/my-letter-to-the-surgeon-who-performed

38    https://pubmed.ncbi.nlm.nih.gov/35300570/

39    https://www.youtube.com/watch?v=Vn6J-iAcYWc

40    https://pubmed.ncbi.nlm.nih.gov/31604554/

41    Commun Integr Biol. 2009 May-Jun; 2(3): 279–281. doi: 10.4161/cib.2.3.8227

42    https://pubmed.ncbi.nlm.nih.gov/9989430/

43    https://pubmed.ncbi.nlm.nih.gov/9570031/

44    https://www.sciencedirect.com/science/article/abs/pii/S088421751534363X

45    https://pubmed.ncbi.nlm.nih.gov/25505951/

46    https://pubmed.ncbi.nlm.nih.gov/20105662/

47    https://www.who.int/publications/i/item/WHO-HEP-NFS-21.45

48    https://openbooks.org/books-we-donate/

49    https://www.texaspolicy.com/of-drag-queens-and-parental-empowerment/

50    https://gardenstatefamilies.org/parents-outrage-at-kinnelon-pearl-r-miller-middle
      -school/

51    https://www.plannedparenthood.org/about-us/newsroom/press-releases/planned
      -parenthood-los-angeles-announces-landmark-program-and-partnership-of-high
      -school-based-wellbeing-centers-across-l-a-county

## CHAPTER TWELVE

1     https://www.globenewswire.com/news-release/2020/03/31/2009112/0/en/Sex
      -Reassignment-Surgery-Market-to-hit-USD-1-5-Bn-by-2026-Global-Market
      -Insights-Inc.html

2     https://twitter.com/mscots41/status/1511988114046267397

3     https://twitter.com/mscots41/status/1511988114046267397

4     https://exulansic.substack.com/p/phalloplasty-philes-the-hotdog-with

5     https://www.hopkinsmedicine.org/health/treatment-tests-and-therapies/phalloplasty
      -for-gender-affirmation

6     https://exulansic.substack.com/p/phalloplasty-philes-the-hotdog-with

7     Ibid.

8     Ibid.

9     Ibid.

10    Ibid.

11    https://substack.com/profile/56208027-exulansic

12    https://exulansic.substack.com/p/phalloplasty-philes-the-hotdog-with

13    Ibid.

14    Combaz N, Kuhn A. Long-Term Urogynecological Complications after Sex
      Reassignment Surgery in Transsexual Patients: a Retrospective Study of 44 Patients and
      Diagnostic Algorithm Proposal, Am J Urol Res. 2017;2(2): 038-043.

15    https://archive.ph/dA1wn

16    Potter E, Sivagurunathan M, Armstrong K, Barker LC, Du Mont J, Lorello GR,
      Millman A, Urbach DR, Krakowsky Y. Patient reported symptoms and adverse
      outcomes seen in Canada's first vaginoplasty postoperative care clinic. Neurourol
      Urodyn. 2023 Feb;42(2):523-529. doi: 10.1002/nau.25132. Epub 2023 Jan 11.
      PMID: 36630152.

17    https://www.genderdysphoriaalliance.com/post/meet-scott-newgent

18  Ibid.

19  Ibid.

20  https://www.youtube.com/@shifterofshape

21  Annie M.Q. Wang, Vivian Tsang, Peter Mankowski, Daniel Demsey, Alex Kavanagh, Krista Genoway, Outcomes Following Gender Affirming Phalloplasty: A Systematic Review and Meta-Analysis, Sexual Medicine Reviews, 2022 Aug 25.Online ahead of print. DOI: 10.1016/j.sxmr.2022.03.002

22  Ortengren CD, Blasdel G, Damiano EA, Scalia PD, Morgan TS, Bagley P, Blunt HB, Elwyn G, Nigriny JF, Myers JB, Chen ML, Moses RA. Urethral outcomes in metoidioplasty and phalloplasty gender affirming surgery (MaPGAS) and vaginectomy: a systematic review. Transl Androl Urol. 2022 Dec;11(12):1762-1770. doi: 10.21037/tau-22-174. PMID: 36632157; PMCID: PMC9827403.

23  van der Loos, Maria, Klink DT, Hannema SE, Bruinsma S, Steensma TD, Kreukels BPC, Cohen-Kettenis PT, de Vries ALC, den Heijer M, Wiepjes CM. Children and adolescents in the Amsterdam Cohort of Gender Dysphoria: trends in diagnostic- and treatment trajectories during the first 20 years of the Dutch Protocol. J Sex Med. 2023 Feb 27;20(3):398-409. doi: 10.1093/jsxmed/qdac029. PMID: 36763938.

24  Hess J, Henkel A, Bohr J, Rehme C, Panic A, Panic L, Rossi Neto R, Hadaschik B, Hess Y. Sexuality after Male-to-Female Gender Affirmation Surgery. Biomed Res Int. 2018 May 27;2018:9037979. doi: 10.1155/2018/9037979. PMID: 29977922; PMCID: PMC5994261.

25  Rossi Neto R, Hintz F, Krege S, Rubben H, Vom Dorp F. Gender reassignment surgery—a 13 year review of surgical outcomes. Int Braz J Urol. 2012 Jan-Feb;38(1):97-107. doi: 10.1590/s1677-55382012000100014. PMID: 22397771.

26  https://www.researchgate.net/publication/308491141_Lethal_Necrotizing _Cellulitis_Caused_by_ESBL-Producing_E_Coli_after_Laparoscopic_Intestinal _Vaginoplasty.

27  https://www.youtube.com/watch?v=PqisKeHKPzs&t=12s

28  Ibid.

29  https://www.youtube.com/watch?v=3QMaJdXSmHg

30  Zwickl S, Burchill L, Wong AFQ, Leemaqz SY, Cook T, Angus LM, Eshin K, Elder CV, Grover SR, Zajac JD, Cheung AS. Pelvic Pain in Transgender People Using Testosterone Therapy. LGBT Health. 2023 Jan 4. doi: 10.1089/lgbt.2022.0187. Epub ahead of print. PMID: 36603056.

31  Poorthuis MHF, Yao P, Chen Y, Guo Y, Shi L, Li L, Chen Z, Clarke R, Yang L; China Kadoorie Biobank Collaborative Group. Risks of Stroke and Heart Disease Following Hysterectomy and Oophorectomy in Chinese Premenopausal Women. Stroke. 2022 Oct;53(10):3064-3071. doi: 10.1161/STROKEAHA.121.037305. Epub 2022 Jul 13. PMID: 35862220; PMCID: PMC9508951.

32  https://www.youtube.com/watch?v=3XTg2lEJiVs

33  van der Loos, Maria, Klink DT, Hannema SE, Bruinsma S, Steensma TD, Kreukels BPC, Cohen-Kettenis PT, de Vries ALC, den Heijer M, Wiepjes CM. Children and adolescents in the Amsterdam Cohort of Gender Dysphoria: trends in diagnostic- and treatment trajectories during the first 20 years of the Dutch Protocol. J Sex Med. 2023 Feb 27;20(3):398-409. doi: 10.1093/jsxmed/qdac029. PMID: 36763938.

34  https://www.youtube.com/watch?v=9EYdzTPaguU

35  https://twitter.com/libsoftiktok/status/1563245685138345984?ref_src
    =twsrc%5Etfw%7Ctwcamp%5Etweetembed%7Ctwterm%5E156324782605
    7846784%7Ctwgr%5Ef62b0b81f74c910f82e349b6a5edb68c02b67edb%7
    Ctwcon%5Es3_&ref_url=https%3A%2F%2Fwww.bizpacreview.com%2F20
    22%2F08%2F27%2Fdetransitioner-regrets-surgery-blames-woke-docs-i-was
    -brainwashed-by-the-trans-community-1278097%2F
36  https://www.youtube.com/watch?v=PqisKeHKPzs&t=12s
37  https://www.reddit.com/r/detrans/comments/srpp27/the_rdetrans_demographic
    _survey_screened_and/
38  https://pubmed.ncbi.nlm.nih.gov/34665380/
39  Hakeem, A. (2007). Trans-sexuality: A case of the "Emperor's New Clothes." In:
    Morgan, D., & Ruszczynski, S. (Eds.). (2007). Lectures on Violence, Perversion and
    Delinquency (1st ed.). Routledge, pp. 179-192. https://doi-org.ezproxy.lib.utexas
    .edu/10.4324/9780429476648.
40  Hakeem, A. (2007). Trans-sexuality: A case of the "Emperor's New Clothes." In:
    Morgan, D., & Ruszczynski, S. (Eds.). (2007). Lectures on Violence, Perversion and
    Delinquency (1st ed.). Routledge, pp. 179-192. https://doi-org.ezproxy.lib.utexas
    .edu/10.4324/9780429476648.
41  https://www.transgendertrend.com/interview-az-hakeem/.
42  D'Angelo R, Syrulnik E, Ayad S, Marchiano L, Kenny DT, Clarke P. One Size Does
    Not Fit All: In Support of Psychotherapy for Gender Dysphoria. Arch Sex Behav.
    2021 Jan;50(1):7-16. doi: 10.1007/s10508-020-01844-2. Epub 2020 Oct 21.
    PMID: 33089441; PMCID: PMC7878242.
43  Dhejne C, Lichtenstein P, Boman M, Johansson AL, Långström N, Landén M.
    Long-term follow-up of transsexual persons undergoing sex reassignment surgery:
    cohort study in Sweden. PLoS One. 2011 Feb 22;6(2):e16885. doi: 10.1371/journal.
    pone.0016885. PMID: 21364939; PMCID: PMC3043071.
44  Littman L. Individuals Treated for Gender Dysphoria with Medical and/or Surgical
    Transition Who Subsequently Detransitioned: A Survey of 100 Detransitioners. Arch
    Sex Behav. 2021 Nov;50(8):3353-3369. doi: 10.1007/s10508-021-02163-w. Epub
    2021 Oct 19. PMID: 34665380; PMCID: PMC8604821.
45  Dahlen S, Connolly D, Arif I, Junejo MH, Bewley S, Meads C. International
    clinical practice guidelines for gender minority/trans people: systematic review
    and quality assessment. BMJ Open. 2021 Apr 29;11(4):e048943. doi: 10.1136
    /bmjopen-2021-048943. PMID: 33926984; PMCID: PMC8094331.
46  van der Sluis WB, Bouman MB, Meijerink WJHJ, Elfering L, Mullender MG, de
    Boer NKH, van Bodegraven AA. Diversion neovaginitis after sigmoid vaginoplasty:
    endoscopic and clinical characteristics. Fertil Steril. 2016 Mar;105(3):834-839.e1.
    doi: 10.1016/j.fertnstert.2015.11.013. Epub 2015 Nov 26. PMID: 26632208.
47  https://www.youtube.com/watch?v=MLxkykG1R88
48  https://www.womenshealthmag.com/health/a30631270/jazz-jennings-surgery
    -complications/
49  https://www.tandfonline.com/doi/full/10.1080/0092623X.2022.2121238
50  Cohen-Kettenis, P. T., Delemarre-van de Waal, H. A., & Gooren, L. J. G. (2008). The
    treatment of adolescent transsexuals: Changing insights. Journal of Sexual
    Medicine, 5, 1892–1897. doi:10.1111/j.1743-6109.2008.00870.

51 https://wpath.org/about/mission-and-vision

52 https://nypost.com/2023/02/09/whistleblower-lifts-lid-on-st-louis-kids-gender-clinic/

53 https://wpath.org/publications/soc

54 Ibid.

55 van der Sluis, W. B., de Nie, I., Steensma, T. D., van Mello, N. M., Lissenberg-Witte, B. I., & Bouman, M.-B. (2021). Surgical and demographic trends in genital gender-affirming surgery in transgender women: 40 years of experience in Amsterdam. *British Journal of Surgery, 109*, 8–11. doi:10.1093/bjs/znab213

56 https://adflegal.org/sites/default/files/2022-03/BPJ-v-West-Virginia-State-Board-Ed-2022-02-23-Levine-Expert-Report.pdf

57 Ibid.

58 Ibid.

59 Personal conversation 1/6/2023 and email 4/3/23.

60 https://wpath.org/about/history

61 https://adflegal.org/sites/default/files/2022-03/BPJ-v-West-Virginia-State-Board-Ed-2022-02-23-Levine-Expert-Report.pdf

62 https://adflegal.org/sites/default/files/2022-03/BPJ-v-West-Virginia-State-Board-Ed-2022-02-23-Levine-Expert-Report.pdf

63 Lisa Mac Richards, *Bias, not evidence dominates WPATH transgender standard of care*, Canadian Gender Report, October 1, 2019 http://genderreport.ca/bias-not-evidence-dominate-transgender-standard-of-care/.

64 https://wpath.org/publications/soc

65 https://quillette.com/2022/01/06/a-transgender-pioneer-explains-why-she-stepped-down-from-uspath-and-wpath/

66 https://wpath.org/publications/soc

67 https://www.dailywire.com/news/levine-opens-wpath-conference-with-activist-manifesto-this-is-a-call-to-action

68 https://www.beyondwpath.org/

69 https://cranects.com/non-binary-surgery/

70 Clayton A. The Gender Affirmative Treatment Model for Youth with Gender Dysphoria: A Medical Advance or Dangerous Medicine? Arch Sex Behav. 2022 Feb;51(2):691-698. doi: 10.1007/s10508-021-02232-0. Epub 2021 Nov 22. PMID: 34811654; PMCID: PMC8888500.

## CHAPTER THIRTEEN

1 https://www.amazon.com/Desist-Detrans-Detox-Getting-Gender/dp/B0932G8CF7

2 Based on testimonials from family members, in the later stages of dementia, an affected family member may know their name at times, and other times will no longer be able to recall their own name. According to the Best Friends Approach blog at https://bestfriendsapproach.com/call-me-by-my-name-using-the-preferred-name-in-dementia-care/, "A person's name is probably the last word recognized at the close of life, said Dr. William Markesbery, a noted neurologist who directed the Sanders-Brown Center on Aging. Sometimes the simplest gift is the most precious and the most enduring."

## CONCLUSION

[1]    Levine, S. (2017). Ethical Concerns About Emerging Treatment Paradigms for Gender Dysphoria. *Journal of Sex & Marital Therapy* at 7. DOI: 10.1080/0092623X .2017.1309482.

[2]    https://www.fda.gov/drugs/postmarket-drug-safety-information-patients-and -providers/testosterone-information

[3]    https://pitt.substack.com/p/to-my-daughters-therapist-you-were

[4]    https://www.thefp.com/p/i-felt-bullied-mother-of-child-treated

[5]    https://www.msn.com/en-us/health/medical/transgender-women-face-prostate -cancer-risk-says-first-of-its-kind-study-from-ucsf/ar-AA1awW3e

[6]    https://glbtrt.ala.org/rainbowbooks/

[7]    https://www.washingtonexaminer.com/restoring-america/community-family /washington-state-bill-hides-runaway-children-from-transgender-unsupportive- parents

[8]    https://www.carouseltheatre.ca/classes/drag-camp-2023/

[9]    https://link.springer.com/article/10.1007/s10508-023-02576-9

[10]    https://www.fairforall.org/open-letters/archives-of-sexual-behavior/

[11]    As written in the Torah.

[12]    Babylonian Talmud, Tractate Shabbat, page 104a.

## APPENDIX ONE

[1]    Pediatrics (2018) 142 (4): e20182162

[2]    www.TheGenderBook.com

[3]    wwwTheGenderBook.com/anatomy

[4]    https://pubmed.ncbi.nlm.nih.gov/11534012/

[5]    https://pubmed.ncbi.nlm.nih.gov/12476264/

## APPENDIX THREE

[1]    29 U.S.C. Sec. 701 et seq.

[2]    20 U.S.C. Sec. 1400 et seq.

[3]    *Letter to Ruscio*, 115 LRP 18601 (FPCO 2014); *Irvine (CA) Unified School District*, 14 EHLR 353 (OCR 1989).

[4]    *Letter to Anonymous*, 111 LRP 18281 (FPCO 2010); *Montgomery County Pub. Schs.*, 111 LRP 55173 (SEA Maryland 2011); *Letter to Shuster*, 108 LRP 2302 (OSEP 2007); *Letter to MacDonald*, 20 IDELR 1159 (OSEP 1993); *FPCO Policy Letter* (FPCO—October 2, 1997).

[5]    *Brownsburg Cmty. Sch. Corp.*, 59 IDELR 146 (SEA Indiana 2012); *Washoe County Sch. Dist.*, 114 LRP 25728 (SEA Nevada 2014)(since school never printed the e-mails of a child's recreational activities observation, maintained them as part of the educational records, or kept them in storage or a secure database, they were not FERPA records); *Middleton-Cross Plains Area Sch. Dist.*, 115 LRP 31928 (SEA Wisconsin 2015) (school was not required to provide parents with access to e-mails not maintained in the student's cumulative file). In *S.A. v. Tulare County Office of Educ.*, 53 IDELR 111 (E.D. Cal. 2009), the federal district court held that e-mails are only education records if saved on a permanent secure database or printed and stored in the student's file.

6      34 C.F.R. §99.4
7      20 U.S.C. §1232g(d), 34 C.F.R. 99.5(a)
8      34 C.F.R. §300.625(b)
9      34 C.F.R. §99.10(b), 34 C.F.R. §300.613(a)
10     *Letter re: Regional Multicultural Magnet Sch. Dist.*, 108 LRP 29577 (FPCO 2008);
       *Letter to Anonymous*, 113 LRP 14615 (FPCO 2013)
11     20 U.S.C. §1232g(g)
12     34 C.F.R. §99.64(c); *Letter to Anonymous*, 113 LRP 28738 (FPCO 2013).
13     34 C.F.R. §99.65
14     34 C.F.R. §99.66
15     *Letter to Sanders*, 107 LRP 64190 (FPCO 2007)
16     34 C.F.R. §99.67

# Acknowledgments

The opinions expressed here are mine, but through the years, I have benefitted from the friendship and work of many colleagues, researchers, and journalists, some of them giants in this field. A partial list:

E. Abbruzzese, Michael Biggs, Jennifer Bilek, Alex Capo, Michelle Cretella, Kara Dansky, Susan and Marcus Evans, Walt Heyer, Hacsi Horvath, Paul Hruz, Michael Laidlaw, Patrick Lappert, Diana Lightfoot, Lisa Littman, Steven Marmer, Paul McHugh, Joe McIlhaney, Quentin Van Meter, Andre Van Mol, Leor Sapir, Lauren Schwartz, Debra Soh, Dan Weiss, Colin Wright, Joe Zanga, and Ken Zucker.

For your excellent legal appendices, thank you Vernadette Broyles, Joel Thornton, and Ernie Trakas of Child & Parental Rights Campaign.

I was assisted and inspired by Alix Aharon, Erin Brewer, Kathleen Dooley, Exulansic, Elana Fishbein, Erin Friday, B. Halperin, Tom Hampson, Maria Keffler, Stacy Manning, Carrie Mendoza, J. Reath, Steven Schwartz, Alec Torres, and Mike and Emily Welch.

A.C., you played a major role in this endeavor. Whatever I needed, day or night, you were there. You always had my back, and I am so grateful for that.

Dr. Stephen Levine, thank you for supervising my clinical work, sharing your wisdom and knowledge, and providing a historic perspective on a complex subject. I have benefited immensely from our time together and from your papers and expert reports.

Many people have important things to say, but not everyone is given a voice. I owe a great debt of gratitude to Matt Walsh and Justin Folk, for including me in The Daily Wire's *What Is a Woman?*, Dennis Prager,

Kelsey Bolar of Independent Women's Forum, Jan Jekielek from The Epoch Times's *American Thought Leaders*, Pete Hegseth from Fox Nation's *The Miseducation of America I* and *II*, and to Dr. Jordan B. Peterson for having me on his podcast.

Thank you, John Colapinto, for writing *As Nature Made Him: The Boy Who Was Raised as a Girl.*

At Skyhorse, my gratitude goes to Tony Lyons for recognizing the urgent need for this book, and to Hector Carosso for his wise editorial counsel and patience with my endless additions and revisions. Thanks also to Brian Richardson for working with me on the cover design and creating a perfect finished product.

I am grateful to Harry Crocker at Regnery for recommending Brian Robertson, my agent. Brian doggedly pursued the best placement for my book, was a valued thought partner, and provided a calm presence during apocalyptic moments.

I appreciate my patients and their parents. Thank you for trusting me, teaching me, sharing your secrets, and forgiving my mistakes.

Beth Swift—you deny it, but I know you're hiding a pair of angel's wings. Your support and hands-on assistance for these fifteen years have been indispensable. You've helped me in more ways than I can count. Without your dedication, my job would have been heavier, maybe impossible.

To my children and their spouses, you keep me anchored in what really matters. It's in your homes that I escape the world's madness. Thank you for always welcoming me with smiles. You and your precious children buoy my spirits and give me hope.

C, for months you filled my fridge with homemade delicacies, and I will never forget that.

Finally, I express gratitude to the Almighty for the gift of life and for waking up each morning able to walk, speak, and think. *Modeh Ani.*